West Coast Plays

The Shrunken Head of Pancho Villa
Luis Valdez

Chekhov in Yalta
John Driver and Jeffrey Haddow

And the Soul Shall Dance
Wakako Yamauchi

Surface Tension
Laura Farabough

Catholic Girls
Doris Baizley

The Reactivated Man
Curtis Zahn

Home Free
Robert Alexander

PUBLISHED BY THE CALIFORNIA THEATRE COUNCIL

© Copyright 1982, California Theatre Council

Winter and Spring 1982

West Coast Plays is published four times a year (Spring, Summer, Fall, and Winter) in Berkeley, California, by the California Theatre Council. Subscriptions are available at $20 per year. Send checks or money order to West Coast Plays, P.O. Box 7206, Berkeley, CA 94707.

This project is supported by grants from the National Endowment for the Arts, the Coordinating Council of Literary Magazines, The Zellerbach Family Fund, and The San Francisco Foundation.

West Coast Plays prints only plays which have been produced in a theater on the Pacific Coast of the Americas and can consider only those scripts which have been recommended by a member of the advisory board.

ISBN: 0-934782-11-3

The California Theatre Council is a non-profit service organization whose goals are:

To promote the development and support of non-profit theater in California

To work to increase communication within the theater community and to assist theatrical organizations with funding information, technical advice, and other matters

To provide legislators, arts agencies, and the general public with information on the special concerns of the California non-profit community.

While all the arts have broad areas of common concern, theater has its own special problems, a fact sometimes overlooked by granting agencies and unknown to much of the public. The CTC was formed in 1974 to explore and address the unique problems of the non-profit theater in California and it bases its purposes, goals, and objectives upon the multifaceted needs of the state's theatrical communities. Theatrical activity in California is intense, varied, and reflects the extraordinary ethnic, geographic, and economic diversity of the state. The strongest element in support of the CTC's need and effectiveness is the scope of its membership — organizations spanning the spectrum of California non-profit theater with budgets ranging from $10,000 to $7,000,000 per year. Member theaters encompass every demographic and geographic area and present traditional, ethnic, alternative, and experimental theater.

EDITOR

Rick Foster

REGIONAL EDITORS

Richard Edwards and Lisa Shipley, Seattle
Susan LaTempa, Los Angeles
Edward Weingold, San Francisco

Contents

The Shrunken Head of Pancho Villa
Luis Valdez

A Mi Padre, Francisco "Pancho" Valdez

The Shrunken Head of Pancho Villa was first presented at the Studio Theatre, San Jose State University, San Jose, on January 14, 1965 with the following cast:

PEDRO	William Pendergrast
CRUZ	Carol Pendergrast
BELARMINO	Iver Flom
LUPE	Sally Kemp
JOAQUIN	D. Fred Kahn
MINGO	Dan Zanvettor
CHATO	Davoud Ismaili
POLICEMAN	Gary Sacco
NELLIE	Gretchen Green

Directed by Luis Valdez
Settings by Dan Zanvettor
Costumes by Margaret Ann Crain
Lighting by William Pendergrast *and* Dan Zanvettor
Musical arrangement by Kent Newman

The play was later the first full-length production of El Teatro Campesino, which performed it with the following cast:

PEDRO	Luis Valdez
CRUZ	Donna Haber
JOAQUIN	Danny Valdez
LUPE	Guadalupe Trujillo
MINGO	Agustin Lira
CHATO	Ruben Rodriquez
BELARMINO	Guadalupe Saavedra
COP	Corky Sartwell

Directed by Luis Valdez
Designs by Dave Purdy

PERSONAJES

PEDRO, the jefito, an old Villista con huevos.
CRUZ, the madre, long-suffering but loving.
JOAQUIN, the youngest son, a vato loco and a Chicano.
LUPE, the daughter.
MINGO, the son, a Mexican-American.
CHATO, Joaquin's camarada.
BELARMINO, the oldest son.
LA JURA, a police officer.

SCENE

The interior of an old house: a large, imposing two-story building sagging into total dilapidation. The front room with tall cracked windows; doors to a stairwell and the kitchen; and an adjoining room with a curtained doorway, once a study now also a bedroom. This front room, which is the center of the play's action, has been repainted with a true Mexican folk taste. Bright reds, yellows and blues try to obscure the shabby, broken-down "chingado" quality of it all.

NOTE ON STYLE

The play is not intended as a "realistic" interpretation of Chicano life. The symbolism emerging from the character of Belarmino influences the style of acting, scene design, make-up, etc. The play therefore contains realistic and surrealistic elements working together to achieve a transcendental expression of the social condition of La Raza in los Estados Unidos. The set, particularly, must be "real" for what it represents; but it must also contain a cartoon quality such as that found in the satirical sketches of Jose Clemente Orozco or the lithographs of Jose Guadalupe Posada. In short, it must reflect the psychological reality of the barrio.

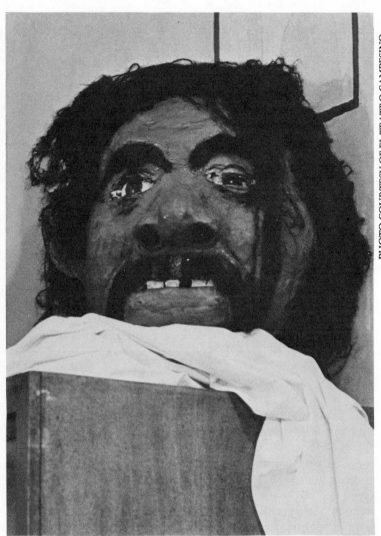

The Shrunken Head of Pancho Villa

Luis Valdez

PROLOGUE

FRANCISCO VILLA, born 1878—died 1923*

Campesino, bandit, guerrilla, martyr, general, head of Northern Division of the Revolutionary Army, and finally an undying legend.

He is born and christened Doroteo Arango in the town of Rio Grande, state of Durango. In 1895, when he is 17, he is outlawed for kiling an *hacendado,* a landowner—a member of the ruling class who had raped his sister. He is caught, but escapes and he takes the name of Francisco Villa. Thus, during the years between 1896 and 1909, the legend of Pancho Villa is born. The legend of the providential bandit: rob the rich to give to the poor. And the poor give him their faith.

1910 brings the beginning of the Mexican Revolution. Pancho Villa enlists his band of men as a guerrilla force. Minor victories grow into major victories: San Andres, Camargo, Juarez, Torreon, Zacatecas, Irapuato, Queretaro. The bandit force becomes a Revolutionary Army with horses, trains, cavalry, artillery, and a mass of 50,000 men. The peasant outlaw evolves into one of the most brilliant military strategists of our century.

November 27, 1914: Pancho Villa and Emiliano Zapata meet in Mexico City. It is a triumph for the poor, the campesinos, the disinherited. Pancho Villa tries out the Presidential chair, yet neither he nor Zapata are compromising types. They are not politicians.

1915: Against the recommendations of his advisors, Woodrow Wilson, President of the United States recognizes the rival

---

*As produced by El Teatro Campesino, this short biography formed the narrative of a slide show that opened the play, showing photographs from the life and career of Francisco Villa.

Carranzista government, and permits Carranza to transport troops over American soil and thus outflank Villa's Division del Norte at Agua Prieta. Villa is defeated. It is the beginning of the end.

1916: Villa retaliates with a raid on Columbus, New Mexico. He is declared an outlaw by the Carranza government, and Wilson sends General John J. Pershing into Mexican Territory on a "punitive expedition" looking for Pancho Villa. Pershing fails, and Villa resumes his guerrilla warfare. His military strength however is flagging.

1919: Emiliano Zapata is murdered on April 10 in Chinameca.

1920: July 28. Francisco Villa surrenders the remains of his army to the government. He settles in Canutillo and lives peacefully.

July 23, 1923: Pancho Villa is ambushed and he dies in the streets of Parral, Chihuahua. His body is dumped into an unmarked grave. Three years later it is disinterred and the corpse is decapitated. The head is never found. This is the story of a people who followed him beyond borders, beyond death.

A C T   O N E

A *sharp-stringed guitar plays* "La Cucaracha." *It is afternoon.*
    PEDRO, *the aged father of the family, is asleep on a broken-down couch. He is on his back—his paunch sagging—and snoring loudly. He has long, drooping white moustaches and toussled white hair.*
    The guitar concludes "La Cucaracha" *with a sharp, final note.* PEDRO, *as if by cue, shouts violently.*

PEDRO: (*In his sleep.*) VIVA VILLAA!!

BELARMINO *screams from the curtained bedroom. It is the cry of a full-grown man. He starts singing with vengeance.*

BELARMINO: Aarrrrrrgh! (*Sings.*)

> LA CUCARACHA! LA CUCARACHA
> YA NO QUIERE CAMINAR
> PORQUE LE FALTA, PORQUE NO TIENE
> MARIJUANA QUE FUMAR!

CRUZ: (*Running from the kitchen.*) Dios mio, you see what you do, hombre? You have wake up your own son! (BELARMINO *repeats "La Cucaracha," getting louder and more viciously impatient.* CRUZ, *distraught, runs into the curtained bedroom. From off.*) Belarmino, Belarmino, my son, go to sleep. Go to sleep. A la rrurru, niño, duermete ya. (BELARMINO *dozes off singing and is finally silent.* CRUZ *emerges, sighing with relief.*) Gracios a dios! He's asleep! (*To* PEDRO, *a harsh whisper.*) Be quiet, you old loco! You know he always wakes up hungry. I got enough trouble catching your son's lices so they don' eat us alive! You are crawling with them already.

PEDRO: (*In his sleep.*) Señores, I am Francisco Villa! (*Scratches.*)
CRUZ: Sweet name of God.
PEDRO: Pancho Villa!
CRUZ: Pedro!
PEDRO: I am Pancho Villa!
CRUZ: Yes, with lices!
PEDRO: Viva Villa!
CRUZ: Que hombre. (*She goes to him.*)
PEDRO: VIVA PANCHO VEE-
CRUZ: (*Pulls his leg.*) PEDRO!
PEDRO: Yah! (*He wakes up.*) Uh!
CRUZ: Stop shouting, hombre.
PEDRO: Uh. (*He goes back to sleep, scratching his belly.*)
CRUZ: Viejo loco. Pancho Villa. I don' know what goes through that head he gots. (JOAQUIN *rushes in and stops, panting against the door. His shirt is torn.*) Joaquin! What happen to you?
JOAQUIN: Nothing.
CRUZ: What did you do?
JOAQUIN: Nothing.
CRUZ: What happen to your shirt?
JOAQUIN: Nothing!
CRUZ: Don' you know nothing but nothing?
JOAQUIN: (*Pause.*) I beat up some vato.
CRUZ: Another fight, my son?
JOAQUIN: I never start it. Dumb gavacho. He come up to me and says "Heh, Pancho!"
PEDRO: (*In his sleep.*) Uh?
CRUZ: You hit him for that?
JOAQUIN: Well, how would you like it, man? I wasn' looking for

no trouble. I even take Pancho at first, which was bad enough, but then he call me a lousy Pancho, and I hit the stupid vato in the mouth.

CRUZ: Dios mio! (*Pause.*) What is wrong with you hombre? Don' you think? You on patrol!

JOAQUIN: Parole.

CRUZ: Si. (*Sighs.*) and mañana it will be the jail again, no? How come you this way, hijo? Your brother Mingo he never fight so much.

JOAQUIN: He was pus-pus.

CRUZ: (*Miserable*) Don' you know nothing else? Your brother he's coming from the war today with muchos medals, Joaquin. That is not so pus-pus. If he fight, he do it in the right place. Only you turn out so lousy.

JOAQUIN: (*Fiercely.*) I ain' lousy, ma!

CRUZ: (*Pause.*) You goin to hit me in the mouth too, my son? (JOAQUIN *starts to go.*) What you doin?

JOAQUIN: Splittin'!

CRUZ: Joaquin!

JOAQUIN: (*He stops.*) Stop bugging me, jefita!

CRUZ: (*With deep concern.*) What trouble you so much, hijo?

JOAQUIN: The gavachos.

LUPE: (*Comes in from the kitchen.*) Mama, the beans are ready! You wan' me to bring 'em?

CRUZ: No, Lupe, Belarmino is asleep.

LUPE: What happen to our favorite jailbird?

JOAQUIN: Shut up!

LUPE: Been out duk'ing again, huh? Rotten pachuco.

CRUZ: Guadalupe, don' say that.

LUPE: It's true. He barely got outa jail yesterday, and now look at him. He don' even care that Mingo's coming home from the war. I bet he's just jealous.

JOAQUIN: Of what?

LUPE: His medals.

JOAQUIN: Screw his medals!

CRUZ: Joaquin! Don' you even feel glad your brother's come home alive and safe?

JOAQUIN: Simon, it make me feel real patriotic.

LUPE: Liar! Just wait till Mingo gets here. He'll cool your bird. Lousy hoodlum.

JOAQUIN: Lousy, huh? Well, how about this? (*He grabs* LUPE *and pretends to set a louse loose in her hair.*) Ha! Who's lousy now, man?

LUPE: Ayy, Mama! Mama!

CRUZ: Haven' you do enough already, muchacho?

JOAQUIN: I was only joking.

CRUZ: But Belarmino—

JOAQUIN: I was only joking, man! I don' got no piojos.

LUPE: That's what you think.

JOAQUIN: Shut up!

LUPE: You lousy Mexican!

CRUZ: Stop it, señorita. Din't I tell you to go water the beans?

LUPE: No!

CRUZ: Go water the beans! (*Pause.*) Andale. Go, Guadalupe. (LUPE *exits.*)

JOAQUIN: And stay out!

CRUZ: You stop too, Joaquin. Wha's wrong with you anyways? Are you as loco as your padre?

JOAQUIN: Loco?

CRUZ: Making noise! This morning your poor brother he eat 50 plates of beans and 100 tortillas. This afternoon I fine 30 lices on him—do you hear, hombre? 30! My poor Belarmino, some of this days if he don' eat us out of the house, his lices they will do it. (*She turns and notices* JOAQUIN *scratching his head.*) Joaquin, what you doing?

JOAQUIN: (*Stops.*) What? (*Lowers his hand.*)

CRUZ: You was scratching your head! Blessed be the Señor! Come here, sit down.

JOAQUIN: (*Guiltily.*) What?

CRUZ: (*Inspecting his head.*) Dios mio, this all we need.

JOAQUIN: (*Angry.*) What?

CRUZ: For you to catch the lices, muchacho.

JOAQUIN: (*Tries to rise.*) Lices!

CRUZ: Don' move. (JOAQUIN *remains still.*) Joaquin! I think I find one! No . . . si . . . si! It is one. It gots little legs!

JOAQUIN: (*Jumps up.*) Let's see.

CRUZ: Put him up to the light, my son. (*Pause.*) It is . . . one lice, no?

JOAQUIN: A louse.

CRUZ: What is that?

JOAQUIN: One lice.

CRUZ: May the Señor help us all! (BELARMINO *grunts.*) Ay. Now he's waking up again. I better fix his frijolitos. (*Exits to kitchen.*)

JOAQUIN: Me too, huh señora? My pipes are rumbling.

PEDRO: Si, mi general. I hear the rumbling. The gringos got cannons y aeroplanos, pero no se apure . . . mi General! Que paso con su cabeza? Muchachos, abusados! Alguien se robo la cabeza de Pancho Villa! Ayyy.

JOAQUIN: (*Shaking him.*) Pa! 'apa!

PEDRO: (*Awaking.*) Uh? What?

JOAQUIN: You have a nightmare.

PEDRO: How you know?

JOAQUIN: You shout. Something about Pancho Villa and his head. I don' know. It was in Spanish.

PEDRO: Huh. (*Sits up.*) Where's your madre?

JOAQUIN: In the kitchen

PEDRO: Frying beans no doubt, *eh?* Only I never get to try 'em. The loco in the room over theres always eat 'em first. Curse the day all my sons was born starving in the land of the gringos! (*He finds an empty wine bottle under the couch.*) Ay, here it is. No, hombre, my little bottle is dead. Oye, my son, you got enough maybe for one . . . bueno, you know, eh?

JOAQUIN: Nel, I'm sorry, jefito.

PEDRO: No, don' start wis your "I'm sorrys." Don' you find work yet?

JOAQUIN: Work?

PEDRO: Field work.

JOAQUIN: You mean like farm labor?

PEDRO: Man's work!

JOAQUIN: Cool it, ese, I just get here. They work me enough in the can. I pull off more than a year wisout pay.

PEDRO: Bueno, it's your own fault. For your itchy fingers . . . stealing tires.

JOAQUIN: What tires?

PEDRO: Pos what ones? They din' catch you red-handed?

JOAQUIN: Simon, but it wasn' tires. They arrest me for a suspect together with nine other vatos. Then there at the station the placa give us all matches, and the one wis the short one was guilty. They catch me red-handed! But I din't swipe no tires.

PEDRO: No, eh? Well, I hope maybe you learn something.

JOAQUIN: No sweat, jefito. I learn to play the guitar.

PEDRO: Tha's all?

JOAQUIN: Nel, I sing too. Honest. Loan me your guitar, I show you.

PEDRO: No, Joaquin, I don' like to loan that guitar. I have too many years with it, since the Revolucion! Que caray, what happen if you break it. Ees too old.

JOAQUIN: What about when I fix it that time?

PEDRO: When?

JOAQUIN: When you smash it on Mingo's head.

PEDRO: Oh si. But the babozo he talk back to me, tha's how come. Bueno, que caray, go bring it pues— I want to see if you really know how to play it.

JOAQUIN: Orale. (*He goes into the side room and comes out with an old guitar.*)

PEDRO: What you play? Corridos, rancheras?

JOAQUIN: Rhythm and Blues.

PEDRO: (*Pause.*) What about "Siete Leguas"?

JOAQUIN: What about it?

PEDRO: You see, you don' know nothing.

JOAQUIN: What's "Siete Leguas"?

PEDRO: "Seven Leguas"! How you say leguas in—

JOAQUIN: Uh, leaguews.

PEDRO: What?

JOAQUIN: Lea-gews.

PEDRO: That's right. "Siete Leguas." The song of the horse of Pancho Villa. The horse he mos' estimated. (*Solemnly.*) He ride that horse until the day he die.

JOAQUIN: The general?

PEDRO: No, the horse. After that Pancho Villa buy a Chivi. Maybe it was a Ford? No, it was a Chivi. 1923! That was the year they kill him, you know. A revolutionary giant like he was.

JOAQUIN: Aaah, he wasn' a giant.

PEDRO: Oh, caray, you don' know, my son! Francisco Villa was a man to respect. A man to fear! A man con muchos . . . ummmhhh (*Huevos.*) He rob from the rich to give to the poor— like us. That's why the poor follow him. Any time he could rise 50,000 men by snapping his fingers. You should have see what he do to the gringos.

JOAQUIN: The gavachos?

PEDRO: No, the gringos. In them times they was only call gringos. Not gavachos. Pancho Villa have 'em running all over Mexico.

JOAQUIN: What was they doing in Mexico?

PEDRO: Chasing him! But they never catch him. He was too smart, eh? Too much cabeza. He ride on Siete Leguas and stay in the

mountains. Then he ride his men around the back, and they kill
gringos until they get tired! Sometimes they even get more tire'
than picking potatoes, but they go back to the mountains to
rest.

JOAQUIN: (*Impressed.*) Heh, man, tha's too much.

PEDRO: I myself ride with him, you know. See this scar? (*Points to
his neck.*) From a bullet. And listen to this: VIVA VILLAAAA!

CRUZ: (*In the kitchen.*) Pedro, hombre! You wake your son!

PEDRO: (*Shouts back.*) Oh, you and that crazy loco! (*To* JOAQUIN.)
Huh, that stinking madre of yours! All she live for is to feed that
bean belly! He has curse my life.

JOAQUIN: What about Pancho Villa? When he got the Chivi? I bet
he run down a lotta gavachos, huh? Squashed 'em!

PEDRO: (*With exaggeration.*) Oh si! He—(*Pause.*) The Chivi? No,
hombre, when he get the Chivi then they get him. Right in
Chihuahua too, in Parral. He was just driving down the street
one day, not bothering nobody, when they shoot him down and
kill him. (*Mournful pause.*) So . . . they bury him, and then in
the night three years later, somebody come and—ZAS! They cut
off his head.

JOAQUIN: His *head?*

PEDRO: Chattap! (*Whispering.*) You want Belarmino to hear?

JOAQUIN: How come they cut off his head? Who done it?

PEDRO: Pos who you think?

JOAQUIN: Los gavachos!

PEDRO: (*Nods.*) Maybe they still even got it too. To this day
nobody has find it.

JOAQUIN: Hijola, how gacho, man. (*Pause.*) How did that song
goes?

PEDRO: "Siete Leguas"?

JOAQUIN: Simon.

PEDRO: (*Sings.*) "Siete Leguas, el caballo que Villa mas estimabaaa."

BELARMINO: (*In his room.*) Ay! Yai! Yai! Yai!

PEDRO: Oh-oh, now we do it.

CRUZ: (*Entering.*) What have you do, hombre?

PEDRO: NOTHING. (BELARMINO *yells and howls, sings "La Cucaracha."*)

CRUZ: No, eh? (*Shouting back.*) Lupe, bring the tortillas!

PEDRO: We eat now?

CRUZ: You wait!

PEDRO: I don' wan to wait! (BELARMINO *yells.*)

CRUZ: Lupe, bring the beans too ! (*She goes into the bedroom.*)

PEDRO: I don' got to wait! I wan' to eat — EAT! Quiero tragar! (*LUPE comes out of the kitchen with beans and tortillas.* JOAQUIN *grabs a tortilla with a laugh.*)

LUPE: You pig!

PEDRO: (*Turns around.*) Pig?

LUPE: I meant Joaquin. (*She goes into the bedroom quickly.*)

PEDRO: Sinverguenzas! Who's the boss here pues? Who buys the eats!

CRUZ: (*Inside the room.*) El Welfare!

PEDRO: And before that?

CRUZ: Your son, Mingo.

PEDRO: Mingo? (*Throws his arms out in a helpless gesture.*) So this is what I get, eh? In 1927 I come here all the way from Zacatecas. For what? CHICKENSQUAT? Everybody talks back, that . . . that loco in there eats before his padre does, and Mingo . . . Mingo . . . Where's Mingo?

JOAQUIN: (*Eating the rolled up tortilla.*) Not home from the war yet.

MINGO *walks into the room through the front door. He is in a soldier's uniform and carries a sack with his stuff in it.*

MINGO: Somebody say war?

LUPE: (*Peeking out of* BELARMINO'*s room.*) Mama, Mingo's home!

CRUZ: (*Coming out with the bowl of beans.*) My son! (*She embraces him and cries.*)

PEDRO: Bueno, bueno, lemme see him. He's my son too!

MINGO: Hello, Pa. (*Offers his hand.*)

PEDRO: Halo que? Give me one abrazo, I'm your padre! (*He hugs him.*) Tha's it — strong like a man. Look, vieja, see how much medals he gots?

LUPE: Hi Mingo, remember me?

MINGO: Sure. Maria!

LUPE: Maria!

MINGO: (*Pause.*) Rosita?

LUPE: Lupe!

MINGO: Oh, yeah, Lupe.

PEDRO: And over heres you got your brother Joaquin.

MINGO: Hi, punk. Shake.

JOAQUIN: Orale. (*They shake hands.*)

CRUZ: Well, my son, sit down. Rest. You must be tired.

MINGO: Not at all, mom.

CRUZ: Tienes hambre?

MINGO: What's for dinner?

CRUZ: Papas con huevos.

MINGO: What else?

LUPE: Huevos con papas.

MINGO: Is that all?

JOAQUIN: Papas a huevo.

MINGO: No thanks. I had a steak in town.

CRUZ: Oh. Well, thank God you have come home safe and sound. (*She takes him to the couch.*) Look, sit down over here. Tell us about . . . . (*She sees the wine bottle.*) Pedro hombre, this dirty bottle!

MINGO: Still at it, huh pa?

PEDRO: No, only from time to times, hijo. For the cough. (*He coughs.*)

LUPE: Tell us of the war, Mingo.

CRUZ: What's wrong with you, women? Your brother he want to forget such things. It already pass, gracias a dios.

PEDRO: Huh, it pass. You mean we don' suppose to know where the muchacho was? War is war! If the sons fight today, we fight yesterday. Mira, when I was with Pancho Villa, we kill more Americanos than—

MINGO: Americanos? Americans!

BELARMINO: (*In his room.*) ARRRRRGGGHHH!

MINGO: (*Alarmed.*) What the hell's that?

CRUZ: Belarmino! Lupe, please give him the beans that was left. I had forgot he din't finish eating.

LUPE: He never finish eating. (*She exits.*)

MINGO: Mom, who's Belarmino?

CRUZ: (*Surprised.*) Pos . . . you know, hijo. You don' remember?

PEDRO: Of course, he remember! Caray, how he's going to forgot that animal? Don' let him bother you, my son. Come here, tell me your plans. What you going to do now?

MINGO: Well, 'apa, I been thinking. (*Long pause.*)

PEDRO: He's been thinking, que bueno. What you been thinking, hijo?

MINGO: I been thinking I wanna help the family!

CRUZ: Ay, mijito! (*She embraces him.* PEDRO *shakes his hand.*)

MINGO: As a matter of fact, I gotta surprise for you. I bet you din't expect me till tonight, right? Well, you know how come I'm home early? I bought a new car!

JOAQUIN: A new car!

CRUZ: A new car!

LUPE: (*Reentering.*) A new car!

BELARMINO *grunts three times, mimicking the sound of the words, "A new car."*

CRUZ: Dios mio!

LUPE: We din't even hear you drive up!

MINGO: Natch. She's as quiet as a fly in the beans. Mom, sis— hold on to your frijole bowl. There she is! (*Points out the window.*) A new Chevrolet!

LUPE: A Chevi! Mama, un Chevi!

CRUZ: Blessed be the name of the Señor. That one is ours, Mingo?

MINGO: All ours, only forty more payments to go. (*Everyone looks out the window except* PEDRO.) What's wrong, pa? Ain't you going to see?

PEDRO: For what? They going to come for it in two months.

MINGO: Not this baby. I'm gonna keep up all my payments.

PEDRO: Tha's what I used to say. I never make it.

MINGO: I know, but I ain't you. (*Pause.*) I mean it wasn' necessary, dad. Give me one good reason why you didn't keep good credit. Just one!

PEDRO: (BELARMINO *grunts hungrily in his room.*) There it is.

CRUZ: Guadalupe, go. (LUPE *exits to room.*)

MINGO: (*Pause. Everybody dejected.*) You know what's wrong with you people? You're all defeated! Just look at this place! Well, it ain't gonna get me down. I learned some skills in the Marines, and I'm gonna use 'em in the best place I know to get ahead!

PEDRO: Where?

MINGO: The fields.

JOAQUIN: A farm labor? (*Laughs.*) You going to be a farm labor?

MINGO: Listen you cholo.

CRUZ: Mingo, no!

PEDRO: Callate el hocico, babozo.

MINGO: What's he ever done but land in jail, mom? What you ever done? (JOAQUIN *blows a raspberry in his face.*)

CRUZ: Joaquin, es-stop it.

MINGO: You drop-out. You high school drop-out!

CRUZ: Mingo, please—

MINGO: You know what you're gonna end up like? Like the old man—a stinking *wino!*

PEDRO: WHAT?!

MINGO: (*Embarrassed pause.*) Aw, come on, dad. I din' mean no- thing bad. Look, let's face it, okay? You're just a wino, right? Like I'm a Marine. What's wrong with that? There's a million of 'em. Today I was even going to buy you a bottle of Old Crow.

PEDRO: Whiskey?

MINGO: Damn rights. $6.50 a quart. It's better than that 35 cent stuff you been drinking. From now on it's nothing but the best for us. Only we gotta be realistic. Plan everything. Okay, Tomahawk, you'll be working with me. You got a job now?

JOAQUIN: Chale.

MINGO: You mean dad's the only one working?

PEDRO: (*Pause.*) Eh . . . no, I don' work neither, Mingo.

MINGO: Then how do you support yourselfs?

JOAQUIN: How come you don' tell him, pa? The jefitos are on welfare, ese.

MINGO: Welfare? WELFARE! (*He turns away, sick.*)

CRUZ: We always been poor, my son.

MINGO: (*Determined.*) That's true, mom. But now things are gonna be different. I'm here now, and we're going to be rich— middle class! I didn't come out the war without learning nothing.

JOAQUIN: Then how come you going back to the fields? Nobody get rich in that jale.

MINGO: No, huh? (*He embraces* CRUZ *and* PEDRO.) Well, thanks to this old man and old lady, who were smart enough to cross the border, we live in the land of opportunity. The land I risk my life for. The land where you can start at the bottom, even in the fields, and become a rich man before you can say—

BELARMINO: ARRRGGGHHH! (LUPE *comes running with her blouse torn on one side.*)

LUPE: AY! Mama! He eat all the beans then he try to bite me!

CRUZ: Por dios. The poor man.

LUPE: The poor man? He's a pig. Look at the hole he made.

CRUZ: Alright pues, I see it.

LUPE: And he give me his piojos.

CRUZ: No matter. Go bring more tortillas!

MINGO: Wait a minute, *wait a minute!* Mom, for the last time, who's in there?

CRUZ: Your older brother, hijo. Belarmino.

MINGO: Brother? I don't remember no other brother. What's wrong with him, how come he shouts?

PEDRO: Hay, pos 'ta loco el babozo.

CRUZ: (*Surprised.*) He's sick . . . but you should know. You used to play with him when you was little.

MINGO: Ma, don' lie to me. Are we so poor we gotta take in braceros? Or maybe it's a wetback you're hiding?

JOAQUIN: (*A whisper to* PEDRO.)Or maybe he suffering from shell-shock?

MINGO: I ain't suffering from nothing, man!

JOAQUIN: Take it easy, carnal, cool it.

MINGO: Well, ma, is that guy a wetback?

CRUZ: No, he's your brother.

MINGO: Brother, huh? We'll soon find out! (*He charges into the bedroom.*)

BELARMINO: (*After a pause.*) ARRRRRRRGGGGHH.

MINGO: (*Running out.*) ARRRRGGGGHH! He ain't got a body. He's just a . . . HEAD!

Curtain.

A C T   T W O

Three months later. The walls of the house are moderately speckled with red cockroaches of various sizes. LUPE *is standing behind* PEDRO, *who is asleep on a chair, delousing him. On an old sofa in the corner, a white lace veil covers* BELARMINO — *like a child. The radio is blaring out frantic mariachi music, "La Negra."* LUPE *finds something in* PEDRO'*s hair.*

LUPE: (*Gasps.*) Lousy cucaracha!

CRUZ: (*Shouting from the kitchen.*) Negra, shut off the noises, diablo! (*Pause.*) Negra! Belarmino is sleeping!

LUPE: Mama, stop calling me negra.

CRUZ: Shut off the noises, sonavavichi!

LUPE: (*Shuts off radio.*) Okay pues, I did, man! (BELARMINO *grunts from under the veil.*) What you want? (BELARMINO *grunts harder.*) No, no more radio. Did't you hear mi 'ama? Go to sleep! (BELARMINO *grunts again.*) Ay, that stupid cabeza! (*She removes the veil and* BELARMINO *is seen for the first time: he is the head of a man about 30-35 years old. That is all. He has no body. He has long hair and a large mustache. His black eyes are deep and expressive. The head is otherwise only distinguished by its tremendous size. A full eighteen inches in diameter.*)

BELARMINO: (*Singing.*) "La Cucarachaa!"

LUPE: Shut up! (BELARMINO *laughs idiotically.*) Idiot, because of you I'm like a slave in this house. Joaquin and Mingo and e'rybody goes to town but they never let me go. I gotta be here — ready to stuff you with frijoles. Like a maid, like a negra.

CHATO: (*At the front door.*) Hi, negra.

LUPE: (*Covering* BELARMINO.) What you call me?

CHATO: N—othing.

BELARMINO: Callate el hocico!

CHATO: Why!

LUPE: Mi papa, he's asleep.

CHATO: Oh! Heh, tha's Belarmino behind there, huh?

LUPE: Where at?

CHATO: Under that velo. (*Points to veil.*)

LUPE: No! My brother's a man, how could he fit in there?

CHATO: You know. (*He laughs.*)

LUPE: Look, Chato, if you come to make fun of us you better cut it out, man. Belo's sick, he don'—(BELARMINO *grunts.*) Okay, okay hombre. In a minute. Here, have a cockroach. (*She takes a cockroach off the wall and gives it to him.*)

CHATO: (*Open mouthed.*) How come he eats cockaroaches?

LUPE: Because he's hungry, dumbbell.

CHATO: I'm not a dumb-bell!

LUPE: Oh no, *you're* real smart. Only you don't even know how to read or write. You think we din't go to the second grade together? Menso.

CRUZ: (*In the kitchen.*) Guadalupe?

LUPE: Si, mama? (*She makes a sign to* CHATO *not to say anything.*)

CRUZ: Who you talking to?

LUPE: Belarmino, mama. I'm cleaning his cucarachas.

CRUZ: Okay pues, don' let him eat 'em.

CHATO: (*Looking under the veil.*) En la Madre, what a big head.

LUPE: (*Turning, whispering furiously.*)What you doing? Let him alone! Nobody tell you to come in. Get out!

CHATO: How come?

LUPE: Because.

CHATO: Huy, huy que touchy. Come on, esa. Don' play hard-to-get.

LUPE: (*Menacing the fly-spray pump.*) Look stupid, I'll hit you.

CHATO: Okay, don't get mad. I come over to see Mingo. He don' pay me yet.

LUPE: Liar. He said he pay you two days ago.

CHATO: What days ago? I been searching for a week for him. He haven't pay me nothing. I go to the rancho, he ain't there. I come over here—same story. This whole thing is beginning to smell. (BELARMINO *farts loudly.*) Sacos! de potatoes. Heh, wha's wrong with this ruco?

LUPE: None of your business. Pig!

CHATO: Din' he just learn to talk too?

LUPE: No!

CHATO: Joaquin says he sings *"La Cucaracha."*

LUPE: He's crazy, man.

BELARMINO: (*Singing.*) LA CUCARACHA, LA CUCARACHA!

CHATO: No que no? That cat do okay.

LUPE: Oh, how you know? I'm sick and tired of this freak. Feeding him beans, taking out his louses. Listening to that stupid little song. That's all he knows. He don' talk. If he wants to eat he still shout or grunts like he's doing it all my life. I almost can't stand it no more!

CHATO: (*Putting his arm around her.*) Okay pues, mi honey. Don't cry. Some of these days I'm going to take you away from all this.

LUPE: What all this?

CHATO: This poverty, this cucarachas, this . . . this . . . .

LUPE: This what?

CHATO: You know . . . Belarmino. I don' say nothing, but . . .well there's the Raza, no? El chisme. People talk.

LUPE: (*Sobering.*) What they say?

CHATO: Well, you know . . . dicen que tu carnal es una cabeza.

LUPE: Una what?

CHATO: Cabeza.

LUPE: Sorry, guy. I don' speak Spanish.

CHATO: Una HEAD! (PEDRO *wakes, goes back to sleep with a grunt.*) Tha's what they say. No arms, no legs, no nothing. Just a head. (*Laughs.*)

LUPE: You black negro! You dirty Mexican! (*She attacks* CHATO.)

CHATO: Orale, hold it there! (*He grabs her.*)

LUPE: Let me go, Chato.

CHATO: Who's a dirty Mexican!

LUPE: You, and ugly too. And more blacker than a Indian.

CHATO: Huy, huy, huy, and you like cream, uh. I'm dark because I work in the fields all day in the sun. I get burn! But look here. (*Shows her his armpit.*) See? Almost tan.

LUPE: You're loco.

CHATO: Chure, loco about you, mi vida. Don' make me suffer. I don' care if Belarmino's a cabeza.

LUPE: Chato, mi papa'll wake up.

CHATO: So what? Te digo que te quiero, que te amo, que te adoro.

LUPE: My mother's in the kitchen.

CHATO: Tu eres mi sol, mi luna, mi cielo . . .

LUPE: Chatito, por favor.

CHATO: Mis tamales, mis tortillas, mis frijoles!

CRUZ: (*Entering from the kitchen.*) GUADALUPE!

LUPE: (*Matter-of-factly.*) Mi mama.

CHATO: (*Turns.*) Buenas tardes. (*He runs out.*)

CRUZ: Si, buenas tardes, you shameless goddammit! (*Turns.*) Pedro!

PEDRO: (*In his sleep.*) Si, mi General?

CRUZ: Pedro, hombre wake up!

PEDRO: Viva Villa.

CRUZ: You old loco.

PEDRO: Viva Pancho Vi—(CRUZ *pulls his leg.*) Yah! Uh? Que paso?

CRUZ: Chato!

PEDRO: (*Jumps up.*) Chato? (*Pause.*) Chato who?

CRUZ: He was after Lupe, hombre!

PEDRO: (*Heads for kitchen.*) Where's he at?

CRUZ: (*Pulling him back.*) He went that way! Go, hombre! Serve for something!

PEDRO: Where's my rifle! WHERE'S MY GUN?

LUPE: (*Throws herself upon him.*) No, Papa!

PEDRO: You chattap! WHERE'S MY GUN, WOMEN!

CRUZ: (*Pause.*) You don' got a gun, Pedro. (*Silence.*)

LUPE: I din' do—

PEDRO: CHATTAP! Dios mio, how lousy. (*He grabs his wine bottle beside the chair.*) You see? This is what I get for coming to the land of the gringos. No respect! I should have stay in Zacatecas. (*He heads for the door.*)

CRUZ: Pedro, where you going?

PEDRO: Where I feel like it, sabes? To look for work.

CRUZ: At sundown?

PEDRO: La night shift, mujer! Maybe I go back to Zacatecas.

CRUZ: Oh si, hitchi-hiking.

PEDRO: Callate si no quieres que te plante un guamaso! Vieja desgraciada!

MINGO *enters dressed in new khaki work clothes, complete with new hat and boots. He carries a clipboard with papers and a money box.*

MINGO: Home sweet home! E'erybody yelling as usual? What was Super-Mex running about?

CRUZ: Who?

MINGO: Chato. He come flying outa here like the immigration was after him.

CRUZ: He was after Lupe.

MINGO: (*To* PEDRO.) Where were you, man?

CRUZ: Your padre was asleep.

MINGO: (*Deliberately.*) Oh.

PEDRO: (*Sensing disrespect.*) Oh, what?

MINGO: Oh, nothing — dad.

PEDRO: Some of this days, cabron, you going to say "oh, something else." Then we see who's boss around here. (*To* LUPE). I take care of you later, señorita. (*He exits.*)

CRUZ: Dios mio, that old loco. Now he won' be home until it is so late. Then he gots to cross the tracks in the dark. (*To* LUPE.) You see? You see what you do?

LUPE: I din' do nothing! Chato grab me!

MINGO: What you mean he grabbed you? Just took a little grab, huh?

LUPE: No, he was telling me about Belo. The whole neighborhood's talking about him! They say he don' got no arms or legs or nothing. That he's a —

CRUZ: What?

LUPE: You know what. (*Uncomfortable pause.*)

CRUZ: No, I don' know. My son is sick! How can they say such things?

MINGO: Forget 'em, ma. They do it from envy.

LUPE: Envy, of Belo?

MINGO: Of me! Since they always pass the time drunk or begging on welfare, they can't stand a man who betters himself. But they ain't seen nothing yet. Mom, sit down over here. I got something to tell you. You too, negra.

LUPE: Don' call me negra, Mingo.

MINGO: Can't you take a joke?

LUPE: No!

MINGO: Sit down. (*She sits.*) Okay now. Ma, remember that place where we picked prunes for so many years? On Merd Road? (CRUZ *nods.*) Well, it's called Merde Boulevard now. They cut down the orchard and built new houses on the land. They got a big sign up: Prune Blossom Acres. And right under it: No Down Payment To Vets. You know what it means, ma? I'm a vet and we're gonna get a new house!

LUPE: A new house! Mama, a new house!

MINGO: (*Laughs.*) I thought that'd grab you. Well, mom, what do you say? Shall we move outa this dump? (CRUZ *is silent, she stands.*) Heh, what's wrong?

CRUZ: This ain't a dump, Mingo. It is the house of your padre.

MINGO: Padre, madre, so what? I'm talking about Prune Blossom Acres. America's at our doorstep. All we have to do is take one step.

CRUZ: What about Belarmino?

MINGO: Somebody can carry him, what else? Put him in a shoebox.

LUPE: He don't fit in a shoebox.

MINGO: Not a real shoebox, stupid. A cardboard box. We can put holes in it so he can breathe. That ain't no problem.

CRUZ: I know, Mingo, but . . . it is not the same. In this barrio they don' care.

MINGO: I care!

CRUZ: And the gringos?

MINGO: Whatta you mean, gringos?

CRUZ: Who else lives in new houses?

MINGO: Americans, ma.   American citizens like me and y— (*Pause.*) Aw, whatta you trying to do? Get me defeated too? You wanna spend the rest of your life in this stinking barrio? What about all the gossiping beanbellies? You know they're laughing at this head.

CRUZ: This what?

MINGO: (*Pause.*) Shorty.

LUPE: That's not what I heard.

MINGO: You shut up, sister.

CRUZ: His name ain't Chorti, Mingo.

MINGO: For pete's sake, Ma, I'm trying to help out here! He's my brother so I call him Shorty. What's wrong with that? He's short. The important thing's the lies people are telling about us, about Shorty, about me. I don't owe them peons nothing.

JOAQUIN: (*Standing in the doorway.*) Simon, just pay Chato what you owe him. Come on in, ese, don' be chicken.

MINGO: And what do I owe him?

JOAQUIN: His pay.

CHATO: Buenas tardes. (*He hides behind* JOAQUIN)

CRUZ: You say that before, sinverguenza! (CHATO *runs out again.*) You dare to come in after he try to steal our respect?

CHATO: (*Reentering.*) Aw, I din't come to steal nothing. I come because you robbing me!

CRUZ: What?

CHATO: Well, maybe not you, but Mingo? Tell you right off the bat, Doña Cruz, this vato's nothing but a crooked contractor!

MINGO: Crooked?

LUPE: Mingo?

CRUZ: My son?

BELARMINO: AAARRRRGH!

CRUZ: (*To* BELARMINO.) Ay no, my son, not you. You ain't crooked.

MINGO: What the hell you trying to say, Chato?

JOAQUIN: What you think, you din't hear him? He says the big war hero's a thief just like e'rybody else! So you was going to get rich working in the fields, uh? Free country and all that chet! Simon, I believe it now. Anybody can get rich if he's a crooked farm labor contractor. Only this time it's no dice, ese. Chato's my friend. Pay him.

MINGO: I already paid him! If you don't believe me, look here in my paybook. Here's everybody that receive their wages. See . . . what's signed here? (*He shows* CHATO.)

CHATO: I don' know, ees in Spanish.

MINGO: Spanish? It's your name, stupid. Chato Reyes. You sign it yourself.

JOAQUIN: Nel, carnal, we got you there. Chato don' know how to read or write.

MINGO: (*Pause.*) Of course he don't know — that's how come his "X" is here instead of his name. See? (*He shows the* "X".) Okay, Chato, if you want to prove that this ain' your "X" or that I haven't pay you, you got to take me to court, right? But just to show you I ain' crooked, I'm gonna pay you again. Sit down. (CHATO *and* MINGO *sit down.*) Alright, how many days do you work?

CHATO: Four.

MINGO: Four days, at ten hours each, is 40 hours. 40 hours at 85¢ an hour is . . . $34, right?

CHATO: Si, muchas gracias.

MINGO: One moment, social security.

CHATO: But I don't got a card.

MINGO: You an American citizen?

CHATO: Simon.

MINGO: Good. You can still pay. That's $15, plus a dollar fine for not having a card. That leaves $18, right?

CHATO: Simon, gracias.

MINGO: Hold it, income tax. 50% of 18 is 9. That leaves you $9, correct?

CHATO: Orale, gra—

MINGO: The lunches. Five tacos at 40¢ each, one chili pepper at 15¢ and a large-size coca cola at 35¢ . . . that's $2.50 a day. $2.50 for four days are-

CHATO: Heh, cut it out!

MINGO: What's wrong, a mistake?

CHATO: Simon, that ain't right! I don't pay for mordidas.

MINGO: (*Standing up.*) Morididas! What you referring to?

CHATO: Pos what? The tacos. They have bites.

CRUZ: Bites?

CHATO: Mordidotas.

LUPE: Oh-Oh, I know who done 'em.

CRUZ: You shut up, woman. (*To* MINGO, *smiling.*) I don't know who could have do it, my son. I put 'em in new everyday.

MINGO: Well, (*He sits.*) one cent discount for each taco for the bites are . . . 39¢ five times. $1.95, plus the chili pepper, the coke, etc . . . $2.45 a day. For four days that's $9.80. You had 9 dollars; you owe me 80 cents.

CHATO: OWE?

MINGO: There's the proof. Pay me. (CHATO *looks at the paper.*)

JOAQUIN: Lemme see that, ese. (*He takes the paper.*)

MINGO: (*Taking the paper from* JOAQUIN.) How about it, Chato? You pay me or what you gonna do?

BELARMINO: AARRRRRRRRRGGGGGGGGHHHHHHHH!

CRUZ: Ay mijo! (*She goes to quiet* BELARMINO.)

CHATO: Ay see you! (*He runs toward the door.*) And ees true what I say! You stupid, chet contractor! T'ief!

MINGO: Thief! You come here and say that you little—

CHATO: Ay! (*He runs out.*)

BELARMINO: AARRRRRRGGGGGGHHH!

CRUZ: Mingo, please, don' make so much fuss.

MINGO: Fuss? What you talking, señora? Din' you hear what—

CHATO: (*Peeking in again.*) I forget to say somet'ing. Stay wis you stinking head! (*He ducks out quickly.*)

CRUZ: Stinking head? Pos mira que jijo de—! (*At the door shouting.*) Arrastrado! Analfabeto! MUERTO DE HAMBRE!

MINGO: Mom!

CRUZ: YOU GODAMMIT!

MINGO: Okay, ma, that's enough! (*He pulls her back.*)

CRUZ: He call your brother a stinking head. (BELARMINO *farts sonorously.* JOAQUIN *leaves.*)

LUPE: Ay! It's true! (*Everybody moves away from* BELARMINO *except* CRUZ.) It's true. He's disgusting.

CRUZ: And what you think you are, estupida? Don' think I forget what you do with Chato, eh? Go make tortillas.

LUPE: For what? Belarmino eat 'em all.

CRUZ: No matter, go do it.

LUPE: He eat all the lunches.

MINGO: Lunches?

CRUZ: Don' talk back, I tell you. Go make tortillas!

LUPE: Oh no! I'm not a tortilla factory.

CRUZ: Pos mira que—(CRUZ *starts to hit* LUPE.)

MINGO: Wait a minute, WAIT A MINUTE, MA! What's this about the lunches?

LUPE: It's Belarmino, Mingo. We make 200 tacos for the lunches tomorrow and he already eat 150! He never get full. That's why Chato's tacos have bites, because mi 'ama give 'em to Belo.

MINGO: You give 'em to him, ma? The tacos we sell to the men?

CRUZ: He was a little hungry, my son.

MINGO: A little hungry! What about all the beans he's already eating? You seen the bills at the store lately? He's eating more and more every week.

LUPE: And that's not all, Mingo. He's also crawling wis more and more lices! And he eats cucarachas, and he stinks! I can't stand him no more. He's just a stupid . . . HEAD!

CRUZ: (*Pause. She slaps* LUPE.) Your brother is not a head.

MINGO: I oughta knock your stupid lips off.

LUPE: (*Anger, disgust.*) Go to hell. I'll never use 'em! Give 'em to Belo so he can eat *more!* I rather get married so I can suffer in my own house, even if it's with the ugliest, most stupidest man in the world. It can't be worser than this. One of this days Belarmino's gonna grunt or yell for his frijoles, and I won't be here to stuff his throat. You going to *see!* (*She goes out crying.*)

JOAQUIN: (*Reenters.*) Ma? This a piojo?

MINGO: Piojo? A louse!

JOAQUIN: One lice.

CRUZ: This ain't a piojo, my son. Ees one little . . . cucaracha, que no?

BELARMINO: ARRRRGGGHHH!

CRUZ: Ay! (*She removes* BELARMINO'*s veil.*) Dios mio!

MINGO: What the hell's on his face?

JOAQUIN: Cucarachas! (BELARMINO'S *face is covered with cockroaches of various sizes.*)

BELARMINO: (*Smiling, singing.*)

> LA CUCARACHA, LA CUCARACHA!
> YA NO PUEDE CAMINAR
> PORQUE LE FALTA, PORQUE NO TIENE
> MARIJUANA QUE FUMAR!

ACT THREE

SCENE ONE

Later that same night. BELARMINO *is on top of an old table, asleep.* JOAQUIN *staggers in drunk, singing, smoking a hand-rolled cigarette.*

JOAQUIN: (*Singing.*)

> I'm gonna sing this corrido
> And I'm feeling very sad
> Cause the great Francisco Villa
> Some vato cut off his head.
>
> La Cucaracha, La Cucaracha
> She don' wanna go no more
> You give her pesos and marijuana
> Cuca open up her door!

(*Sees* BELARMINO, *moves toward him.*)

> When they murder Pancho Villa
> His body they lay to rest
> But his head somebody take it
> All the way to the U.S.

> La Cockaroacha, La Cockaroacha
> She don' wanna caminar
> Porque le falta, porque no tiene
> She's a dirty little whore!

(*Pause.*) Heh, Belo? You a wake, ese? Come on, man. Get your butt up! Oh yeah . . . you don't got one, huh? (*Laughs.*) So what? Get up! (*Pulls his hair.*)

BELARMINO: (*Roars.*) LA CUCARACHAAA!

JOAQUIN: Tha's all you know, huh stupid? (*Mocks him.*) "Cucaracha!" (*Pause.*) Oh, a real one, eh? They even coming outa your nose, ese. Look at her . . . she's a dirty little whore. A putita. (*Holds out the small cockroach with his fingers in front of* BELARMINO'S *eyes.*) Puuu-teee-tita! (*Laughs, throws it down, squashes it.*) Well, what you looking so stupid about? It was only a stinking cockaroach. Dumb Mexican . . . not you, ese, this stupid cucaracha I squash. They love to be step on. (*Laughs.*) You know what happen tonight, man? I been all over the barrio running away from vatos. Simon, all my friends and camaradas. Like a big chingon I get 'em at work with Mingo, and he chisle 'em. Now I'm the patsy and they wanna knife me. Even Chato. He's telling e'rybody you're a head, ese. (*Laughs.*) With no guts.

BELARMINO: (*As if disembowled.*) ARRRGGGGGHHHH!

JOAQUIN: (*Whispering.*) Heh, MAN, CUT IT OUT! Shh, the jefita's gonna hear. Okay, you ask for it! (*He covers* BELARMINO *with his coat.*) Shhh. (BELARMINO *yells, muffled.* JOAQUIN *laughs.*) Come on, ese, be a sport. You wan' me to throw you out the window? (BELARMINO *stops shouting.* JOAQUIN *gives him a tug.*) Heh? (*No response.* JOAQUIN *peeks under the coat.*) You awright?

BELARMINO: Simon!

JOAQUIN: (*Covers him quickly.*) Dumb head. (*Pause.*) Heh, he say something. He's learning to talk! (*Uncovers him again.*)

BELARMINO: Cabron!

JOAQUIN: Spanish.

BELARMINO: (*Grunts.*) Uh, toque! Toque, cigarro!

JOAQUIN: What, you want' a toke? (*He holds out the cigarette.* BE-LARMINO *puffs on it eagerly.*) No, man don't just puff on it. You gotta inhale it. See, like this. (JOAQUIN *inhales.*) Take in a little air wis it.

BELARMINO: (*Grunts.*) Uh-uh, toque! (JOAQUIN *holds out the cigarette again.* BELARMINO *puffs noisely then sniffs vociferously.*)

JOAQUIN: How you like it, bueno?

BELARMINO: (*Holding his breath.*) Bueno.

JOAQUIN: (*Laughs.*) Chet, man, you just as bad as me. A lousy Mexican!

BELARMINO: ARRRGGGHHH! (JOAQUIN *covers him with his coat.*)

CRUZ: (*Runs in the front door.*) Joaquin!

JOAQUIN: Hi, Jefita.

CRUZ: What you doing? Where's Chorty?

JOAQUIN: (BELARMINO *grunts under the coat.*) He went out to take a piss.

CRUZ: Wha's that?

JOAQUIN: What? Oh, that — my coat. (BELARMINO *grunts.*)

CRUZ: Valgame dios, do you got Belarmino in there, Joaquin?

JOAQUIN: Nel, there's nobody under here. (*Lifts coat.*) See? Nobody! (*He laughs.*)

CRUZ: Belarmino! (*She goes to him.* BELARMINO *grunts, moans, breathes hard.*) He shrink —

JOAQUIN: (*Moving away from* BELARMINO.) Don' let him fool you, jefita. Maybe you think the vato grunts and tha's it, but he talks. (CRUZ *looks at him.*) No chet, I mean no lie. He do it. And it's not only "La Cucaracha." He swing in pure words, huh, ese? Simon, he just barely talk to me. Go on, ask him something.

CRUZ: (*Emotionally.*) Mijito . . . my Chorti, ees true? You can talk at last? Ees me, your madre. Speak to me! (BELARMINO *grunts.*) Ay, dios, he can talk ingles.

JOAQUIN: That was a grunt. Come on, Belo. Talk right. (BELARMINO *laughs idiotically.*) Nel, ese, don' act stupid. This is the jefita. She want to hear you talk. (BELARMINO *grunts and makes idiotic noises.*) Come on, man!

BELARMINO: ARRRGGGH!

CRUZ: Tha's enough, Joaquin. You scare him. I don' know how you can make fun of your poor brother.

JOAQUIN: But he can talk, señora. He's faking.

CRUZ: Tha's enough! Din' I tell you not to bother him? I have enough to worry with your sister. She run out like crazy this afternoon, and haven' come back. Maybe she want to elope with Chato?

JOAQUIN: Pos so what? Chato's a good vato.

CRUZ: A good vato. An ignorant who let the contractors rob him!

JOAQUIN: Simon, and who's the contractor? Mingo!

CRUZ: Shut up, liar! Thief!

JOAQUIN: T'ief?

CRUZ: Since you was born you have give me nothing but trouble.

Going out in the streets at night, coming late, landing in jail. I don' got no more hope in you. Or in Lupe. The only one who haven' come out bad is my poor Chorti who's only hungry all the time. Why don' you rob something for your brother to eat, eh? Serve for something. (*Weeps.*) Valgame dios, nobody care about my poor sick Belarmino. Only his madre. (*She starts to go out.*)

BELARMINO: Mama.

CRUZ: (*Without turning.*) No, don' call me, Joaquin.

JOAQUIN: But I din'—

CRUZ: No, I tell you, comprende, sanavavichi! I got to be out in the street. Maybe with the help of the Virgen, your sister come back. (*Exits.*)

BELARMINO: Pobre viejita.

JOAQUIN: Pobre nothing! If you care so much, how come you keep your mouth shut when it count?

BELARMINO: (*Brusquely, furiously.*) No seas torpe! Si todo el mundo se da cuenta que puedo habrar, van ha saber quien soy. O mejor dicho, quien fui. Me vienen ha mochar la lengua o toda la maceta de una vez! Que no sabes que estamos en territorio enemigo?

JOAQUIN: Orale pues, cool it, ese! You don't gotta make a speech. (*Pause.*) Man, what a trip! You know what? I think I been smoking too much. You din' really say all that, right? Simon, it's all in my head.

BELARMINO: Pos quien sabe lo que dices, vale.

JOAQUIN: What?

BELARMINO: Que no hablo ingles. El totache. Hablame in espanish.

JOAQUIN: Sorry, man, I don' speak it. No hablo español.

BELARMINO: Mendigos pochos. (*Pause.*) Mira, chabo . . . ah, you . . . Mexicano, no?

JOAQUIN: Who me? Nel, man, I'm Chicano.

BELARMINO: No seas pendejo.

JOAQUIN: Who you calling a pendejo!

BELARMINO: You, tu, tu Mexican! Pendejo! Mira, esperate . . . ahhh, you Mexican, me Mexican . . . ahhh, this one familia Mexican, eh? Mingo, no! Mingo es gringo. Comprendes?

JOAQUIN: Heh, yeah, now you talking my language!

BELARMINO: Mingo ees gavacho, eh?

JOAQUIN: Simon, and a t'ief.

BELARMINO: Okay maguey. Now . . . you don' puedes atinar quien soy?

JOAQUIN: Wait a minute man . . . Slower, I can't do what?

BELARMINO: Atinar.

JOAQUIN: Atinar . . . that's *guess*. I can't guess what?

BELARMINO: Quien soy.

JOAQUIN: Who you are. (*Pause.*) Who?

BELARMINO: Pos guess. You have hear . . . el Pueblo de Parral?

JOAQUIN: Parral?

BELARMINO: Chihuahua!

JOAQUIN: Oh, simon. Tha's the town where they kill Pancho Villa and they cut off his . . . (*Pause.*) HEAD.

BELARMINO: Exactamente.

JOAQUIN: Did you ever have a horse?

BELARMINO: Siete Leguas.

JOAQUIN: And a Chivi?

BELARMINO: One Dodge.

JOAQUIN: 1923?

BELARMINO: Simon — yes.

JOAQUIN: (*Pause.*) I don' believe it. You? The head of Pancho . . .

BELARMINO: Belarmino please! (*Secretively.*) Muchos carefuls. I only trust you. Ees one secret politico, comprendes?

JOAQUIN: (*Shocked.*) Simon, I don't tell nobody. (*Pause.*) Only the jefita. MAAA! (*He runs out the front door.*)

BELARMINO: OYE! (*Alone.*) Chi . . . huahua! Que feo no tener cuerpo, erdad de dios!

PEDRO *is heard in the kitchen, yelling and singing drunkenly.* BELARMINO *feigns sleep.* PEDRO *enters with a wine bottle, and cartridge belts criss-crossed on his chest.*

PEDRO: (*Sings.*)
> "Adios torres de Chihuahua,
> Adios torres de Canteraaa!
> Ya vino Francisco Villaaa,
> Pa' quitarles lo pantera.
> Ya llego Francisco Villa
> Ha de volver la fronteraaa!"

(*Shouts,*) Ay, yai, yai, YAI! I'm home, cabrones. Your padre is home. come out! come out from your holes! I am home!! (*Pause.*) Where's e'rybody at? (*He goes to* BELARMINO.) Oye, Wake up, loco! (*He pulls* BELARMINO'*s hair.*)

BELARMINO: (*Opening his eyes.*) ARRRRGGH! LA CUCARACHAA!

PEDRO: (*Furiously, in case of insult.*) What?

BELARMINO: Cucaracha.

PEDRO: (*Pause.*) You know "Siete Leguas"? (*Sings.*) "Siete Leguas el caballo que Villa mas— "

BELARMINO: AY, YAI, YAI!

PEDRO: Heh, you do that pretty good, cabron. (CRUZ *runs in the front door.* JOAQUIN *follows her.*)

CRUZ: Pedro, what are you doing?

PEDRO: I am talking to my son.

CRUZ: Talking? (*She glances at* JOAQUIN.)

JOAQUIN: Din' I tell you? He can talk, huh pa? (BELARMINO *grunts and spits at* JOAQUIN *Orale, carnal, take it easy. You can trust the jefitos . . .* (BELARMINO *spits, hits* JOAQUIN'S *shirt.*) Un pollo! (*He exits upstairs.*)

CRUZ: It ees true, Pedro, my son talks?

PEDRO: Who? This animal? No, wha's wrong wis you, not even with a gallon of vino. (BELARMINO *laughs idiotically.*) You see? How can this idiota talk? He don' know nothing.

CRUZ: He is still your son, Pedro.

PEDRO: Pos who knows, verdad? A man almost forty years old which he don' even know his own padre? That is no son. You got this one for you, woman.

CRUZ: Tha's not true, Pedro. He look like you.

PEDRO: Oh yes, the face!

CRUZ: And the hair, the eyes, the mustaches.

PEDRO: CHICKENSQUAT! Those are things a madre notice. A padre he wants a son with a strong back. And arms and legs to help him work! You cheat me, woman. Caray, I will never forget the day Belarmino was born. 1928 and my first son! They run to the field to get me, and when I arrive . . . there you was with the niño in your arms . . . his big eyes looking out, his mouth open . . . with ears, a nose, and mucho hair, everything his madre want. Then I open the blanket: NOTHING. *Nothing for his padre! Dios mio, what a lousy son!*

CRUZ: (*Hurt.*) Yes, lousy, but it hurt me to have him.

PEDRO: Pos I give him to you then. For your pains. I give 'em to you all. Joaquin, Mingo, Lupe, and the head for good measure. (JOAQUIN *enters with guitar.*) Anyway, I'm going to across the border. My carrilleras and my 30-30 is all I take. Wis that I come, wis that I go.

JOAQUIN: And your guitar, jefito?

PEDRO: You keep it, hijo. Of all my sons I like you the most, because you're the only one who understand the Revolucion. Maybe this guitarrita serve to remind you of your padre . . . when he's dead.

CRUZ: You're crazy, viejo.

PEDRO: Well, you will see. I going back to Zacatecas, to my tierra, to die.

CRUZ: (*Relieved.*) Okay pues, go die! I don' care. Right now I'm worry about my Lupe. (*She wraps her shawl around her neck.*)

PEDRO: Where you going, to the street again like a crazy loca?

CRUZ: I'm going over to Señora Reyes house. Maybe Chato come back. I don' even know what to think, dios mio. (*Exits.*)

PEDRO: Stinking vieja.

JOAQUIN: Heh, pa, can I go to Mexico with you?

PEDRO: For what? You din' come from over theres, you was born over heres.

JOAQUIN: So what, maybe I gotta get outa town? I mean the U.S.

PEDRO: Can you ride a horse?

JOAQUIN: No, pero—

PEDRO: Or eat chili peppers?

JOAQUIN: No, but—

PEDRO: Ah! And tortillas, my son. How to know a good woman by her tortillas. You got to know. One don' buy burro just because she gots long eyelashes.

JOAQUIN: Okay pues, but you know what? I find the head of Pancho Villa!

PEDRO: (*Pause.*) When?

JOAQUIN: Today . . . tonight!

PEDRO: You crazy. How you going to find the head of the General? Pos mira . . . go say it up in the sierra, que! Where they believe you.

JOAQUIN: You wanna see it?

PEDRO: (*Pause.*) El General?

JOAQUIN: Pancho Villa himself.

PEDRO: You sure ees him? How you know? He don' be in bad shape?

JOAQUIN: He's like new.

PEDRO: (*Lowers his head emotionally.*) I don' believe it . . . after so many years? Just imagine, to rescue the General's head from the hands of the gringos, then to take it back to Mexico con honor!

In a big train like the old days! Que caray, maybe even the Revolucion break out again! Maybe they give us a rancho — in Zacatecas. Ay, yai, yai! Think we better be careful, my son. (*Pause.*) Oye, you hide it good? If we lose that head again — !

JOAQUIN: Nel, he's here in the house.

PEDRO: Who know about it?

JOAQUIN: Nobody, just me and you, and the General.

PEDRO: General? He's dead.

JOAQUIN: He ain' dead.

PEDRO: What you mean, hombre? They kill him.

JOAQUIN: Not all of him.

PEDRO: Yes, all of him!

JOAQUIN: Nel, he lives. Pancho Villa lives!

PEDRO: (*Pause.*) You chure?

JOAQUIN: Simon, and there he is! (*Points to* BELARMINO.)

PEDRO: (*Scandalized.*) Belarmino! Pos que jijos—! What you thinking, babozo? Laughing at your padre?

JOAQUIN: No, jefito! He prove it to you himself. Just give him a chance! (*Goes to* BELARMINO.) Heh, General? General Villa?

PEDRO: (*Pulls his hair.*) Wake up, bruto.

BELARMINO: AARRRAAGGHH!

JOAQUIN: Uh, General, here's one of your Villistas . . . my jefito. You know him already, tell him something, okay? Just a word or two.

BELARMINO: (*Smiles.*) UHHH.

JOAQUIN: He's warming up.

PEDRO: For what, more frijoles? No Joaquin, this go beyond a joke. I never going to forgive you this.

JOAQUIN: But he's Pancho Villa, 'apa. He tell me.

PEDRO: What I care what this animal tell you? How he's going to be the great Centauro del Norte? Pancho Villa was a giant, a legend, a big hombre!

JOAQUIN: Simon, and this a big hombre's head.

PEDRO: CHICKENSQUAT! Not in one thousand years can you compare this chompetita to the head of my General! Men like Pancho Villa ain't born no more, just lousies like this one. And cowards! T'iefs! Useless cabrones! Tha's all I got for sons.

MINGO: (*Standing in the front.*) And we're only chips off the old block, no pa? (PEDRO *turn toward* MINGO *who is dressed in casual bowling clothes. He also carries a bowling bag.*)

PEDRO: Pos you tell me. What block you talking about?

MINGO: Skip it. What was the yelling about?

PEDRO: This pachuco . . . lying to his padre.

JOAQUIN: I din' lie, jefito.

PEDRO: Chatap! Pos this one . . . still at it, hombre? (*To* MINGO.) What you think he was saying, my son? That Belarmino is my General Villa! Mira . . . lousy godamit. (*To* JOAQUIN.) Why don' you be smart like your brother here. He don' go around wis stupid babozadas. He is a serious hombre con respeto y dinero.

JOAQUIN: Orale, cool it pues.

PEDRO: Culo . . . a quien le dices culo! I still haven' die, cabron. I still the boss in this house.

JOAQUIN: Okay, okay. Keep your house. (*Gets the guitar and heads for the door.*)

PEDRO: Oye, oye, and my guitarra?

JOAQUIN: You give me it. Wan't it back?

PEDRO: No for what I want that junk?

JOAQUIN: Here. (*Gives him the guitar.*) I get a new one. Orale, carnal, hand over 75 bolas.

MINGO: Bolas?

JOAQUIN: Bones, maracas, bills, ese.

MINGO: Seventy-five dollars? What the hell for?

JOAQUIN: My cut, ese! I get the workers, you screw 'em, we split the take.

MINGO: You're crazy.

JOAQUIN: Simon, real loco. But I ain't stupid. All the vatos in the barrio go to work for you because I ask 'em!

MINGO: So what? I paid you 50¢ a head for that truckload you round up and that was it.

JOAQUIN: Nel, ese, you din' tell me you was going to burn 'em. Like Chato! Social security, income tax . . . that's a lotta chet, mano. You got itchy fingers too, que! You pocket them coins yourself.

MINGO: (*Calm.*) Can you prove it?

JOAQUIN: I see you do it!

MINGO: Then call the cops. Go on! Who you think the law's gonna believe, me or you?

JOAQUIN: (*Pause.*) Eh, jefe, you loan me your guitar?

PEDRO: Now you wan' it back, eh? Bueno, take it. (JOAQUIN *grabs the guitar and lifts it to smash it on* MINGOs *head.*) FOR YOU TO PLAY IT!! (JOAQUIN *stops.*)

JOAQUIN: Don' you see he's cheating us?

PEDRO: I don' see nothing!

JOAQUIN: The General see it!

PEDRO: No que General ni nada! (JOAQUIN *leaves with the guitar.*) Useless! Huh, as if all people don' be crooked. No hombre, we all looking to see what we scratch up. (*Drinks from his bottle. It is empty.*) Chihuahua, it is finish. Bueno, no matter?

Tha's how come we got money — for necessaries. Of all my sons I like you the most — porqué tienes intelegencia, hijo lo juro por los cielos. Andale, my son, let loose one pesito to go for more. But this time we get a big one, eh?

MINGO: No, señor.

PEDRO: Bueno, a small one pues.

MINGO: No! Don' you understand? There's no money for booze.

PEDRO: Mira, mira, don't play the crooked contractor wis me, eh? I ain' Joaquin. All I ask is for 35 centavitos.

MINGO: I don't give a damn. That money ain't gonna support your habit. I want this family to be decent and that's how it's gonna be.

PEDRO: Oh si, eh? Well, who are you to decide everything? I'm your padre.

MINGO: You're nothing. If it wasn' for me, we'd still be in the gutter, like usual. Confess it. You could never handle Shorty's hunger. You had to drag us all to the fields together with mi 'ama. And for what? We still ended up owing the store just to feed the head! That head's a pushover for me. From now on, I'm in charge here and you can do what you damn well please.

PEDRO: (*Pause.*) Pos I think I damn well please to give you some chingasos well-planted, sabes?

MINGO: If you can. Don' forget I was a Marine.

PEDRO: And I was a Villista!

MINGO: You want me to give you a judo chop?

PEDRO: (*He runs to the door.*) Joaquin! Joaquin! Bring me my guitarra!

MINGO: The guitar? You going to play or fight?

PEDRO: I going to smash it on your head, pendejo!

MINGO: What's the matter, old man? Not so good with your fists anymore? Been picking fruit too long? Come on, gimme a try! This hand only broke a Chink's red neck once. WHACK! Come on, wetback, get a taste of an American fighting man overseas! Come, farm laborer! Greaser! Spic! Nigger! (*Pause.*) GRINGO!

PEDRO: (*The dam breaks.*) VIVA VILLAAAAA! (PEDRO *leaps on* MINGO *and they wrestle.* MINGO *quickly subdues him giving him a couple of efficient judo chops. He pins him down and sits on him.*)

MINGO: All right, green-carder, you give up?

PEDRO: Cabron.

MINGO: What?

PEDRO: Cabron!

MINGO: That's what I thought you said.

PEDRO: Joaquin!

MINGO: He ain't coming back man. You think he wants that guitar smashed? Besides you ran him out. You better give up. What you say? No hard feelings? Look, I'll even get up. (*He rises.*) Come on, Pete, be a sport. Don't be a bad loser. (*Nudges him with his foot.*) Come on, I don't like to see you sprawled out like that.

PEDRO: Get away, cabron! Get away!

MINGO: Okay, stay down. I don't give a damn. (*Exits.*)

PEDRO: Now I don't got any sons . . . except Belarmino. He was the first. I like him the most. Besides, he always remind me of Pancho Villa. (*He gets up and removes his cartridge belts.*) Eh, my son? You see this carrilleras? They're from the Revolucion. They

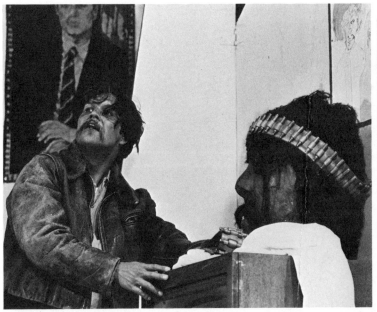

don' got any bullets but I give 'em to you, eh? (*He places the belts around* BELARMINO.) Now you look like the General. You remember Pancho Villa? There was a man, a giant . . . he rob the rich to give to the poor. You should have see him when we take Zacatecas. (*He begins to walk around the room imagining the scene he describes.*) All the trains, the smoke, the people climbing all over like lices. (*Laughs.*) Caray, there was nothing like the trains. (*Train whistle in the distance.*) They would gather at the crossings.

(*Under his voice: "Marcha de Zacatecas."*) Here comes Pancho Villa, they would say. Ahi viene Pancho Villa! And mi General he would come to the back of the car. VIVA VILLA! VIVA VILLA! Here come Pancho Villa! (*One final war cry.*) A ZACATECAAASS!

The music is like the sound of a train pulling in. PEDRO *runs out in the direction of the train whistle. The sounds end abruptly and all that remains is the ringing of a small bell at a distant railroad crossing. This fades into the sound of a church bell. Light and sound fade.*
    BELARMINO *is left illuminated by a single ray of light. He screams, a sorrowful cry of death. Darkness. Curtain.*

SCENE   TWO

The front room. Morning. Church bells. A guitar plays "Siete Leguas." A procession in black enters. CRUZ *in mourning,* MINGO *holding her. Then* LUPE *and* CHATO, *carrying* BELARMINO *wrapped in a sarape.*

LUPE: I'll put Belarmino away, mama. (*Goes into bedroom.*)
CRUZ: (*Sitting on the couch.*) The Señor knows what we shall do now, my sons.
MINGO: Pa was a good guy.
JOAQUIN: You liar!
MINGO: You insulting his memory already? (*Pause.*) I'll let that one go this time.
LUPE: (*Reentering.*) He's asleep.
CRUZ: He was tired poor man.
MINGO: I don' think we shoulda take him.
CRUZ: It was his padre, my son.
MINGO: He sang "La Cucaracha," din't he? Pa was my pa too, ma. I wanted him to have a good quiet funeral. What was the name of that other "bit" you did?
JOAQUIN: "Siete Leguas."
MINGO: What?
JOAQUIN: Seven . . . leaguews. (*He chokes up with grief.*)
CHATO: That's okay, ese, e'rybody like what you did.
LUPE: It was so sad to see them let mi 'apa down into his grave and all the time Belarmino singing "La Cucaracha." E'rybody think you like it like that, mama.
CRUZ: We should have had a wake.
MINGO: You still on that, ma? The funeral parlor did the job.
CRUZ: They din' let me see him.

MINGO: There was nothing left to see. I mean, what you expect them to do? That train hit him. I'm not even sure it was him when I identified him. Maybe it wasn't. Maybe he went back to Mexico like he always wanted? That's possible.

JOAQUIN: Why don't you shut up!

CRUZ: We should have had a wake! (*She breaks down crying.*)

LUPE: Chato, help me. (LUPE *and* CHATO *take* CRUZ *upstairs, crying.*)

MINGO: Everything's gonna be okay, ma. You'll see. I order him a stone with his name in Spanish, and a saying: "Here lies our Dad, By Angels Guarded— " (CRUZ *has gone upstairs.*)

JOAQUIN: Tried to feel sad but only farted. (*Laughs until he cries.*)

MINGO: (*Going over to him, whispering.*) What the hecks the matter with you, tomahawk? Pa's dead. Don't you appreciate that? (*Pause.*) Heh, are you crying?

JOAQUIN: Lemme alone, ese.

MINGO: Listen, Joaquin, things ain't been the best between us but maybe we ought to sit down and talk, huh? Man to man? I'm your legal guardian now.

JOAQUIN: What you mean?

MINGO: I'm responsible for you. For the whole family. I wanna help you, Tomahawk.

JOAQUIN: Help me what?

MINGO: Help you. You wanna join the Marines? I'll sign for you. Sure, the service'll make a man outa you. Look what it did for me. How about it?

JOAQUIN: Nel, I awready tried. They don' like my record.

MINGO: That bad, huh? Well, how about night school? (JOAQUIN *makes a face.*) Okay then, come and work with me.

JOAQUIN: I awready worked with you.

MINGO: You still think I cheated your friends?

JOAQUIN: I know!

MINGO: Boy, that's rich. You know what's wrong with you? You can't imagine anybody making an honest buck. This is a free country, man. There's no law against making money.

JOAQUIN: How about being a Chicano?

MINGO: Is *that* what's eating you?

JOAQUIN: How come we're poor? How come mi jefito die like that?

MINGO: Not because he was a Mexican!

JOAQUIN: You ever have the placa work you over in jail, ese? Rubber hoses on the ribs? Calling you greaser! Mexican bastard!

MINGO: I've never been in jail remember?

JOAQUIN: You're still a greaser.

MINGO: Why you little punk, don't aim your inferiority complex at me. You're so twisted with hate you can't see straight.

JOAQUIN: Simon, I'm cross-eyed. But you wanna be a gavacho so bad, you can't see nothing. You hated mi 'apa. You hate all of us! You and your new clothes and bowling ball and shit. Well, take a good look, ese. We're greasy and lousy but we're your family!

MINGO: Damn rights, my family! But you don't have to be greasy and lousy!

JOAQUIN: You don't have to be a gavacho!

MINGO: Listen, man, there's only one thing I ever wanted in this life. That's not to be poor. I never got that until I become a Marine. Now I want it for the family. Is that so bad? You wanna go on this way, with that stupid head eating and stinking and farting?

JOAQUIN: He's the General!

MINGO: Come off it, buddy. Shorty ain't Pancho Villa. He's nothing but a mouth. I know, I have to feed it.

JOAQUIN: If you ever feed him nothing again, I'll kill you.

MINGO: Okay. But how are you going to feed it? On welfare, like the old man used to do it?

JOAQUIN: You don' even respect mi 'apa now! When he's dead!

MINGO: That's a damn lie! I loved that old wino.

JOAQUIN: Pinchi buey.

MINGO: What did you call me!!!

JOAQUIN: Pinchi puto desgraciado!

MINGO: You talk to me in English!

JOAQUIN: (*Swings guitar at him.*) FUCK YOU! (*Runs out.*)

MINGO: (*Running to the door.*) You godamned delinquent! I'd turn you in if pa wasn' dead today.

Curtain.

ACT FOUR

Six months later. It is winter. The walls of the house are covered with red cockroaches of various sizes. LUPE *is studying the walls, carrying a fly-swatter. She is pregnant, but is nevertheless knocking down cockroaches energetically and capturing them in her apron.* BELARMINO *is on top of an old, broken-down* TV *set. His eyes are wide open, following every move that* LUPE *makes. The door to the side bedroom is new and has "Private" painted on it in big black letters.*

LUPE: Cucarachas . . . big fat cucarachas. There's one! (*She knocks it down.*) Gee man, this is a big one!

BELARMINO: NARRH!

LUPE: No, you pig! This is mine and I'm gonna eat it by myself.

BELARMINO: NAAARRRRGGGH!

LUPE: Pediche! You ain' hungry. You just don' want me to have it, huh? Well now you going to have to eat it! And I hope you choke! (*She crams it into* BELARMINO'*s mouth.*)

CRUZ: (*In the kitchen.*) Guadalupe?

LUPE: Si, mama? (*She backs away from* BELARMINO.)

CRUZ: (*Enters.*) Did Belarmino shout? (BELARMINO *spits out the cockroach.*) Una cucaracha!

LUPE: It's not my fault, man. I can't watch him all the time.

CRUZ: Ay, little woman. Go bring the tortillas.

LUPE: There's no more.

CRUZ: And the dozen there was?

LUPE: I ate 'em. (*Pause.*) Well, what you want? I was hungry! Besides, there's plenty of food there—bread, steaks, milk, eggs, orange juice.

CRUZ: It all belong to Mingo.

LUPE: Sure, pure American food. Well, what about us? Are we suppose to eat cucarachas? (*Angry.*)

CRUZ: No! Now stop this foolishness and go make tortillas, andale.

LUPE: Tortillas . . . I should work in a taco bar. (*Exits, angry.*)

CRUZ: (*Loud voice.*) And don' touch Mingo's food! (BELARMINO *growls.*) Si, my son, I know. She coming with your frijolitos. You mus' be very hungry, no? You have eat nothing for days. (*Pause.*) Here. Eat one little cucaracha, eh? But don' spit out the shell. I don' want your sister to know. Here.

MINGO: (*In the kitchen.*) Aha, I caught you!

CRUZ: Mingo! (*She turns, searching for him. Noises come from the kitchen. A chair falls, a glass breaks. We hear the voices of* MINGO *and* LUPE, *arguing.*)

MINGO: Drinking my orange juice, eh? What you eating?

LUPE: None of your business!

MINGO: What's that?

LUPE: Give 'em back!

MINGO: You crazy?

LUPE: Gimme 'em back!

MINGO: Oh no, sister, we're going to see ma.

LUPE: No, Mingo, please—ay!

MINGO: Shut up! (MINGO *comes in from the kitchen, pushing* LUPE *in front with her arm twisted behind her back.* MINGO *is dressed in fashionable casual clothing.*) Heh, ma, you know what this pig was eating?

CRUZ: (*Resigned.*) Cucarachas.

MINGO: How do you know?

CRUZ: What's wrong with you, woman? You want to kill that child you carry? You going to be a madre.

LUPE: I'm not either. I don' got no baby. Only a belly full of cocoaroaches! And I'm still hungry. We never have any meat in this house! (*Exits.*)

MINGO: (*Shouting after her.*) Meat? Well, tell your Chatito to get a goddamn job! How d'yuh like that? What's her husband for? Just to keep her pregnant? Tell the bum to go to work.

CRUZ: It is winter, Mingo. There's no work in the fields.

MINGO: Then to the breadlines, lady. The welfare department. Anyway that's all they know.

BELARMINO: (*With rage.*) ARRRRRGGGGGGH!

MINGO: Heh!

CRUZ: Belarmino, behave.

MINGO: (BELARMINO *stares at him with hate.*) Look at him, señora, look! He's enrage! Well now I seen everything. This freak getting insulted. (BELARMINO *growls with rage.*)

CRUZ: My son, calm down!

MINGO: Let him blow his top. He can't do nothing anyway. Maybe he's been eating my food, too, no ma? You sure you ain't slip him one of my TV dinners?

CRUZ: No, Mingo, your poor brother he haven' eat nothing in four days.

MINGO: So what?

CRUZ: Look how skinny he is. He's shrinking on me, and he still don' wanna eat nothing.

MINGO: Maybe he knows something I know.

CRUZ: (*Suspiciously.*) What?

MINGO: (*Calmly, deliberately.*) That he ain't got no guts.

CRUZ: (*Alarmed.*) Don' say that!

MINGO: It's a fact.

CRUZ: No!

MINGO: Look at him!

CRUZ: He's sick.

MINGO: (*With meaning.*) He ain't got a body, señora. (CRUZ *stares at him unbelievingly.*) Let's face it, okay? He's a head. (CRUZ *turns away shaking her head.*) You gotta accept it, ma. Shorty's a head and that's it.

CRUZ: No.!

MINGO: (*Angered.*) Then where's all the food going that he's eating? I become a contractor to make more money, but each week that I make more, he eat more. Last week it was $127. By himself! Beans and tortillas!! He blew my whole check. (BELARMINO *laughs.*) Shut up!

BELARMINO: ARRGGH!

MINGO: All these years we been poor and stinkin', working the fields, for what? To stuff his fat belly which he don't even got! What kinda stupid, useless life is that? I don't wanna end up like dad. I wanna get outa this slum!

CRUZ: Por favor, Mingo, no more.

MINGO: Look, ma, I wanna help you. I'll even let Lupe and Chato freeload on us for the winter, if you do one thing.

CRUZ: What?

MINGO: Stop wasting money on beans and tortillas. Admit Shorty's a head.

CRUZ: No!

MINGO: Ma, it's nothing but dumb pride. Be realistic. Be practical.

CRUZ: (*Determined.*) My son is not a head!

MINGO: (*Pause.*) Okay, suit yourself. Just don't expect me to pay the bills at the store no more. (*Adds quickly.*) But don't worry, I'm still gonna help the family— with my example. See that little red sports car in front of the house? It's mine.

CRUZ: Yours?

MINGO: I trade it in for my Chivi. I also took 200 bucks outa the bank and bought new clothes. See? Everything new. You should see how great it feels! Instead of the head, I'm spending money where it counts: on self-improvement. And with my credit, I can get anything else I want. Thirty dollar shoes, color TV, a Hi-Fi stereo, a new bowling ball, steak dinners, cocktails! I can even go to college. Sure, State College! The G.I. Bill will foot the bill. Heh, you get that? G.I. Bill foot the bill? I know it's below your mental intelligence to comprehend the simplicity . . . (*During this speech* MINGO's *voice changes from a Chicano accent to the nasal tones of an Anglo; he also begins to talk down his nose at his mother.*)

CRUZ: Mijo!

MINGO: (*Coming to his senses.*) Que?

CRUZ: What about us?

MINGO: Well . . . hustle! Din't Joaquin go to work?

CRUZ: He say he have little jobs to do.

MINGO: What little jobs?

CRUZ: I don' know.

MINGO: What about mi 'apa? He can still work. Where is he, boozing again?

CRUZ: (*With fearful surprise.*) Tu padre esta muerto!

MINGO: Muerto? Dead? (*Laughs.*) You're kidding.

CRUZ: For six months. That train kill him. (*She crosses herself.*)But . . . how did you forgot? Wha's happen to you, Mingo?

MINGO: Six months?

JOAQUIN: (*Outside the house.*) Viva mi jefito! (*Shouts of Viva.*) Viva Pancho Villa! (*More Vivas.*)

BELARMINO: AY, YAI, YAI, YAI, YAI! (*Outside the house we hear the music of a band. Drums and trumpets sound with revolutionary enthusiasm.*)

MINGO: What the hell's that? (*Goes to the front door.*)

CRUZ: Mariachis.

MINGO: The hell, it's a pachuco band.

CRUZ: No, ees a Charro. It's . . . Joaquin!! And Chato!

A police siren sounds in the distance. There is immediate confusion outside. "En la madre, the fuss!" "Le's go!" "No, don' run!" etc. Various voices, besides the voices of JOAQUIN *and* CHATO, *indicate there is a small group of young men outside, which now breaks out running in all directions.* CHATO *runs in, frightened, dressed in huarache sandals and white mexican peasant clothing. He wears a straw hat, and carries a drum and a trumpet. He enters tripping over his feet, making noise, trying to hide.*

CRUZ: Chato, hombre, wha's happen?

CHATO: The placa!

MINGO: The police? What did you do?

CHATO: I din' do nothing!

JOAQUIN: (*Outside.*) Open the door, sergeant!

CRUZ: Joaquin!

JOAQUIN: (*Still outside.*) Sergeant, the door!

MINGO: How come you're dressed like that? You look like a peon.

JOAQUIN: (*Still outside.*) CHATO!

CHATO: Yes, my General! (*He opens the door.*)

JOAQUIN: It's about time, *corporal!* (JOAQUIN *enters dressed in the traditional costume of the Mexican charro, complete with a pair of cartridge belts crisscrossed on his chest. Hanging from one shoulder on a strap, he carries a 30-30 carbine. On his shoulders he carries two big sacks, one on each side.*) Here you are, jefita. (*He lowers the sacks.*) One hundred pounds of flour . . . and a hundred pounds of beans, like I promised you.

MINGO: Where did you get this?

JOAQUIN: I'm sorry, I don' speak gavacho.

MINGO: Don't act stupid. where did you get these sacks? You swipe 'em, huh?

JOAQUIN: (*Ignores him.*) And this is for you, jefita. (*From his jacket he pulls out a beautiful white rebozo — a shawl.*)

CRUZ: Where did you got this, hijo?

MINGO: He swipe 'em, don' I tell you, señora? (*He grabs* JOAQUIN *by one arm.*) You going to have to return them!

JOAQUIN: 'tas lucas, Gringo.

MINGO: Gringo?

JOAQUIN: Mingo el gringo.

BELARMINO: (*Joyfully.*) AY, YAI, YAI, YAI!

JOAQUIN: VIVA VILLAA! (*To* BELARMINO.) And this is for you, mi General. A box of cigars. (*He offers him one.*) You wan' one! (BELARMINO *smiles, grunts affirmatively.*) Orale, pues.

CRUZ: No, Joaquin, your brother don' smoke.

BELARMINO: (*Growling.*) ARRGH!

CRUZ: (*Backs up.*) Ay dios.

JOAQUIN: At your orders, mi General. (*Gives him a cigar.*) Que le haga buen provecho y que — (*Pause.*) Corporal, a match! (*Chato comes forward with a match.*) Que Viva la Revolucion. (BELARMINO *smokes contentedly, making a lot of smoke.*)

MINGO: I don't believe it. (*Laughs.*) So this is the General, eh? Who the hell do you guys think you are? The Cisco Kid and Pancho?

CHATO: No, he's Pancho. (*Points to* BELARMINO.)

MINGO: You lousy clown! I oughta call the cops right now.

CRUZ: No, Mingo.

MINGO: Don't worry señora. The cops are already after 'em. I bet they even end up in jail tonight. For thiefs!

JOAQUIN: And you? You're the one that oughta be in jail for cheating the jefitos, the family, La Raza! You pinchi sell-out traitor!

CRUZ: Joaquin!

MINGO: No, no, señora. Let him spill the beans.

JOAQUIN: We rob the rich to give the poor, like Pancho Villa! But you . . .

MINGO: I worked to fill all of your stinking bellies! Especially your beloved General there. I got tired of stuffing his guts with . . .

JOAQUIN: What guts?

MINGO: (*Pause.*) I won't argue that.

JOAQUIN: Simon, because he don' got any. He's a head and tha's all.

CRUZ: No, head, no!

JOAQUIN: The head of Francisco Villa! No, my General?

BELARMINO: (*Triumphantly.*) AY, YAI, YAI!

LUPE: (*Entering.*) Ay! (*She doubles up with pain.*) Ay, mama!

CHATO: Mi honey! (*He goes to her side.*)

CRUZ: Lupe, wha's wrong?

MINGO: It's the cockaroaches she ate.

LUPE: Ay! Ay, mama, help me.

CRUZ: Si, mijita. Diosito santo, maybe she's going to have the baby?

CHATO: Baby?

CRUZ: Si, hombre, your son. Help me with her.

CHATO: Heh, ese, I going to have a son.

CRUZ: Joaquin, no you—Mingo! Go call the doctor!

JOAQUIN: Nel, jefita. I'll go!

MINGO: Not dressed like that! I'll go!

JOAQUIN: Dressed like what?!

MINGO: Like a stinking Mexican!

JOAQUIN: You dirty cabron, I'm proud to be a stinking Mexican! You're dress like a gavacho! Through and through!

MINGO: You're the one that's through, Mex! You can't even bring a sack of beans home without stealing it!

JOAQUIN: Simon, but I swipe from the supermarket not the poor! It's no crime to be a thief if you steal from thiefs!

MINGO: Who told you that?

CRUZ: (*Entering.*) Mingo, pronto! Go bring the doctor! Your sister . . .

JOAQUIN: Who you think? The one and only who knows. And that ain't all! He also tell me that he wasn' hungry for food all this time. He was hungry for justice!

MINGO: (*Laughs.*) Justice?

JOAQUIN: Social justice!

CRUZ: Mijos!

MINGO: What social, stupid? You don' even know what the word means!

JOAQUIN: That's what you think but we've had it wis your bones, ese! We're going to get rid of all the gavacho blood-suckers like you. The contractors, the judges, the cops, the stores!

MINGO: Bandit!

JOAQUIN: Simon, like Pancho Villa!

MINGO: You want me to give you a judo chop?

JOAQUIN: Pos ponte, ese!

CRUZ: Hijos, por favor . . .

MINGO: Greasy, low, ignorant, lousy . . .

JOAQUIN: Viva La Raza! (*They start to fight.*)

CRUZ: HIJOS DE SU CHINGADA MADRE! (CRUZ *is holding the 30-30 carbine.*)

MINGO: Ma!

CRUZ: Shut up! Now you going to calm down and sit down like hombrecitos or I pump holes in you! (*Ferociously.*) Okay, MARCH! (*She pushes them toward the sofa, with the carbine.*) Caramba, if you want to fight like dogs tha's how they going to treat you.

MINGO: But I din't.

JOAQUIN: Yo no hice . . .

CRUZ: Silencio! (JOAQUIN *and* MINGO *sit on the sofa.*) Now you, Mingo you goin' for the doctor, and bring him here, understand? Don' make me beg you again. And you, Joaquin. You goin' to take off that crazy clothes and you going to return everything you steal.

JOAQUIN: For what? So the fuzz can get me? Nel, jefita, I'm sorry. I rather go to the mountains and take the General with me. My jefito rode with Pancho Villa, now it's my turn!

CRUZ: NO!

JOAQUIN: Simon, Viva La Revolucion!

CRUZ: No, I tell you! Ees time you know . . . your padre never was in the Revolucion.

JOAQUIN: Chale.

CRUZ: He was in Arizona all those years, working in the mines. For the gringos.

JOAQUIN: Aaah, tha's a lotta chet. And the scar he have here in the neck, from the bullet?

CRUZ: Belarmino bite him there before you was born.

JOAQUIN: (*Desperate.*) And this cartridge belts? And this 30-30? You going to tell me they're not from the Revolucion?

CRUZ: No, because they are.

JOAQUIN: Okay, then, mi 'apa use them. Who else could have use them?

CRUZ: (*Pause.*) I use them, Joaquin! (JOAQUIN *and* MINGO *are shocked.*) Si, mis hijos, your madre rode with Pancho Villa! And tha's how I'm certain Belarmino ees not the General. (*Someone knocks at the door rudely. Silence, another knock.*)

POLICE: (*Outside.*) Okay, I know you're in there! Open up!

JOAQUIN: (*Runs to the window.*) La jura!

MINGO: The cops! Din't I tell you, señora? They're looking for him!

CRUZ: Ay dios! My son, pronto, hide. (*She puts the sombrero over* BELARMINO.)

MINGO: No, Ma! How can you tell him to hide? It's the law! (*He peeks out the window.*) For Pete's sake, this is embarrassing. All the neighbors are watching.

POLICE: (*Knocking furiously.*) OPEN UP IN THE NAME OF THE LAW, GODAMMIT!

CRUZ: Mingo, do something.

JOAQUIN: Don' ask nothing from that sonavavichi, jefita. (*More knocks.*) Open the door!

CRUZ: No, Joaquin, they get you. (*More strong knocks then the sound of glass and wood breaking.*) Ay dios!

POLICE: (*Entering with his club.*) What the hell's going on here? (*The* POLICEMAN *is dressed in a uniform that half resembles a highway patrolman's and half, a soldier's. He wears a helmet with the letters "M-P" printed in black. As soon as he barges in* JOAQUIN *takes the carbine from* CRUZ.)

JOAQUIN: (*Lifting the rifle.*) Put your stinking gavacho hands up!

CRUZ: Joaquin!

JOAQUIN: (*The* POLICEMAN *goes for his gun.*) Ah! Don't try it, man! I fill you full of holes!

POLICE: You're gonna regret this, boy.

JOAQUIN: Tha's what you think, man. (*He takes the officer's gun.*) Heh, wait a minute. Wha's that on your hat — M-P? Ain't you a city cop?

POLICE: What's the difference? You pachucos no le gusta mucho los cops right? Maybe it's Military Police — maybe its Mexican Patrol. We're looking for a couple of suspects. Supermarket thiefs. "El Ladron de los Supermercados."

CRUZ: Ladron? Ay no, forgive him, señor! He's a good boy. Him and Chato din' do nothing.

POLICE: Who's Chato?

CHATO: (*Entering the room.*) Heh, Doña Cruz, my wife is very — (*Sees the officer.*) Lonely! (*He exits.*)

POLICE: Heh!

JOAQUIN: Ah, ah! Cool it, gringo!

POLICE: You cholos are in mucho hot water, you savvy that? When did you swipe the car outside?

JOAQUIN: What car?

POLICE: The red sports car!

MINGO: (*Entering from his room.*) Sports car? Oh no, officer, that's my car!

POLICE: Who the hell are you?

MINGO: (*Pause.*) NOBODY! I don't have nothing to do with these people. I just room here. I'm a college student.

CRUZ: Tell him, Mingo, explain — you got the words.

MINGO: What my landlady here means, officer, is that the punk you want is right there. He's the Supermarket Thief.

JOAQUIN: Simon, ees me! But so what, you can't do nothing! Maybe the Revolucion break out right now. What you say, General? We go to the mountains?

BELARMINO: AY, YAI, YAI, YAI!

POLICE: Now what?

JOAQUIN: Pancho Villa!

POLICE: What the hell's going on in this place?

JOAQUIN: I'm going to blow you to pieces, that's what. One side, jefita!

CRUZ: Oh, Joaquin, that carabina don' shoot. It don' got bullets.

MINGO: It's not loaded.

POLICE: Not loaded?! (*He tries to jump* JOAQUIN.)

CRUZ: NO! (*She steps in front of the officer.*) Por favor, señor, don' take him.

POLICE: Get outa my way, lady!

MINGO: Get away, landlady!

JOAQUIN: Hold 'em there, jefita! (JOAQUIN *pulls gun. He runs to* BELARMINO.)

CRUZ: Joaquin, what you doing?

JOAQUIN: I'm going to the mountains with my General!

CRUZ: No, hijo, you drop him! (MINGO *knocks down* JOAQUIN'S *gun.*)

JOAQUIN: VIVA LA REVOLUCION!

POLICE: Why you little son of a—

CRUZ: JOAQUIN!

MINGO: I'll help you get him, officer!

POLICE: (*Chasing* JOAQUIN.) I warn you, punk! It'll go worse for you resisting arrest! (*Everyone chases* JOAQUIN *around the room, trying to catch him and* BELARMINO. CHATO *peeks in.*)

CHATO: Heh, ese, throw it over here! Over here! (JOAQUIN *throws* BELARMINO *like a ball.*)

MINGO: Stay out of this, Chato!

CHATO: (*To* JOAQUIN.) Run, ese, run!

JOAQUIN: Not wisout the General!

CRUZ: Gimme him, Chato!

JOAQUIN: Throw it back, ese! (CHATO *throws* BELARMINO *back to* JOAQUIN, *but* CRUZ *catches him. The police officer nabs* JOAQUIN. CRUZ *takes* BELARMINO *back to the* TV *set and examines him. In a corner of the room, the officer beats* JOAQUIN.)

CHATO: Orale, watcha eso! (*The officer pulls out handcuffs.*)

CRUZ: No! Not those, señor! (*She goes to* JOAQUIN, *leaving* BELARMINO *on top of the* TV *set.*) Por favor, he's my son, señor! Mijo!

POLICE: Sorry, Lady, I'm only doing my job. (JOAQUIN *resists and the officer beats the sadistic hell out of him.*) It's only my job.

CRUZ: (*Embracing* JOAQUIN.) Hijo, mijo!

POLICE: Lady, I— (*Tries to pull her away.*)

JOAQUIN: Leave her alone!

POLICE: Shut your mouth, boy! (*He pulls* CRUZ *away.*) Alright, señora.

CRUZ: Joaquin!

JOAQUIN: (*Blood on his nose.*) Don' worry, jefita. I ain' scared of 'em. You'll see. I going to return with 50,000 vatos on horses

and Chivis! Lemme go, huh? (CRUZ *silently makes the sign of cross on* JOAQUIN*'s forehead with her thumb.*)

POLICE: Okay, boy, let's go!

MINGO: Here's your gun, officer.

POLICE: That's okay, boy. Just put it in my holster.

JOAQUIN: I'm coming back, jefita! I'm coming back! VIVA VIL-LAAAAAA! (*The officer takes him out.*)

CRUZ: Joaquin! Joaquin, my son!! (*She weeps at the front door. Silence.* MINGO *approaches* CRUZ.)

MINGO: (*Pointing to* BELARMINO.) Look, señora, there's your son.

CHATO: Hijo? Hijo de su! Lupe's gonna have my son! We need a doctor! Orale, brother-in-law, loan me your sports car to go fast. Ees for your carnala.

MINGO: What are you talking about?

CHATO: Tu sister, Lupe!

MINGO: I don't have a sister.

CHATO: La Negra!

MINGO: Negra? Not my sister, boy. You trying to be funny? I just room here.

BELARMINO: DESGRACIADO!

MINGO: Who said that?

CHATO: Not me.

BELARMINO: TRAIDOR A TU RAZA!

CRUZ: Ees Belarmino. He's talking!

MINGO: What did he say?

BELARMINO: LAMBISCON!

MINGO: Obscenity, obscenity.

BELARMINO: CABRON!

CRUZ: Ay dios! (*Crosses herself.*) Belarmino, don' say that!

BELARMINO: PENDEJO!

CRUZ: Ay dios! (*Crosses herself.*)

MINGO: I'll shut him up! (*He approaches* BELARMINO.)

BELARMINO: BEBOZO!

CRUZ: Ay dios, mi Chorti! (*She approaches* BELARMINO.)

BELARMINO: SINVERGUENZA!

CRUZ: Ees the devil!

CHATO: Nel, ees the General!

MINGO: I'll fix this General!

BELARMINO: AARRRGGHH! (*He bites* MINGO.)

CRUZ: Dios. (*Crosses herself.*)

BELARMINO: (*Getting up steam.*) AMERICANIZADO, DESHECHADO, DESARRIAGADO, DESVERGONZADO, INTERESADO, TAPADO—

CHATO: Go, go, General!

BELARMINO: AGARRADO, EMPAPADO, FIJADO, MALHABLADO, TROMPESADO, AHOGADO, CHIFLADO!

MINGO: Shut up! Shut up! Speak English! (CHATO *whistles.*)

CRUZ: Chato, don' do that, por dios! Go bring the doctor! And a priest!

CHATO: Priest?

CRUZ: Tell him to bring Holy Water! Andale, run! (CHATO *exits.*)

BELARMINO: NI SABES QUIEN SOY! NI SABES QUIEN SOY!

MINGO: Speak English! Speak English!

BELARMINO: PANCHO VILLA!

MINGO: SPEAK ENGLISH! (*Goes on repeating.*) SPEAK ENGLISH! SPEAK ENGLISH! SPEAK ENGLISH! SPEAK ENGLISH! SPEAK ENGLISH!

BELARMINO: (*Simultaneously with* MINGO.) PANCHO VILLA, PANCHO VILLA, PANCHO VILLA, PANCHO VILLA!

CRUZ: (*Simultaneously, kneeling, crossing herself hysterically.*) DIOS, DIOS, DIOS, DIOS, DIOS, DIOS, DIOS, DIOS, DIOS, DIOS, DIOS!!

Curtain

ACT FIVE

Two years later. A winter night. The walls of the house are still covered with cockroaches. Some of them have grown to a tremendous size. CRUZ *is sitting on the sofa, with* BELARMINO *to her side. A kerosene heater is nearby flickering with a weak, useless flame and heating absolutely nothing. Everything looks more run down than ever.*

CRUZ: (*Singing sadly.*)

> Adios torres de Chihuahua
> Adios torres de Cantera
> Ya vino Francisco Villa
> Pa' quitarles lo pantera
> Ya llego Francisco Villa
> Ha de volver la Frontera.

(BELARMINO *esta roncando.*) Ay, my little Chorti. What a good hombre you are. I would not be sorprise if some of these days the Señor he give you a big body for being so good, no? Not a little body but a great big body with arms and legs strong like a macho. Tha's how Pedro always want you to be. May God keep him in peace. (*Crosses herself. We hear a terrible cry more animal than human coming from the kitchen.* CRUZ *rises and calls.*) Guadalupe, what you doing to the niña? (*More cries.*) Lupe! (*The cries stop.*) Don' you know how to feed her yet? (*Lupe enters with a small bundle. She looks like* CRUZ *in hair style and dress, having taken on the role of a mother.*)

LUPE: How can I feed him? He bit the nipple on the bottle and eat it. Look he's all cover with bean soup.

CRUZ: What is she shewing?

LUPE: A cucaracha. (*Pause.*) Oh, don' look at me like that, man. He like 'em. At least I peel off the shell first.

CRUZ: Que muchacha, What kind of little mother you be, eh? You want to kill her?

LUPE: He's not a her, mama!

CRUZ: How you know? He don' get mustaches. His uncle Chorti was born wis mustaches.

LUPE: I don' care I know. I'm his madre.

BELARMINO: (*In his sleep.*) La tuya.

LUPE: There he goes again, man.

CRUZ: He's sleeping.

BELARMINO: (*Dreaming.*) Señores, I am Francisco Villa.

LUPE: See? He's dreaming just like mi 'apa used to do it.

BELARMINO: Pancho Villa!

CRUZ: My son?

LUPE: Why don' you pull his leg. (*Laughs.*)

CRUZ: You chattap. You think your son gots so much?

BELARMINO: I am Pancho Villa.

CRUZ: No, my son, you're Belarmino.

BELARMINO: VIVA VILLA!

LUPE: Shut him up, man! He's scaring my baby. Pull his ear!

BELARMINO: VIVA PANCHO VI—(CRUZ *pulls his ear.*) YAH-aay jijos! Who pull my ear?

CRUZ: I do it, my son. You was having a bad dream.

LUPE: And it gets worser every day. Look like that's all you learn to talk for. I'm Pancho Villa! Pancho Villa!

BELARMINO: I also talk something else, baboza jija de la—

LUPE: Ah ah. Speak English. Without English there's no welfare.

BELARMINO: How I'd like to keek your butt.

LUPE: Well, try it . . . Shorty! (*Laughs.*)

CRUZ: Stop it, Negra. You should have more respect for your older brother. Since Mingo leave and Joaquin's in jail, he's the man of the man of the house.

LUPE: The head of the house.

BELARMINO: Chattap! Your madre's right. I'm in charge.

LUPE: Of what, our starvation?

CRUZ: (*Sighs.*) If Mingo was here, we wouldn't have to worry about nothing. He always work so hard.

BELARMINO: Chure, on us! Forget Mingo, señora. Mingo go away forever. I'm here and I take care of you now. Just wait till the Revolucion.

LUPE: What Revolucion? What we need is welfare so we can eat.

CRUZ: I only pray to Dios Nuestro Señor that Joaquin come back from jail serious. Ready to marry and settle down and support a family.

BELARMINO: Si, like *our* family, for one ejemplo, no? Huevonas! I know what you up to. You itching for Joaquin to come so he can support you! Well, what happen to all that pedo about welfare? We got a right to it. I'm disable.

CRUZ: They want to come to investigate first.

BELARMINO: To investigate? Wha's that?

LUPE: They wanna see how come you don' get a job.

BELARMINO: Huy, pos let 'em come. I don' hide nothing.

LUPE: You got nothing to hide.

BELARMINO: (*An angry burst.*) Tu ya me estas caendo gorda, sabes? Vale mas que te calles el hocico! Yo mando en esta casa y me tienes que guardar respeto! *Malcriada, Pendeja, Malhablada!!!* (*Pause.*) Chihuahua, what a relief. There's nothing like saying what you got to say in Spanish. Like chili in the beans. But I say the same thing in English if you push me, eh? You godamit!

LUPE: Ay, okay pues. Don' bite me.

BELARMINO: Well, don' come too close. Ma? What time is Joaquin coming from the jail?

CRUZ: I don' know, my son. I'm worry already. Chato go to get him this morning and ees already night. (*There is a knock at the door.*) Ay! Maybe tha's him?

LUPE: No, I bet it's the welfare man.

CRUZ: No, ees my son. I feel it's Joaquin.

LUPE: No, señora, why should Joaquin knock? He lives here.

CRUZ: But maybe he's . . .

BELARMINO: Bueno pues, don' just argue. Open the door!

CRUZ: (*Hesitant.*) Ay dios. You open it, Lupe . . . I can't do it.

LUPE: (*Opens the door.*) There's nobody.

CRUZ: Nobody? (*She goes to the door.*)

BELARMINO: Look outside, maybe he's outside! Stinking viejas! If I had your legs I would have already run around the house. You don' see nobody?

CRUZ: Nothing. I wonder who it is? (LUPE *crosses the door.*)

CHATO: (*Outside.*) Orale, don' close it! I'm coming!

LUPE: It's Chato! (CHATO *enters, dressed in* PEDRO's *old clothes. He has a mustache now, and in appearance and behavior he has begun to resemble* PEDRO.) What a joke you trying to pull, hombre? Knocking at the door.

CHATO: What door? Vieja sonsa! I din' knock.

BELARMINO: Where's Joaquin?

CRUZ: Yes, Chato. Where's my son? (CHATO *says nothing.*)

BELARMINO: Well talk, hombre!

CHATO: I din' find him.

CRUZ: What?

CHATO: I went to the prison door and wait, but he din' come out.

CRUZ: Ay no, my poor son! They din' let him come out!

LUPE: Din' I tell you? He haven' change. He do something and they take away his parole.

CHATO: They din' neither! I ask 'em. They let him out today.

BELARMINO: Then where's he at? Babozo, maybe you miss him.

CHATO: Nel, I notice good all the vatos that come out. Joaquin wasn' nobody of 'em. I mean . . . nobody look like Joaquin.

BELARMINO: Me lleva la . . . ! What you think Joaquin look like? Like Joaquin! A muchaco wis arms and legs! Did you look good by the road? Maybe he come walking?

CHATO: Nel, I look up and down. I even run outa gas and have to leave my carucha by the road. I din' have even enough to buy a gallon of gas. (*Pause.*) Don' worry, Doña Cruz. Maybe Joaquin come in the bus or something. He'll come today. (*Pause.*) What about here? Did the welfare vato come? (*There is another knock at the door.*)

CRUZ: Ees my son! (*She goes to the door and opens it.*)

BELARMINO: Ees him? (*Pause.*) How do he look? No la jodan pues! Tell me who is it?

CRUZ: Ees nobody. (*She closes the door. There is another knock at the door. Stronger this time.*)

BELARMINO: Epale! They knocking over here, señora! (CHATO *opens the door to the side room "*MINGO's room*". *MINGO* is standing in the doorway. He is dressed in a professional gray suit and is carrying a briefcase. He wears a smart hat and glasses, shoes shined, etc. His face is unusually pale; in fact, it almost looks bleached.*)

PHOTO COURTESY OF EL TEATRO CAMPESINO

MINGO: Good evening, is this the home of Mr. Belarmine?

LUPE: Who?

MINGO: Belarmine, I believe it is?

LUPE: Oh. You mean Belarmino!

BELARMINO: Abusados, raza, es el vato de la welfare.

LUPE: Yes, this is the home of Mr. Belarmino. Come in please.

MINGO: (*With an anglo accent.*) Muchas gracias. (*Enters, takes off his hat.*)

CRUZ: (*Approaching* MINGO, *awed.*) Mingo? My son, my Domingo! (*She leaps at him and hugs him.*) You come home!

MINGO: I beg your pardon!

LUPE: (*Trying to pull* CRUZ *away.*) Mama! Please! This gentleman isn' Mingo! Mingo's gone! (CRUZ *backs up.*) This is my mother, please excuse her. She thinks you're my brother who went away.

CRUZ: (*Touching* MINGO'S *face.*) Como te llamas?

MINGO: (*Pause.*) Mi nombre is Sunday, señora.

LUPE: You speak Spanish?

MINGO: Un poquito. It's part of my job.

LUPE: You see, ma? He's call Sunday, not Domingo. Let him talk with Belarmino.

MINGO: Gracias, let me see . . . Usted es Mr. Belarmine?

CHATO: No, him.

MINGO: Him?

BELARMINO: Quihubole, chabo.

MINGO: Mucho gusto. I have here your application to receive county welfare aid, and oh, do you speak English?

BELARMINO: Oh yes, more better than a gringo.

LUPE: Belo!

MINGO: Ha ha. It's okay, I don't mind. It may surprise you to know that I'm Mexican-American and fully aware of the sympathies of the culturally deprived. Now Mr. Belarmine, all we want and need before your case goes through is a few personal facts about yourself for our records. Me entiende?

BELARMINO: (*Nods.*) Picale a la burra.

MINGO: Well, for example. You've applied for our disability coverage. so we need to know who you sleep with.

BELARMINO: Que?

MINGO: Do you sleep alone?

BELARMINO: None of you bis'ness! Pos mira . . . sonavavichi!

LUPE: Belo!

MINGO: I'm sorry, but we need to know.

CRUZ: He sleep with me.

MINGO: Oh yeah? And where's your husband, señora?

BELARMINO: Esta muerto!

MINGO: Let her answer please!

CRUZ: He is dead.

MINGO: Well, I don't mean to question your traditional moral values, but don't you think it's wrong just to shack up with this fellow? You're both old enough to know better. Why don't you get married?

CRUZ: Because he's my son!

MINGO: Oh. Oh!

BELARMINO: Cochino.

MINGO: Well, what kind of disability do you have?

BELARMINO: Pos take a good look.

MINGO: (*He looks.*) Hmm. You did have a rather serious accident, didn't you? Have you tried to find any work at all?

BELARMINO: Doing what, being a futbol?

MINGO: Do you have any stocks or bonds or private property?

BELARMINO: Huuuy.

MINGO: Well?

BELARMINO: Nothing, nada, ni madre!

MINGO: Good. I guess that does it. We have your application with all other facts and with this, we'll be able to push your case through. But there's just one more thing.

BELARMINO: Pues si, there's always just one more thing.

MINGO: I would suggest you get a haircut.

BELARMINO: Haircut?

MINGO: A crewcut.

CRUZ: No! No, señor, please. Not his hair! When he was born like he is, I promise the Virgin never to cut his hair if she let him live.

MINGO: Oh, I see. An old supersti— religion, huh? Well, I was only thinking of your health. I know it's hard in these barrios to keep the city clean, but we gotta give it that old 100% try, know what I mean? I'm going to let you in on a little secret, maybe you'll feel better. Once a long time ago . . . I was poor too. That's right. I also used to live in a lousy dump with cockroaches a lot like this one. Everything was almost exactly like this . . . but that was a lotta years back . . . in another barrio . . . another town . . . another time. (*Snapping out of it.*) Now I'm middle class! I got out of the poverty I lived in because I cared about myself. Because I did something to help myself. I went to college. So now I'm a social worker helping out the poor! Which means that I want to help you to take full advantage of what our society has to offer. There's nothing to lose and everything to gain, believe me!

BELARMINO: I believe you. When do the checks come?

MINGO: Oh, I figure in about thirty days.

BELARMINO: Thirty days!

LUPE: But we don' got nothing to eat.

MINGO: I'm sorry but that's the best we can do.

LUPE: What about Aid to Needy Children?

MINGO: What needy children?

LUPE: My baby. (*She shows him the baby.*)

MINGO: Cute. But what does he need?

LUPE: Look. (*She opens the blanket.*)

MINGO: (*Double take at* BELARMINO *then down at the baby again.*) Another one! What happen?

LUPE: He's sick. Like his uncle.

MINGO: Runs in the family, huh? Well, I'll tell you. There's a good chance you might be able to get some kind of help, but nothing before 30 days at least.

BELARMINO: Okay, that do it! Señora, fry me some cucarachas! I hungry.

CHATO: Don' worry, Doña Cruz. I bet Joaquin gets some coins.

MINGO: Joaquin who? Another man in the family?

BELARMINO: Simon limon, more man than you think! Es mas hombre que la ching —

CRUZ: Mingo! Oh, Joaquin, no-Lupe, ah, tu — Chorti!

MINGO: Joaquin . . . ? Oh yeah! I forgot! Where is this Joaquin? (*No one says anything.*) Okay, let me put it different. Where was this Joaquin? In prison?

CHATO: How you know?

MINGO: And he was just released today?

CRUZ: Yes, on patrol.

BELARMINO: Parole.

MINGO: What's he like? Tall, short, light, dark?

CRUZ: Yes, tha's him! Why?

MINGO: Because tonight when I was coming across town I passed by this good looking Mexican walking along the road. It was pretty cold, so I gave him a lift. He'd just gotten out on parole this morning.

CRUZ: Joaquin, ees my Joaquin!

CHATO: Where's he at?

MINGO: Outside in my car. I forgot he came with me. I'll go get him.

CRUZ: Ay dios! My son is outside!

MINGO: Oh, another thing. It looks like the prison term helped him a lot. He seems very reformed, rehabilitated. Lots of spunk. A clean cut American boy! Be right back. (*He exits.*)

BELARMINO: AY, YAI, YAI! Now you going to see the Revolucion burst out! Joaquin is back!

CRUZ: (*Overexcited.*) Viva la Revolucion!! (*Pause.*) I mean gracias a dios, my son is back.

LUPE: I bet you pass up Joaquin when he was walking, huh? Menso!

CHATO: Como que menso? Quieres que te meta un guamazo en el hocico? Huh, pos mira? Who's the boss around heres pues? (*He goes to door.*)

CRUZ: You hear what the social worker says, Lupe? My Joaquin is change, he's serious and reform.

BELARMINO: He don' say that. He say he got lots of spunk. He's revolutionary!!

CHATO: (*At the window.*) Here they come! (*Pause*) Que caray! Tha's not Joaquin!

CRUZ: What?

LUPE: (*At the window.*) Oh no, Joaquin!

BELARMINO: Que, what you see?

MINGO: (*Opening the door.*) Okay, folks, here he is! (MINGO *comes in.*) Well, Jack, come in. This is where you live.

CRUZ: (*Standing in the doorway.*) Dios mio, my son. (*She weeps.*)

JOAQUIN *comes into the house. He is well dressed,* BUT HE HAS NO HEAD.

BELARMINO: Chingado, they got him.

MINGO: You see? Rehabilitated. He even grew a little. Congratulations, Jack, I know now you'll make it. Well, I guess I better be on my way. Don't forget the crewcut and general cleanliness, okay? Buenas noches. (*Exits.*)

LUPE: I don' think he looks so bad, mama. He look cleaner.

CHATO: Quihubole, ese. (*Shakes* JOAQUIN's *hand.*) No wonder I din' reco'nize him on the road.

LUPE: You shut up. I think Joaq—Jack's gonna be okay, ma. He can still find a job in the fields. Now we can all plan together for the future. Like my son he's not going to have a poor life like us. I'm going to make sure he study so he can go to college someday like Mr. Sunday. With the help of God, my son will grow to be a decent man. Maybe someday he even find a body he can . . . (*Pause.*)

BELARMINO: (*Quickly.*) Heh, señora, bring Joaquin over here! I want to see him. Pos what you know? Look at the big arms he gots . . . and the big body! Oye, Ma, I got an idea.

LUPE: No you don't! I see him first!

BELARMINO: What firs'? I got years waiting for him! Anyway he don' even fit that little head you got.

CRUZ: What you two arguing?

BELARMINO: Pos what? There's the body and here's the head. Le's get together! Pick me up!

CRUZ: But how, hombre? Joaquin is your brother.

BELARMINO: Pos there you are. We keep it in the family. Pick me up somebody!

CRUZ: No, Belarmino.

BELARMINO: Orale, Chato, gimme a lift!

CRUZ: No, I say!

LUPE: See? He's mine, huh mama?

CRUZ: Neither his or yours or nobody but me. Joaquin is mine. Buenas noches. Come on, my son. (*Exits with* JOAQUIN.)

BELARMINO: Heh! Wait, señora! Wait one minute!

CRUZ: Callate tu, cabezon!

LUPE: You see, stupid? We both lose! Come on, Chato. (*Exits.*)

BELARMINO: (*Shouting after* LUPE.) Both lose, eh? Bueno, we see who have more pull wis the old lady! Stinking woman! They don' understand Revolucion for nothing. We men must carry on the fight. We machos! No, Chato?

CHATO: Simon, we machos!

LUPE: (*Shouting.*) Chato, come to bed!

CHATO: Oh, that vieja apestosa! Buenas noches, ese.

BELARMINO: Buenas noches. (CHATO *exits.*) Well, here I sit . . . broken hearted. But tha's okay cause I still got time to wait. Sooner or later, the jefita gots to come across wis Joaquin's body. All I need is to talk sweet when she give me my beans eh? In other words, organize her. Those people don' even believe who I am. Tha's how I wan' it. To catch 'em by surprise. So don' worry, my people, because one of this days Pancho Villa will pass among you again. Look to your mountains, your pueblos, your barrios. He will be there. Buenas noches.

Curtain

Chekhov in Yalta

(Featuring a Rare and Delightful Visit
by the Moscow Art Theater)

John Driver and
Jeffrey Haddow

Chekhov in Yalta was first presented at the Mark Taper Forum, Los Angeles, on May 24, 1981, with the following cast:

FYOKLA	Lois Foraker
ANTON PAVLOVICH CHEKHOV	Robin Gammell
MAXIM GORKY	Keene Curtis
IVAN ALEXEIVICH BUNIN	James R. Winker
MASHA CHEKHOV	Marian Mercer
OLGA LEONARDOVA KNIPPER	Penny Fuller
VLADIMIR NEMIROVICH—DANCHENKO	Dana Elcar
PEASANTS	Douglas Blair
	Edward Fabry
LILINA STANISLAVSKI	Andra Akers
LUZHKI	Michael Bond
MOSKVIN	Jeffrey Combs
KONSTANTIN SERGEIEVICH STANISLAVSKI	Rene Auberjonois

Directed by Ellis Rabb *and* Gordon Davidson
Scenery by Douglas W. Schmidt
Costumes by John Conklin
Lighting by Martin Aronstein
Music composed by Catherine MacDonald
Fight and dance choreography by Anthony DeLongis
Production coordination by Frank Bayer

SETTING

Anton Chekhov's villa in Yalta.

TIME

ACT I, Scene 1: A spring morning in 1900.
ACT I, Scene 2: The next evening.
ACT II: Sunday morning, one week later.

CHARACTERS

FYOKLA: 21. Chekhov's maid.

ANTON PAVLOVICH CHEKHOV: 40. Writer and doctor.

MAXIM GORKY: 32. Writer of the people. Living in Yalta to treat his consumption.

IVAN ALEXEIVICH BUNIN: 30. Popular writer of aristocratic descent. Summering in Yalta.

MASHA CHEKHOV: Mid-thirties. Anton's unmarried sister and housekeeper.

OLGA LEONARDOVA KNIPPER: Thirtyish. Leading lady of the Moscow Art Theater.

VLADIMIR NEMIROVICH-DANCHENKO: 41. Co-director and business manager of the Moscow Art Theater.

LUZHKI: Mid-thirties. Fat, sentimental actor of the Moscow Art Theater.

MOSKVIN: Late twenties. Young, acrobatic character man with the Moscow Art Theater.

LILINA STANISLAVSKI: 34. A delicate beauty and wife of Stanislavski. Actress and costume designer for the Moscow Art Theater.

KONSTANTIN SERGEIEVICH STANISLAVSKI: 37. Co-director and artistic force behind the Moscow Art Theater.

Chekhov in Yalta
John Driver and Jeffrey Haddow

ACT ONE

SCENE ONE

Lights up on the patio terrace of ANTON CHEKHOV's *villa in Yalta. Downstage left, a path leads off toward the sea. Upstage left is a stone wall beyond which is a Tartar cemetery. Stage right, a walkway skirts the side of the villa leading off upstage towards the front of the house. Farther right can be seen the edge of a sub-tropical forest bordered by a well-tended row of acacia trees. The rear facade of the three-story villa dominates the upstage area. Two entrances lead from the patio into the house, one small entrance stage left to the kitchen, and one larger double-door arrangement opening into the parlor. On the terrace is a grouping of wicker furniture— armchairs, sofa, table. Upstage left is a small gazebo, and downstage left is a bench. It is spring. Morning fog covers the ground. In the distance can be heard the sound of the sea. A boat whistle blows.*

The maid, FYOKLA, *an unself-consciously voluptuous creature in her early twenties, enters carrying a samovar which she places on a table. She runs off into the kitchen and immediately returns with a tea set and tray.* FYOKLA *looks around, taps a glass of tea and, while the cup fills, she wipes the dew from the chairs.*

FYOKLA: (*Realizing the tea is overflowing.*) Oh, oh. (*She rushes over and turns off the spigot.*) It's too much work for me. I'm all alone here. (*Pours tea from the tray back into the samovar and wipes glasses with her apron.*)

ANTON CHEKHOV *enters. He is forty but looks much older. Dropping his medical bag, he sinks exhaustedly into a wicker armchair.*

CHEKHOV: A stomach ache! Madame Tolstoy had a stomach ache. This time I thought it was something serious, but no, Tolstoy told me she'd consumed three bowls of cold borscht just before going to bed. What could I do? I held her hand, made sympathetic noises, and gave her a placebo. The treatment took five minutes. Then, for the rest of the night, I had to sit and listen to Tolstoy expound on the simplicity of the Russian soul.

FYOKLA: You must be exhausted. Can I bring you something?

CHEKHOV: Just a glass of tea would be fine, Fyokla. (FYOKLA *starts to samovar.*) Maybe I'll have a roll and butter too. (FYOKLA *starts into kitchen. The story stops her.*) You know, I saw a curious thing on the way back here. A drunken ice merchant had run his cart into a ditch. He was sitting on a block of ice, sobbing and tearing his hair out. It almost made the trip worthwhile. I can probably turn that into a very amusing story. Fyokla, my notebook. Eh, it's a wonder I get any writing done at all. If it's not a peasant or casual acquaintance looking for free medical advice, it's some society woman pushing her romantic drivel under my nose for criticism. (FYOKLA *starts into the kitchen.*) Wait. Semyon!

FYOKLA: Beg pardon, sir?

CHEKHOV: That's a good name for an ice man. Semyon. (FYOKLA *shrugs and exits into the house.*) God I'm hungry. Must be the sea air. The fog is burning off. The weather's going to be perfect today. I'm so bored here, unimaginably bored. (*Coughs.*) Oh Yalta, Yalta, my warm Siberia. (FYOKLA *reenters with rolls.*) Ah, thank you. Fyokla, take my bag inside, please.

FYOKLA: Yes, sir. (FYOKLA *bends over to pick up bag.*)

CHEKHOV: Wait. Come here, Fyokla. Last night as I was leaving, I saw you walking in the cemetery with a young man.

FYOKLA: We were picking mushrooms.

CHEKHOV: If Masha were here, I'd be spared this discussion, but since she isn't . . . You should be aware that your nocturnal harvesting companion is known throughout the district as a notorious cad. You mustn't throw yourself away on men who are attracted only by your . . . most obvious assets. When they've finished with you, they'll discard you like an empty tin of peaches. You wouldn't want to cause a scandal, would you?

FYOKLA: Oh, no, sir.

CHEKHOV: That will be all, Fyokla. By the way, I'm looking forward to mushrooms for lunch.

FYOKLA: Yes, sir, I'll go to the market and buy some. (FYOKLA *exits.*)

CHEKHOV: Hm. The body of a goddess. The brain of a flea. (*Taking out his notebook.*) Where was I? Oh, yes, Semyon, the ice merchant. One day, while he's making his rounds, he receives word that his nagging, gluttonous wife has choked to death on a piece of black bread. That's good. That's funny.

Enter MAXIM GORKY, *tall, dark, with Tartar features, flowing black hair, in peasant blouse, breeches, and riding boots. With him is* IVAN BUNIN, *elegant, aristocratic. They are carrying on a mock duel with fishing poles.*

GORKY: Parasite!

BUNIN: Hypocrite!

GORKY: Tsarist pig!

BUNIN: Crass peasant!

CHEKHOV: Fyokla! (BUNIN *scores a hit.*)

BUNIN: Aha! A hit!

GORKY: (*Grabs* BUNIN'*s pole and snaps it in two.*) Touché!

CHEKHOV: Fyokla! Bunin and Gorky are here.

BUNIN: You're a barbarian, Gorky.

CHEKHOV: How can you let three of the world's greatest writers languish from thirst?

BUNIN: Zola is here?

GORKY: Turgenev? I thought he was dead. (FYOKLA *enters and serves tea.* GORKY *swipes the notebook away from* CHEKHOV.) Ah, ah. None of that today.

CHEKHOV: What are you talking about?

BUNIN: Gorky's just formed a writers' union.

GORKY: And today we're on strike.

BUNIN: Like all strikes, Anton, it's merely an excuse to go fishing. And to that end . . . (*Handing* CHEKHOV *a sack.*) we've come bearing a gift.

CHEKHOV: Worms. How nice.

GORKY: (*Quietly.*) Come here and look, but keep talking. (GORKY *crosses to wall.*)

BUNIN: They're fat ones too, Anton.

GORKY: From the cemetery. You can find all sorts of crawling things in the cemetery. (*He indicates that two men are behind the wall.*)

CHEKHOV: So? A couple of gravediggers playing cards.

GORKY: They're secret police.

CHEKHOV: Around my house? Why? Do they suspect me?

GORKY: They suspect everybody.

BUNIN: It's the leaflets. He's writing those leaflets again.

GORKY: You accuse *me* of subversion? Maxim Gorky? Imperial Russia's most obedient citizen? Besides, you can't prove it's my writing.

BUNIN: I recognize the juvenile rhetoric.

GORKY: Look at the one on the right. See the bulge in his blouse? That's an oak truncheon filled with lead. They say he's killed five men with it. They don't dare arrest me. The public outcry would be too great.

BUNIN: I can hear the crowds now, yelling, "Give us Barrabas!"

GORKY: They've heard us. (GORKY, BUNIN, *and* CHEKHOV *move away from the wall to the samovar.*)

CHEKHOV: Maxim, why do you put yourself in such danger for a few worthless pieces of paper? (FYOKLA *enters with sandwiches and serves tea.*) Fyokla, have you seen my fishing pole?

FYOKLA: No, sir.

CHEKHOV: Well, find it, and bring it here, please. Maybe this bait will change my luck.

BUNIN: (*Drinks tea, spits it out.*) Ptooey! Yeccchh.

GORKY: Wonderful tea. My grandmother made tea like this.

FYOKLA: I'll make a new pot.

BUNIN: Oh, don't waste it. I can always use it to clean my shotgun.

CHEKHOV: My fishing pole, Fyokla.

FYOKLA: Yes, sir. (FYOKLA *exits.* GORKY *begins tying his fly to his leader.* BUNIN *repairs his pole.*)

CHEKHOV: Maxim, you're too impatient. Change and growth will only come when the season is right and the ground has been carefully prepared.

GORKY: Yes, but the ground must be scorched, cleansed by fire then plowed under. Ground covered with ashes is fertile ground.

CHEKHOV: But to burn, to tear down. No, give the people books, teach them to read, make them healthy . . .

GORKY: I want to see it in my lifetime. The solution is quick and simple. Chop off the head of the Imperial eagle.

CHEKHOV: For God's sake, Gorky, keep your voice down.

BUNIN: You look tired, Anton. You really should rest for a while.

CHEKHOV: I was at Tolstoy's all night.

BUNIN: Oho. That's enough to exhaust a plow horse. Take a nap. We'll come back later.

CHEKHOV: No, no, don't go. His wife was ill. You won't believe what Tolstoy came up with this time. He said he couldn't tolerate Shakespeare's plays.

BUNIN: What conceit!

GORKY: Only Tolstoy could get away with that.

CHEKHOV: Then he said my plays were even worse. (*Imitating Tolstoy.*) "Nothing happens in your plays, Anton." (*Silence.*) He must have seen Stanislavski's production of *Seagull.* All those pauses. (*Pause.*) I almost fell asleep myself. I know many people say Konstantin Sergeivich is a genius, but the things he did to my play. Granted, it was supposed to be night but the lights were so dim the audience could hardly see the stage. And that constant cacophany of nightingales, hoofbeats, creaking gates, rustling leaves, strange noises in the forest. And his brilliant idea of a plague of imaginary insects. All through the first act the players kept slapping themselves so loudly you couldn't hear what they were saying. In the next play I write, I'll have someone make an entrance in every scene just to say, "What a marvelous place! There are no mosquitoes."

BUNIN: Anton, you must admit, the acting at the Moscow Art is more real than at other theaters. Sometimes Stanislavski's off the mark but he's bold. He's an experimenter.

CHEKHOV: My plays are not laboratory animals.

BUNIN: And when he's on stage the man is amazing—such presence, such style . . .

CHEKHOV: Such an idiot. He can't even remember his lines.

GORKY: Has the company left Sebastopol yet?

CHEKHOV: Yes. Tomorrow they'll descend on Yalta like locusts. Oh, I want both of you here for a little reception I'm giving after the performance tomorrow night.

BUNIN: Watch out for Olga Knipper, Anton. She's got her sights on you. Your sister tells me you write to her three times a week.

CHEKHOV: Yes, I bore her with the details of my tedious existence, and she sends me back news of Moscow.

BUNIN: That's not what I've heard.

GORKY: Aha, a new tenant for the notorious beach house. One actress moves out, another moves in. I hope at least you changed the sheets.

CHEKHOV: Not a word about Komisarevskaya to anyone.

GORKY: The secret of social success unveiled! Become a playwright and beautiful actresses will tug at your breeches.

CHEKHOV: Pleasure always has its price, my friends. In the three days she was here the demure Komisarevskaya became a tyrannical Amazon possessed with a single-minded hunger for matrimony. Thank God she had an engagement to star in an Ibsen play in Rostov. Ach, Ibsen, now there's an atrocious playwright.

GORKY: Nothing happens in his plays.

BUNIN: Imagine naming a play after a bird.

CHEKHOV: Why does the Moscow Art insist on doing my plays the same way they do Ibsen's? I write comedies. (BUNIN *whistles a little tune. Awkward silence. Sound of the sea.*)

GORKY: Wind is from the south today. You can hear the breakers.

CHEKHOV: Ivan, how would you describe the sea?

BUNIN: The sea . . . The sea. A well of tears . . . fallen from the eyes of the Mother of Life. A restless opalescent tabletop . . . reflecting the depths of cosmic sorrow.

CHEKHOV: Maxim?

GORKY: The enormous black sea appears calm. But beneath that serene facade lies a monstrous denizen of discontent covered with scales of razor-sharp steel. It is an embryo, never having seen the light, never having breathed the air of freedom. For centuries it has gathered size and substance. It is waiting, waiting for the right moment to burst from its womb and cut the night fog with the fiery blue sword of Justice.

BUNIN: Thank God. For a second there I thought you were going to get political.

CHEKHOV: I was looking over some of my old copybooks, and I came across this quote. In my opinion it is the most perfect description of the sea ever written. "The sea is huge." (GORKY *and* BUNIN *assent. Awe.*) I always carry it with me as a reminder to write simply.

FYOKLA: (*Enters with fishing pole.*) It was on the piano.

CHEKHOV: Well, philosophy never accomplished anything. Let's go fishing. (*The three begin tying on their flies.*)

BUNIN: Anton, could I borrow your magnifying glass? (CHEKHOV *hands* BUNIN *the magnifying glass.*)

GORKY: Damn! This is all tangled up. (BUNIN *looking at his lure through the magnifying glass, gets an idea. He trains a pinpoint of light on* GORKY's *bald spot. Silence, punctuated by an occasional cough from* GORKY *and* CHEKHOV.)

BUNIN: My, you two are having such a nice cough together.

GORKY: (*Jumping up.*) AAAAARGHHHH! (GORKY *grabs* BUNIN, *tears his shirt.*)

BUNIN: So vulgar.

Enter MASHA CHEKHOV, ANTON's *sister. She is a plain, matronly woman who has devoted much of her life to looking after her brother's welfare. She is followed by* OLGA KNIPPER, *vibrant, strong-willed, charismatic leading lady of the Moscow Art Theater.*

MASHA: (*Seeing* BUNIN.) Ivan.

CHEKHOV: Masha! (MASHA *rushes to* ANTON *and kisses him.*)

MASHA: Dear brother.

CHEKHOV: What are you doing here?

MASHA: We came early. How nice to see you again, Ivan.

BUNIN: Masha.

MASHA: And you, Maxim.

GORKY: Masha.

CHEKHOV: Olga!

OLGA: We tried to telephone, but you know how temperamental those machines are. We can't stay long. We just stopped to bring Masha home.

BUNIN: (*Bowing.*) Mademoiselle Knipper.

OLGA: Monsieur Bunin.

MASHA: Ivan, what happened to your shirt?

BUNIN: I was attacked by an animal.

MASHA: Well, it can be mended. The tear is on the seam.

CHEKHOV: You'll all be staying here tonight, then?

Enter VLADIMIR NEMIROVICH-DANCHENKO, *dapper, bearded managing director of the Moscow Art Theater.* FYOKLA *enters from kitchen.*

NEMIROVICH: I'm afraid not. Half the scenery isn't even assembled yet. But I promise you, after the performance tomorrow night your villa will become the Pension Moscow Art.

CHEKHOV: Nemirovich!

NEMIROVICH: Anton Pavlovich, how are you?

CHEKHOV: Fine, fine. Ivan Bunin, Maxim Gorky, this is Vladimir Nemirovich-Danchenko, director of the Moscow Art Theater.

NEMIROVICH:Co-director.

CHEKHOV: Ah, yes. With Konstantin . . . what's his name.

MASHA: Why are you alone here, Fyokla? Where's the footman?

FYOKLA: He disappeared last Thursday.

CHEKHOV: With the silver tea set and my new beaver hat.

MASHA: How can I possibly get everything ready by tomorrow? Come, Fyokla. (MASHA *and* FYOKLA *exit.*)

CHEKHOV: Sit down, sit down everybody.

GORKY: Olga Leonardova, may I say you were wonderful as Arkadina in *The Seagull.*

CHEKHOV: Oh, I'm sorry, you two haven't met, have you? Olga Knipper, Maxim Gorky.

NEMIROVICH: Gorky, why didn't you come backstage to see us while you were in Moscow?

GORKY: I was under surveillance. Still am as a matter of fact. I didn't want to get you involved in that.

NEMIROVICH: Ah, yes. I've heard you attract police like baklava draws flies.

CHEKHOV: When did you leave Moscow?

NEMIROVICH: On the twelfth.

GORKY: Then you were there when it happened. The students must have marched right past your theater.

CHEKHOV: What are you talking about?

NEMIROVICH: You didn't hear about it? People were killed. Students and Cossacks fighting in the streets.

CHEKHOV: There was no mention of it in the newspapers.

GORKY: (*Contemptuously.*) The newspapers.

NEMIROVICH: A large group of students were demonstrating about something or other and the Cossacks wouldn't let them pass.

GORKY: The bastards!

NEMIROVICH: At first everyone just stopped and looked at each other. Then, one student began shouting slogans and the rest of them lost their heads.

OLGA: Just outside the entrance to the theater I watched as a Cossack cut off a boy's hand.

NEMIROVICH: Several students were trampled to death.

OLGA: The gutters ran with blood. (MASHA *enters.*)

GORKY: They'll pay for this. For each one killed, a thousand will rise up to take his place.

BUNIN: I can't believe there are that many suicidal fools, even in Russia.

MASHA: At the station we saw them loading coffins onto the mail train.

GORKY: Wait till the workers start joining the students.

MASHA: God help us. (FYOKLA *enters carrying a tray of oysters.*)

CHEKHOV: Oysters! Where did they come from?

MASHA: I brought them packed in ice all the way from Sebastopol.

CHEKHOV: Ah, Masha, you know so well how to make me happy. You all must be hungry.

NEMIROVICH: Ravenous.

GORKY: How many dead?

CHEKHOV: Can't we talk about something else?

BUNIN: For Maxim there is no other subject.

GORKY: Everything is political. Even those oysters. A metaphor for the masses.

BUNIN: Perfect. After all, they are lazy and stupid. Day in, day out, lying passively on the bottom doing nothing.

GORKY: Not at all. They're working, always working, silently producing pearls to hang about the necks of bourgeois swine.

OLGA: But Maxim, what about the oysters that don't produce pearls?

CHEKHOV: They, my dear actress, make excellent appetizers. (*Everyone digs into the oysters.* CHEKHOV *has serious coughing fit.* MASHA *rushes to him.*)

PHOTO BY JAY THOMPSON

OLGA: Are you all right?

CHEKHOV: I'm fine. You see? I've stopped.

MASHA: Come on, Antosha. You need to lie down.

CHEKHOV: Nonsense. I'm perfectly well. I must have choked on a pearl.

OLGA: I'll help you upstairs.

MASHA: I can manage myself, thank you. (MASHA *leads* CHEKHOV *into house.*)

BUNIN: He was worn out. We should have left him alone. (GORKY *coughs.*) Maybe we should put you to bed too.

NEMIROVICH: Good lord, does everyone in Yalta have consumption?

BUNIN: Almost everyone. But you needn't worry. It isn't thought to be contagious.

NEMIROVICH: I know that. You certainly look healthy enough.

BUNIN: Oh, yes, I live here not because it's therapeutic, but because it's fashionable. And the fishing is superb. Well, Maxim, shall we?

GORKY: By all means. (*To others.*) Until tomorrow. (*They start to leave.* FYOKLA *runs in with jar full of brown liquid.*)

FYOKLA: Wait, Ivan Alexeivich! (*Hands* BUNIN *the jar.*)

BUNIN: What's this?

FYOKLA: It's tea. For your shotgun. (BUNIN *and* GORKY *laugh and exit.* FYOKLA *exits.*)

NEMIROVICH: Anton looks terrible. I hope he's not too ill to write.

OLGA: Your concern for his health is touching.

NEMIROVICH: I'm very concerned for him. The last thing in the world I want right now is for Anton Chekhov to die.

OLGA: You think he's that ill?

NEMIROVICH: He certainly looks it. Olga, if we don't have a financial success this season — and that means a new Chekhov play — the doors of the Moscow Art will close forever. Why do you think we're here?

OLGA: I thought we were simply on tour.

NEMIROVICH: It's up to you to make sure Anton continues to be our playwright.

OLGA: Oh, no. You can't use me like you did in former times. I'm not your adoring student anymore.

NEMIROVICH: Sometimes I miss those former times.

OLGA: How's your wife?

NEMIROVICH: As promiscuous as possible at her age.

OLGA: You two have so much in common. But this time you're going too far.

NEMIROVICH: What are you talking about?

OLGA: Your current asault on Madame Stanislavski is a mistake.

NEMIROVICH: I have no intention . . .

OLGA: You have every intention. The longing looks across the room, the significant smiles, the well-chosen words of extravagent praise. Don't forget, you played that game with me. But I'm strong, Lilina is not.

NEMIROVICH: You have an over-active imagination.

OLGA: Do I? Stanislavski may not be able to see anything beyond the footlights, but you can't fool me. Lilina is terribly insecure right now about her marriage and her work. She pours valerian drops into her tea and still she can't sleep.

NEMIROVICH: Does Anton love you?

OLGA: Don't change the subject.

NEMIROVICH: Lilina is not entirely unresponsive to my advances, and she's old enough to know what she's doing. End of discussion. Now, does Anton love you?

OLGA: Who knows?

NEMIROVICH: You can't give up now, Olga. The stakes are too high. After all, what actress wouldn't want to be Madame Chekhov?

OLGA: You underestimate me.

NEMIROVICH: I underestimate everyone. Maybe that's why I'm such a good businessman. (MASHA *enters.*) Masha, may I use your telephone?

MASHA: You can try.

NEMIROVICH: How is Anton Pavlovich?

MASHA: A little better now, thank you. (NEMIROVICH *exits.*) I'm so worried. He seems much worse.

OLGA: Oh, you're exaggerating.

MASHA: He had an attack! He coughed up blood. I was a fool to stay in Moscow so long.

OLGA: Your brother died of consumption, didn't he?

MASHA: Yes. Poor Nikolai. He was a wonderful artist. His illustrations for Anton's stories were so sensitive. He was quite young. Anton took it very hard. (*Pause.*)

OLGA: I did as you asked. I watched Bunin's eyes.

MASHA: What do you think?

OLGA: Oh, Masha, I can't lie to you.

MASHA: (*Crying.*) I knew it. He likes pretty women. There's no chance for me. What can I do, Olga? I love him.

OLGA: Then tell him that.

MASHA: No, I couldn't. You see, Ivan and I have become friends. We talk, we have long conversations. But the subject is always Anton. To him, I'm only Chekhov's spinster sister. (*She cries more.*)

OLGA: A spinster! Don't be ridiculous, Masha. You're younger than I am.

MASHA: I am?

OLGA: I . . . think so.

MASHA: But you have charm, Olga. You know how to talk to men. (*Hopefully.*) You could even talk to Bunin about me.

OLGA: Oh, Masha, I have no talent as a go-between, and I hardly know the man.

MASHA: Please . . .

OLGA: And if he's not interested in you?

MASHA: Then I'll forget all about him.

OLGA: Well . . .

MASHA: Thank you, thank you. Oh, Olya, Olya, what would I do without you?

OLGA: All right, I'll do it. But from now on, you must be completely honest with me.

MASHA: I've always been honest with you.

OLGA: Not when it comes to Anton.

MASHA: I just don't want you to be hurt, Olya. He's not as good as you think he is.

OLGA: What does that mean?

MASHA: Nothing.

OLGA: You see? You're holding back.

MASHA: Less than a month ago, Komisarevskaya was here.

OLGA: What?

MASHA: For three days.

OLGA: And how many nights?

MASHA: He calls her his Russian Duse.

OLGA: His Russian Duse.

MASHA: I shouldn't have told you! I shouldn't have.

OLGA: I will talk to Bunin, and I'll be as honest with you as you've been with me. Komisarevskaya, that scheming bitch.

MASHA: I'm sorry I told you.

OLGA: Why? It's the truth, isn't it?

MASHA: But it's so unfair. Oh, Olya, how can we go on living with this hopelessness? (*They cry and embrace.* CHEKHOV *enters.*)

CHEKHOV: Did Stanislavski direct this scene?

MASHA: What are you doing down here? Go back to bed. I sent for Dr. Altschuler. He'll be here soon.

CHEKHOV: What do I need a doctor for? I am a doctor. I take my pulse. (*Can't find it.*) Strange, it was here yesterday. Ah, there it is. And when I look at Olga, it's twice as fast. I'm healthy as a bull. Masha, bring my cigars.

MASHA: I will not let you smoke while I'm in this house.

CHEKHOV: Fine, bring me my cigars and leave. (MASHA *storms out.*)

Olga. (*They kiss passionately.*) Mmmm. Can't do that in a letter.

OLGA: You've tried, Anton.

CHEKHOV: The things we've done on paper. Well, what do you think of my prison?

OLGA: Palms, hibiscus, bougainvillia—the air is perfume.

CHEKHOV: Thank God the villa's finally finished. I planted all the acacias myself.

OLGA: Why didn't you come to Moscow?

CHEKHOV: I was going through a bad period then. That Prussian tyrant Altschuler forbade me to travel.

OLGA: You should have told me, Anton. Why can't you trust me?

CHEKHOV: But I do, you know I do, my little Russian Bernhardt.

OLGA: Bernhardt? Why not Duse?

CHEKHOV: Duse? Oh, no, Duse is a tragic figure. (FYOKLA *enters with humidor.*)

FYOKLA: Your cigars, sir.

CHEKHOV: (*Tries to open the humidor. It's locked.*) Fyokla, it's locked. Where's the key?

FYOKLA: Masha has it.

CHEKHOV: Well, tell Masha to bring it to me.

FYOKLA: She's not here. She went to market. (*Starts out, comes back.*) Oh, here's your matches. (FYOKLA *exits.*)

CHEKHOV: Could I borrow one of your hairpins? (OLGA *gives him one.*) I've built a little house on the beach.

OLGA: Don't tell me, very private, two rooms, the sound of the sea . . .

CHEKHOV: Four rooms. And it's particularly romantic when moonlight streams through the bedroom window.

OLGA: Is that where you made love to Komisarevskaya?

CHEKHOV: The devil made this lock.

OLGA: I said . . .

CHEKHOV: I may be sick, but I'm not deaf. Ah, Knipschutz, you're taking this whole matter much too seriously.

OLGA: And you're not taking me seriously at all.

CHEKHOV: What a part I've written for you in *The Three Sisters*.

OLGA: The mistress of a famous writer?

CHEKHOV: That wouldn't be quite accurate, would it? Not yet.

OLGA: Love is no joke, Anton. People shoot themselves over it.

CHEKHOV: Why make such a fuss? What will it all matter in a hundred years?

OLGA: Oh, then why write, why build beach houses? Why not just . . .

CHEKHOV: Die?

OLGA: You do have consumption, darling.

CHEKHOV: I have a slight cough due to the dampness in the air.

OLGA: You need treatment. Let me help you.

CHEKHOV: There is one thing you can do. Dr. Altschuler has prescribed the beach house cure.

OLGA: I wonder how many actresses have fallen for that?

CHEKHOV: Let's see . . . (*Counting on his fingers.*) . . . one, two, three . . .

OLGA: Am I just another one of your short stories?

CHEKHOV: No. Sometimes I wish you were. But you're not. (NEMIROVICH *enters.*)

NEMIROVICH: Olga, we must be off.

OLGA: Well, until tomorrow.

CHEKHOV: Until tomorrow night. There'll be a full moon.

OLGA: Dreamer.

NEMIROVICH: Good-bye, Anton Pavlovich.

CHEKHOV: Good-bye. Oh, Nemirovich, do you happen to have a cigar?

NEMIROVICH: Shouldn't smoke, Anton. Bad for the lungs.

OLGA: Goodbye, Anton.

CHEKHOV: Goodbye. (NEMIROVICH *and* OLGA *exit.*) Semyon the ice man. Where was I? Damn! Olga makes me nervous. Even when she's not here she invades my privacy. I can't get any work done. Why do I bother with this inconsequential tripe? Vanity. How long will my work outlive me? Twenty years? Twenty-five years? No, let's be honest, seven. (*Takes out a notebook.*) What was it she said? "Love is no laughing matter. People shoot themselves over it." I can't use that. It sounds like fiction. But it's not fiction. (*Writing.*) "Sounds like fiction but it's not fiction." (*Goes back to work on the humidor lock.*) Oh, Knipper, we could share beautiful evenings in the beach house, but you want more than that. You deserve more. I can't let you betroth yourself to my misery. The bacillus *will* devour me. It's coming as surely as the tide. I'll be like Nikolai. I'll sleep all day, my face will be flushed and bloated, my clothes will hang on my emaciated body and flap in the wind, my hands won't have the strength to hold even a pencil. I'll have to be bathed. Me! Who can't even bear to be seen without a tie. (*The lock springs open.* CHEKHOV *takes out a cigar and lights it.*) No, no wife. I have work to do. (*Coughs.*)

Lights fade to black.

ACT ONE

SCENE TWO

The following night. Sound of a door bell. Shouts. Groups heard singing Russian folk songs accompanied by guitar. OLGA, BUNIN, GORKY, NEMIROVICH, MASHA, *and* FYOKLA *burst into the terrace carrying bottles of wine and vodka. With them are* LUZHKI, *a fat, sentimental actor,* MOSKVIN, *a young acrobatic character man, and* LILINA, *the delicately beautiful wife of Stanislavski.*

Dancing and singing continue, LUZHKI *playing guitar, until final spectacular Cossack dance by* MOSKVIN. *Applause. Silence. Crickets.*

OLGA: Fyokla, bring some glasses. (FYOKLA *exits.*)

NEMIROVICH: Where's Stanislavski?

LILINA: He's still at the theater. You know Kostya, he can never resist lecturing, even if only one person is listening.

BUNIN: Would somebody tell me why all the actors were crying during the second act?

MOSKVIN: We were drunk.

LILINA: Just before the curtain went up, Luzhki filled the samovar with vodka.

LUZHKI: It was the best performance of *Vanya* we ever did.

GORKY: Anton Pavlovich left before it was over.

EVERYONE: He did? Is he ill?. . . etc.

NEMIROVICH: You know he can't stand crowds.

MASHA: I'd better go see if he's all right.

OLGA: I'll go with you. (MASHA *and* OLGA *exit into house.*)

LUZHKI: Where are those glasses? (FYOKLA *enters with glasses.*)

NEMIROVICH: It's one o'clock already.

EVERYONE: No. It couldn't be . . . etc.

LILINA: Moscow seems a million miles away.

LUZHKI: (*Crying.*) Ah, Moscow, Moscow.

MOSKVIN: Warm night.

LILINA: It was terribly hot onstage.

BUNIN: At least there's a cool breeze tonight.

NEMIROVICH: Why discuss it? There's nothing to be done about the weather.

LUZHKI: It's in God's hands.

GORKY: Why should that be?

LILINA: Why?

GORKY: Why should God control the weather and man have nothing whatsoever to say about it? When there's a storm is it God who gets shipwrecked? Is it God who freezes to death catching fish to feed His starving family? God doesn't depend on the wheat, God's skin doesn't blister in the desert. It's quite clear. God forfeited His rights by His apathy. (NEMIROVICH *is asleep.*)

BUNIN: Gorky, you've whipped us all into a frenzy. (MOSKVIN *burlesques a fit of frenzy culminating in a backflip.*)

LUZHKI: Fyokla, you have some fish in the house? Maybe a little herring? I'm hungry.

GORKY: Fish would be nice.

LUZHKI: (*Draining the last drop of vodka.*) The vodka's finished. Anybody want more?

LILINA: You do.

BUNIN: (*Starting toward the house.*) I know where Anton Pavlovich keeps his private stock.

GORKY: Anyone else drinking beaujolais? (GORKY *and* BUNIN *exit into house.*)

LUZHKI: I can't drink another drop.

EVERYONE: What?

LUZHKI: Unless we have music. Moskvin, did you see? Anton Pavlovich has a piano inside. Come play.

LILINA: Luzhki, Moskvin's tired. What do you think he is, a trained monkey? (MOSKVIN *exits imitating monkey.* LUZHKI *shrugs and follows.* LILINA *gazes at* NEMIROVICH, *then starts toward house. Singing and piano are heard.*)

NEMIROVICH: (*Catching* LILINA'*s arm.*) My blood boils for you.

LILINA: Why, Vladimir, why this sudden ardor after all these years?

NEMIROVICH: Feel my forehead, I'm on fire. (OLGA *enters.*) You see, if the hat comes down to the eyebrows, the face is obscured. Other than that, your designs for the Hauptmann play are exquisite.

LILINA: Why, thank you, Vladimir Ivanovich.

OLGA: Can't you two talk about anything but the theater?

LILINA: Is Anton Pavlovich all right?

OLGA: He's fine. Masha's watching over him like a mother hen.

NEMIROVICH: Ladies, if you'll excuse me. (NEMIROVICH *exits.* LILINA *takes out needlepoint. Begins to work.*)

OLGA: If you confine a man to a sickroom, he'll become a sick man. It's all so negative. He must be infused with the will to cure himself. (LILINA *breaks down.*) Lilina, what's the matter? It's Nemirovich, isn't it? That snake.

LILINA: No. It's everything. Everything.

OLGA: Something's come between you and Konstantin. Is it another woman?

LILINA: Yes. The theater. The theater is his mistress. He's slipping away from me, Olga. His mind never leaves the stage. The gentle, considerate Kostya I knew has been replaced by a caricature of a great artiste. My presence does nothing but irritate him. I suppose I remind him that he's mortal. He wants me to stop acting.

OLGA: He said that?

LILINA: It's the subtext of everything he says. You've seen how he abuses me with his criticism.

OLGA: He abuses everyone.

LILINA: You don't have to go home with him. (*Pause.*) What will happen to us? The government is spying on the theater, everyone is spouting high-minded words about revolution. A month ago, a group of drunken workers from Kostya's factory stood under our bedroom window in the middle of the night shouting horrible obscenities. And that riot last week. I keep seeing those bodies in the street.

OLGA: The other day there was no bread in the shops.

LILINA: Where is it all leading, Olga? The ground is moving under our feet.

OLGA: Lilina, look, you've sewn your ring into the pattern.

LILINA: (*Ripping the cloth violently.*) What's wrong with me? I can't even act anymore. There's a hollowness now, and the audience can feel it.

OLGA: You're imagining that.

LILINA: Well, there's one thing I'm not imagining. Kostya sees me as an annoying piece of baggage that won't stay home in the closet. Look at me. There are dark circles under my eyes. I'm not attractive anymore.

OLGA: Lilina, what are you talking about? When we're onstage together, I work twice as hard, and still everyone is watching you. Nemirovich has surely been taken by your charms.

LILINA: Yes. Oh, Olga, I'm tempted, but it's impossible.

OLGA: Be careful. He has an uncanny talent for sniffing out unsatisfied women. (MASHA *enters.*)

MASHA: He looks like a little boy when he sleeps. So peaceful. He hasn't taken his medicine for several days. That wouldn't have happened if I'd been here. He needs me, Olga.

OLGA: I think this may be good time to have that little chat with Bunin.

MASHA: Oh, yes, yes!

NEMIROVICH: (*Poking head in.*) Come join us, ladies. How can we dance without you? Lilina?

LILINA: I'd love to. (LILINA *exits with* NEMIROVICH.)

OLGA: Go ahead, Masha. Tell Bunin I want to have a word with him.

MASHA: Don't you think tomorrow would be better? What if he rejects me? I couldn't take it. I'll kill myself. I'll enter a convent.

OLGA: Very well, I won't talk to him.

MASHA: All right, all right. (MASHA *exits.*)

OLGA: Poor Masha, so desperate and so alone. (*Finds* CHEKHOV'*s hat on bench.*) I wish I could put this on and know your thoughts . . . Oh God, I'm tired of casual affairs. Please don't let this be another one. (*Lauhter is heard from the house.* BUNIN *enters.*)

BUNIN: Olga Leonardova, is something wrong?

OLGA: What do you mean?

BUNIN: Well, Gorky was in the middle of a humorous anecdote when Masha woke me and said you wanted to see me. She was pale as chalk. What is it?

OLGA: Oh, it's nothing, really, Ivan Alexeivich. I simply wanted to have a little chat with you.

BUNIN: Ah, a chat.

OLGA: Actually, I need your advice.

BUNIN: Well, I must warn you, I'm much better at pointless conversation.

OLGA: Forgive me if I don't mention names, but I have a friend who is in love with a certain man.

BUNIN: Ah, a friend.

OLGA: But she's very shy, and she's not sure how this man feels about her.

BUNIN: Why are you telling *me* all this?

OLGA: I value your opinion. You're an astute judge of character. I see that especially in your poetry.

BUNIN: Continue.

OLGA: The man in question is everything a woman could want: good-looking, talented, very intelligent . . .

BUNIN: And your friend?

OLGA: She would make an excellent wife. In fact, they would make an ideal couple, if the man loved my friend as much as she loves him.

BUNIN: Is this mysterious man a writer?

OLGA: I think you understand who we're talking about.

BUNIN: Oh, yes, it's quite obvious, isn't it? But I don't believe the woman loves the man as deeply as you say.

OLGA: Take my word for it, she does, and she must know the man's true feelings for her. What do you think?

BUNIN: I think you're absolutely wrong for him.

OLGA: What?

BUNIN: If Anton marries you, he'll be committing suicide.

OLGA: Oh my God!

BUNIN: You know how sick he is. In his condition, he's an easy mark for a beautiful woman like you. If he tries to keep up with your hyper-active Moscow social life, he'll be dead before the honeymoon's over.

OLGA: How vicious!

BUNIN: No, just frank.

OLGA: If you were a woman, I'd say you were jealous.

BUNIN: I'm sorry. I do like you. But this is not the time in Anton's life for you or anyone else. (OLGA *laughs.*) Did I say something funny?

OLGA: The man in my little story was not Anton.

BUNIN: You said he was a writer.

OLGA: That's right.

BUNIN: (*Astonished.*) Gorky?

OLGA: No.

BUNIN: (*Surprise.*) Ahhh! (*Pause.*) Don't tell me you're in love with me.

OLGA: The woman is Masha.

BUNIN: Masha! (*Laughs. Stops laughing.*) Masha. (*Sound from the house.* CHEKHOV *has come downstairs. Enter* CHEKHOV *followed by* NEMIROVICH, LILINA, LUZHKI, MOSKVIN, GORKY, *and* MASHA.)

NEMIROVICH: What didn't you like about the production?

MASHA: (*To* OLGA, *whispering.*) Olga, what did he say?

OLGA: Later.

LUZHKI: It was me. It was me. I put the vodka in the samovar. I ruined everything. (*He eats a herring.*)

NEMIROVICH: Anton, you know these provincials. If you don't give them slapstick they lose interest. (MOSKVIN *does raspberry, pratfall, picks himself up by the collar.*)

GORKY: What can you expect from an audience of merchants?

LUZHKI: They didn't even cry.

CHEKHOV: They're not supposed to cry.

LUZHKI: They're not? (*To* NEMIROVICH.) They're not? But it's so moving when Vanya tries to shoot the professor.

CHEKHOV: It's not moving. It's funny.

LUZHKI: That's funny?

CHEKHOV: The play is practically a vaudeville. How could you misinterpret it so? I wrote it all down. And that's another thing, why do you improvise?

NEMIROVICH: Don't be too hard on Stanislavski. Learning lines is not his forte.

CHEKHOV: But tonight he replaced one of my monologues with a speech from *Hedda Gabler*.

NEMIROVICH: He did?

> FYOKLA *enters with tray of hors d'oeuvres. She trips, falls, with a crash, and several people help her pick up the food.* KONSTANTIN SERGEIEVICH STANISLAVSKI, *flamboyant co-director of the Moscow Art Theater, sweeps into the scene. No one notices.*

STANISLAVSKI: Hello, everyone. I'm here.

CHEKHOV: Ah, Konstantin Sergeievich, we were just talking about you.

STANISLAVSKI: Nothing bad I hope. (*Chuckles. Sits in* CHEKHOV'*s chair.*) The show was rather good tonight, I thought. (*Pause.*)

LILINA: Isn't the garden lovely, Kostya?

OLGA: Anton Pavlovich planted all the acacias himself.

STANISLAVSKI: (*Dejected, to* CHEKHOV.) You didn't like it. You left early.

CHEKHOV: I liked Moskvin. (MOSKVIN *bows.*) He wasn't bad. (MOSKVIN *shrugs.*) But it wasn't my play.

STANISLAVSKI: What do you mean. We did our best to present the reality of your text. We used real food, real tea, we created the atmosphere of a real country dacha with the sounds of birds, cows, crickets.

CHEKHOV: The stage is not a barnyard. The stage is not life. It is the quintessence of life.

STANISLAVSKI: I spoke to a critic after the show. He loved it. I remember his exact words. He said . . . uh, . . . well, he was impressed with the, let me see, yes, "the twilight mood of melancholy."

CHEKHOV: What melancholy? There isn't even one death.

STANISLAVSKI: Anton, you seem to be unaware of the depth of your gift.

CHEKHOV: When I write, I know exactly what I'm doing. *Uncle Vanya* is a comedy.

STANISLAVSKI: Certainly it has its comic moments, yes, but on the whole anyone would have to agree, it's a tragedy.

LUZHKI: Why don't we take a vote?

STANISLAVSKI: When I'm wrong, I'm the first to admit it. (MOSKVIN *whistles.*)

LUZHKI: How many think *Uncle Vanya* is a comedy? (*Nobody. Then* CHEKHOV, *then* MASHA, *then* GORKY *raise their hands.*)

GORKY: An artist must always be supported in his own opinions about his work . . . even when he's wrong.

NEMIROVICH: Anton, try to look at it as a practical solution to a creative problem. Most playgoers come to the theater to cry.

CHEKHOV: Sheep. Let them cry at weddings and funerals.

NEMIROVICH: And if they cry, they tell their friends, and their friends buy tickets. No tears, no Moscow Art.

CHEKHOV: But surely they want to laugh, too.

STANISLAVSKI: There's too much truth in your plays.

CHEKHOV: Sometimes the truth is comical. Even ridiculous.

STANISLAVSKI: Then why don't they laugh at it?

CHEKHOV: Because you make them cry.

LUZHKI: It's my fault. It's all my fault.

STANISLAVSKI: Your plays touch people. They move people. They strike a responsive chord, Anton Pavlovich. I remember when we were in rehearsal for our first production of *Seagull.* Quite frankly, I have to admit it, I, Konstantin Stanislavski, did not understand the play. I thought, my God, the audience will be throwing cabbages at us by the end of the first act. It was only the encouragement and the prophetic genius of Nemirovich-Danchenko that prevented me from losing all hope. You see, our very survival depended on the reception of this play. The theater had spent its last ruble on the production. Our noble experiment to change the course of theatrical history was in danger of being dashed on the reefs of financial ruin. And, as if that weren't enough, Masha, who loves you with all of her generous heart, forgive me for telling your little secret, Masha, sent us letters, telegrams, and finally, two days before our opening night she came to the theater in person. She spoke quietly through her sobs. You were ill, she cried, very ill, and then this dear, sensitive creature actually fell to her knees before the entire company and begged us, implored us, beseeched us not to open the play. She said, and these were here exact words, "If this play

fails, uh . . . (MOSKVIN *makes motion of hammer and nail.*)
. . . it will drive the final nail into Anton's coffin." But it was
too late. We had to go on. Opening night before the curtain
went up we were terrified. Upon this one cast of the die depended not only the fate of the Moscow Art Theater but perhaps
the very life of our revered Chekhov as well. The boards of the
stage had become a gallows and we the executioners. Everything
seemed to be against us. Olga Leonardova was running a high
fever, Lilina was groggy from too many valerian drops. I personally was so overcome with tension that I had to sit with my back
to the audience in order to stop my legs from shaking. Fortu-
nately, I had staged myself with my back to the audience.

LUZHKI: A great innovation.

STANISLAVSKI: Thank you. In the first five minutes, three sound
cues were missed. I could see Masha in her box, clutching at her
handkerchief. Nemirovich was pacing up and down the lobby.
He couldn't even bring himself to watch the performance. The
audience was cool, uncertain. We played without thinking, as if
we were possessed. The first act ended, the curtain fell, and there
was total silence. We knew we were lost. Olga fainted, I sank to
my bench, Luzhki broke down, Lilina ran offstage, and Moskvin
squatted with his head between his legs . . . Then, suddenly
there was an explosion of applause! They cheered, they
screamed, they stamped their feet. The curtain rose and caught
us in our ridiculous positions. We took call after call. They
shouted again and again for the author. Our theater was saved,
and our own Anton Chekhov was baptized as Russia's greatest
living playwright . . . where is he? (CHEKHOV *has exited quietly
during the speech.*) Did I say something wrong? (*Sits.*) What does
he have against me? He doesn't like me as an actor, he doesn't
like me as a director, I don't even think he likes me as a person.

MASHA: I'm sorry, Konstantin. Antosha simply cannot tolerate
praise, particularly in public. (MASHA *exits.* GORKY *already
drunk, pulls cork from a wine bottle with loud pop.* GORKY *and*
LILINA *exit into house.* OLGA *starts to leave.*)

LUZHKI: Olya, could I borrow five rubles till Friday?

OLGA: Get if from Moskvin. (MOSKVIN *pulls his pockets inside out and
makes a sad face.*)

LUZHKI: Him? He'd let his grandmother eat hailstones.

OLGA: You already owe me twenty-six rubles. Isn't that right,
Moskvin? (MOSKVIN *nods.*) Last week your uncle in Kiev died.
You said you had some money coming.

LUZHKI: The estate's not settled yet.

BUNIN: Here, Luzhki. Five rubles?

LUZHKI: Oh, I couldn't. I hardly know you. Actually I need ten if you can spare it. (BUNIN, LUZHKI *and* MOSKVIN *exit.* OLGA *makes sure no one is watching, and exits along the down-left path.* FYOKLA *is cleaning and watching* STANISLAVSKI. *Piano can be heard from within.*)

FYOKLA: Pardon me, I thought your speech was . . . was . . .

NEMIROVICH: Brilliant?

FYOKLA: Yes, brilliant! Thank you, thank you. (*She runs off, embarassed.*)

STANISLAVSKI: Nice girl, who is she? (*To* NEMIROVICH.) Vladimir, what does Anton Pavlovich expect of me? You know, I don't think he understands his own plays. With any other director, *Uncle Vanya* would be inaccessible to the public.

NEMIROVICH: It's the best thing you've done.

STANISLAVSKI: Mark my words, Chekhov will not be remembered. Now, Potapenko or Griboyedov—those are names that will echo down the halls of history. (*Hears piano, under.*) He steals from Ibsen.

NEMIROVICH: Oh, Kostya, he doesn't steal.

STANISLAVSKI: He's boring. His characters do nothing but chase each other's wives. (LILINA *enters.*)

LILINA: Kostya, it's late.

STANISLAVSKI: We should make a new policy. From now on, we only do plays by deceased writers. They don't make such a fuss when you improve on their work.

LILINA: Kostya, I'm going to bed. Good night Vladimir.

NEMIROVICH: Good night, Lilina. (LILINA *exits.*)

STANISLAVSKI: We need that new play of his. What's it called? *The Three Brothers?*

NEMIROVICH: *Sisters.*

STANISLAVSKI: I hope there's a good man's role in it. Where's Lilina? (*Enter* BUNIN *and* GORKY, *both drunk.*)

GORKY: I'm surrounded and suffocated by enemies of the people.

STANISLAVSKI: Ah, Maxim Alexeievich, at last I have the opportunity to tell you how much I admire your work.

NEMIROVICH: Yes, Maxim, have you ever considered writing for the theater?

GORKY: As a matter of fact, I am working on a play.

STANISLAVSKI: Wonderful! What's it about?

GORKY: Starvation, poverty, humiliation, the absurdity of life in Russia.

STANISLAVSKI: We really need a comedy.

NEMIROVICH: We need anything you write, Maxim.

GORKY: I'll only give it to you one one condition. It has to be free.

NEMIROVICH: Free?

GORKY: No admission charge.

STANISLAVSKI: We do have very cheap seats.

GORKY: Free.

NEMIROVICH: Well, we'd love to do that of course, but there are costs involved in running a theater: scenery, costumes, props . . .

STANISLAVSKI: Sound effects.

NEMIROVICH: We have to heat the theater.

GORKY: You think you're artists? You're businessmen. You, Konstantin Sergeievich, you own a factory, your father was a rich merchant. And you, Nemirovich-Danchenko, married to a wealthy baroness, what do you know about the misery of a peasant's existence?

BUNIN: I've heard they often seek relief from their terrible lives by fornicating with chickens.

GORKY: Bunin, Bunin, Bunin. The Bunins have always had their tongues securely up the Tsar's anus. (*Makes move to attack* BUNIN, *falls over chair.*) Ummmgah!

NEMIROVICH: (*Helping him up.*) Perhaps after a good night's rest we can discuss the proposition.

GORKY: Don't touch me, shithead.

BUNIN: Remarkable command of the language.

GORKY: I feel . . . I feel . . . (*Runs off. Sound of retching, off.*) Jesus, oh God . . . (*Retch.*)

BUNIN: There. That's the opening monologue from his play.

STANISLAVSKI: Bunin, you should join our company. You'd be a fine actor, I can tell.

BUNIN: Never. I'm far too humble to be an actor.

GORKY: (*Stumbles back on.*) Forgive me . . . forgive m . . bleeahh. (*Passes out.*)

BUNIN: He's quite lucid tonight. (*Takes off his jacket. Puts it under* GORKY's *head.*) Look at him, the Voice of the People, the model peasant in his rustic blouse of Japanese silk, his Italian leather boots with silver buckles. (*Takes bottle from* GORKY's *hand.*) And see what he drinks? Only the finest French beaujolais. Do you know how much rent he pays on his villa? It's not difficult to be a peasant when you have money. Yet it's strange how I envy this man. I can only mouth flowery platitudes to a race of dying dinosaurs, while he embodies the future. (LUZHKI *and* MOSKVIN *enter singing. They stop, swaying.*)

LUZHKI: Look, Moskvin, the moon! And, there, Venus is rising.

GORKY: (*Coming to. Singing.*)

> I took home a lady named Venus
> And assured her that no one had seen us.
> While I stroked her fair skin,
> Her mother walked in,
> Just as Venus was kissing my . . .

(*Passes out. Everyone, tensed for the word, relaxes.*)

STANISLAVSKI: When I was young, I played in an operetta called *Queen of the Night*. And in it there was a glorious speech about the moon. I still remember it. "Oh, Moon . . ." (*Pause.*)

BUNIN: (*Helping* GORKY *up.*) I'll lug the guts into the neighbor room.

STANISLAVSKI: Macbeth. I love Macbeth.

MOSKVIN: Hamlet.

STANISLAVSKI: Moskvin, you talk to much.

LUZHKI: You watch that tongue of yours, Moskvin. Come on, it's late. (MOSKVIN *and* LUZHKI *follow* BUNIN *and* GORKY *into the house.* FYOKLA *enters, cleaning.*)

NEMIROVICH: I think I'll retire for the night. What about you Konstantin?

STANISLAVSKI: No, it's such a pleasant evening.

NEMIROVICH: Ah, good night then.

STANISLAVSKI: See you in the morning. (NEMIROVICH *exits.*) Ma, me, mi, mo, mu. Ma, me, mi, mo, mu. Oh, Moon . . . (*Begins to weep.* FYOKLA *comes closer, also begins to cry.* STANISLAVSKI *sees her.*) Why are you crying, girl?

FYOKLA: Because you're crying, sir.

STANISLAVSKI: No, no, I'm just practicing.

FYOKLA: Practicing? You mean you were acting?

STANISLAVSKI: Ah, no, it was more than acting. I was actually experiencing great sorrow.

FYOKLA: I believed you.

STANISLAVSKI: And see, now I'm cheerful. I'm speaking to you as if nothing happened. What's your name, girl?

FYOKLA: Fyokla, sir.

STANISLAVSKI: Don't be deceived, my dear Fyokla. It's not as easy as I make it appear to be. Years of labor and sacrifice must be invested in the theater, and even then, without the God-given gift of Talent, an actor can never be more than a mere gramophone mechanically reproducing the speech and gestures of others.

FYOKLA: How can a person tell if she has a gift?

STANISLAVSKI: Whenever a young would-be actress asks me that question, I give her a simple exercise to perform. I tell her to imagine herself arriving home after the most rapturous afternoon of her life. The rich young man she loves has proposed to her. (*Moving table.*) Now, this table will represent a table, and this napkin will be a telegram informing you that your father has just died. The door is upstage center.

FYOKLA: Where?

STANISLAVSKI: There. You come in, see the telegram, read it, and react. Do you understand?

FYOKLA: Yes, yes.

STANISLAVSKI: Good, proceed.

FYOKLA: (*Enters laughing, melodramatic gestures, sees telegram, does long take, picks it up, drops pose.*) Shouldn't you write the message on this?

STANISLAVSKI: No, no, no, use the magic "if."

FYOKLA: If?

STANISLAVSKI: Pretend.

FYOKLA: Oh. (*Staring at the napkin.*) But, sir, I can't read.

STANISLAVSKI: Pretend you can read. Try it again. And don't move your arms about like that.

FYOKLA: (*Enters, does the same scene with arms stiffly at sides, gets to telegram.*) Can I move my arms to pick up the telegram?

STANISLAVSKI: Yes. (FYOKLA *picks up telegram.*)

PHOTO BY JAY THOMPSON

FYOKLA: Oh, Papa. (*Swoons mechanically, looks at* STANISLAVSKI *expectantly.*)

STANISLAVSKI: In all my twenty years in the theater, I have never seen anything so intolerably bad.

FYOKLA: (*Crying.*) I'm a gramophone! I'm a gramophone!

STANISLAVSKI: Now that's the kind of reaction you should have had to the telegram. (FYOKLA *cries more.*) You see? Acting is not a child's game. It is a monumental task. The actor must work with all the perserverance of a grunting, sweating fieldhand.

MASHA: (*Offstage.*) Fyokla!

FYOKLA: Teach me more. Please, teach me more, right now!

STANISLAVSKI: Shhh. It's late. Your mistress calls. We mustn't wake everyone. Another time.

FYOKLA: No, now.

STANISLAVSKI: I've already given you far too much for one evening. Why you could work on that little scene for . . . two years.

MASHA: (*Offstage.*) Fyokla!

FYOKLA: Coming. (*Halfway to door, stops, stamps foot.*) No, I'm going to practice my acting. I'll be in the cemetery under the willow tree if you want to give me more exercises. (*Exits to the cemetery.*)

STANISLAVSKI: Ah, she's hopeless. But, God knows, people have been known to do quite well without the slightest trace of intelligence. (LILINA *enters.*)

LILINA: Kostya, please come to bed.

STANISLAVSKI: Ah, Lilina. Would you bring me my make-up case? It's just inside the door. (LILINA *exits.*) The willow tree. Hmmm. (LILINA *returns with kit.*)

LILINA: Kostya. It'll be morning soon.

STANISLAVSKI: (*Kneads putty, sets up mirror on bench.*) You must be tired. Go to bed.

LILINA: I want you to come to bed with me, Kostya.

STANISLAVSKI: Are you blind? Can't you see I'm building a nose?

LILINA: Kostya . . .

STANISLAVSKI: Kostya, Kostya, Kostya! Leave me alone.

LILINA: This is important.

STANISLAVSKI: Important? This nose is the single most important external detail of my Dr. Astrov. (*Looks for something in kit.*)

LILINA: I've got to talk to you.

STANISLAVSKI: It's the wrong time to talk now.

LILINA: It's always the wrong time to talk.

STANISLAVSKI: We talk all the time.

LILINA: No, we don't. You talk. I listen.

STANISLAVSKI: You left the top off the clown white again. Details, my dear, details. Attention to detail is everything.

LILINA: I need attention, Kostya. Maybe you don't feel it, but our marriage is falling apart, and I'm afraid.

STANISLAVSKI: Rubbish! It's a phase, like the moon. It'll pass, Lilina, how many times do I have to tell you . . . the spirit gum goes to the right of the brushes, and the face powder should always be set alongside the dry rouge. Is that so difficult to remember?

LILINA: Why, no. I'll rearrange it right now. (*She picks up the kit and dashes it to the floor.*)

STANISLAVSKI: Have you gone mad, woman? It's taken me twelve years to assemble that kit. Pick it up immediately and put everything back . . . in the correct order! (*Picks up mirror, putty, stalks toward house, changes mind, goes off toward cemetery.*)

For LILINA, *anger turns to resignation. She stoops to reassemble kit.* NEMIROVICH *enters. He begins to help her. He takes rouge, makes up* LILINA's *lips, and kisses her. He stands, tries to lead her.*

NEMIROVICH: Come to my room. (*She resists. He puts a hand down her robe. She begins to swoon.*)

MASHA: (*Entering.*) Oh, I was looking for Fyokla.

NEMIROVICH: Haven't seen her.

MASHA: Lilina, would you like to come have some tea?

LILINA: No.

NEMIROVICH: Good night, Masha. (MASHA *exits.*) Come to my room.

LILINA: No, go away. (*Embraces him. Pushes him away. Runs towards the cemetery. Stops.* NEMIROVICH *calmly walks to her, puts his arm around her. He leads her into house.*)

Sound of sea. CHEKHOV *and* OLGA *enter.*

OLGA: I can't imagine what happened to it.

CHEKHOV: Did you look in the bushes? I might have thrown it out the window in the heat of the moment.

OLGA: Oh, no. What if someone finds it. We'd better go back.

CHEKHOV: Oh, here it is! (*Opens jacket. He is wearing* OLGA's *corset.*)

OLGA: Anton, take that off.

CHEKHOV: Why, Olga, what sort of man do you think I am?

OLGA: A shameless rake. (*Chuckles.*) I never thought I'd see it. The great Chekhov without his starched collar.

CHEKHOV: Did I cut such a ridiculous figure?

OLGA: No, it was heavenly. I was beginning to think that collar was a permanent part of your body.

CHEKHOV: And you, my dear actress, always in such control on the stage. It was a great pleasure to see you so . . . (OLGA *puts hand over* CHEKHOV's *mouth.*)

OLGA: Antosha . . . In that moment I was transported away from Russia, away from time, away from the Earth. Yet I was still with you. (*Moment of silent affection.*) Do you love me?

CHEKHOV: My little cantaloupe . . .

OLGA: Cantaloupe, melon, pumpkin. Antosha, I think I deserve to know what's under this pile of fruits and vegetables. Everyone knows of our relationship. In one week I'm returning to Moscow, and the vultures from the press will be waiting. What will I tell them?

CHEKHOV: Tell them I'm paralyzed from the waist down.

OLGA: Be serious, damn you.

CHEKHOV: Come to Italy with me.

OLGA: Yes, affairs are taken for granted there. You know what the gossip-mongers are calling me? A social-climbing vampire.

CHEKHOV: What do you care what they say?

OLGA: They're dragging my name through the mud.

CHEKHOV: You're an actress. Any publicity is good publicity.

OLGA: I will not be treated like a whore.

CHEKHOV: I've been much more discreet than Nemirovich ever was. (OLGA *slaps him.*) I'm sorry, Olya, you know I never wanted a virgin hausfrau.

OLGA: Why should you? Masha fills that role very well.

CHEKHOV: I need you, Olga. When you're away from me, I feel more alone than I've ever felt.

OLGA: I'll give up the theater for you.

CHEKHOV: No!

OLGA: You're not pleased?

CHEKHOV: You'd hate me for it.

OLGA: I see. You need me but you don't want me to be with you.

CHEKHOV: We both have our work to consider. If I let you give up yours, you *would* resent it.

OLGA: Not if we were married. (CHEKHOV *coughs.*) Your cough is timed so conveniently.

CHEKHOV: Sounds quite natural, doesn't it?

OLGA: I'm confused. Just how sick are you, Doctor? I think it's about time you gave me an honest diagnosis.

CHEKHOV: Marriage is for healthy people.

OLGA: You can be cured. We can have a future. Do you believe that?

CHEKHOV: Faith is not my strong point.

OLGA: Well, then here are some hard, cold facts for you. I'm not Komisarevskaya. I don't bargain with my flesh. I gave you everything for only one reason. I love you deeply. But you're not the only one who's running out of time. I want to have children. Set a date, Anton, or get another mistress. (*She exits.*)

CHEKHOV: (*Takes humidor from hiding place, it is empty.*) Oh, Masha. (STANISLAVSKI *enters with nose.*)

STANISLAVSKI: Anton Pavlovich, what do you think of the new Dr. Astrov?

CHEKHOV: God forbid he should sneeze. Join me for a drink, Konstantin?

STANISLAVSKI: (*Taking nose off and putting it carefully on the bench.*) Yes, I do believe I . . .(*Sees make-up kit.*) Damn! (*Gets down to putting stuff back.* CHEKHOV *gives* STANISLAVSKI *drink.*) Thank you.

CHEKHOV: Do you have a cigar, Kostya?

STANISLAVSKI: Yes, yes. (*Hands* CHEKHOV *cigar.*)

CHEKHOV: Ah, you smoke my brand.

STANISLAVSKI: Yes, Masha gave me a whole box.

CHEKHOV : Hm. Cheers.

STANISLAVSKI: Cheers.

CHEKHOV: Another?

STANISLAVSKI: Please. Such an enchanting night. I took a stroll through the cemetery.

CHEKHOV: (*Brushing dirt from* STANISLAVSKI's *jacket.*) Looks like you took a crawl through the cemetery.

STANISLAVSKI: (*Lying.*) Yes, I tripped over a shovel, fell on a fresh grave.

CHEKHOV: What happened to your make-up?

STANISLAVSKI: Accident.

CHEKHOV: One more?

STANISLAVSKI: Why not? (*Finishing up. Snapping case shut.*) Women.

CHEKHOV: So demanding.

STANISLAVSKI: So impulsive.

CHEKHOV: So yielding.

STANISLAVSKI: Yes. To women.

CHEKHOV: What would we do without them?

STANISLAVSKI: Get some work done.

CHEKHOV: Become extinct.

STANISLAVSKI: Ah, memento mori. Isn't it curious how sex and death are so intimately related?

CHEKHOV: Are they? I think that's perverse.

STANISLAVSKI: How can you say that? The greatest literary minds have made the comparison.

CHEKHOV: And now you.

STANISLAVSKI: What was it Tolstoy said? In death, the individual soul . . .

CHEKHOV: . . . merges ecstatically with the cosmic ocean.

STANISLAVSKI: Yes!

CHEKHOV: (*Coughs*) But the old man was wrong about that. Death is the final curtain. Finita la Commedia.

STANISLAVSKI: It's getting light.

CHEKHOV: Pretty.

STANISLAVSKI: Ah, the ocean. I was walking on the beach tonight when suddenly I stopped and stood transfixed by the waves. I was struck with an incredible revelation. Anton, the sea is huge. (CHEKHOV *takes out notebook, rips out page, throws it away.*)

CHEKHOV: One last drink.

STANISLAVSKI: No, thank you.

CHEKHOV: A nightcap.

STANISLAVSKI: Well, in that case . . . (*Sits heavily on nose.*)

CHEKHOV: You're sitting on your nose.

STANISLAVSKI: What? Oh, oh.

CHEKHOV: What a nice tie you're wearing.

STANISLAVSKI: Hm? Yes, Lilina made it.

CHEKHOV: Nice. I admire your marriage. Not everyone can be as fortunate as you've been with Lilina.

STANISLAVSKI: Ah, but I haven't the slightest doubt that were you and Knipper to wed, your marriage would be every bit as idyllic as my own.

CHEKHOV: How is Moscow?

STANISLAVSKI: The same. Oh, there's a new restaurant.

CHEKHOV: I heard. (*Pause.*)

STANISLAVSKI: We're making history, Anton. Already our names are being spoken of with excitement and respect in Paris, London, New York. We are becoming demi-gods of the stage. True, it's difficult for our personal lives, but Lilina will come to accept it. She'll have to. I'm so glad we're having this little talk. Oh, yes, we've had our differences. I know, sometimes I can be a pompous ass.

CHEKHOV: You're absolutely right.

STANISLAVSKI: No, no, don't be kind. I can, I can be. But I want you to know, I do everything in my power to make your plays work.

CHEKHOV: I know. I appreciate it, but you don't have to go to all that trouble.

STANISLAVSKI: Why, if it weren't for you and *The Wild Duck* . . .

CHEKHOV: *The Seagull.*

STANISLAVSKI: Whoops, wrong bird. (*Pause.*) We have to work together. After all, if you've got a play but no director, you don't have a play.

CHEKHOV: No play.

STANISLAVSKI: And if you've got a director but no play, you don't have a play.

CHEKHOV: No play.

STANISLAVSKI: We need each other.

CHEKHOV: You're absolutely right. (*They get up, unsteadily walk toward house.* STANISLAVSKI *throws his arm around* CHEKHOV.)

STANISLAVSKI: Anton?

CHEKHOV: What?

STANISLAVSKI: Are you wearing a corset? (*They exit into house. Morning sounds. Lights fade.*)

ACT TWO

One week later. Sunday morning. Church bells are heard in the distance. Clouds are gathering. OLGA *and* FYOKLA *bustle about setting up for a party.*

OLGA: Fyokla, set the plates there and put the silverware in neat rows on the side. (OLGA *sets glasses around the samovar.*)

FYOKLA: Madame Knipper, may I ask you a professional question?

OLGA: Professional?

FYOKLA: Yes. Where did you learn acting?

OLGA: I studied with Nemirovich at his school in Moscow. Oh, I hope it doesn't rain.

FYOKLA: Was he a good teacher?

OLGA: Yes, he's excellent, especially with beginners. Napkins! Go get napkins. (FYOKLA *turns to leave, stops, breaks down.*) Fyokla, what's the matter?

FYOKLA: Oh, nothing. Just practicing. (FYOKLA *exits.* MASHA *enters on* LUZHKI's *arm.*)

MASHA: Olga, look. I didn't have to go to church alone today.

LUZHKI: It was my pleasure, Masha. You saved my soul. If not for you, I would've had nothing to put in the offering plate. I'll pay you back, though.

MASHA: (*Sees the table-setting.*) Olga! You used Mother's lace. I told you not to start without me. And the good crystal.

OLGA: What good is it if you never use it?

MASHA: Change it immediately. Fyokla! (FYOKLA *enters.*) Bring the linen tablecloth. (FYOKLA *exits.*)

OLGA: There's no time.

LUZHKI: Where's the food? Kneeling makes me hungry. Maybe in the kitchen? (*He exits.*)

MASHA: And why have you set it like a buffet instead of a proper dinner?

OLGA: I arranged things so they could be carried into the house quickly if it rains.

MASHA: It won't rain. (FYOKLA *comes back with the linen.*)

OLGA: Take that back inside and bring the napkins. (FYOKLA *exits.*)

MASHA: That lace will be ruined if it rains.

OLGA: You said it wouldn't rain. (MASHA *pours herself a drink.*)

MASHA: Olga, we have a way of doing things here. There is time and place for everything in this house. Using fine lace outdoors in a buffet setting is vulgar. I don't want people to think I have no taste. Oh, it's not your fault. You couldn't have known the lace was being saved for an occasion.

OLGA: This *is* an occasion.

MASHA: A *special* occasion.

OLGA: And what would you consider special enough? Anton's wedding, perhaps?

NEMIROVICH: (*Entering.*) Ah, Masha, you're back. Where's Luzhki?

MASHA: In the kitchen.

NEMIROVICH: I should have known. What a lovely setting.

OLGA: How much time do we have?

NEMIROVICH: I told Moskvin and Gorky to keep Anton fishing at least until noon. (LILINA *enters.*)

LILINA: Can I help?

NEMIROVICH: Good morning, Lilina. Did you sleep well?

LILINA: Very well, thank you.

NEMIROVICH: How's Kostya's speech coming along?

LILINA: I don't know. He's getting into make-up right now.

NEMIROVICH: Make-up for a speech? God help us. Where is he?

LILINA: Upstairs.

NEMIROVICH: Ladies, if you'll excuse me. (NEMIROVICH *exits.* FYOKLA *enters.*)

FYOKLA: Ma, me, mi, mo, mu. (FYOKLA *exits.*)

LILINA: Masha, I'm sorry I didn't wake up early enough to go to services with you.

MASHA: Well, you were probably exhausted. (*She exits.*)

OLGA: She's upset because her house has been invaded by libertines.

LILINA: She wouldn't complain if she were one of them.

OLGA: Hmmm. Quite a change has come over you in the last week, Lilina. Infidelity seems to agree with you.

LILINA: Olga, someone might hear.

OLGA: Lord knows, I'm not criticizing you.

LILINA: I do feel marvelous. I keep waiting for the guilt to come. I know it's building up somewhere inside me but so far . . .

OLGA: I know that euphoria, Lilina. I know it well. But don't forget, you're on the road. It's easy to live dangerously when you're away from home.

LILINA: I don't intend to bring any of it back to Moscow if that's what you mean.

OLGA: Nemirovich may not feel the same way. You're walking a tightrope, darling. If you lose your balance, you'll bring the theater down on all of us. (*Enter* STANISLAVSKI *and* NEMIROVICH.)

NEMIROVICH: I tell you Konstantin, he'll walk out.

STANISLAVSKI: We've been on very good terms lately. (FYOKLA *enters with hors d'oeuvres.*)

OLGA: Not now. If you bring them out now, they'll attract ants. (OLGA *takes the hors d'oeuvres back to the kitchen.*)

NEMIROVICH: This party is a tribute to him.

STANISLAVSKI: Exactly, leave it to me.

MASHA: (*Offstage.*) Fyokla, the pieroshki! I need you. (FYOKLA *exits.*)

STANISLAVSKI: Don't worry, Vladimir. This will be very funny. A tour de force.

NEMIROVICH: Anton won't like it. When it comes to his plays, he has no sense of humor.

LILINA: You see? That's exactly what I said.

STANISLAVSKI: What do you know? (*To* NEMIROVICH.) I tell you my presentation is clever enough to amuse even the stoical Chekhov.

LILINA: It's silly.

STANISLAVSKI: It's what?

NEMIROVICH: You'll make a complete fool of yourself.

STANISLAVSKI: Such a coward. Look at the fear in his eyes. Always so afraid to offend. In this case, Vladimir, your financial expertise is irrelevant.

NEMIROVICH: Not quite. He almost gave *Uncle Vanya* to the Maly Theater because of your stupidity. If you insult him again, we'll lose the new play.

STANISLAVSKI: You're wrong, you're wrong, you're wrong, you're wrong!

LILINA: Don't be such a baby, Kostya.

STANISLAVSKI: This is between Nemirovich and myself, Lilina. Leave us alone.

LILINA: But Kostya . . .

STANISLAVSKI: I told you to keep out of this.

NEMIROVICH: It's too risky.

STANISLAVSKI: Everything's too risky for you. Why in Christ's name did you ever get into the theater?

LILINA: Don't swear.

NEMIROVICH: I absolutely forbid you to do this.

STANISLAVSKI: How dare you forbid me to do anything!

LILINA: Please, Kostya, I think Vladimir is right this time.

STANISLAVSKI: This matter involves a creative judgment, Lilina, something I've found to be notably lacking in your mind.

NEMIROVICH: He'll walk out, I'm telling you.

STANISLAVSKI: Very well, when Chekhov comes in, we'll all get down on our knees and kiss his feet.

LILINA: Vladimir, when he's in this state of mind, there's no use arguing with him.

STANISLAVSKI: Is this the way you support me?

LILINA: It's for your own good.

STANISLAVSKI: I should strike you, Lilina, but I want you to see that I still have some measure of self-control. However, I'm warning you. Don't say another word. Just go to the kitchen with the other women. That's where you belong. (LILINA *starts to leave.*) You can't stop me, Vladimir, I'm going to do it.

NEMIROVICH: Fine. You're the one who'll destroy the theater. The responsibility will be on your shoulders.

LILINA: Vladimir and I are lovers. (NEMIROVICH *freezes.* STANISLAVSKI *turns.*)

STANISLAVSKI: What?

LILINA: Vladimir and I are lovers.

NEMIROVICH: Oh, Lilina.

STANISLAVSKI: Cuckold?

NEMIROVICH: It's not true. Lilina, what a cruel joke!

STANISLAVSKI: I've done nothing to deserve this.

LILINA: What have I done? Oh my God, what have I done?

NEMIROVICH: Why did you tell him?

STANISLAVSKI: Why did you do it?

LILINA: I only wanted to get your attention. (LILINA *exits.* NEMIROVICH *starts out.*)

STANISLAVSKI: Must you go so soon? (NEMIROVICH *sits. Pause.*)

NEMIROVICH: Looks like rain.

STANISLAVSKI: Stabbed in the back and the knife twisted. What sort of treacherous fiend are you that you would risk everything we've worked for these past three years solely for the gratification of your indiscriminate lust?

NEMIROVICH: I'm sorry, I'm sorry. It was . . . foolish.

STANISLAVSKI: Sorry? Foolish? The end of the Moscow Art Theater is no mere folly. You have deprived the Twentieth Century of its most significant theatrical institution. Our relationship is severed. Utterly. (*Pause.*)

NEMIROVICH: You can have my wife. Then we'll be even.

STANISLAVSKI: Bastard. You try to run a theater without me. Oh, you have a head for figures and a nose for new plays, but you have no artistic spine. You'll flounder on the rocks of mediocrity.

NEMIROVICH: Hah! I'd like to see *you* manage a company. After one production, your actors would be reduced to eating roots and leaves.

STANISLAVSKI: Oh, how you flatter yourself. Your duties could be performed better by a monkey with an abacus.

NEMIROVICH: You fool. I've written some of the most popular plays we've done.

STANISLAVSKI: Popular, that's the key word, isn't it? Drawing room excrement.

NEMIROVICH: It was I who brought Anton Chekhov to the Moscow Art.

STANISLAVSKI: You have my undying gratitude for that.

NEMIROVICH: I do all the work while you wallow shamelessly in undeserved applause.

STANISLAVSKI: I'll never speak to you again.

NEMIROVICH: This could be a blessing in disguise.

STANISLAVSKI: Contemptuous worm!

NEMIROVICH: Pretentious windbag!

STANISLAVSKI: You're nothing but a clerk! A drab clerk!

NEMIROVICH: And you're a selfish, pig-headed peacock! I see Lilina was right about you. You haven't mentioned her once. Ah, but I'm sure all these emotions you're cataloguing will be very useful on the stage. (STANISLAVSKI *swings at* NEMIROVICH *who ducks and grabs a chair—holding it out in front of him like a lion-tamer.* MOSKVIN, GORKY, *and* BUNIN *enter with* CHEKHOV.)

CHEKHOV: (*Holding up bunch of fish.*) Moskvin, you're a born fisherman. (*Sees* STANISLAVSKI *and* NEMIROVICH.) What's all this? (*Awkward pause.*)

STANISLAVSKI: Surprise! (MASHA, LUZHKI, FYOKLA, *and* LILINA *enter carrying trays of food and glasses.*)

EVERYONE: Surprise!

STANISLAVSKI: The chair will be just fine there, Vladimir. I'll be waiting for your introduction. (*Exits hurriedly.*)

NEMIROVICH: Uh, Anton Pavlovich, please sit down. We of the Moscow Art are proud and happy to show our appreciation for your invaluable contribution to our theater by throwing this little party for you. (*Applause.*)

CHEKHOV: I can't tell you how sorry I am that you've gone to all this trouble. (*General disappointment.*) But I promise you, no matter how unbearable the praise becomes, I will try with all my heart to avoid leaving.

EVERYONE: Hurrah!

MASHA: Everybody help yourselves. (*She is holding a tray of glasses filled with champagne.*)

OLGA: Take a glass, everyone.

MOSKVIN: To Chekhov!

BUNIN: To Chekhov! A truly civilized human being. (*Scattered Nastrovya's.*)

GORKY: To Chekhov! A man who knows better than any other playwright in Russia, how to treat chronic hemorrhoids. (*More Nastrovya's.*)

STANISLAVSKI: (*Pokes his head in.*) Nemirovich!

NEMIROVICH: Ladies and Gentlemen, in the theater it is often said of people, "You are dispensable. If you do not perform well, you can be replaced." It has even been said, and not entirely in jest, that my job could be filled by a monkey with an abacus. The same could not possibly be said for my esteemed partner. So here, with an entertainment entirely of his own devising, sans abacus, is Konstantin Sergeievich Stanislavski. (*Enter* STAN-ISLAVSKI *made up as a ludicrous parody of* CHEKHOV.)

STANISLAVSKI: No applause. Please, I want no appreciation. You have been a great inspiration to me during your visit to my humble estate. By the way I planted all the acacias myself. In honor of this occasion I've penned a new tragedy . . . uh, comedy. I'm nervous. Now, rather than hand this play over to the Moscow Art Theater to be violated by that imbecile, Stanislavski, I have decided to read selected scenes so their correct interpretation will not be a matter of dispute. Ladies and gentlemen, my latest play, *Uncle Cuckoo.* The play opens with no offstage sound effects.

CHEKHOV: (*Stands.*) Bravo! (*Sits.*)

STANISLAVSKI: Enter the country doctor and well-known writer Pavel Antonovich and his sister, Marfa. Pavel studies his feet carefully and says, "The night is so still." (MOSKVIN, LUZHKI, BUNIN, *and* GORKY *imitate cows, sheep, cuckoos, chickens, etc.* STAN-ISLAVSKI *cuts them off.*) Marfa replies, "Would you like some tea?" End of Act One. At the beginning of Act Two, the company of a famous Moscow theater arrive at the doctor's estate in Yalta. Pavel says, "Marfa, allow me to introduce to you the actress Olgavina Leonarova and Aniusha Lilina, the actors Luzka Morozovich and Gimpel Grabowski Muskvinovich Goldberg. And you remember Stanislav Danchenko-Nemirovski, also called Popki. This is my sister, Marfa Yegorovna Lydia Babakina Chekonte, also known as Marfoosha, Yegoosha, Shooroochka, Ziuziushka, and Babababakinushka." End of Act Two. In Act Three all the minor characters become involved in amorous triangles . . . (*Pause. He begins to drop character and break down.*). . . in which everyone is making romantic overtures to everyone else . . . (*Looks at* NEMIROVICH *and* LILINA.). . . except their respective spouses. (*He loses control completely.*) It's all too funny. I can't go on. (*Exits. General applause.*)

BUNIN: What twilight melancholy!

LUZHKI: Bravo, Stanislavski!

MOSKVIN: What an actor!

GORKY: What a ham.

CHEKHOV: There you see? I told you I write comedies.

OLGA: Eat! Drink! Help yourselves, everyone.

MASHA: (*Inebriated.*) Yes! Listen to Olga; she's the mistress here now.

GORKY: When did Masha start drinking?

BUNIN: I've never seen her like this. (CHEKHOV *takes* MASHA's *drink away from her. She goes and pours another.*)

GORKY: Poor Masha. People just can't adjust to change. I've seen it more and more lately. (CHEKHOV *and* OLGA *cross to* GORKY *and* BUNIN.) Anton, you know that old squire on the hill, Babyatkin?

CHEKHOV: Yes, I was called to his estate once to treat his gout.

GORKY: Did you know his land is being divided and parceled out to creditors? But what does he do? He stares out the window while workmen chop down his trees and plow up his gardens. They're carrying away his furniture while he smokes his Egyptian cigarettes and tells visitors how his banker has everything under control.

CHEKHOV: What a shame. Babyatkin's gardens were the pride of Yalta.

GORKY: You see what I'm saying? When people ignore change it comes that much more quickly.

BUNIN: Leaving smoking craters of rotting corpses where once there were gardens.

OLGA: Maxim, if there is a revolution, what will happen to you?

BUNIN: Oh, he'll be all right. Minister of Culture for the new Peasant Tsar.

NEMIROVICH: And you, Ivan Alexeievich, what about you?

BUNIN: There's no question about it, I'd be shot. Excuse me.

MASHA: Ivan, I have to speak with you.

BUNIN: Yes, yes, but later. Attention everyone, although Tolstoy was unable to attend today, he did send a gift for our guest of honor. Anton Pavlovich, would you accept it, please. (CHEKHOV *takes package from* BUNIN. *Unwraps it.*)

CHEKHOV: Ahh, it's a photograph of himself. It's inscribed, "Remember, there is no death. Affectionately, Lev." Good. I can give up my medical practice. (NEMIROVICH *walks Center.*)

NEMIROVICH: Luzhki, we're ready.

LUZHKI: Moskvin. (LUZHKI *and* MOSKVIN *exit.*)

NEMIROVICH: Several months ago . . . (FYOKLA *runs in.*) What is it?

FYOKLA *whispers to* NEMIROVICH.

NEMIROVICH: (*To others.*) There are two men out front who wish to speak with Alexei Peshkov. (*Scattered* Who?'s.)

CHEKHOV: Gorky, don't go.

GORKY: Don't worry, it's just routine. Please go on with your party. (*Exits.* STANISLAVSKI *enters.*)

NEMIROVICH: Several months ago, we prevailed upon your dear sister to lend us a photograph of yourself. (LUZHKI *and* MOSKVIN *enter carrying a large painting covered by a protective cloth.*) From the brush of the great Sokovkin . . . (NEMIROVICH *removes the cloth with a flourish. It is upside down.* MOSKVIN *and* LUZHKI *turn the portrait of* CHEKHOV *around.*)

CHEKHOV: It's so gloomy. (*Everyone is upset.*)

NEMIROVICH: Sokovkin is quite an admirer of yours.

STANISLAVSKI: He's seen every one of your plays.

LUZHKI: When he came backstage after *Vanya,* he was still crying.

CHEKHOV: Aha. I'm very touched by the sentiment behind this gift. I am. Truly. Fyokla, fetch the humidor. The man in this picture is so morose. It's fine, thank you. Now I have some trifling presents for you. (FYOKLA *bring the humidor and script. From the humidor,* CHEKHOV *takes medallions and hands them out.*)

LUZHKI: They're little books.

MOSKVIN: There's a seagull on the cover.

LUZHKI: And they're engraved: "To an actor who knows how to fill the stage." Lilina, what does yours say?

LILINA: "Your costumes are always fitting."

LUZHKI: Moskvin, read yours. (MOSKVIN *shakes his head.* LUZHKI *grabs it and reads.*) "A rare combination of humility and talent."

CHEKHOV: Read them later.

STANISLAVSKI: Wait, wait, everybody. Listen to this. "My plays would never be the same without you." (*Pleased, then does take.*)

LUZHKI: Knipper's! Let's hear Knipper's!

OLGA: No, no.

EVERYONE: Read it, Knipper, read it!

OLGA: (*Flustered.*) I can't. It's too personal.

EVERYONE: Ahhh. (*Applause.* MASHA *laughs like a hyena.*)

CHEKHOV: And finally, I want to make the only real contribution I can to the Moscow Art Theater. (*Holds up script.*)

STANISLAVSKI: It's *The Three Siblings!* (*Both* NEMIROVICH *and* STANISLAVSKI *reach for it, check themselves, and walk away.*)

CHEKHOV: Well, it's here if you want it.

OLGA: (*Raising glass.*) Long life to *The Three Sisters!*

BUNIN: And to Anton Pavlovich! (*Nastrovya's all around.* GORKY *staggers in, knocks painting off easel. He has a bloody nose and mouth.*)

NEMIROVICH: My God, it's Gorky!

MASHA: What happened to him? (CHEKHOV *moves to* GORKY, *starts to examine him.*)

STANISLAVSKI: A doctor. Someone get a doctor.

NEMIROVICH: (*Grabs* STANISLAVSKI's *arm.*) A doctor, Konstantin . . . (*Indicates* CHEKHOV.)

STANISLAVSKI: Ah, yes, of course, a doctor. (*Realizes* NEMIROVICH *is touching him, pulls his arm away. Pause.*)

BUNIN: Maxim, was it the two from the cemetery?

GORKY: Yes.

BUNIN: What did they do to you?

GORKY: Nothing, until I called the Tsar's mother a syphilitic slut.

BUNIN: You fool.

CHEKHOV: Nothing seems to be broken.

GORKY: He wrapped his shirt around the truncheon.

CHEKHOV: Don't talk. I only hope you're not bleeding internally. Masha, bring cold compresses. Fyokla, get my bag.

NEMIROVICH: I can't believe they'd go this far. And right on your doorstep, Anton.

LILINA: There must have been some mistake.

GORKY: No mistake. The secret police found the printing press, tortured the printer. He told them who wrote the leaflets.

BUNIN: Are you sure they weren't literary critics? (GORKY *laughs, then clutches his stomach in pain.*)

CHEKHOV: Moskvin, Luzhki, gently . . . To the sofa in the sitting room. (MOSKVIN *and* LUZHKI *carry* GORKY *into house. Everyone follows but* NEMIROVICH. NEMIROVICH *picks up the play.* STANISLAVSKI *reenters watching.* NEMIROVICH *offers him the script.*)

STANISLAVSKI: (*Snatching the script.*) You knew it, didn't you? (*Pause.*) You knew you could do as you liked, and the collaboration would continue. (*Pause.*) If I do this play with you, what kind of a man will you think I am?

NEMIROVICH: A smart man. This production will allow the Twentieth Century's most significant theatrical institution to survive another six months.

STANISLAVSKI: You've never had any difficulty separating business affairs and personal adventures, have you?

NEMIROVICH: None, whatsoever.

STANISLAVSKI: With me, if my dinner doesn't digest well, I become an insufferable martinet at rehearsal.

NEMIROVICH: Why let something so trivial get in the way of your work?

STANISLAVSKI: We're not talking about a slice of tainted veal, are we?

NEMIROVICH: Ah, Kostya, for me, an interlude with a desirable woman is like a game of chance.

STANISLAVSKI: A toss of the dice, a spin of the wheel, a bet on a horse?

NEMIROVICH: Exactly.

STANISLAVSKI: Well, you shouldn't have taken the mare from my stable.

NEMIROVICH: Why don't we read the play together?

STANISLAVSKI: How was she with you? Did she moan with pleasure?

NEMIROVICH: Let's drop this.

STANISLAVSKI: Did she dab perfume between her breasts? Did she call out your name?

NEMIROVICH: It's over.

STANISLAVSKI: How did she compare with the others? I suppose I'll learn what you taught her.

NEMIROVICH: Your capacity for melodrama is boundless.

STANISLAVSKI: Rivaled only by your cold-blooded lechery. I came out here with the intention of killing you.

NEMIROVICH: Nonsense.

STANISLAVSKI: Oh, yes, I did. A crime of passion. No court in Russia would ever convict me.

NEMIROVICH: Oh, really, Konstantin.

STANISLAVSKI: My God, did you share a brandy with her afterwards?

NEMIROVICH: Cognac. (STANISLAVSKI *pulls out a pistol.*) Wait. No! Don't shoot.

STANISLAVSKI: You are a coward, Nemirovich.

NEMIROVICH: I think under the circumstances I'm handling myself pretty well. What do you want?

STANISLAVSKI: I want to put a lead ball through your heart. Nothing more.

NEMIROVICH: Mother of God. Please help me!

STANISLAVSKI: Bastard! You'll burn in hell!

NEMIROVICH: No! (STANISLAVSKI *fires.* NEMIROVICH *falls, screams, twitches.*) I'm hit! I'm killed! What's this? (*Holds up wadding.*) A wad of cotton?

STANISLAVSKI: (*Tapping the script with the pistol.*) I'll read it first. (*Heads to up-center door, turns.*) I may be a cuckold, but I'm also Russia's greatest living actor. (*He exits.* BUNIN *enters, followed by* MOSKVIN, LUZHKY, *and* MASHA.)

MASHA: Good lord!

MOSKVIN: What happened?

BUNIN: What's going on here? We heard a shot.

NEMIROVICH: Uh, uh, . . . nothing. Stanislavski was testing a pistol for our next show. Obviously the charge was too loud.

BUNIN: Obviously. That was bad timing, I'm afraid. After what happened to Gorky, everyone's a little jumpy.

LUZHKI: My heart leapt into my throat!

NEMIROVICH: How is Gorky? (*Boat whistle.* NEMIROVICH *looks at his watch.*) We have to be packed and on our way to the dock within the hour. Luzhki, Moskvin, make sure everything is ready. (*Exit* NEMIROVICH, LUZHKI, *and* MOSKVIN. BUNIN *pours himself a drink.*)

MASHA: (*Fanning herself.*) It's too hot for all this excitement.

BUNIN: Perhaps the rain will bring some relief. You wanted to talk?

MASHA: Yes. Would you pour me another one?

BUNIN: Are you sure?

MASHA: Yes. I like the rain. Papa liked the rain. During spring showers he used to sit under the veranda at our dacha in Melicovo like an emperor surveying his domain. He was so confident, so certain his seeds would sprout. Oh, why can't life be as predictable as nature?

BUNIN: It is. Or at least as unpredictable. A frost in June is like a sudden relapse of an old illness. An unexpected flood is like a revolution.

MASHA: I wish I had your brain, Ivan. A poet's mind. What a wonderful thing!

BUNIN: Wonderful, and utterly useless.

MASHA: Oh, wait, I just remembered, I have something for you. (*Runs out, comes back with shirt.*) It's been ready for a week.

BUNIN: (*Holds it up.*) Masha, it's good as new. Thank you.

MASHA: (*Throws her arms around* BUNIN.) Marry me, Ivan. Please marry me.

BUNIN: I do believe you've lost your mind.

MASHA: I'd make a perfect wife. You'll always have clean shirts. Your house will be well kept.

BUNIN: You've had too much to drink.

MASHA: I need you to love me.

BUNIN: Isn't there anything else I can do for you instead?

MASHA: Don't laugh at me. Who could manage your affairs better than I could?

BUNIN: There's one thing you're overlooking, Masha. I don't care for you.

MASHA: In time you could learn to like me. I wouldn't be any trouble.

BUNIN: You're not being very convincing about that.

MASHA: Ivan, don't deny yourself this happiness. Listen to me. I know I'm not good-looking.

BUNIN: Please, Masha, stop being so pathetic.

MASHA: (*Dropping to her knees.*) Try. You could love me, I know you could. (BUNIN *tries to exit, but she holds his leg.*) Can't you see how much I want you?

BUNIN: At least let's get away from the house. (*He drags her a few steps.*)

MASHA: You're my last chance. (*He pulls out of his boot and backs off quickly.*)

BUNIN: I'm sorry, I'm sorry. (*He exits.* MASHA *throws his boot after him.*)

MASHA: Don't run away. What a fool I am! A drunken fool. (CHEKHOV *enters, smoking a cigar.*)

CHEKHOV: (*Calling into house.*) He'll be all right. Just let him rest. What a day. (MASHA *takes* CHEKHOV's *cigar and throws it on the ground.*) Why did you do that?

MASHA: I have a bad habit of trying to stop you from killing yourself.

CHEKHOV: What harm can there be in one cigar?

MASHA: One more cigar, one more drink, one more night without sleep. I don't care. Do what you like. Marry your actress. She'll put you in a coffin quicker than anything you could do to yourself. I'm going to Moscow.

CHEKHOV: I think you should sober up first.

MASHA: I have to get away from Yalta now.

CHEKHOV: I need you here, Masha.

MASHA: You, Antosha, you forced me into this. You manipulated my life so that I've ended up with nothing. I just proposed to Bunin.

CHEKHOV: And?

MASHA: He fled in terror. You didn't have to use your influence this time.

CHEKHOV: When have I ever stopped you from doing anything?

MASHA: Fourteen years ago. Do you want the exact date? Alexander, the bank clerk. He wanted to marry me.

CHEKHOV: I never said no.

MASHA: You delivered a silent ultimatum. If I had married him, a great chasm would have opened between us.

CHEKHOV: The choice was always yours. You merely showed some good sense. He would have gone with other women. You deserved a better man.

MASHA: Ha! If I had brought home the King of Spain, you would have said he wasn't good enough for me.

CHEKHOV: Stop lying to yourself. You've had a reasonably happy life.

MASHA: Happy? How can a person with no future be happy?

CHEKHOV: You're too upset to travel.

MASHA: You're going to marry her, aren't you?

CHEKHOV: I don't feel well.

MASHA: That won't work this time. My bags are already packed.

CHEKHOV: You packed your bags to go to Moscow, and then you spoke to Bunin about marriage?

MASHA: I knew it was hopeless. (*Starts to door. Stops.*) I'll stay if you want me to.

CHEKHOV: No, no, go on.

MASHA: Well, you do have Fyokla. (*Exits.*)

CHEKHOV: (*Setting up the portrait.*) I really don't feel well. (*Looking at the painting.*) But if I felt like he looks, I'd be dead. (OLGA *enters.*)

OLGA: (*Holding out locket.*) What does this mean?

CHEKHOV: What it says.

OLGA: It's blank.

CHEKHOV: I was at a loss for words.

OLGA: Things can't stay the way they are, Anton, and silence won't change them.

CHEKHOV: I didn't say no.

OLGA: That simply won't do. (*Taking* CHEKHOV's *hand and giving him the locket.*) Thank you, Anton. We'll see each other in Moscow I'm sure. (*Starts to leave.*)

CHEKHOV: Olga.

OLGA: Please, there's no point in prolonging this. I give you the last week with no regrets. Good-bye.

CHEKHOV: I love you.

OLGA: Don't insult my intelligence.

CHEKHOV: It's true. Believe me, Olya, it's true.

OLGA: (*Uncertain.*) No, you're incapable of it.

CHEKHOV: Yes, I was until this week. Olya, I'm gravely ill. I know I've denied it and laughed it off, but that's a symptom of the disease. I'm a model consumptive. It was the same with Nikolai. To the end, he pretended his ruddy cheeks were a sign of good health. I've had the bacillus for eleven years.

OLGA: No.

CHEKHOV: Yes, eleven years.

OLGA: No!

CHEKHOV: It's invaded my intestines. The day before yesterday I passed blood.

OLGA: You should be in a sanitorium.

CHEKHOV: Yalta is the biggest open-air sanitorium in Russia. I am receiving treatment with every breath I take.

OLGA: We'll go to the mountains. Patients sicker than yourself have recovered there.

CHEKHOV: One in a thousand.

OLGA: That's good enough for me.

CHEKHOV: Oh, I do love you, Olya. In the last few days I've done nothing but stare into the abyss, and it's made me see how absurd it is to fear your love.

OLGA: I want you to live, Anton Pavlovich Chekhov.

CHEKHOV: It's important that everybody lives.

OLGA: But especially you. You inspire others to go on living.

CHEKHOV: You see? You refuse to accept the inevitable. It's one thing for a doctor to watch his patients waste away, but when it's someone you love . . . You can't know what it was like sitting by Nikolai's bedside those last months. My conscience will not allow you to suffer an experience like that.

OLGA: No matter what your conscience says, Anton, you want me to be with you, don't you?

CHEKHOV: Yes.

OLGA: I'll do anything for you. I'll make love to you, I'll bathe your forehead, I'll walk through hell with you, and if the worst should happen, I'll be with you when you die.

CHEKHOV: (*Breaking down.*) I'm afraid. I'm so afraid. (OLGA *cradles him in her arms.*) How futile! You make me yearn for a miracle. (*He holds up the locket.*) I'll have a wedding date engraved on this. (*They kiss.*) I promise you, by the end of summer we'll be together. (*Enter* STANISLAVSKI *and* MOSKVIN.)

STANISLAVSKI: At first glance it seems Vershinin is my part, but the play is actually centered around Toozenbach. The fire is exciting, isn't it? But why does it take place offstage? If we put it onstage, now that would be a challenge! (*Notices* CHEKHOV.) Anton, what would you think of putting the fire onstage?

CHEKHOV: That's an awful idea.

STANISLAVSKI: Just think of it. A packed house of theatergoers confronted with the spectacle of a roaring inferno.

CHEKHOV: Lovely.

STANISLAVSKI: I think we could stage it so it would be quite safe.

CHEKHOV: No. I would rather the play were not produced at all.

STANISLAVSKI: Maybe we could work out a compromise.

CHEKHOV: No. (*He exits with* OLGA. NEMIROVICH *enters.*)

NEMIROVICH: Moskvin, where's Luzhki?

MOSKVIN: I don't know.

NEMIROVICH: Well, find him. The carriages will arrive any minute now. (MOSKVIN *and* NEMIROVICH *exit.* LILINA *enters with suitcases.*)

STANISLAVSKI: Lilina, the bags go out front. (*Gently.*) Never mind, I'll get them.

LILINA: Sit down, Kostya. I'm sorry I caused you so much pain.

STANISLAVSKI: Yes, you did. I hate you for it, and I don't know if I can ever forgive you. But I understand why it happened. I abused and ignored you. You merely defended yourself.

LILINA: Yes.

STANISLAVSKI: It made me think what it would be like to lose you. How incomplete my image would be.

LILINA: Your image!

STANISLAVSKI: I've become too attached to it, haven't I? My artistic persona, my public mask.

LILINA: You've become the mask. What happened to the old Kostya?

STANISLAVSKI: I suppose he was the one who was hurt by what you did. I shouldn't neglect him, Lilina. He's the only part of me that's not acting.

LILINA: Kostya, everything will be all right if we just take the time to talk to each other.

STANISLAVSKI: I couldn't agree more . . . Oh, oh, I forgot my make-up kit. (STANISLAVSKI *runs off.* LILINA *picks up the suitcases, drops* STANISLAVSKI'*s bag, and exits with her own.* LUZHKI *and* MOSKVIN *enter.*)

LUZHKI: I'm sorry, I'm sorry. I guess I dozed off. (OLGA *and* NEMIROVICH *enter.*)

OLGA: Surprise, everybody. Masha is coming with us. (STANISLAVSKI *enters with make-up kit.*)

NEMIROVICH: Everyone, hurry! Kostya, won't it be wonderful to get back to Moscow? We must have dinner at the new restaurant.

STANISLAVSKI: If you're talking about dining socially, I'm afraid I reserve that for my friends. (BUNIN, GORKY, MASHA, *and* CHEKHOV *enter.* BUNIN *is supporting* GORKY.)

LUZHKI: Hey, look who's up and about.

BUNIN: He is risen.

GORKY: Take care, comrades. Never forget, Moscow is the belly of the beast.

MASHA: Antosha, promise me you'll get plenty of sleep.

CHEKHOV: Don't worry.

MASHA: There's fresh sausage hanging in the pantry. I laid in a good supply of tinned salmon. Fyokla has detailed instructions about your medicines. And don't work too hard.

NEMIROVICH: But do keep writing, old boy, and come to Moscow as soon as you can to help us with *The Three Sisters.*

STANISLAVSKI: But not if it will endanger your health in any way. (LILINA *enters.*)

NEMIROVICH: Enough. It's late.

MASHA: Good-bye, Antosha. Are you sure you can manage without me?

CHEKHOV: I'll be fine, Masha. Good-bye.

MASHA: Good-bye.

BUNIN: Good-bye, Masha.

MASHA: Good-bye. (MASHA *exits.*)

LILINA: Thank you, Anton. Thank you for everything.

LUZHKI: Anton Pavlovich, I tell you I hate to leave this place. The good food, good drink. I have an idea. As an incentive to make you join us in Moscow sooner, I will wait until you get there to pay you the fifteen rubles I owe you. Moskvin, don't stand there like an idiot. Let's go.

MOSKVIN: Good-bye.

CHEKHOV: Good-bye Moskvin.

MOSKVIN: (*Embracing* LUZHKI.) Good-bye.

LUZHKI: What are you doing?

CHEKHOV: Oh, Moskvin.

MOSKVIN: Yes.

CHEKHOV: Remember, I wrote the part of Toozenbach for you. (STANISLAVSKI *chokes.* MOSKVIN *and* LUZHKI *exit.* LILINA *points at suitcase and leaves.* STANISLAVSKI *picks it up and follows.* OLGA *crosses to* CHEKHOV. *He takes her hand.*) I'll envy the rat that lives below the floor of your theater. (OLGA *and* CHEKHOV *embrace.*)

NEMIROVICH: Olga, it's time. (OLGA *turns and raises hand in farewell gesture.* CHEKHOV *responds by holding up locket.* OLGA *exits.*) Good-bye, Anton Pavlovich.

CHEKHOV: Good-bye and thank you for understanding my work, Vladimir Ivanovich. But next time you're on tour, do what Stanislavski did—take a tumble with the maid. (NEMIROVICH *exits bewildered.* LUZHKI *runs in.*)

LUZHKI: I forgot to say good-bye to you. Good-bye.

CHEKHOV: Good-bye.

NEMIROVICH: (*Offstage.*) Luzhki! The first carriage has already left.

LUZHKI: Coming! (*Exits.*)

BUNIN: Well, good-night, Anton.

CHEKHOV: Good-night, Ivan. Gorky, you shouldn't walk home.

GORKY: Right, Doctor. (*Holds up bottle of wine.*) I intend to stagger every inch of the way. (BUNIN *and* GORKY *exit.*)

> CHEKHOV *sits on bench.* FYOKLA *enters with suitcase. She is dressed to travel. She approaches* CHEKHOV *but he does not see her. Offstage the carriage can be heard reining up.* FYOKLA *exits hurriedly. A few seconds later we hear the sound of the carriage leaving. Pause.*

CHEKHOV: They're gone. Now maybe I can have some peace. Fyokla! Bring my notebook! So, *The Three Sisters* are on their way to Moscow. If I could only go with them. I can see rehearsals, now. He'll have the whole cast snapping twigs to simulate the sound of the fire. (*Laughs.*) Oh, Knipper, what hast thou wrought? Chekhov married at this point in his life? Fyokla! (*Listens. Sea.*) In a hundred years, all this might be washed into the sea. (*Thunder.*) Maybe sooner. Fyokla! Let it rain. The storm is nothing. The *fear* of the storm is everything. (*Thunder.*)

Anton Chekhov has made a decision! It's life that matters, not vapid stories and silly vaudevilles. Let it rain! (*Thunder. He has an attack of coughing.*) Nikolai!

If I only have time. Why, why now? Why did I wait so long?

I'm living my life in reverse. A lovestruck schoolboy at death's door, an optimist with lungs full of blood. (*Thunder. The rain begins.* CHEKHOV *starts to the house, covers the portrait with the protective cloth, thinks, then uncovers the painting again. He exits into the house.*) Fyokla!

And the Soul Shall Dance
Wakako Yamauchi

And The Soul Shall Dance was first performed by the East West Players, Los Angeles, in March of 1977. The production had the following alternating casts:

MURATA	Jim Ishida
HANA	J. Maseras Pepito, Pat Li
MASAKO	Mimosa Iwamatsu, Denice Kumagai
OKA	Keone Young, Yuki Shimoda
EMIKO	Shizuko Hoshi, Haunani Minn
KIYOKO	Susan Inouye, Diane Takei

Directed by **Mako** *and* **Alberto Isaac**
Sets and lights by **Rae Creevey**
Costumes by **Betty Muramoto**

CHARACTERS

MURATA, 40, Issei farmer.
HANA, Issei wife of Murata.
MASAKO, 11, Nisei daughter of the Muratas.
OKA, 45, Issei farmer.
EMIKO, 30, wife of Oka.
KIYOKO, 14, Oka's daughter.

PLACE AND TIME

The action of the play takes place on and between two small farms in Southern California's Imperial Valley in the early 1930's.

And the Soul Shall Dance
Wakako Yamauchi

ACT ONE

SCENE ONE

Summer 1935, afternoon. Interior of the Murata house. The set is spare.
There is a kitchen table, four chairs, a bed, and on the wall, a calendar
indicating the year and month: June, 1935. There is a doorway leading to
the other room. Props are: a bottle of sake, *two cups, a dish of chiles, a*
phonograph, and two towels hanging on pegs on the wall. A wide wooden
bench sits outside.

The bathhouse has just burned to the ground due to the carelessness of
MASAKO, Nisei *daughter, 11. Off stage there are sounds of* MURATA,
40, Issei farmer, putting out the fire.

Inside the house HANA MURATA, *Issei wife, in a drab house dress,*
confronts MASAKO *(wearing summer dress of the era).* MASAKO *is sullen*
and somewhat defiant. HANA *breaks the silence.*

HANA: How could you be so careless, Masako? You know you
should be extra careful with fire. How often have I told you?
Now the whole bathhouse is gone. I told you time and again,
when you stoke a fire, you should see that everything is swept
into the fireplace. (MURATA *enters. He's dressed in old work clothes.*
He suffers from heat and exhaustion.)

MURATA: (*Coughing.*) Shack went up like a match box . . . This
kind of weather dries everything . . . just takes a spark to make
a bonfire out of dry timber.

HANA: Did you save any of it?

MURATA: No. Couldn't . . .

HANA: (*To* MASAKO.) How many times have I told you . . .
(MASAKO *moves nervously.*)

MURATA: No use crying about it now. *Shikata ga nai.* It's gone
now. No more bathhouse. That's all there is to it.

HANA: But you've got to tell her. Otherwise she'll make the same
mistake. You'll be building a bathhouse every year. (MURATA
removes his shirt and wipes off his face. He throws his shirt on a chair
and sits at the table.)

MURATA: *Baka!* Ridiculous!

MASAKO: I didn't do it on purpose. (*She goes to the bed, opens a book.* HANA *follows her.*)

HANA: I know that but you know what this means? It means we bathe in a bucket . . . inside the house. Carry water in from the pond, heat it on the stove . . . We'll use more kerosene.

MURATA: Tub's still there. And the fireplace. We can still build a fire under the tub.

HANA: (*Shocked.*) But no walls! Everyone in the country can see us!

MURATA: Wait 'til dark then. Wait 'til dark.

HANA: We'll be using a lantern. They'll still see us.

MURATA: Angh! Who? Who'll see us? You think everyone in the country waits to watch us take a bath? Hunh! You know how stupid you sound? Ridiculous!

HANA: (*Defensively.*) It'll be inconvenient. (HANA *is saved by a rap on the door.* OKA, *Issei neighbor, 45, enters. He is short and stout, dressed in faded work clothes.*)

OKA: Hello! Hello! Oi! What's going on here? Hey! Was there some kind of fire? (HANA *rushes to the door to let* OKA *in. He stamps the dust from his shoes and enters.*)

HANA: Oka-san! You just wouldn't believe . . . We had a terrible thing happen.

OKA: Yeah. Saw the smoke from down the road. Thought it was your house. Came rushing over. Is the fire out? (MURATA *half rises and sits back again. He's exhausted.*)

MURATA: (*Gesturing.*) Oi, oi. Come in . . . sit down. No big problem. It was just our bathhouse.

OKA: Just the *furoba,* eh?

MURATA: Just the bath.

HANA: Our Masako was careless and the *furoba* caught fire. There's nothing left of it but the tub. (MASAKO *looks up from her book, pained. She makes a very small sound.*)

OKA: Long as the tub's there, no problem. I'll help you with it. (*He starts to roll up his sleeves.* MURATA *looks at him.*)

MURATA: What . . . now? Now?

OKA: Long as I'm here.

HANA: Oh, Papa. Aren't we lucky to have such friends?

MURATA: (*To* HANA.) Hell, we can't work on it now. The ashes are still hot. I just now put the damned fire out. Let me rest a while. (*To* OKA.) Oi, how about a little *sake?* (*Gesturing to* HANA.) Make *sake* for Oka-san. (OKA *sits at the table.* HANA *goes to prepare the sake. She heats it, gets out the cups and pours it for the men.*) I'm tired . . . I am *tired.*

HANA: Oka-san has so generously offered his help . . . . (OKA *is uncomfortable. He looks around and sees* MASAKO *sitting on the bed.*)

OKA: Hello, there, Masako-chan. You studying?

MASAKO: No, it's summer vacation.

MURATA: (*Sucking in his breath.*) Kids nowadays . . . no manners . . .

HANA: She's sulking because I had to scold her. (MASAKO *makes a small moan.*)

MURATA: Drink Oka-san.

OKA: (*Swallowing.*) Ahhh, that's good.

MURATA: Eh, you not working today?

OKA: No . . . no . . . I took the afternoon off today. I was driving over to Nagatas' when I saw this big black cloud of smoke coming from your yard.

HANA: It went up so fast . . .

MURATA: What's up at Nagatas'? (*To* HANA.) Get the chiles out. Oka-san loves chiles. (HANA *opens a jar of chiles and puts them on a plate. She serves the men and gets her mending basket and walks to* MASAKO. MASAKO *makes room for her on the bed.*)

OKA: (*Helping himself.*) Ah, chiles. (MURATA *looks at* OKA, *the question unanswered.*) Well, I want to see him about my horse. I'm thinking of selling my horse.

MURATA: Sell your horse!

OKA: (*He scratches his head.*) The fact is, I need some money. Nagata-san's the only one around made money this year, and I'm thinking he might want another horse.

MURATA: Yeah, he made a little this year. And he's talking big . . . big! Says he's leasing twenty more acres this fall.

OKA: Twenty acres?

MURATA: Yeah. He might want another horse.

OKA: Twenty acres, eh?

MURATA: That's what he says. But you know his old woman makes all the decisions. (OKA *scratches his head.*)

HANA: They're doing all right.

MURATA: Henh. Nagata-kun's so hen-pecked, it's pathetic. Peko-peko. (*He makes motions of a hen pecking.*)

OKA: (*Feeling the strain.*) I better get over there.

MURATA: Why the hell you selling your horse?

OKA: I need cash.

MURATA: Oh, yeah. I could use some too. Seems like everyone's getting out of the depression but the poor farmers. Nothing changes for us. We go on and on planting our tomatoes and summer squash and eating them . . . Well, at least it's healthy.

HANA: Papa, do you have lumber?

MURATA: Lumber? For what?

HANA: The bath.

MURATA: (*Impatiently.*) Don't worry about that. We need more *sake* now. (HANA *rises to serve him.*)

OKA: You sure Nagata-kun's working twenty more acres?

MURATA: Last I heard. What the hell; if you need a few bucks, I can loan you . . .

OKA: A few hundred. I need a few hundred dollars.

MURATA: Oh, a few hundred. But what the hell you going to do without a horse? Out here a man's horse is as important as his wife.

OKA: (*Seriously.*) I don't think Nagata will buy my wife. (*The men laugh, but* HANA *doesn't find it so funny.* MURATA *glances at her. She fills the cups again.* OKA *makes a half-hearted gesture to stop her.* MASAKO *watches the pantomine carefully.* OKA *swallows his drink in one gulp.*) I better get moving.

MURATA: What's the big hurry?

OKA: Like to get the horse business done.

MURATA: Ehhhh . . . relax. Do it tomorrow. He's not going to die, is he?

OKA: (*Laughing.*) Hey he's a good horse. I want to get it settled today. If Nagata-kun won't buy, I got to find someone else. You think maybe Kawaguchi . . .?

MURATA: Not Kawaguchi . . . Maybe Yamamoto.

HANA: What is all the money for, Oka-san? Does Emiko-san need an operation?

OKA: Nothing like that . . .

HANA: Sounds very mysterious.

OKA: No, mystery, Mrs. No mystery. No sale, no money, no story.

MURATA: (*Laughing.*) That's a good one. "No sale, no money, no . . ." Eh, Mama. (*He points to the empty cups.* HANA *fills the cups and goes back to* MASAKO.)

HANA: (*Muttering.*) I see we won't be getting any work done today. (*To* MASAKO.) Are you reading again? Maybe we'd still have a bath if you . . .

MASAKO: I didn't do it on purpose.

MURATA: (*Loudly.*) I sure hope you know what you're doing, Oka-kun. What'd you do without a horse?

OKA: I was hoping you'd lend me yours now and then . . . (*He looks at* HANA.) I'll pay for some of the feed.

MURATA: (*Emphatically waving his hand.*) Sure! Sure!

OKA: The fact is, I need that money. I got a daughter in Japan and I just got to send for her this year. (HANA *comes to life. She puts down her mending and sits at the table.*)

HANA: A daughter? You have a daughter in Japan? Why, I didn't know you had children. Emiko-san and you . . . I thought you were childless.

OKA: (*Scratching his head.*) We are. I was married before.

MURATA: You son-of-a-gun!

HANA: Is that so? How old is your daughter?

OKA: Kiyoko must be . . . fifteen now. Yeah, fifteen.

HANA: Fifteen! Oh, that *would* be too old for Emiko-san's child. Is Kiyoko-san living with relatives in Japan?

OKA: (*Reluctantly.*) Yeah, with grandparents. With Shizue's parents. Well, the fact is, Shizue, that's my first wife, and Emiko were sisters. They come from a family with no sons. I was a boy when I went to work for the family . . . as an apprentice . . . they're blacksmiths. Later I married Shizue and took on the family name—you know, *yoshi*—because they had no sons*. My real name is Sakakihara.

MURATA: Sakakihara! That's a great name!

HANA: A magnificent name!

OKA: No one knows me by that here.

MURATA: Should have kept that . . . Sakakihara.

OKA: (*Muttering.*) I don't even know myself by that name.

HANA: And Shizue-san passed away and you married Emiko-san?

OKA: Oh, yeah. Well, Shizue and I lived with the family for a while and we had the baby . . . that's, you know, Kiyoko . . . (*The liquor has affected him and he's become less inhibited.*) Well, while I was serving apprentice with the family, they always looked down their noses at me. After I married, it got worse . . . That old man . . . Angh! He was terrible! Always pushing me around, making me look bad in front of my wife and kid. That old man was mean . . . ugly!

---

*Yoshi is a procedure wherein a man is married into a family that has no sons and is obliged to carry the wife's family name and continue the lineage.

MURATA: Yeah, I heard about that apprentice work—*detchi-boko* . . . Heard it was damned humiliating.

OKA: That's the God's truth!

MURATA: Never had to do it myself. I came to America instead. They say *detchi-boko* is bloody hard work.

OKA: The work's all right. I'm not afraid of work. It's the humliation! I hated them! Pushing me around like I was still a boy . . . Me, a grown man! And married to their daughter! (MURATA *groans in sympathy.*) Well, Shizue and I talked it over and we decided the best thing was to get away. We thought if I came to America and made some money . . . you know, send her money until we had enough, I'd go back and we'd leave the family . . . you know, move to another province . . . start a small business, maybe in the city, a noodle shop or something.

MURATA: That's everyone's dream. Make money, go home and live like a king.

OKA: I worked like a dog. Sent every penny to Shizue. And then she died. She died on me! (HANA *and* MURATA *observe a moment of silence in respect for* OKA's *anguish.*)

HANA: And you married Emiko-san.

OKA: I didn't marry her. They married her to me! Right after Shizue died.

HANA: But Oka-san, you were lucky . . .

OKA: Before the body was cold! No respect! By proxy. The old man wrote me they were arranging a marriage by proxy for me and Emiko. They said she'd grown to be a beautiful woman and would serve me well.

HANA: Emiko-san *is* a beautiful woman.

OKA: And they sent her to me. Took care of everything! Immigration, fare, everything.

HANA: But she's your sister-in-law—Kiyoko's aunt. It's good to keep the family together.

OKA: That's what I thought. But hear this: Emiko was the favored one. Shizue was not so pretty, not so smart. They were grooming Emiko for a rich man—his name was Yamoto—lived in a grand house in the village. They sent her to schools; you know, the culture thing: tea ceremony, you know, all that. They didn't even like me, and suddenly they married her to me.

MURATA: Yeah. You don't need all that formal training to make it over here. Just a strong back.

HANA: And a strong will.

OKA: It was all arranged. I couldn't do anything about it.

HANA: It'll be all right. With Kiyoko coming . . .

OKA: (*Dubiously.*) I hope so . . . I never knew human beings could be so cruel. You know how they mistreated my daughter? You know after Emiko came over, things got from bad to worse and I *never* had enough money to send to Kiyoko.

MURATA: They don't know what it's like here. They think money's picked off the ground here.

OKA: And they treated Kiyoko so bad. They told her I forgot about her. They told her I didn't care—they said I abandoned her. Well, she knew better. She wrote to me all the time and I always told her I'd send for her . . . soon as I got the money. (*He shakes his head.*) I just got to do something this year.

HANA: She'll be happier here. She'll know her father cares.

OKA: Kids tormented her for not having parents.

MURATA: Kids are cruel.

HANA: Masako will help her. She'll help her get started at school. She'll make friends . . . she'll be all right.

OKA: I hope so. She'll need friends. (*He considers he might be making a mistake after all.*) What could I say to her? Stay there? It's not what you think over here? I can't help her? I just have to do this thing. I just have to do this one thing for her.

MURATA: Sure . . .

HANA: Don't worry. It'll work out fine. (MURATA *gestures to* HANA. *She fills the cups.*)

MURATA: You talk about selling your horse, I thought you were pulling out.

OKA: I wish I could. But there's nothing else I can do.

MURATA: Without money, yeah . . .

OKA: You can go into some kind of business with money, but a man like me . . . no education . . . there's no kind of job I can do. I'd starve in the city.

MURATA: Dishwashing, maybe. Janitor . . .

OKA: At least here we can eat. Carrots, maybe, but we can eat.

MURATA: All the carrots we been eating 'bout to turn me into a rabbit. (*They laugh.* HANA *starts to pour more wine for* OKA *but he stops her.*)

OKA: I better not drink any more. Got to drive to Nagata-san's yet. (*He rises and walks over to* MASAKO.) You study hard, don't you? You'll teach Kiyoko English, eh? When she gets here . . .

HANA: Oh, yes. She will.

MURATA: Kiyoko-san could probably teach her a thing or two.

OKA: She won't know about American ways . . .

MASAKO: I'll help her.

HANA: Don't worry, Oka-san. She'll have a good friend in our Masako. (*They move toward the door.*)

OKA: Well, thanks for the *sake*. I guess I talk too much when I drink. (*He scratches his head and laughs.*) Oh. I'm sorry about the fire. By the way, come to my house for your bath . . . until you build yours again.

HANA: (*Hesitantly.*) Oh, uh . . . thank you. I don't know if . . .

MURATA: Good! Good! Thanks a lot. I need a good hot bath tonight.

OKA: Tonight, then.

MURATA: We'll be there.

HANA: (*Bowing.*) Thank you very much. *Sayonara.*

OKA: (*Nodding.*) See you tonight. (OKA *leaves.* HANA *faces her husband as soon as the door closes.*)

HANA: Papa, I don't know about going over there.

MURATA: (*Surprised.*) Why?

HANA: Well, Emiko-san . . .

MURATA: (*Irritated.*) What's the matter with you? We need a bath and Oka's invited us over.

HANA: (*To* MASAKO.) Help me clear the table. (MASAKO *reluctantly leaves her book and begins to clear the table.*) Papa, you know we've been neighbors already three, four years and Emiko-san's never been very hospitable.

MURATA: She's shy, that's all.

HANA: Not just shy . . . she's strange. I feel like she's pushing me off . . . she makes me feel like—I don't know—like I'm prying or something.

MURATA: Maybe you are.

HANA: And never put out a cup of tea . . . If she had all that training in the graces . . . why, a cup of tea . . .

MURATA: So if you want tea, ask for it.

HANA: I can't do that, Papa. She's strange . . . I don't know . . . (*To* MASAKO.) When we go there, be very careful not to say anything wrong.

MASAKO: I never say anything anyway.

HANA: (*Thoughtfully.*) Would you believe the story Oka-san just told? Why, I never knew . . .

MURATA: There're lot of things you don't know. Just because a

man don't . . . talk about them, don't mean he don't feel
. . . don't think about . . .

HANA: (*Looking around.*) We'll have to take something . . . There's
nothing to take . . . Papa, maybe you can dig up some carrots.

MURATA: God, Mama, be sensible. They got carrots. Everybody's got
carrots.

HANA: Something . . . maybe I should make something.

MURATA: Hell, they're not expecting anything.

HANA: It's not good manners to go empty-handed.

MURATA: We'll take the *sake*. (HANA *grimaces.* MASAKO *sees the record
player.*)

MASAKO: I know, Mama. We can take the Victrola! We can play
records for Mrs. Oka. Then nobody has to talk. (MURATA *laughs.*)

Fade out.

SCENE TWO

*That evening. We see the exterior wall of the Okas' weathered house. There
is a workable screen door and a large screened window. Outside there is a
wide wooden bench that can accomodate three or four people. There is one
separate chair and a lantern stands against the house.*

*The last rays of the sun light the area in a soft golden glow. This light
grows gray as the scene progresses and it is quite dark at the end of the scene.*

Through the screened window, EMIKO OKA, *Issei woman, 30, can be
seen walking erratically back and forth. She wears a drab cotton dress but
her grace and femininity come through. Her hair is bunned back in the style
of Issei women of the Era.*

*OKA sits cross-legged on the bench. He wears a Japanese summer robe
(yukata) and fans himself with a round Japanese fan.*

The Muratas enter. MURATA *carries towels and a bottle of* sake.
HANA *carries the Victrola, and* MASAKO *a package containing their*
yukatas.

OKA: (*Standing to receive the Muratas.*) Oh, you've come. Welcome!

MURATA: Yah . . . . Good of you to ask us.

HANA: (*Bowing.*) Yes, thank you very much. (*To* MASAKO.) Say
"hello," Masako.

MASAKO: Hello.

HANA: And "thank you."

MASAKO: Thank you. (OKA *makes motion of protest.* EMIKO *stops her
pacing and watches from the window.*)

HANA: (*Glancing briefly at the window.*) And how is Emiko-san this evening?

OKA: (*Turning toward the house.*) Emi! Emiko!

HANA: That's all right. Don't call her out. She must be busy.

OKA: (*Half rising.*) Emiko! (EMIKO *comes to the door.* HANA *starts a deep bow toward the door.*)

MURATA: *Konbanwa!* (*"Good evening!"*)

HANA: *Konbanwa*, Emiko-san. I feel so bad about this intrusion. Your husband has told you, our bathhouse was destroyed by fire and he graciously invited us to come use yours. (EMIKO *shakes her head.*)

OKA: I didn't have a chance to . . . (HANA *recovers and nudges* MASAKO.)

HANA: Say hello to Mrs. Oka.

MASAKO: Hello, Mrs. Oka. (HANA *lowers the Victrola on the bench.*)

OKA: What's this? You brought a phonograph?

MASAKO: It's a Victrola.

HANA: (*Laughing indulgently.*) Yes. Masako wanted to bring this over and play some records.

MURATA: (*Extending the wine.*) Brought a little *sake* too.

OKA: (*Taking the bottle.*) Ah, now that I like. Emiko, bring out the cups. (*He waves at his wife, but she doesn't move. He starts to ask again, but decides to get them himself. He enters the house and returns with two cups.* EMIKO *seats herself on the single chair. The Muratas unload their paraphernalia;* OKA *pours the wine, the men drink,* HANA *chatters and sorts the records.* MASAKO *stands by, helping her.*)

HANA: Yes, our Masako loves to play records. I like records too . . . and Papa, he . . .

MURATA: (*Watching* EMIKO.) They take me back home. The only way I can get there . . . in my mind.

HANA: Do you like music, Emiko-san? (EMIKO *looks vague but smiles faintly.*) Oka-san, you like them, don't you?

OKA: Yeah. But I don't have a player. No chance to hear them.

MURATA: I had to get this for them. They wouldn't leave me alone until I got it. Well . . . a phonograph . . . what the hell, they got to have *some* fun.

HANA: We don't have to play them, if you'd rather not . . .

OKA: Play. Play them.

HANA: I thought we could listen to them and relax. (*She extends some rcords to* EMIKO.) Would you like to look through these, Emiko-san? (EMIKO *doesn't respond. She pulls out a sack of Bull*

Durham and starts to roll a cigarette. HANA *pushes* MASAKO *to her.*)
Take these to her. (MASAKO *moves toward* EMIKO *with the records.*
MASAKO *stands watching her as she lights her cigarette.*) Some of
these are very old. You might know them, Emiko-san. (*She sees*
MASAKO *watching* EMIKO.) Masako, bring those over here. (*She
laughs uncomfortably.*) You might like this one, Emiko-san
. . . (*She starts the player.*) Do you know it? (*The record whines out*
"Kago No Tori." EMIKO *listens with her head cocked. She smokes her
cigarette. She becomes wrapped in nostalgia and memories of the past.*
MASAKO *watches her carefully.*)

MASAKO: (*Whispering.*) Mama, she's crying. (*Startled,* HANA *and*
MURATA *look toward* EMIKO.)

HANA: (*Pinching* MASAKO.) Shhh. The smoke is in her eyes.

MURATA: Did you bring the record I like, Mama? (EMIKO *rises
abruptly and enters the house.*)

MASAKO: There were tears, Mama.

HANA: From yawning, Masako. (*Regretfully, to* OKA.) I'm afraid
we've offended her.

OKA: (*Unaware.*) Hunh? Aw . . . no . . . pay no attention . . .
no offense . . . (MASAKO *looks toward the window.* EMIKO *stands
forlornly and slowly drifts into a dance.*)

HANA: I'm very sorry. Children, you know . . . they'll say
anything, anything that's on their minds. (MURATA *notices*
MASAKO *watching* EMIKO *through the window and tries to divert her
attention.*)

MURATA: The needles. Masako, where're the needles?

MASAKO: (*Still watching.*) I forgot them. (HANA *sees what's going on.*
OKA *is unaware.*)

HANA: Masako, go take your bath now. Masako . . . (MASAKO
reluctantly picks up her towel and leaves.)

OKA: Yeah, yeah . . . take your bath.

MURATA: (*Sees* EMIKO *still dancing.*) Change the record, Mama.

OKA: (*Still unaware.*) That's kind of sad.

MURATA: No use to get sick over a record. We're supposed to
enjoy. (HANA *stops the record.* EMIKO *disappears from the window.*
HANA *selects a lively* ondo—*"Tokyo Ondo."*)

HANA: We'll find something more fun. (*The three begin to tap to the
music.*) Can't you just see the festival? The dancers, the bright
kimonos, the paper lanterns bobbing in the wind, the fireflies
. . . How nostalgic . . . Oh, how nostalgic . . .

From the side of the house EMIKO *appears. Her hair is down, she wears an old straw hat. She dances in front of the Muratas. They're startled. After the first shock, they watch with frozen smiles. They try to join* EMIKO's *mood but something is missing.* OKA *is grieved. He finally stands as though he's had enough.* EMIKO, *now close to the door, ducks into the house.*

HANA: That was pretty . . . very nice . . . (OKA *settles down and grunts.* MURATA *clears his throat and* MASAKO *returns from her bath.*)

MURATA: You're done already? (*He's glad to see her.*)

MASAKO: I wasn't very dirty. The water was too hot.

MURATA: Good! Just the way I like it.

HANA: Not dirty?

MURATA: (*Picking up his towel.*) Come on, Mama . . . scrub my back.

HANA: (*Laughing embarrassedly.*) Oh, oh . . . well . . . (*She stops the player.*) Masako, now don't forget . . . crank the machine and change the needle now and then.

MASAKO: I didn't bring them.

HANA: Oh. Oh . . . all right. I'll be back soon . . . don't forget . . . crank. (*She leaves with her husband.* OKA *and* MASAKO *are alone.* OKA *is awkward and falsely hearty.*)

OKA: So! So you don't like hot baths, eh?

MASAKO: Not too hot.

OKA: (*Laughing.*) I thought you like it real hot. Hot enough to burn the house down. That's a little joke. (MASAKO *busies herself with the records to conceal her annoyance.*) I hear you're real good in school. Always top of the class.

MASAKO: It's a small class. Only two of us.

OKA: When Kiyoko comes, you'll help her in school, yeah? You'll take care of her . . . a favor for me, eh?

MASAKO: Okay.

OKA: You'll be her friend, eh?

MASAKO: Okay.

OKA: That's good. That's good. You'll like her. She's a nice girl too. (OKA *stands, yawns, and stretches.*) I'll go for a little walk now. (*He touches his crotch to indicate his purpose.* MASAKO *turns her attention to the records and selects one, "The Soul Shall Dance," and begins to sway to the music. The song draws* EMIKO *from the house. She looks out the window, sees* MASAKO *is alone and begins to slip into a dance.*

EMIKO: Do you like that song, Masa-chan? (MASAKO *is startled and draws back. She remembers her mother's warning. She doesn't know what to do. She nods.*) That's one of my favorite songs. I remember in Japan I used to sing it so often . . . my favorite song . . . (*She sings along with the record.*)

> Akai kuchibiru
> Kappu ni yosete
> Aoi sake nomya
> Kokoro ga odoru . . .

Do you know what that means, Masa-chan?

MASAKO: I think so . . . The soul will dance?

EMIKO: Yes, yes, that's right.

> The soul shall dance. Red lips against a glass
> Drink the green . . .

MASAKO: Wine?

EMIKO: (*Nodding.*) Drink the green wine.

MASAKO: Green? I thought wine is purple.

EMIKO: (*Nodding.*) Wine is purple . . . but this is a green liqueur. (EMIKO *holds up one of the china cups as though it were crystal, and looks at it as though the light were shining through it and she sees the green liquid.*) It's good . . . it warms your heart.

MASAKO: And the soul dances.

EMIKO: Yes.

MASAKO: What does it taste like? The green wine . . .

EMIKO: Oh, it's like . . . it's like . . . (*The second verse starts.*

"*Kurai yoru no yume, Setsunasa yo, Aoi sake nomya, Yume mo odoru . . .*")

MASAKO: In the dark night . . .

EMIKO: Dreams are unbearable . . . insufferable . . . (*She turns sad.*)

MASAKO: Drink the . . .

EMIKO: (*Nodding.*) Drink the green wine . . .

MASAKO: And the dreams will dance.

EMIKO: (*Softly.*) I'll be going back one day . . .

MASAKO: To where?

EMIKO: My home . . . Japan . . . my real home. I'm planning to go back.

MASAKO: By yourself?

EMIKO: (*Nodding.*) Oh, yes. It's a secret. You can keep a secret?

MASAKO: Unhn. I have lots of secrets . . . . all my own . . . (*The music stops. EMIKO sees OKA approaching and disappears into the house. MASAKO attends to the record and does not know EMIKO is gone.*) Secrets I never tell anyone.

OKA: Secrets? What kind of secrets? What did she say?

MASAKO: Oh. Nothing.

OKA: What did you talk about?

MASAKO: Nothing . . . Mrs. Oka was talking about the song. She was telling me what it meant . . . about the soul.

OKA: (*Scoffing.*) Heh! What does she know about soul? (*Calming down.*) Ehhh . . . some people don't have them . . . souls.

MASAKO: (*Timidly.*) I thought . . . I think everyone has a soul. I read in a book . . .

OKA: (*Laughing.*) Maybe . . . maybe you're right. I'm not an educated man, you know . . . I don't know too much about books. When Kiyoko comes you can talk to her about it. Kiyoko is very . . .(*From inside the house, we hear EMIKO begin to sing loudly at the name KIYOKO as though trying to drown it out. OKA stops talking. Then resumes.*) Kiyoko is very smart. You'll have a good time with her. She'll learn your language fast. How old did you say you are?

MASAKO: Almost twelve. (*By this time OKA and MASAKO are shouting, trying to be heard above EMIKO's singing.*)

OKA: Kiyoko is fifteen . . . . Kiyoko . . . (*OKA is exasperated. He rushes into the house seething. MASAKO hears OKA's muffled rage. "Behave yourself," and "kitchigai" come through. MASAKO slinks to the window and looks in. OKA slaps EMIKO around. MASAKO reacts to the violence.* OKA *comes out.* MASAKO *returns to the bench in time. He pulls his fingers through his hair and sits next to* MASAKO. *She very slightly draws away.*) Want me to light a lantern?

MASAKO: (*Shaken.*) No . . . ye- . . . okay . . .

OKA: We'll get a little light here . . . (*He lights the lantern as the Muratas return from their bath. They are in good spirits.*)

MURATA: Ahhhh . . . Nothing like a good hot bath.

HANA: So refreshing . . .

MURATA: A bath should be taken hot and slow. Don't know how Masako gets through so fast.

HANA: She probably doesn't get in the tub.

MASAKO: I do. (*Everyone laughs.*) Well I do. (EMIKO *comes out. She has a large purple welt on her face. She sits on the separate chair, hands folded, quietly watching the Muratas. They look at her with alarm.* OKA *engages himself with his fan.*)

HANA: Oh!   Emiko-san . . . what . . . ah-ah . . . whaa . . . (*She draws a deep breath.*) What a nice bath we had . . . such a lovely bath. We do appreciate your hos . . . pitality. Thank you so much.

EMIKO: Lovely evening, isn't it?

HANA: Very lovely. Very. Ah, a little warm, but nice . . . Did you get a chance to hear the records? (*Turning to* MASAKO.) Did you play the records for Mrs. Oka?

MASAKO: Ye- . . . no . . . The needle was . . .

EMIKO: Yes, she did. We played the records together.

MURATA: Oh, you played the songs together?

EMIKO: Yes . . . yes . . .

MURATA: That's nice . . . Masako can understand pretty good, eh?

EMIKO: She understands everything . . . everything I say.

MURATA: (*Withdrawing.*) Oh, yeah? Eh, Mama, we ought to be going . . . (*He closes the player.*) Hate to bathe and run but . . .

HANA: Yes, yes. Tomorrow is a busy day. Come, Masako.

EMIKO: Please . . . stay a little longer.

MURATA: Eh, well, we got to be going.

HANA: Why, thank you, but . . .

EMIKO: It's still quite early.

OKA: (*Indicating he's ready to say goodbye.*) Enjoyed the music. And the *sake.*

EMIKO: The records are very nice. Makes me remember Japan. I sang those songs . . . those very songs . . . Did you know I used to sing?

HANA: (*Politely.*) Why, no . . . no. I didn't know that. You must have a very lovely voice.

EMIKO: Yes.

HANA: No, I didn't know that. That's very nice.

EMIKO: Yes, I sang. My parents were very strict . . . they didn't like it. They said it was frivolous. Imagine?

HANA: Yes, I can imagine. Things were like that . . . in those days singing was not considered proper for nice . . . I mean, only for women in the profess- . . .

MURATA: We better get home, Mama.

HANA: Yes, yes. What a shame you couldn't continue with it.

EMIKO: In the city I did do some classics: the dance, and the *koto,* and the flower, and of course, the tea . . . (*She makes the proper gesture for the different disciplines.*) All those. Even some singing . . . classics, of course.

HANA: (*Politely.*) Of course.

EMIKO: All of it is so disciplined . . . so disciplined. I was almost a *natori.*

HANA: Oh! How nice.

EMIKO: But everything changed.

HANA: Oh!

EMIKO: I was sent here to America. (*She glares at* OKA.)

HANA: Oh, too bad . . . I mean, too bad about your *natori.*

MURATA: (*Loudly to* OKA.) So did you see Nagata today?

OKA: Oh, yeah. Yeah.

MURATA: What did he say? Is he interested?

OKA: Yeah. Yeah. He's interested.

MURATA: He likes the horse, eh?

OKA: Ah . . . yeah.

MURATA: I knew he'd like him. I'd buy him myself if I had the money.

OKA: Well, I have to take him over tomorrow. He'll decide then.

MURATA: He'll buy . . . he'll buy. You'd better go straight over to the ticket office and get that ticket. Before you — ha-ha — spend the money.

OKA: Ha-ha. Yeah.

HANA: It'll be so nice when Kiyoko-san comes to join you. I know you're looking forward to it.

EMIKO: (*Confused.*) Oh . . . oh . . .

HANA: Masako is so happy. It'll be good for her too.

EMIKO: I had more freedom in the city . . . I lived with an aunt and she let me . . . She wasn't so strict. (MURATA *and* MASAKO *have their gear together and stand ready to leave.*)

MURATA: Good luck on the horse tomorrow.

OKA: Yeah, thanks.

HANA: (*Bowing.*) Many, many thanks.

OKA: (*Nodding toward the* sake.) Thanks for the *sake.*

HANA: (*Bowing again.*) Goodnight, Emiko-san. We'll see you again soon. We'll bring the records too.

EMIKO: (*Softly.*) Those songs . . . those very songs . . .

MURATA: Let's go, Mama. (*The Muratas pull away. Light follows them and grows dark on the Okas. The Muratas begin walking home.*)

HANA: That was uncomfortable.

MASAKO: What's the matter with . . .

HANA: Shhhh!

MURATA: I guess Oka has his problems.

MASAKO: Is she really *kitchigai?*

HANA: Of course not. She's not crazy. Don't say that word, Masako.

MASAKO: I heard Mr. Oka call her that.

HANA: He called her that?

MASAKO: I . . . I think so.

HANA: You heard wrong, Masako. Emiko-san isn't crazy. She just likes her drinks. She had too much to drink tonight.

MASAKO: Oh.

HANA: She can't adjust to this life. She can't get over the good times she had in Japan. Well, it's not easy . . . but one has to know when to bend . . . like the bamboo. When the winds blow, bamboo bends. You bend or crack. Remember that, Masako.

MURATA: (*Laughing wryly.*) Bend, eh? Remember that, Mama.

HANA: (*Softly.*) You don't know . . . it isn't ever easy.

MASAKO: Do you want to go back to Japan, Mama?

HANA: Everyone does.

MASAKO: Do you, Papa?

MURATA: I'll have to make some money first.

MASAKO: I don't. Not me. Not Kiyoko . . .

HANA: After Kiyoko-san comes, Emiko will have company and things will straighten out. She has nothing to live on but memories. She doesn't have any friends. At least I have my friends at church . . . at least I have that. She must get awful lonely.

MASAKO: I know that. She tried to make friends with me.

HANA: She did? What did she say?

MASAKO: Well, sort of . . .

HANA: What did she say?

MASAKO: She didn't say anything. I just felt it. Maybe you should be her friend, Mama.

MURATA: Poor woman. We could have stayed longer.

HANA: But you wanted to leave. I tried to be friendly. You saw that. It's not easy to talk to Emiko. She either closes up, you can't pry a word from her, or else she goes on and on . . . all that . . . that . . . about the *koto* and tea and the flower . . . I mean, what am I supposed to say? She's so unpredictable. And the drinking . . .

MURATA: All right, all right, Mama.

MASAKO: Did you see her black eye?

HANA: (*Calming down.*) She probably hurt herself. She wasn't very steady.

MASAKO: Oh, no. Mr. Oka hit her.

HANA: I don't think so.

MASAKO: He hit her. I saw him.

HANA: You saw that? Papa, do you hear that? She saw them. That does it. We're not going there again.

MURATA: Aww . . . Oka wouldn't do that. Not in front of a kid.

MASAKO: Well, they didn't do it in front of me. They were in the house.

MURATA: You see . . .

HANA: That's all right. You just have to fix the bath-house. Either that or we're going to bathe at home . . . in a bucket. We're not going . . . we'll bathe at home. (MURATA *mutters to himself.*) What?

MURATA: I said all right, it's the bucket then. I'll get to it when I can. (HANA *passes* MURATA *and walks ahead.*)

Fade out.

SCENE   THREE

Same evening. Lights crossfade to the exterior of the Oka house. The Muratas have just left. EMIKO sits on the bench. Her back is to OKA. OKA, still standing, looks at her contemptuously as she takes the bottle and one of the cups to pour herself a drink.

OKA: Nothing more disgusting than a drunk woman. (EMIKO *ignores him.*) You made a fool of yourself. *Washi baka ni shite!* You made a fool of me! (EMIKO *doesn't move.*)

EMIKO: One can only make a fool of one's self.

OKA: You learn that in the fancy schools, eh? (EMIKO *examines the pattern on her cup.*) Eh? Eh? Answer me! (EMIKO *ignores.*) I'm talking to you. Answer me! (*Menacing.*) You don't get away with that. You think you're so fine . . . (EMIKO *looks off into the horizon.* OKA *turns her roughly around.*) When I talk, you listen! (EMIKO *turns away again.* OKA *pulls the cup from her hand.*) Goddamnit! What'd you think my friends think of you? What kind of ass they think I am? (*He grabs her shoulders.*)

EMIKO: Don't touch me . . . don't touch me.

OKA: Who the hell you think you are? "Don't touch me, don't touch me." Who the hell! High and mighty, eh? Too good for me, eh? Don't put on the act for me . . . I know who you are.

EMIKO: Tell me who I am, Mister Smart Peasant.

OKA: Shut your fool mouth, Goddamnit! Sure! I'll tell you. I know all about you . . . Shizue told me. The whole village knows.

EMIKO: Shizue!

OKA: Yeah! Shizue. Embarrassed the hell out of her, your own sister.

EMIKO: Embarrassed? I have nothing to be ashamed of. I don't know what you're talking about.

OKA: (*Derisively.*) You don't know what I'm talking about. I know. The whole village knows. They're all laughing at you. At me! Stupid Oka got stuck with a second-hand woman. I didn't say anything because . . .

EMIKO: I'm not second-hand!

OKA: Who you trying to fool? I know. Knew long time ago . . . Shizue wrote me all about your affairs in Tokyo. The men you were mess- . . .

EMIKO: Affairs? Men?

OKA: That man you were messing with . . . I knew all along. I didn't say anything because you . . . I . . .

EMIKO: I'm not ashamed of it.

OKA: You're not ashamed! What the hell! Your father thought he was pulling a fast one on me . . . thought I didn't know nothing . . . thought I was some kind of dumb ass . . . I didn't say nothing because Shizue's dead . . . Shizue's dead. I was willing to give you a chance.

EMIKO: (*Laughing.*) A chance?

OKA: Yeah! A chance! Laugh! Give a *joro* another chance. Sure, I'm stupid . . . dumb.

EMIKO: I'm not a whore. I'm true . . . he knows I'm true.

OKA: True! Ha!

EMIKO: You think I'm untrue just because I let . . . let you . . . There's only one man for me.

OKA: Let me (*Obscene gesture.*) you? I can do what I want with you. Your father palmed you off on me—like a dog or cat—an animal . . . couldn't do nothing with you. Even that rich dumb Yamato wouldn't have you. You father—greedy father—so proud . . . making big plans for you . . . for himself. Ha! The whole village laughing at him . . . (EMIKO *hangs her head.*) Shizue told me. And she was working like a dog . . . trying to keep your goddamn father happy . . . doing my work and yours.

EMIKO: My work?

OKA: Yeah, your work too! She killed herself working! She killed herself . . . (*He has tender memories of his dull, uncomplaining wife.*) Up in the morning getting the fires started, working the bellows, cleaning the furnace, cooking, and late at night working with the sewing . . . tending the baby . . . (*He mutters.*) The goddamn family killed her. And you . . . you out there in Tokyo with the fancy clothes, doing the (*He sneers.*) dance, the tea, the flower, the *koto,* and the . . . (*Obscene gesture.*)

EMIKO: (*Hurting.*) Achhhh . . .

OKA: Did you have fun? Did you have fun on your sister's blood? (EMIKO *doesn't answer.*) Did you? He must have been a son-of-a-bitch . . . What would make that goddam greedy old man send his prize mare to a plow horse like me? What kind of bum was he that your father . . .

EMIKO: He's not a bum . . . he's not a bum.

OKA: Was he Korean? Was he *Etta?* That's the only thing I could figure.

EMIKO: I'm true to him. Only him.

OKA: True? You think he's true to you? You think he waits for you? Remembers you? *Aho!* Think he cares?

EMIKO: (*Nodding quietly.*) He does.

OKA: And waits ten years? *Baka!* Go back to Japan and see. You'll find out. Go back to Japan. *Kaire!*

EMIKO: In time.

OKA: In time? How about now?

EMIKO: I can't now.

OKA: Ha! Now! Go now! Who needs you? Who needs you? You think a man waits ten years for a woman? You think you're some kind of . . . of . . . diamond . . . treasure . . . he's going to wait his life for you? Go to him. He's probably married with ten kids. Go to him. Get out! Goddamn *joro*. . . Go! Go! (OKA *sweeps* EMIKO *off the bench*.)

EMIKO: (*Hurting*.) Ahhhh! I . . . I don't have the money. Give me money to . . .

OKA: If I had money I would give it to you ten years ago. You think I been eating this *kuso* for ten years because I like it?

EMIKO: You're selling the horse . . . Give me the . . .

OKA: (*Scoffing*.) That's for Kiyoko. I owe you nothing.

EMIKO: Ten years, you owe me.

OKA: Ten years of what? Misery? You gave me nothing. I give you nothing. You want to go, pack your bag and start walking. Try cross the desert. When you get dry and hungry, think about me.

EMIKO: I'd die out there.

OKA: Die? You think I didn't die here?

EMIKO: I didn't do anything to you.

OKA: No, no you didn't. All I wanted was a little comfort and . . . you . . . no, you didn't. No. So you die. We all die. Shizue died. If she was here, she wouldn't treat me like this . . . (*He thinks of his poor dead wife*.) Ah, I should have brought her with me. She'd be alive now. We'd be poor but happy . . . like . . . like Murata and his wife . . . and the kid . . .

EMIKO: I wish she were alive too. I'm not to blame for her dying. I didn't know . . . I was away. I loved her. I didn't want her to die . . . I . . .

OKA: (*Softening*.) I know that. I'm not blaming you for that . . . And it's not my fault what happened to you either . . . (EMIKO *is silent and* OKA *mistakes that for a change in attitude. He is encouraged*.) You understand that, eh? I didn't ask for you. It's not my fault you're here in this desert . . . with . . . with me . . . . (EMIKO *weeps*. OKA *reaches out*.) I know I'm too old for you. It's hard for me too . . . but this is the way it is. I just ask you be kinder . . . understand it wasn't my fault. Try make it easier for me . . . for yourself too. (OKA *touches her and she shrinks from his touch*.)

EMIKO: Ach!

OKA: (*Humiliated again.*) Goddamn it! I didn't ask for you! *Aho!* If you was smart you'd done as your father said . . . cut out that *saru shibai* with the *Etta* . . . married the rich Yamoto. Then you'd still be in Japan. Not here to make my life so miserable. (EMIKO *is silent.*) And you can have your *Etta* . . . and anyone else you want. Take them all on . . .(OKA *is worn out. It's hopeless.*) God, why do we do this all the time? Fighting, fighting all the time. There must be a better way to live . . . there must be another way. (OKA *waits for a response, gives up, and enters the house.* EMIKO *watches him leave and pours herself another drink. The storm has passed, the alcohol takes over. She turns to the door* OKA *disappeared into.*)

EMIKO: Because I must keep the dream alive . . . the dream is all I live for. I am only in exile now. Because if I give in, all I've lived before . . . will mean nothing . . . will be for nothing . . . Because if I let you make me believe this is all there is to my life, the dream would die . . . I would die . . . (*She pours another drink and feels warm and good.*)

Fade out.

A C T   T W O

S C E N E   O N E

Mid-September, afternoon. Muratas' kitchen. The calendar reads September. MASAKO *is at the kitchen table with several books. She thumbs through a Japanese magazine.* HANA *is with her sewing.*

MASAKO: Do they always wear kimonos in Japan, Mama?

HANA: Most of the time.

MASAKO: I wonder if Kiyoko will be wearing a kimono like this?

HANA: (*Peering into* MASAKO's *magazine.*) They don't dress like that . . . not for every day.

MASAKO: I wonder what she's like.

HANA: Probably a lot like you. What do you think she's like?

MASAKO: She's probably taller.

HANA: Mr. Oka isn't tall.

MASAKO: And pretty . . .

HANA: (*Laughing.*) Mr. Oka . . . Well, I don't suppose she'll look like her father.

MASAKO: Mrs. Oka is pretty.

HANA: She isn't Kiyoko-san's real mother, remember.

MASAKO: Oh. That's right.

HANA: But they are related. Well, we'll soon see.

MASAKO: I thought she was coming in September. It's already September.

HANA: Papa said Oka-san went to San Pedro a few days ago. He should be back soon with Kiyoko-san.

MASAKO: Didn't Mrs. Oka go too?

HANA: (*Glancing toward the Oka house.*) I don't think so. I see lights in their house at night.

MASAKO: Will they bring Kiyoko over to see us?

HANA: Of course. First thing, probably. You'll be very nice to her, won't you? (MASAKO *leaves the table and finds another book.*)

MASAKO: Sure. I'm glad I'm going to have a friend. I hope she likes me.

HANA: She'll like you. Japanese girls are very polite, you know.

MASAKO: We have to be or our Mamas get mad at us.

HANA: Then I should be getting mad at you more often.

MASAKO: It's often enough already, Mama. (*She opens a hardback book.*) Look at this, Mama . . . I'm going to show her this book.

HANA: She won't be able to read at first.

MASAKO: I love this story. Mama, this is about people like us — settlers — it's about the prairie. We live in a prairie, don't we?

HANA: Prairie? Does that mean desert?

MASAKO: I think so.

HANA: (*Nodding and looking bleak.*) We live in a prairie.

MASAKO: It's about the hardships and the floods and droughts and how they have nothing but each other.

HANA: (*Nodding.*) We have nothing but each other. But these people — they're white people.

MASAKO: (*Nodding.*) Sure, Mama. They come from the east. Just like you and Papa came from Japan.

HANA: We come from the far far east. That's different. White people are different from us.

MASAKO: I know that.

HANA: White people among white people . . . that's different from Japanese among white people. You know what I'm saying?

MASAKO: I know that. How come they don't write books about us . . . about Japanese people?

HANA: Because we're nobodies here.

MASAKO: If I didn't read these, there'd be nothing for me . . .

HANA: Some of the things you read, you're never going to know.

MASAKO: I can dream though.

HANA: (*Sighing.*) Sometimes the dreaming makes the living harder. Better to keep your head out of the clouds.

MASAKO: That's not much fun.

HANA: You'll have fun when Kiyoko-san comes. You can study together, you can sew, and sometime you can try some of those fancy American recipes.

MASAKO: Mama, you have to have chocolate and cream and things like that.

HANA: We'll get them. (*We hear the putt-putt of* OKA's *old car.* MASAKO *and* HANA *pause and listen.* MASAKO *runs to the window.*)

MASAKO: I think it's them!

HANA: The Okas?

MASAKO: It's them! It's them! (HANA *stands and looks out. She removes her apron and puts away her sewing.*)

HANA: Two of them. Emiko-san isn't with them. Let's go outside.

OKA *and* KIYOKO, *14, enter.* OKA *is wearing his going-out clothes: a sweater, white shirt, dark pants, but no tie.* KIYOKO *walks behind him. She is short, chunky, broadchested and very self-conscious. Her hair is straight and banded into two shucks. She wears a conservative cotton dress, white socks and two inch heels.* OKA *is proud. He struts in, his chest puffed out.*

OKA: *Hello, hello . . . We're here. We made it!* (*He pushes* KIYOKO *forward.*) This is my daughter, Kiyoko. (*To* KIYOKO.) Murata-san . . . remember I was talking about? My friends . . .

KIYOKO: (*Barely audible, bowing deeply.*) *Hajime mashite yoroshiku onegai shimasu . . .*

HANA: (*Also bowing formally.*) I hope your journey was pleasant.

OKA: (*While the women are still bowing, he pushes* KIYOKO *toward* MASAKO.) This is Masako-chan; I told you about her . . . (MASAKO *is shocked at* KIYOKO's *appearance. The girl she expected is already a woman. She stands with her mouth agape and withdraws noticeably.* HANA *rushes in to fill the awkwardness.*)

HANA: Say hello, Masako. My goodness, where are your manners? (*She laughs apologetically.*) In this country they don't make much to-do about manners. (*She stands back to examine* KIYOKO.) My, my, I didn't picture you so grown up. My, my . . . Tell me, how was your trip?

OKA: (*Proudly.*) We just drove in from Los Angeles just this morning. We spent the night in San Pedro and the next two days we spent in Los Angeles . . . you know, Japanese town.

HANA: How nice!

OKA: Kiyoko was so excited. Twisting her head this way and that—couldn't see enough with her big eyes. (*He imitates her fondly.*) She's from the country, you know . . . just a big country girl. Got all excited about the Chinese dinner—we had a Chinese dinner. She never ate it before. (KIYOKO *covers her mouth and giggles.*)

HANA: Chinese dinner!

OKA: Oh, yeah. Duck, pakkai, chow mein, seaweed soup . . . the works!

HANNA: A feast!

OKA: Oh, yeah. Like a holiday. Two holidays. Two holidays in one.

HANA: (*Pushes* MASAKO *forward.*) Two holidays in one! Kiyoko-san, our Masako has been looking forward to meeting you.

KIYOKO: (*Bowing again.*) *Hajime mashite . . .*

HANA: She's been thinking of all sorts of things she can do with you: sewing, cooking . . .

MASAKO: Oh, Mama. (KIYOKO *covers her mouth and giggles.*)

HANA: It's true, Kiyoko-san. She's been looking forward to having a best friend. (KIYOKO *giggles again and* MASAKO *pulls away.*)

OKA: Kiyoko, you shouldn't be so shy. The Muratas are my good friends and you should feel free with them. Ask anything, say anything . . . right?

HANA: Of course, of course. (*She is slightly annoyed with* MASAKO.) Masako, go in and start the tea. (MASAKO *enters the house.*) I'll call Papa. He's in the yard. Papa! Oka-san is here! (*To* KIYOKO.) Now tell me, how was your trip? Did you get seasick?

KIYOKO: (*Bowing and nodding.*) Eh ("yes"). A little . . .

OKA: Tell her. Tell her how sick you got. (KIYOKO *covers her mouth and giggles.*)

HANA: Oh, I know, I know. I was too. That was a long time ago. I'm sure things are improved now. Tell me about Japan . . . what is it like now? They say it's so changed . . . modern . . .

OKA: Kiyoko comes from the country . . . backwoods. Nothing changes much there from century to century.

HANA: Ah! That's true. That's why I love Japan. And you wanted to leave. It's unbelievable. To come here!

OKA: She always dreamed about it.

HANA: Well, it's not really that bad.

OKA: No, it's not that bad. Depends on what you make of it.

HANA: That's right. What you make of it. I was just telling Masako today . . . (MURATA *enters. He rubs his hands to take off the soil and comes in grinning. He shakes* OKA's *hand.*)

MURATA: Oi, oi . . .

OKA: Yah . . . I'm back. This is my daughter.

MURATA: No! She's beautiful!

OKA: Finally made it. Finally got her here.

MURATA: (*To* KIYOKO.) Your father hasn't stopped talking about you all summer.

HANA: And Masako too.

KIYOKO: (*Bowing.*) *Hajime mashite* . . .

MURATA: (*Acknowledging with a short bow.*) Yah. How'd you like the trip?

OKA: I was just telling your wife—had a good time in Los Angeles. Had a couple of great dinners, took in the cinema—Japanese pictures, bought her some American clothes.

HANA: Oh, you bought that in Los Angeles.

MURATA: Got a good price for your horse, eh? Lots of money, eh?

OKA: Nagata's a shrewd bargainer. Heh. It don't take much money to make her happy. She's a country girl.

MURATA: That's all right. Country's all right. Country girl's the best.

OKA: Had trouble on the way back.

MURATA: Yeah?

OKA: Fan belt broke.

MURATA: That'll happen.

OKA: Lucky I was near a gasoline station. We were in the mountains. Waited in a restaurant while it was getting fixed.

HANA: Oh, that was good.

OKA: Guess they don't see Japanese much. Stare? Terrible! Took them a long time to wait on us. Dumb waitress practically threw the food at us. Kiyoko felt bad.

HANA: Ah! That's too bad . . . too bad. That's why I always pack a lunch when we take trips.

MURATA: They'll spoil the day for you . . . those barbarians!

OKA: Terrible food too. Kiyoko couldn't swallow the dry bread and bologna.

HANA: That's the food they eat!

MURATA: Let's go in . . . have a little wine. Mama, we got wine? This is a celebration.

HANA: I think so . . . a little . . . (*They enter the house talking.* MASAKO *has made the tea, and* HANA *begins to serve the wine.*) How is your mother? Was she happy to see you?

KIYOKO: Oh, she . . . yes . . .

HANA: I just know she was surprised to see you so grown up. Of course, you remember her from Japan, don't you?

KIYOKO: (*Nodding.*) Eh ("yes"). I can barely remember. I was very young . . .

HANA: Of course. But you do, don't you?

KIYOKO: She was gone most of the time . . . at school in Tokyo. She was very pretty, I remember that.

HANA: She's still very pretty.

KIYOKO: Eh. She was always laughing. She was much younger then.

HANA: Oh now, it hasn't been that long ago. (MASAKO *leaves the room to go outside. The following dialogue continues muted as light goes dim in the house and focuses on* MASAKO. EMIKO *enters, is drawn to the* MURATA *window and listens.*)

OKA: We stayed at an inn on East First Street. *Shizuokaya.* Whole inn filled with Shizuoka people . . . talking the old dialect. Thought I was in Japan again.

MURATA: That right?

OKA: Felt good. Like I was in Japan again.

HANA: (*To* KIYOKO.) Did you enjoy Los Angeles?

KIYOKO: (*Nodding.*) Eh.

OKA: That's as close as I'll get to Japan.

MURATA: *Mattakuna!* That's for sure. (*Outside* MASAKO *becomes aware of* EMIKO.)

MASAKO: Why don't you go in?

EMIKO: Oh. Oh. Why don't you?

MASAKO: They're all grown-ups in there. I'm not grown up.

EMIKO: (*Softly.*) All grown-ups . . . Maybe I'm not either. (*Her mood changes.*) Masa-chan, do you have a boy friend?

MASAKO: I don't like boys. They don't like me.

EMIKO: Oh, that will change. You will change. I was like that too.

MASAKO: Besides, there're none around here . . . Japanese boys . . . There are some at school, but they don't like girls.

HANA: (*Calling from the kitchen.*) Masako . . . (MASAKO *doesn't answer.*)

EMIKO: Your mother is calling you.

MASAKO: (*Answering her mother.*) *Nani?* ("What?")

HANA: (*From the kitchen.*) Come inside now.

EMIKO: You'll have a boy friend one day.

MASAKO: Not me.

EMIKO: You'll fall in love one day. Someone will make the inside of you light up, and you'll know you're in love. (*She relives her own experience.*) Your life will change . . . grow beautiful. It's good, Masa-chan. And this feeling you'll remember the rest of your life . . . will come back to you . . . haunt you . . . keep you alive . . . five, ten years . . . no matter what happens . . . keep you alive.

HANA: (*From the kitchen.*) Masako . . . Come inside now. (MASAKO *turns aside to answer and* EMIKO *slips away.*)

MASAKO: What, Mama? (HANA *comes out.*)

HANA: Come inside. Don't be so unsociable. Kiyoko wants to talk to you.

MASAKO: (*Watching* EMIKO *leave.*) She doesn't want to talk to me. You're only saying that.

HANA: What's the matter with you? Don't you want to make friends with her?

MASAKO: She's not my friend. She's your friend.

HANA: Don't be so silly. She's only fourteen.

MASAKO: Fifteen. They said fifteen. She's your friend. She's an old lady.

HANA: Don't say that.

MASAKO: I don't like her.

HANA: Shhh! Don't say that.

MASAKO: She doesn't like me either.

HANA: Ma-chan. Remember your promise to Mr. Oka? You're going to take her to school, teach her the language, teach her the ways of Americans.

MASAKO: She can do it herself. You did.

HANA: That's not nice, Ma-chan.

MASAKO: I don't like the way she laughs. (*She imitates* KIYOKO *holding her hand to her mouth and giggling and bowing.*)

HANA: Oh, how awful! Stop that. That's the way the girls do in Japan. Maybe she doesn't like your ways either. That's only a difference in manners. What you're doing now is considered very bad manenrs. (*She changes tone.*) Ma-chan . . . just wait— when she learns to read and speak, you'll have so much to say to each other. Come on, be a good girl and come inside.

MASAKO: It's just old people in there, Mama. I don't want to go in.

(HANA *calls* KIYOKO *away from the table and speaks confidentially to her.*)

HANA: Kiyoko-san, please come here a minute. Maybe it's better for you to talk to Masako alone. (KIYOKO *leaves the table and walks to* HANA *outside.*) Masako has a lot of things to tell you about . . . what to expect in school and things . . .

MURATA: (*Calling from the table.*) Mama, put out something . . . chiles . . . for Oka-san. (HANA *leaves the two girls and enters the house.* KIYOKO *and* MASAKO *stand awkwardly,* KIYOKO *glancing shyly at* MASAKO.)

MASAKO: Do you like it here?

KIYOKO: (*Nodding.*) Eh. (*There's an uncomfortable pause.*)

MASAKO: School will be starting next week . . .

KIYOKO: (*Nodding.*) Eh.

MASAKO: Do you want to walk to school with me?

KIYOKO: (*Nodding.*) Ah. (MASAKO *rolls her eyes and tries again.*)

MASAKO: I leave at 7:30.

KIYOKO: Ah. (*There's a long pause.* MASAKO *finally gives up and moves off stage.*)

MASAKO: I have to do something. (KIYOKO *watches her leave and uncertainly moves back to the house.* HANA *looks up at* KIYOKO *coming in alone, sighs, and quietly pulls out a chair for her.*)

Fade out.

SCENE TWO

November night. Interior of the Murata house. Lamps are lit. The family is at the kitchen table. HANA *sews,* MASAKO *does her homework,* MURATA *reads the paper. They're dressed in warm robes and having tea. Outside thunder rolls in the distance and lightening flashes.*

HANA: It'll be *ohigan* (An autumn festival.) soon.

MURATA: Something to look forward to.

HANA: We will need sweet rice for *omochi* (Rice cakes.).

MURATA: I'll order it next time I go to town.

HANA: (*To* MASAKO.) How is school? Getting a little harder?

MASAKO: Not that much. Sometimes the arithmetic is hard.

HANA: How is Kiyoko-san doing? Is she getting along all right?

MASAKO: She's good in arithmetic. She skipped a grade already.

HANA: Already? That's good news. Only November and she skipped a grade! At this rate she'll be through before you.

MASAKO: Well, she's older.

MURATA: Sure, she's older, Mama.

HANA: Has she made any friends?

MASAKO: No. She follows me around all day. She understands okay, but she doesn't talk. She talks like, you know . . . she says "ranchi" for lunch and "ranchi" for ranch too, and like that. Kids laugh and copy behind her back. It's hard to understand her.

HANA: You understand her, don't you?

MASAKO: I'm used to it. (MURATA *smiles secretly.*)

HANA: You should tell the kids not to laugh; after all, she's trying. Maybe you should help her practice those words . . . show her what she's doing wrong.

MASAKO: I already do. Our teacher told me to do that.

MURATA: (*Looking up from his paper.*) You ought to help her all you can.

HANA: And remember when you started school you couldn't speak English either.

MASAKO: I help her. (MURATA *rises and goes to the window. The night is cold. Lightening flashes and the wind whistles.*)

MURATA: Looks like a storm coming up. Hope we don't have a freeze.

HANA: If it freezes, we'll have another bad year. Maybe we ought to start the smudge pots.

MURATA: (*Listening.*) It's starting to rain. Nothing to do now but pray.

HANA: If praying is the answer, we'd be in Japan now . . . rich.

MURATA: (*Wryly.*) We're not dead yet. We still have a chance. (HANA *glares at this small joke.*) Guess I'll turn in.

HANA: Go to bed . . . go to bed. I'll sit up and worry.

MURATA: If worrying was the answer, we'd be around the world twice and in Japan. Come on, Mama. Let's go to bed. It's too cold tonight to be mad. (*There's an urgent knock on the door. The family react to it.*) Dareh da! (Who is it.) (MURATA *goes to the door and pauses.*) Who is it!

KIYOKO: (*Weakly.*) It's me . . . help me . . . (MURATA *opens the door and* KIYOKO *enters. She's dressed in a kimono with a shawl thrown over. Her legs are bare except for a pair of straw zori. Her hair is stringy from the rain and she trembles from the cold.*)

MURATA: My God! Kiyoko-san! What's the matter?

HANA: Kiyoko-san! What is it?

MURATA: What happened?

KIYOKO: (*Gasping.*) They're fighting . . . they're fighting.

MURATA: Ah . . . don't worry . . . those things happen. No cause to worry. Mama, make tea for her. Sit down and catch your breath. I'll take you home when you're ready.

HANA: Papa, I'll take care of it.

MURATA: Let me know when you're ready to go home.

HANA: It must be freezing out there. Try to get warm. Try to calm yourself.

MURATA: Kiyoko-san . . . don't worry. (HANA *waves* MASAKO *and* MURATA *off.* MURATA *leaves.* MASAKO *goes to her bed in the kitchen.*)

HANA: Papa, I'll take care of it.

KIYOKO: (*Looking at* MURATA'*s retreating form.*) I came to ask your help.

HANA: You ran down here without a lantern? You could have fallen and hurt yourself.

KIYOKO: I don't care . . . I don't care.

HANA: You don't know, Kiyoko-san. It's treacherous out there . . . snakes, spiders . . .

KIYOKO: I must go back . . . I . . . I . . . you . . . please come with me.

HANA: First, first, we must get you warm . . . Drink your tea.

KIYOKO: But they might kill each other. They're fighting like animals. Help me stop them! (HANA *goes to the stove to warm a pot of soup.*)

HANA: I cannot interfere in a family quarrel.

KIYOKO: It's not a quarrel . . . it's a . . .

HANA: That's all it is. A family squabble. You'll see. Tomorrow . . . (KIYOKO *rises and puts her hand on* HANA'*s arm.*)

KIYOKO: Not just a squabble . . . please! (*She starts toward the door but* HANA *restrains her.*)

HANA: Now listen. Listen to me, Kiyoko-san. I've known your father and mother a little while now. I suspect it's been like this for years. Every family has some kind of trouble.

KIYOKO: Not like this . . . not like this.

HANA: Some have it better—some worse. When you get married, you'll understand. Don't worry. Nothing will happen. (*She takes a towel from the wall and dries* KIYOKO'*s hair.*) You're chilled to the bone. You'll catch your death . . .

KIYOKO: I don't care . . . I want to die.

HANA: Don't be silly. It's not that bad.

KIYOKO: They started drinking early in the afternoon. They make some kind of brew and hide it somewhere in the desert.

HANA: It's illegal to make it. That's why they hide it. That home brew is poison to the body . . . and the mind too.

KIYOKO: It makes them crazy. They drink it all the time and quarrel constantly. I was in the other room studying. I try so hard to keep up with school.

HANA: We were talking about you just this evening. Masako says you're doing so well . . . you skipped a grade?

KIYOKO: It's hard . . . hard . . . I'm too old for the class and the children . . . (*She remembers all her problems and starts to cry again.*)

HANA: It's always hard in a new country.

KIYOKO: They were bickering and quarreling all afternoon. Then something happened. All of a sudden I saw them on the floor . . . hitting and . . .and . . . He was hitting her in the stomach, the face . . . I tried to stop them, but they were so . . . drunk.

HANA: There, there . . . It's probably all over now.

KIYOKO: Why does it happen like this? Nothing is right. Everywhere I go . . . Masa-chan is so lucky. I wish my life was like hers. I can hardly remember my real mother.

HANA: Emiko-san is almost a real mother to you. She's blood kin.

KIYOKO: She hates me. She never speaks to me. She's so cold. I want to love her but she won't let me. She hates me.

HANA: I don't think that's true, Kiyoko-san.

KIYOKO: I know it's true.

HANA: No. I don't think you have anything to do with it. It's this place. She hates it. This place is so lonely and alien.

KIYOKO: Then why didn't she go back? Why did they stay here?

HANA: You don't know. It's not so simple. Sometimes I think . . .

KIYOKO: Then why don't they make the best of it here? Like you?

HANA: That isn't easy either. Believe me. (*She goes to the stove to stir the soup.*) Sometimes . . . sometimes the longing for homeland fills me with despair. Will I never return again? Will I never see my mother, my father, my sisters again? But what can one do? There are responsibilities here . . . children . . . (*She draws a sharp breath.*) And another day passes . . . another month . . . another year. Eventually everything passes. (*She takes the soup to* KIYOKO.) Did you have supper tonight?

KIYOKO: (*Bowing gratefully.*) Ah. When my . . . my aunt gets like this, she doesn't cook. No one eats. I don't get hungry anymore.

HANA: Cook for yourself. It's important to keep your health.

KIYOKO: I left Japan for a better life here . . .

HANA: It isn't easy for you, is it? But you must remember your filial duty.

KIYOKO: It's so hard.

HANA: But you can make the best of it here, Kiyoko-san. And take care of yourself. You owe that to yourself. Eat. Keep well. It'll be better, you'll see. And sometimes it'll seem worse. But you'll survive. We do, you know . . . we do . . . (*She looks around.*) It's getting late.

KIYOKO: (*Apprehensively.*) I don't want to go back.

HANA: You can sleep with Masako tonight. Tomorrow you'll go back. And you'll remember what I told you. (*She puts her arms around* KIYOKO *who is overcome with self-pity and begins to weep quietly.*) Life is never easy, Kiyoko-san. Endure. Endure. Soon you'll be marrying and going away. Things will not always be this way. And you'll look back on this . . . this night and you'll . . . (*There is a rap on the door.* HANA *exchanges glances with* KIYOKO *and goes to answer it. She opens it a crack.* OKA *has come looking for* KIYOKO. *He's dressed in an overcoat and holds a wet newspaper over his head.*)

OKA: Ah! I'm sorry to bother you so late at night . . . the fact is . . .

HANA: Oka-san . . .

OKA: (*Jovially.*) Good evening, good evening . . . (*He sees* KIYOKO.) Ah . . . there you are . . . Did you have a nice visit?

HANA: (*Irritated.*) Yes, she's here.

OKA: (*Still cheerful.*) Thought she might be. Ready to come home now?

HANA: She came in the rain.

OKA: (*Ignoring* HANA's *tone.*) That's foolish of you, Kiyoko. You might catch cold.

HANA: She was frightened by your quarreling. She came for help.

OKA: (*Laughing with embarrassment.*) Oh! Kiyoko, that's nothing to worry about. It's just we had some disagreement . . .

HANA: That's what I told her, but she was frightened all the same.

OKA: Children are . . .

HANA: Not children, Oka-san. Kiyoko. Kiyoko was terrified. I think that was a terrible thing to do to her.

OKA: (*Rubbing his head.*) Oh, I . . . I . . .

HANA: If you had seen her a few minutes ago . . . hysterical . . . shaking . . . crying . . . wet and cold to the bone . . . out of her mind with worry.

OKA: (*Rubbing his head.*) Oh . . . I . . . don't know what she was so worried bout.

HANA: You. You and Emiko fighting like you were going to kill each other.

OKA: (*There's nothing more to hide. He lowers his head in penitence.*) Aaaaaachhhhhhh . . .

HANA: I know I shouldn't tell you this, but there're one or two things I have to say: You sent for Kiyoko-san and now she's here. You said yourself she had a bad time in Japan, and now she's having a worse time. It isn't easy for her in a strange new country; the least you can do is try to keep her from worrying . . . especially about yourselves. I think it's terrible what you're doing to her . . . terrible!

OKA: (*Bowing in deep humility.*) I am ashamed . . .

HANA: I think she deserves better. I think you should think about that.

OKA: (*Still in his bow.*) I thank you for this reminder. It will never happen again. I promise.

HANA: I don't need that promise. Make it to Kiyoko-san.

OKA: (*To* KIYOKO.) Come with Papa now. He did a bad thing. He'll be a good Papa from now. He won't worry his little girl again. All right? All right? (*They move to the door.*)

KIYOKO: Thank you so much. (*She takes* MURATA's *robe and tries to return it.*)

OKA: Madam. I thank you again.

HANA: (*To* KIYOKO.) That's all right. You can bring it back tomorrow. (*Aside to* KIYOKO.) Remember . . . remember what we talked about. (*Loudly.*) Goodnight, Oka-san. (*They leave.* HANA *goes to* MASAKO *who lies on the bed. She covers her.* MURATA *appears from the bedroom. He's heard it all. He and* HANA *exchange a glance and together they retire to their room.*)

Fade out.

SCENE THREE

The next morning. The Murata house and yard. HANA *and* MURATA
have already left the house to examine the rain damage in the fields.
MASAKO *prepares to go to school. She puts on a coat and picks up her books
and lunch bag. Meanwhile,* KIYOKO *slips quietly into the yard. She
wears a coat and carries* MURATA's *robe and sets it on the outside bench.*
MASAKO *walks out and is surprised to see* KIYOKO.

MASAKO: Hi. I thought you'd be . . . sick today.

KIYOKO: Oh. I woke up late.

MASAKO: (*Scrutinizing* KIYOKO's *face.*) Your eyes are red.

KIYOKO: (*Averting her eyes.*) Oh. I . . . got . . . sand in it. Yes.

MASAKO: Do you want to use eye drops? We have eye drops in the
house.

KIYOKO: Oh . . . no. That's all right.

MASAKO: That's what you call bloodshot.

KIYOKO: Oh.

MASAKO: My father gets it a lot. When he drinks too much.

KIYOKO: Oh . . . (MASAKO *notices* KIYOKO *doesn't have her lunch.*)

MASAKO: Where's your lunch bag?

KIYOKO: I . . . forgot it.

MASAKO: Did you make your lunch today?

KIYOKO: Yes. Yes, I did. But I forgot it.

MASAKO: Do you want to go back and get it?

KIYOKO: No, that's all right. (*They are silent for a while.*) We'll be
late.

MASAKO: Do you want to practice your words?

KIYOKO: (*Thoughtfully.*) Oh . . .

MASAKO: Say, "My."

KIYOKO: My?

MASAKO: Eyes . . .

KIYOKO: Eyes.

MASAKO: Are . . .

KIYOKO: Are.

MASAKO: Red.

KIYOKO: Red.

MASAKO: Your eyes are red. (KIYOKO *doesn't repeat it.*) I . . .
(KIYOKO *doesn't cooperate.*) Say, "I."

KIYOKO: I.

MASAKO: Got . . .

KIYOKO: Got.

MASAKO: Sand . . . (KIYOKO *balks.*) Say, "I."

KIYOKO: (*Sighing.*) I.

MASAKO: Reft . . .

KIYOKO: Reft.

MASAKO: My . . .

KIYOKO: My.

MASAKO: Runch . . .

KIYOKO: Run . . . Lunch. (*She stops.*) Masako-san, you are mean. You are hurting me.

MASAKO: It's a joke! I was just trying to make you laugh!

KIYOKO: I cannot laugh today.

MASAKO: Sure you can. You can laugh. Laugh! Like this! (*She makes a hearty laugh.*)

KIYOKO: I cannot laugh when you make fun of me.

MASAKO: Okay, I'm sorry. We'll practice some other words then, okay? (KIYOKO *doesn't answer.*) Say, "Okay."

KIYOKO: (*Reluctantly.*) Okay . . .

MASAKO: Okay, then . . . um . . . um . . . (*She still teases and talks rapidly.*) Say . . . um . . . "She sells sea shells on the sea shore." (KIYOKO *turns away indignantly.*) Aw, come on, Kiyoko! It's just a joke. Laugh!

KIYOKO: (*Imitating sarcastically.*) Ha-ha-ha! Now you say, "*Kono kyaku wa yoku kaki ku kyaku da!*"

MASAKO: Sure! I can say it! Kono kyaku waki ku kyoku kaku . . .

KIYOKO: That's not right.

MASAKO: Koki kuki kya . . .

KIYOKO: No.

MASAKO: Okay, then. You say, "Sea sells she shells . . . shu . . . sss . . ." (*They both laugh,* KIYOKO *with her hands over her mouth.*)

MASAKO: (*Taking* KIYOKO'*s hands from her mouth.*) Not like that! Like this! (*She gives a big belly laugh.*)

KIYOKO: Like this? (*She imitates* MASAKO.)

MASAKO: Yeah, that's right! You're not mad anymore?

KIYOKO: I'm not mad anymore.

MASAKO: Okay. You can share my lunch today because we're . . .

KIYOKO: "Flends?" (MASAKO *looks at* KIYOKO, *they giggle and move on.* HANA *and* MURATA *come in from assessing the storm's damage. They are dressed warmly.* HANA *is depressed.* MURATA *tries hard to be cheerful.*)

MURATA: It's not so bad, Mama.

HANA: Half the ranch is flooded . . . at least half.

MURATA: No-no. A quarter, maybe. It's sunny today . . . it'll dry.

HANA: The seedlings will rot.

MURATA: No, no. It'll dry. It's all right—better than I expected.

HANA: If we have another bad year, no one will lend us money for the next crop.

MURATA: Don't worry. If it doesn't drain by tomorrow, I'll replant the worst places. We still have some seed left. Yeah, I'll replant . . .

HANA: More work.

MURATA: Don't worry, Mama. It'll be all right.

HANA: (*Quietly.*) Papa, where will it end? Will we always be like this—always at the mercy of the weather—prices—always at the mercy of the Gods?

MURATA: (*Patting* HANA's *back.*) Things will change. Wait and see. We'll be back in Japan by . . . in two years . . . guarantee . . . Maybe sooner.

HANA: (*Dubiously.*) Two years . . .

MURATA: (*Finds the robe on the bench.*) Ah, look, Mama. Kiyoko-san brought back my robe.

HANA: (*Sighing.*) Kiyoko-san . . . poor Kiyoko-san . . . and Emiko-san.

MURATA: Ah, Mama. We're lucky. We're lucky, Mama. (HANA *smiles sadly at* MURATA.)

Fade out.

SCENE FOUR

The following spring, afternoon. Exterior of the Oka house. Oka is dressed to go out. He wears a sweater, long sleeved white shirt, dark pants, no tie. He puts his foot on the bench to wipe off his shoe with the palm of his hand. He straightens his sleeve, removes a bit of lint, and runs his fingers through his hair. He hums under his breath. KIYOKO *comes from the house. Her hair is frizzled with a permanent wave, she wears a gaudy new dress and a pair of new shoes. She carries a movie magazine—Photoplay or Modern Screen.*

OKA: (*Appreciatively.*) Pretty. Pretty.

KIYOKO: (*Turning for him.*) It's' not too *hadeh?* I feel strange in colors.

OKA: Oh no. Young girls should wear bright colors. There's time enough to wear gray when you get old. Old lady colors. (KIYOKO *giggles.*) Sure you want to go to the picture show? It's such a nice day . . . shame to waste in a dark hall.

KIYOKO: Where else can we go?

OKA: We can go to the Muratas.

KIYOKO: All dressed up?

OKA: Or Nagatas. I'll show him what I got for my horse.

KIYOKO: (*Laughing.*) Oh, I love the pictures.

OKA: We don't have many nice spring days like this. Here the season is short. Summer comes in like a dragon . . . right behind . . breathing fire . . . like a dragon. You don't know the summers here. They'll scare you. (*He tousles* KIYOKO's *hair and pulls a lock of it. It springs back. He shakes his head in wonder.*) Goddamn. Curly hair. Never thought curly hair could make you so happy.

KIYOKO: (*Giggling.*) All the American girls have curly hair.

OKA: Your friend Masako like it?

KIYOKO: (*Nodding.*) She says her mother will never let her get a permanent wave.

OKA: She said that, eh? Bet she's wanting one.

KIYOKO: I don't know about that.

OKA: Bet she's wanting some of your pretty dresses too.

KIYOKO: Her mother makes all her clothes.

OKA: Buying is just as good. Buying is better. No trouble that way.

KIYOKO: Masako's not so interested in clothes. She loves the pictures, but her mother won't let her go. Some day, can we take Masako with us?

OKA: If her mother lets her come. Her mother's got a mind of her own . . . a stiff back.

KIYOKO: But she's nice.

OKA: (*Dubiously.*) Oh, yeah. Can't be perfect, I guess. Kiyoko, after the harvest I'll have money and I'll buy you the prettiest dress in town. I'm going to be lucky this year. I feel it.

KIYOKO: You're already too good to me . . . dresses, shoes, permanent wave . . . movies . . .

OKA: That's nothing. After the harvest, just wait . . .

KIYOKO: Magazines . . . You do enough. I'm happy already.

OKA: You make me happy too, Kiyoko. You make me feel good . . . like a man again . . . (*That statement bothers him.*)

One day you're going to make a young man happy. (KIYOKO *giggles.*) Someday we going to move from here.

KIYOKO: But we have good friends here, Papa.

OKA: Next year our lease will be up and we got to move.

KIYOKO: The ranch is not ours?

OKA: No. In America, Japanese cannot own land. We lease and move every two, three years. Next year we going to go someplace where there's young fellows. There's none good enough for you here. (*He watches* KIYOKO *giggle.*) Yeah. You going to make a good wife. Already a good cook. I like your cooking.

KIYOKO: (*A little embarrassed.*) Shall we go now?

OKA: Yeah. Put the magazine away.

KIYOKO: I want to take it with me.

OKA: Take it with you?

KIYOKO: Last time, after we came back, I found all my magazines torn in half.

OKA: (*Looking toward the house.*) Torn?

KIYOKO: This is the only one I have left.

OKA: (*Not wanting to deal with it.*) All right. All right. (*The two prepare to leave when the door opens.* EMIKO *stands there, her hair is unkempt and she looks wild. She holds an empty can in one hand, the lid in the other.*)

EMIKO: Where is it? (OKA *tries to make a hasty departure.*)

KIYOKO: Where is what? (OKA *pushes* KIYOKO *ahead of him, still trying to make a getaway.*)

EMIKO: Where is it? Where is it? What did you do with it? (EMIKO *moves toward* OKA. *He can't ignore her and he stops.*)

OKA: (*With false unconcern to* KIYOKO.) Why don't you walk on ahead to the Muratas?

KIYOKO: We're not going to the pictures?

OKA: We'll go. First you walk to the Muratas. Show them your new dress. I'll meet you there. (KIYOKO *picks up a small package and exits.* OKA *sighs and shakes his head.*)

EMIKO: (*Shaking the can.*) Where is it? What did you do with it?

OKA: (*Feigning surprise.*) With what?

EMIKO: You know what. You stole it. You stole my money.

OKA: *Your* money?

EMIKO: I've been saving that money.

OKA: Yeah? Well, where'd you get it? Where'd you get it, eh? You stole it from me! Dollar by dollar . . . You stole it from me! Out of my pocket!

EMIKO: I saved it!

OKA: From my pocket!

EMIKO: It's mine! I saved for a long time . . . Some of it I brought from Japan.

OKA: *Bakayuna!* What'd you bring from Japan? Nothing but some useless kimonos. (OKA *starts to leave but* EMIKO *hangs on to him.*)

EMIKO: Give back my money! Thief!

OKA: (*Swings around and balls his fists but doesn't strike.*) Goddamn! Get off me!

EMIKO: (*Now pleading.*) Please give it back . . . please . . . please . . . (*She starts to stroke him.* OKA *pulls her hands away and pushes her from him.*) Oni!

OKA: (*Seething.*) Oni? What does that make you? *Oni baba?* Yeah, that's what you are . . . a devil!

EMIKO: It's mine! Give it back . . .

OKA: The hell! You think you can live off me and steal my money too? How stupid you think I am?

EMIKO: (*Tearfully.*) But I've paid . . . I've paid . . .

OKA: With what?

EMIKO: You know I've paid.

OKA: (*Scoffing.*) You call that paying?

EMIKO: What did you do with it?

OKA: I don't have it.

EMIKO: It's gone? It's gone?

OKA: Yeah! It's gone. I spent it. The hell! Every last cent.

EMIKO: The new clothes . . . the curls . . . restaurants . . . pictures . . . shoes . . . My money . . . my going-home money . . .

OKA: You through?

EMIKO: What will I do? What will . . .

OKA: I don't care what you do. Walk. Use your feet. Swim to Japan. I don't care. I give you no more than you gave me. Now I don't want anything. I don't care what you do. (*He walks away.*)

EMIKO *still holds the empty can. Off stage we hear* OKA's *car door slam and the sound of his old car starting off. Accustomed to crying alone, she doesn't utter a sound. Her shoulders begin to shake, her dry soundless sobs turn to a silent laugh. She wipes the dust gently from the can as though comforting a friend. Her movements become sensuous, her hands move on to her own body, around her throat, over her breasts, to her hips, caressing, soothing, reminding her of her lover's hands.*

Fade out.

SCENE FIVE

Same day, late afternoon. Exterior of the Murata house. The light is soft.
HANA *is sweeping the yard;* MASAKO *hangs a glass wind chime on the exposed wall.*

HANA: (*Directing* MASAKO.)There . . . there. That's a good place.

MASAKO: Here?

HANA: (*Nodding.*) It must catch the slightest breeze. (*Sighing and listening.*) It brings back so much . . . That's the reason I never hung one before. I guess it doesn't matter much any more . . .

MASAKO: I thought you liked to think about Japan.

HANA: (*Laughing sadly.*) I didn't want to hear that sound so often . . . get too used to it. Sometimes you hear something too often, after a while you don't hear it anymore . . . I didn't want that to happen. The same thing happens to feelings too, I guess. After a while you don't feel any more. You're too young to understand that yet.

MASAKO: I understand, Mama.

HANA: Wasn't it nice of Kiyoko-san to give us the *furin?*

MASAKO: I love it. I don't know anything about Japan, but it makes me feel something too.

HANA: Maybe someday when you're grown up, gone away, you'll hear it and remember yourself as this little girl . . . remember this old house, the ranch, and . . . your old mama . . .

MASAKO: That's kind of scary. (EMIKO *enters unsteadily. She carries a bundle wrapped in a colorful scarf "furoshiki". In the package are two beautiful kimonos.*)

HANA: Emiko-san! What a pleasant surprise! Please sit down. We were just hanging the *furin.* It was so sweet of Kiyoko-san to give it to Masako. She loves it. (EMIKO *looks mildly interested. She acts as normal as she can throughout the scene, but at times drops her facade, revealing her desperation.*)

EMIKO: Thank you. (*She sets her bundle on the bench but keeps her hand on it.*)

HANA: Your family was here earlier. (EMIKO *smiles vaguely.*) On their way to the pictures, I think. (*To* MASAKO.) Make tea for us, Ma-chan.

EMIKO: Please don't . . .

HANA: Kiyoko-san was looking so nice—her hair all curly . . . Of course, in our day, straight black hair was desirable. Of course, times change.

EMIKO: Yes.

HANA: But she did look fine. My, my, a colorful new dress, new shoes, a permanent wave—looked like a regular American girl. Did you choose her dress?

EMIKO: No . . . I didn't go.

HANA: You know, I didn't think so. Very pretty though. I liked it very much. Of course, I sew all Masako's clothes. It saves money. It'll be nice for you to make things for Kiyoko-san too. She'd be so pleased. I know she'd be pleased . . . (*While* HANA *talks,* EMIKO *plucks nervously at her package. She waits for* HANA *to stop talking.*) Emiko-san, is everything all right?

EMIKO: (*Smiling nervously.*) Yes.

HANA: Masako, please go make tea for us. See if there aren't any more of those crackers left. Or did you finish them? (*To* EMIKO.) We can't keep anything in this house. She eats everything as soon as Papa brings it home. You'd never know it, she's so skinny. We never have anything left for company.

MASAKO: We hardly ever have company anyway. (HANA *gives her daughter a strong look, and* MASAKO *goes into the house.* EMIKO *is lost in her own thoughts. She strokes her package.*)

HANA: Is there something you . . . I can help you with? (*Very gently.*) Emiko-san?

EMIKO: (*Suddenly frightened.*) Oh no. I was thinking . . . Now that . . . now that . . . Masa-chan is growing up . . . older . . .

HANA: (*Relieved.*) Oh, yes. She's growing fast.

EMIKO: I was thinking . . . (*She stops, puts the package on her lap and is lost again.*)

HANA: Yes, she *is* growing. Time goes so fast. I think she'll be taller than me soon. (*She laughs weakly, stops and looks puzzled.*)

EMIKO: Yes. (EMIKO's *depression pervades the atmosphere.* HANA *is affected by it. The two women sit in silence. A small breeze moves the wind chimes. At the moment light grows dim on the two lonely figures.* MASAKO *comes from the house with a tray of tea. The light returns to normal again.*)

HANA: (*Gently.*) You're a good girl. (MASAKO *looks first to* EMIKO *then to her mother. She sets the tray on the bench and stands near* EMIKO *who seems to notice her for the first time.*)

EMIKO: How are you? (HANA *pours the tea and serves her.*)

HANA: Emiko-san, is there something I can do for you?

EMIKO: There's . . . I was . . . I . . . Masa-chan will be a young lady soon . . .

HANA: Oh, well, now I don't know about "lady."

EMIKO: Maybe she would like a nice . . . nice . . . (*She unwraps her package.*) I have kimonos . . . I wore in Japan for dancing . . . maybe she can . . . if you like, I mean. They'll be nice on her . . . she's so slim . . . (EMIKO *shakes out a robe.* HANA *and* MASAKO *are impressed.*)

HANA: Ohhhh! Beautiful!

MASAKO: Oh, Mama! Pretty! (HANA *and* MASAKO *finger the material.*) Gold threads, Mama.

HANA: Brocade!

EMIKO: Maybe Masa-chan would like them. I mean for her school programs . . . Japanese school . . .

HANA: Oh, no! Too good for country. People will be envious of us . . . wonder where we got them.

EMIKO: I mean for festivals . . . *Obon, Hana Matsuri* . . .

HANA: Oh, but you have Kiyoko-san now. You should give them to her. Has she seen them?

EMIKO: Oh . . . no . . .

HANA: She'll love them. You should give them to her . . . not our Masako.

EMIKO: I thought . . . I mean I was thinking of . . . if you could give me a little . . . if you could pay . . . manage to give me something for . . .

HANA: But these gowns, Emiko-san—they're worth hundreds.

EMIKO: I know, but I'm not asking for that. Whatever you can give . . . only as much as you can give.

MASAKO: Mama?

HANA: Masako, Papa doesn't have that kind of money.

EMIKO: Anything you can give . . . anything . . .

MASAKO: Ask Papa.

HANA: There's no use asking. I know he can't afford it.

EMIKO: (*Looking at* MASAKO.) A little at a time.

MASAKO: Mama?

HANA: (*Firmly.*) No, Masako. This is a luxury. (HANA *folds the gowns and puts them away.* MASAKO *is disappointed.* EMIKO *is devastated.* HANA *sees this and tries to find some way to help.*) Emiko-san, I hope you understand . . . (EMIKO *is silent trying to gather her resources.*) I know you can sell them and get the full price somewhere. Let's see . . . a family with a lot of growing daughters . . someone who did well last year . . . Nagatas have no girls . . . Umedas have girls but no money . . . Well,

let's see . . . Maybe not here in this country town.
Ah . . . You can take them to the city, Los Angeles, and sell
them to a store . . . or Terminal Island . . . lots of wealthy
fisherman there. Yes, that would be the place. Why, it's no
problem, Emiko-san. Have your husband take them there. I
know you'll get your money. He'll find a buyer. I know he will.

EMIKO: Yes. (EMIKO *finishes folding and ties the scarf. She sits quietly.*)

HANA: Please have your tea. I'm sorry . . . I really would like to
take them for Masako but it just isn't possible. You understand,
don't you? (EMIKO *nods.*) Please don't feel so . . . so bad. It's
not really a matter of life or death, is it? Emiko-san? (EMIKO
nods again. HANA *sips her tea.*)

MASAKO: Mama? If you could ask Papa . . .

HANA: Oh, the tea is cold. Masako could you heat the kettle?

EMIKO: No more. I must be going. (*She picks up her package and rises
slowly.*)

HANA: (*Looking helpless.*) So soon? Emiko-san, please stay. (EMIKO
starts go.) Masako will walk with you. (*She pushes* MASAKO
forward.)

EMIKO: It's not far.

HANA: Emiko-san? You'll be all right?

EMIKO: Yes . . . yes . . . yes . . .

HANA: (*Calling as* EMIKO *exits.*) I'm sorry, Emiko-san.

EMIKO: Yes . . . (MASAKO *and* HANA *watch as* EMIKO *leaves. The
light grows dim as though a cloud passed over.* EMIKO *exits.* HANA
strokes MASAKO's *hair.*)

HANA: Your hair is so black and straight . . . nice . . . (*They
stand close. The wind chimes tinkle; light grows dim. Light returns to
normal.* MURATA *enters. He sees this tableau of mother and child and
is puzzled.*)

MURATA: What's going on here? (*The two women part.*)

HANA: Oh . . . nothing . . . nothing . . .

MASAKO: Mrs. Oka was here. She had two kimo- . . . . .

HANA: (*Putting her hand on* MASAKO's *shoulder.*) It was
nothing . . .

MURATA: Eh? What'd she want?

HANA: Later, Papa. Right now, I'd better fix supper.

MURATA: (*Looking at the sky.*) Strange how that sun comes and
goes. Maybe I didn't need to irrigate—looks like rain. (*He
remembers and is exasperated.*) Ach! I forgot to shut the water.

MASAKO: I'll do it, Papa.

HANA: Masako, that gate's too heavy for you.

MURATA: She can handle it. Take out the pin and let the gate fall all the way down. All the way. And put the pin back. Don't forget to put the pin back.

HANA: And be careful. Don't fall in the canal. (MASAKO *leaves.*)

MURATA: What's the matter with that girl?

HANA: Nothing. Why?

MURATA: Usually have to beg her to do . . .

HANA: She's growing up.

MURATA: Must be that time of the month.

HANA: Oh, Papa, she's too young for that yet.

MURATA: (*Genially as they enter the house.*) Got to start some time. Looks like I'll be out-numbered soon. I'm out-numbered already. (HANA *glances at him and quietly sets about preparations for supper.* MURATA *removes his shirt and sits at the table with a paper. Light fades slowly.*)

Fade out.

SCENE SIX

Same evening. Exterior, desert. There is at least one shrub. MASAKO *appears, walking slowly. From a distance we hear* EMIKO *singing the song: "And the Soul Shall Dance."* MASAKO *looks around, sees the shrub and crouches under it.* EMIKO *appears. She's dressed in her beautiful kimono tied loosely at her waist. She carries a branch of sage. Her hair is loose.*

EMIKO: *Akai kuchibiru/ Kappu ni yosete/ Aoi sake nomya/ Kokoro ga odoru . . . Kurai yoru no yume/ Setsu nasa yo . . .*

She breaks into a dance, laughs mysteriously, turns round and round, acting out a fantasy. MASAKO *stirs uncomfortably.* EMIKO *senses a presence. She stops, drops her branch and walks off stage singing as she goes.*

EMIKO: *Aoi sake nomya/ Yume mo odoru . . .*

MASAKO *watches as* EMIKO *leaves. She rises slowly and picks up the branch* EMIKO *has left. She looks at the branch, moves forward a step and looks off to the point where* EMIKO *disappeared. Light slowly fades until only the image of* MASAKO'*s face remains etched in the mind.*

Fade out.

KOKORO GA ODORU	AND THE SOUL SHALL DANCE
Akai kuchibiru	Red lips
Cappu ni yosete	Press against a glass
Aoi sake nomya	Drink the green wine
Kokoro ga odoru	And the soul shall dance
Kurai yoru no yume	Dark night dreams
Setsu nasa yo	Are unbearable
Aoi sake nomya	Drink the green wine
Yume mo odoru	And the dreams will dance
Asa no munashisa	Morning's reality
Yume wo chirasu	Scatter the dreams
Sora to kokoro wa	Sky and soul
Sake shidai	Depend on the wine
Futari wakare no	The loneliness of
Samishisa yo	The two apart
Hitori sake nomya	Drink the wine alone
Kokoro ga odoru	And the soul shall dance

Lyrics by Wakako Yamauchi

KAGO NO TORI	THE CAGED BIRD
	(She.)
Aitasa, mita sa ni	In the desire to meet her
Kowa sa wo wasure	And the wish to see her
Kurai yomichi wo	He forgets his fear and
Tada hitori	Walks the dark streets alone.
	(He.)
Aini kita no ni	Though I've come to tryst
Naze dete awanu?	Why do you not come out?
Boku no yobu koye	My voice calling you—
Wasure taka?	Have you forgotten it?
	(She.)
Anata no yobu koye	Your voice calling me
Wasure ma senu ga	I have not forgotten, but
Deru ni derareru	To leave, to be able to leave—
Kago no tori	No choice for the caged bird.

Popular song.

Surface Tension
Laura Farabough

Surface Tension was first produced by Nightfire at The Bay Area Playwrights Festival, August, 1981, with the following cast:

THE YOUNG GUY   John Fox
THE WOMAN   Laura Farabough

Directed by Evie Lewis
Music composed and performed for tape by David Doty
Lighting by Doug Vogel *and* Mary Ann Dunn
Voice of THE YOUNG GUY: Karl Danskin
Voice of THE WOMAN: Laura Farabough
Technical direction by Herb Manly

The revised version, here printed, toured California and the Northwest in early 1982 with the following production changes:

THE YOUNG GUY   Mark Sackett
THE WOMAN   Candra Day

Voice of THE YOUNG GUY: Martin Bates
Voice of THE WOMAN: Jane Robinson
Music performed and recorded by Other Music, San Francisco

NOTE

Surface Tension is a location piece. That is, it cannot be performed in a theater but requires competition-sized swimming and diving pools. All of the dialog is on tape.

Surface Tension
Laura Farabough

SCENE ONE

INCIDENT AT A LAKE

The audience is seated on bleachers facing the pool. There is about ten feet of deck between the audience and the water. The technicians operating the sound and light systems are visible, as are all the artifacts to be used in the play.

The houselights go out. On the rear projection screen (at least four feet by five feet) there appears a slide of two white ducks floating on a swimming pool of blue water. Downstage, on the white, saw-toothed bush the word "Incident" is projected.

Birdcalls and duck calls are heard over the sound system. Segue to music.

The underwater lights are turned on. A spotlight shines on the high diving board. A young guy in blue jeans, hip boots, red shirt, and hunter's hat is crouched at the rear end of the diving board. He hold a white shotgun.

The music is pastoral. All words are on tape.

THE YOUNG GUY: I'm looking. I'm looking. I'm looking. I'm in a blind in the dark. Anything moves, I'm gonna see it, hypnotize it, tease it, make it wanna get hit. Got my finger on the trigger and I'm sharp, I got the touch. No need to hurry, I can wait for the one I want. I'm composed; the way I like to be, doing what I like to do. And what I like to do is hunt.

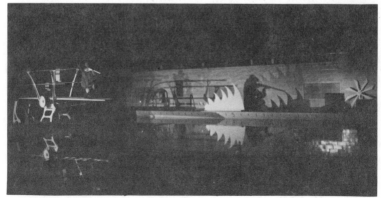

Slowly he extends himself prone on the board and, while aiming the shotgun, he inches his way forward.

A white decoy duck splashes into the water. It slowly moves across the water, heading toward the bush. The hunter aims at it. He blows on a duck call. The sounds of a duck quacking are heard over the speakers.

THE YOUNG GUY: I wish a girl would come to me as quick as that duck. These high school girls don't put out. I need a chance to score and make it work. Yeah, I wish I could get an older woman. Yeah, a college girl! Someone who's been around, knows what it is to have a job, be in trouble, on the run. Stimulated.

He stands on the end of the board, takes aim. Holding the position with his shotgun, he slowly turns around. A woman's legs rise up from behind the bush, toes pointed up. Freeze. The duck is now very close to the bush. The hunter lowers his gun, looks, then quickly takes aim at duck / woman.

THE YOUNG GUY: Now that's the one I want! She's a moving target and I'm in a fixed position.

He shoots. He falls from the high dive into the water. Lights out. Slides out. Music out.

THE YOUNG GUY: Oh, my God! What did I hit?

SCENE TWO

INCIDENT AT A POOL

On the rear projection screen appears a slide of a lifeguard, shown from the neck down, sitting in a lifeguard tower beside the pool. On the bush the word "Coincident" appears.

The lights come up, bright and full. Music begins, uptempo. The WOMAN sits by the bush. She wears a white dress, white sunglasses, and holds a beach bag. She walks around the perimeter of the pool, puts down her bag, takes a pose.

Only now does the YOUNG GUY emerge from underwater. He is wearing red swimming shorts. He goes to the lifeguard tower and sits.

The WOMAN walks to two red light poles (six feet tall, about five feet apart). She attaches two pieces of white tape to the poles so that an "x" is formed between. She stands at the center of the "x."

The music changes to slow. Lights dim. Two sunlamps, atop the poles, come on, shining on the WOMAN. *She begins to take off her dress, lifting it over her head, turning slowly.*

THE WOMAN: I work at the carnival. I can pull a hundred guys a night, easy game. I give him three rings. He throws the first, he misses. He thinks it's a game of chance. I know different; it's my game. He misses again. But the next one's a hit. I say, "What a lucky shot!" If I don't like him, I give him a stuffed animal. I'm a looker. I only take calculated risks.

The dress off, she is wearing a red, one-piece bathing suit. The lifeguard sees her. He stands on the tower and makes an aiming gesture in her direction.

The music returns to uptempo. Sunlamps out. Lighting up full.

The WOMAN *leaves the "x". The lifeguard climbs down from the tower and does slow, stretching exercises, leaning against the tower. He keeps his eye on the* WOMAN.

Moving quickly, she goes to her bag and takes out a red towel, which she spreads downstage. She does fast exercises: jumping jacks. Music changes to slow as the WOMAN *languidly puts on suntan lotion.*

Now the lifeguard is energetic and the music changes to uptempo. The WOMAN *takes off her sunglasses, approaches the racing platforms at the pool's edge. The* YOUNG GUY *gets back on his tower.*

THE YOUNG GUY: These are the rules of swimming safety.

THE WOMAN: I usually just go to the nearest pool . . .

THE YOUNG GUY: One. Do not duck anyone or hold his head under water.

THE WOMAN: Work on my body, get some exercise. (*In slow motion she takes a racing dive position.*)

THE YOUNG GUY: Two. Know your own ability and do not over-estimate it.

THE WOMAN: I survive on my surface appeal.

The rear screen projection slide changes to a close-up of a fish underwater.

THE YOUNG GUY: Three. When swimming underwater, come up to the surface as soon as you feel you need air. Be on the lookout for submerged objects.

THE WOMAN: I like to swim.

She dives into the water, starts swimming. He stands up quickly, watching her swim. He takes a life ring, whose rope is tied to the tower, and throws it into the pool.

THE YOUNG GUY: I'm a looker. I know the signs, what to look for in case of emergency. If there's any trouble, I can react with skill and precision. The trick is keeping a cool head and a sharp lookout. You have to know the difference betwen having fun and being in trouble.

THE WOMAN: (*She continues swimming, changing her stroke with each lap.*) Swimming laps is not much different than being a horse in the field, back and forth, back and forth, my brain just goes dead! I need mental stimulation. I like to imagine that I'm a champion athlete, a swimmer in an Olympic race. I have to keep swimming! I can do it, I've got this race in the bag!

I need a better reason than competition to keep swimming. I'll never make it.

Danger! Yeah, danger! Attack! I saw what they did! They're gonna kill me, maybe worse! I have to jump overboard, into the water, getaway, swimaway, swim for my life.

The lifeguard gets down from his tower, runs to the corner of the deck where several red life rings are stacked. He throws the rings into the pool.

THE YOUNG GUY: Four. When a swimmer is in trouble, get their attention, let them know help is on the way. Avoid panic!

He runs to the next corner and throws in the next group of life rings. She continues to swim.

The rear screen projection changes to a slide of the WOMAN swimming in the pool.

The lifeguard picks up his pace, very agitated. There are two more groups of life rings which he runs to and throws.

The rear screen projection changes to a close-up of a shark in a swimming pool.

THE WOMAN: It's so close! I can see it. I can make it, I can do it. Oh Christ! Sharks! Killers!

The lifeguard dives into the water. He swims frantically as she continues to swim easily.

The rear screen projection changes to a close-up of the WOMAN's hand in the water.

The lifeguard thrashes. If he comes upon a ring he throws it wildly.

THE YOUNG GUY: Where is she? Where is she? Where is she?

She swims to the ladder and climbs from the pool. She has been swimming hard for eight minutes. She goes to her towel, dries off her face, lies down, facing the pool.

THE WOMAN: Well, that's enough of that.

The lifeguard keeps up his frantic search.

THE YOUNG GUY: Is that her? Where'd she go? Is that her? I'm looking. She's been swallowed up!

THE WOMAN: (*Casually watching him, amused.*) Wow. Look at that guy. He's got a lot of energy. He's looking for me.

THE YOUNG GUY: (*Exhausted.*) I can't lose her! What if this were the ocean, she'd really be in trouble. Danger! Sharks. Oh God! I can't see! I need air! (*He collapses and sinks underwater.*)

Lights, slides, and music all out.

SCENE THREE

INCIDENT AT A CARNIVAL

The WOMAN *is near the projection screen. She is lying down, her back arched, head thrown back. A picture of a carnival booth appears on the projection screen. It is a close-up of stuffed dolphins, prizes at a shooting gallery.*

On the bush is projected the word "Simulate." The lights are low, the underwater lights are on. Mysterious music begins.

The WOMAN *slowly rises, moving stealthily to the other side of the pool. She picks up a rope and begins to pull. At the other end of the rope is a long object covered by a white cloth, attached to a red life ring. It looks like a corpse in a shroud.*

THE WOMAN: A good pitchman has a line the peeps can't resist. So I tell'em, "Easy game! Nothing to it! See how it's done. Take a look. Identify what you see. Estimate its speed. Anticipate its upcoming position. Ring a cone and win a prize."

Simultaneously, she lifts the corpse out of the water and the YOUNG GUY, *who has swum across the pool underwater, throws himself across the side, half out of the water.*

The WOMAN *hides the corpse behind a red tile, six of which are lined up along the far side of the pool. The* YOUNG GUY *goes to the high diving board. He does a forward dive with a half twist.*

THE YOUNG GUY: What was that? What happened to me? I almost
drowned rescuing a woman who didn't even need me. I went
after her and she wasn't even there! I have to be more careful.
Crime! Mystery! Cement Shoes! I fall for mystery hook, line,
and sinker. I just transport, you know, telejump into . . . Sam
Spade!

The WOMAN *is engaged in setting up the carnival. Behind each tile is a
pipe stand and on the ground are red poles with white pinwheels
attached. She lifts the poles and places them in the stands, one by one
until all six pinwheels are up.*

The YOUNG GUY *climbs from the pool, goes to the highdive, does an
inward dive, pike position, from the back approach.*

THE YOUNG GUY: I read too much. Most of the time I go to school.
I practice highdiving and compete in shows, meets. It's another
place I like to score. I shoot ducks, skeet, and trap. I'm a pretty
athletic guy. I've got a sensitized imagination, stimulated by
science fiction and detective mysteries.

The WOMAN *continues her tasks as he gets out of the pool, mounts the
highdive, and does a reverse dive, one somersault, tuck position.*

*Along the width-end of the pool are seven white circles, three feet in
diameter. The* WOMAN *goes to the circle closest to her and kneels behind
it. She flips the object into the water, revealing it to be a cone, three feet
tall and sharply pointed, attached to the remaining circles by a line. It*

floats on the water. She goes along the row of circles, repeating her action until all seven cones float on the water, connected by lengths of rope.

THE WOMAN: I started out as a bathing beauty. I love water. It's the perfect playground. I guess you could say I grew up soaking wet. I love swimming pools. You can let your imagination run wild and dangerous in them; they're safe. I used to swim in a friend's pool, and sometimes her daddy would swim laps. In World War II his ship was torpedoed and a shark ate his leg. And I used to think his swimming pool was that same ocean, full of sharks, bloodthirsty, hungry to eat us all. (*She stops, turning to look at the* YOUNG GUY *in the water.*) That guy.

He gets out of the pool, goes to the highdive, and does a back dive, one somersault, tuck position. The WOMAN *has a lead line. She starts to walk, very slowly, pulling the cones across the pool.*

THE WOMAN: My girlfriend and I used to put oranges in our bikini tops and prance around the pool acting like we were Miss Nevada and Miss Coppertone, and I used to hope that her brother would really think I was that stacked. (*She stops, turns, looks at the* YOUNG GUY *in the water.*) That guy in the water.

He gets out of the pool, goes to the highdive, and does a reverse dive, straight position, forward approach. The WOMAN *continues walking.*

THE WOMAN: I learned about kissing in the water. It's easy, you know, to fool around in a swimming pool. Everything just melts away, reasons — "Why not?" — just roll away like water off a duck's back.

On the projection screen the slide changes to a picture of a neon cone — a close-up of a carnival ride. The WOMAN *stops, turns, looks at the man in the water.*

THE WOMAN: That guy in the water makes me feel things. (*He gets out of the pool, goes to the highdive, does a forward flying double somersault. The projection slide changes to another picture of a neon cone.*) I used to love lifeguards, my handsome heroes. I used to dream up disasters and imagine being rescued, held in the water, carried to the safety of a deserted beach. All summer I'd just sit on my little towel until I got so hot I'd just have to dive in and cool off.

There are chance, pick-up connections between the WOMAN *and the*

YOUNG GUY, *based on their familiarity with the music and the language of moves they share. She stops, turns, looks at him in the water.*

THE WOMAN: That guy. (*He gets out of the pool, goes to the highdive, and does a back lay-out.*) I used to love to play the 'pick the duck out of the water' game at the carnival. One time I went out with some girlfriends and met the guy who operated the Scream Machine. He had tatoos, and he was young and goodlooking, and not too stupid. Like that guy in the water. (*She stops, turns, and looks at him in the water.*) And he made me feel things like I'd never imagined. I dropped out of high school and hung out with him for a long time and then we broke up. He joined the Navy, and I worked with the pitchman for Ring a Cone/Win a Prize, and then he split. And now it's my game, and it's been my game for a hell of a long time.

Meanwhile the YOUNG GUY *gets out of the water. He dries himself off with a towel. The* WOMAN *is now at the far end of the pool. The cones form a diagonal line across the pool. She ties off her line. He puts on a white t-shirt, she a pair of jeans and a hunter's hat.*

Sound effects of carnival segue to carnival music. The projection screen slide changes to a full shot of a carnival ride.

The WOMAN *goes to the pinwheels and spins them. Laser light bounces off reflective material on the pinwheels. The* YOUNG GUY *looks toward the woman, runs his hand through his hair, walks a little way toward her.*

THE YOUNG GUY: I wonder what I can pick up at the carnival tonight? Yeah! I can relate to this! I'm not dead from the neck up!

THE WOMAN: (*Leans on the lifeguard tower, looks at him.*) Well, look who's coming my way, that young guy. Oh, I can tell, he's a real winner.

THE YOUNG GUY: (*Approaching her rapidly. She busies herself with the pinwheels then turns, faces him, puts hands on his shoulders.*) Hey, Angel baby, what's your game?

THE WOMAN: What do you want it to be?

She releases him and runs. She stops and looks at him. He follows.

THE YOUNG GUY: What do I get if I win? What's at the top of the line?

THE WOMAN: A mystery prize. Play and find out? (*Again she puts
her hands on his shoulders, then turns to run away.*)

THE YOUNG GUY: Okay. I'm game.

*He follows her. They run around the pool to a red rowboat downstage.
They each grab an end of the boat, swing it back and forth, throw it into
the water. The woman is holding the leadline. She brings the boat
alongside. He gets into the boat, she pushes him out into the pool.*

THE WOMAN: Ring a cone, win a prize.

*He has two red rings which he uses to paddle the boat. He heads for the
furthest one. The* WOMAN *runs back to the pinwheels, picks up three red
rings which she throws to the man. He catches them and tosses one onto
the first cone.*

THE WOMAN: Gotta winner! Solid gold!

*She throws him a prize: a pair of giant sunglasses. He catches them and
starts toward the second cone. She throws him three more red rings. He
catches them and rings the second cone.*

THE WOMAN: Hey! You're pretty sharp. That's two!

*She throws him a giant beer bottle which he catches. He moves on. She
throws two more red rings which he catches and tosses onto the third cone.*

THE WOMAN: You got the touch, killer. That's three!

The next prize is a toy shotgun. She aims it at him, then throws it. He catches it and moves on. He tosses a ring over the fourth cone.

THE WOMAN: Four in a row! You've got a chance to go all the way tonight!

She goes behind the tile to where she stowed the corpse. She drags it out, unwraps it, holds up a lifesized inflatable doll in a red bathing suit. She throws the doll in the water. It floats face up, its arms in the air. The YOUNG GUY *throws himself down in the boat.*

THE YOUNG GUY: Gross! What is it? Don't touch it! Everybody freeze!

THE WOMAN: (*Taking off her jeans.*) Don't get excited.

THE YOUNG GUY: (*Sits back in boat. Acts cool.*) I'm not gonna get excited over that. I practice saving dummies all the time.

She climbs the lifeguard tower, takes a bathing-beauty pose. The projection slide changes to a close-up of cones in a ring-toss game.

THE WOMAN: Why not try for a real one?

THE YOUNG GUY: What, a real dummy?

THE WOMAN: No, a real girl, this is the top of the line, just take a shot at me.

He rings the last cone. The projection slide changes to a neon sign, "Shoot" from a carnival booth. She jumps into the pool and swims toward the boat with only her hand above water. He reaches for her and falls overboard.

THE YOUNG GUY: Oh. What kind of game is this?

Lights, slides, music all out.

SCENE FOUR

INCIDENT AT A BOARDWALK

The projection changes to a picture of the ocean. On the bush is projected the word "Synchronize." Sound of the ocean. Lights come on dimly, underwater lights on.

The YOUNG GUY *and the* WOMAN *sit at the edge of the pool, the boat in the water in front of them. She gets up, puts on her white beach dress and a pair of white high heels. He combs his hair.*

The music is pastoral, romantic.

He helps her into the boat, gets in after her. He guides them across the pool. There is a powerful flashlight in the bottom of the boat which she turns on. They become underlit.

They reach the other side. He gets out, ties off the boat, helps her out. She hands him the flashlight, and he guides their way down the pool deck.

The slide projection changes to a photo of Sutro Baths.

He puts down the flashlight. They get on the one-meter board and together they dive in. They couple-swim, synchronized. They do somer-saults. Her high heels are still on. After a while he gets out, goes to the flashlight, and turns the beam on her. She stops in the water and looks around.

THE WOMAN: Where is he? Where is he? Where'd he go? What are you doing? (*She swims to the edge and looks at him.*)

THE YOUNG GUY: You know, it scares me to death when someone wants me that bad. (*She swims across the pool, gets out by the ladder, stands near him.*)

THE WOMAN: Take it easy. (*She touches his face, walks away from him. She lies down on her back, lifts one leg in the air.*)

THE YOUNG GUY: (*Approaches her, takes off her shoe, throws it behind him.*) Yeah, I like safety but I'm a sucker for danger. (*She lifts her other leg and he takes off that shoe, and tosses it.*)

THE WOMAN: Good. I'll take you someplace I'll bet you've never been before.

SCENE FIVE

INCIDENT AT A BAR

On the projection screen the slide changes to a close-up of a neon sign for a bar. It is a circle with a cocktail glass in it, and the name of the bar, The Circle Club, written around the circle.

Sounds of a barroom: glasses tinkling, bar talk, pool balls. The sounds segue to music.

The WOMAN rolls into the pool. She swims diagonally. The YOUNG GUY rolls in after; he swims "over her." He is holding the flashlight. They meet in the shallow end. He shines the flashlight on them.

THE YOUNG GUY: So what do you do exactly?

THE WOMAN: I'm a sitting duck. I'm a prize in a shooting gallery, what you see is what you get. (*Getting out of the pool, she goes to the sunlamps, takes a pose similar to her pose in scene two. Her white dress is soaking wet.*)

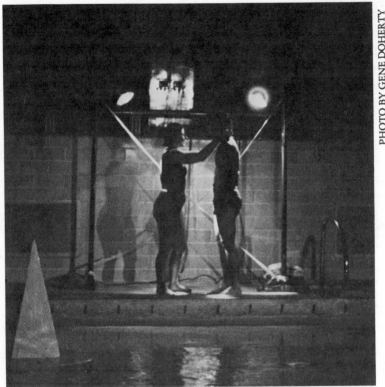

THE YOUNG GUY: I like what I see. (*He gets out of the pool, approaches her. She pulls him into the area of the "x."*)

THE WOMAN: You know, you won the night.

THE YOUNG GUY: Yeah, I know that.

She puts his hands on her body. He is shy. She is helping him. He holds the bottom of her dress, her hands are on top of his; slowly they turn and lift her dress over her head.

THE WOMAN: Honey, I'm fairly dangerous. You're admiring my tail feathers when you ought to be checking out my teeth.

The YOUNG GUY *backs away from her. The sunlamps are on. She is frozen in a pose, bent at the waist with her dress almost off.*

THE YOUNG GUY: Uh, you wanna play some pool?

The WOMAN *takes off her dress, and tosses it. She shrugs, turns around. The* YOUNG GUY *is running away. She follows.*

THE WOMAN: Sure. I'm a pool shark, what're the stakes?

THE YOUNG GUY: Winner's choice. (*He puts on a white jumpsuit and a white bathing cap. He climbs the highdive.*)

THE WOMAN: Great. I'll rack up the balls. It's your shot.

The WOMAN *goes to the fifteen beachballs that are attached into a triangle formation. She eases them into the water, grabs the lead line, and dives in. She swims the balls into position under the diving board. She swims to the side and climbs out.*

On the projection screen the slide changes to a picture of pool balls with a cue ball heading toward them.

The YOUNG GUY *does a cannonball jump. He lands on the balls and sends them flying.*

THE YOUNG GUY: Did I hit it?

Lights, slides, music all out.

SCENE SIX

INCIDENT AT THE SITE

On the projection screen the slide changes to a picture of a corner of a swimming pool. On the bush, the word "Site." Underwater lights on. Music slow.

The YOUNG GUY *has changed clothes underwater. The* WOMAN *throws him a red life ring which is attached to the long line she holds. He grabs onto it and she pulls him across the pool.*

THE WOMAN: That's the game. You win.

He reaches the side, where she is, downstage. He gets out, turns away from her briefly. She takes the ring and lowers it over his head. He turns around, taking the ring away from her. He walks away, throwing the ring into the pool.

THE YOUNG GUY: Uh, I've gotta get up early tomorrow.

She walks away, lies down on the deck and holds her legs up, as she did behind the bush in the opening lake scene.

THE WOMAN: What's your choice?

THE YOUNG GUY: (*Approaches her, touches her feet, walks away.*) I'm going home.

THE WOMAN: (*Goes to him, holds him, lifts her leg onto his thigh.*) Hey lookit! Don't be afraid. I just wanta be your school boy's dream.

He turns away from her, goes to the boat, kneels to undo the tie-off line.

THE YOUNG GUY: I really gotta go. What's it matter to you anyway? You don't even know me. A different guy wins you every night!

The slide projection changes to a picture of a single oar in the pool.
The YOUNG GUY gets in the boat and pushes off. She watches him gliding in the boat.

THE WOMAN: You don't understand! Usually I just send the guys home with a stuffed animal! (*She turns and walks down the deck. She picks up her towel, dress, shoes, and walks to the highdive.*)

He has a red ring which he tosses on the arm of the floating dummy.

THE YOUNG GUY: What a lucky shot!

The WOMAN slowly climbs to the high dive. She walks to the end of the board and looks out.

THE WOMAN: I'm looking. I'm looking. I thought I could be a little younger, and he could be a little older. I guess I misjudged the distance.

She jumps into the water. All lights out except for underwater lights. The woman rises to the surface. Her body forms an "x." On the bush is projected the word "Dissolve."
Music concludes. Lights out.

PHOTO BY GENE DOHERTY

Playwright Development:
Seven Essays and Interviews

Playwright Development

Introduction

The development of new American playwrights has been a matter of some priority for the past two decades. There are classes, workshops, seminars, festivals, reading programs, residencies. Theaters sponsor playwrights units, laboratories, plays in progress, second stages. Formally or otherwise, producers assemble their own "stables" of playwrights. Self-help is at least as important as what existing organizations do for playwrights: Luis Valdez founds El Teatro Campesino to do the kind of theater he envisages; Murray Mednick invents acting exercises which are intrinsic to the creation of his plays (see the interview in *West Coast Plays* 7).

For this issue, *West Coast Plays* commissioned the following seven pieces that cover some of the programs and activities currently or recently to be found in the Western United States. By no means have we assembled a definitive encylcopedia. One important kind of playwright development, the collective, is not treated at all (though Stephen Most's article, "The Ah-pah File," in *West Coast Plays* 8 is a gesture in that direction).

We specifically asked Jerry Patch, literary manager at the South Coast Repertory Theatre, to share his fantasy of what a dramaturg might do, given the funds. His humorous "Hi Tech-ing, Spec-ing and Checking on New Play Development" was the result. James F. Dean's interview with Mako explores the problems faced by a group that needs to develop playwrights for a community that has no theatrical tradition in this country. Aside from these two pieces we have neglected the playwright development work currently being done within theaters, not because we wish to slight the important programs at the Mark Taper Forum, the L.A. Actors' Theatre, The Magic Theatre, The One Act Theatre Company, The Seattle Rep., The Empty Space and elsewhere, but because that kind of playwright development has been well-covered in other publications.

Hi-Teching, Spec-ing, and Checking on New Play Development
Jerry Patch

Imagine what else might be done to develop new plays.

More is being done today to develop new plays and playwrights than at any previous time in history. Several important American institutions exist only for that purpose. Annual playwriting contests offer rich prizes, and continue to proliferate. Most regional theaters have committed some portion of their annual energies and resources to developing new plays and playwrights. Still . . .

Fantasize . . . Okay, suppose the National Science Foundation decided favorably on our grant application to develop new American plays and playwrights. Some avenues of research could be eliminated right away. Computers at MIT and other places have been producing mediocre to bad writing for years. We will continue to deal with playwrights as we have come to know them — in human form. Similarly, the last twenty years have cast doubts on the ability of ingested substances to inspire or enhance a writer's product. Hallucinogens, concentrated protein and other additives have failed to improve artistic writing, especially in the longer forms.

So the standard American playwright with a vision and a voice is square one. Square two is the development process. Plays never seem to be handed over on stone tablets. Instead, they are like buildings: construction envisioned by an architect/playwright, and made material by theatrical developers during a complex process.

The problem is not the nature of the process. Rather, it is the number of things that can go wrong (or worse, go nowhere) during development. Perhaps scientific methods judiciously applied might make the development process more predictable, dependable, and economical.

Fantasize: a panel of applied and behavioral scientists, theater people, and a management planner. They identify common problems of the developement process and suggest means for overcoming them (funded by the grant).

For instance: a theater contemplating development of a play by an unknown playwright has no way of knowing for certain if the writer has the ability to benefit from the process or to improve the work. Our panel constructs a series of tests to measure each candidate's talent, a sort of Stanford-Binet of playwriting potential: the Playwriting Potential Inventory (PPI). Any playwright could be tested by a theater and given a numerical rating. Candidates rated 135 or above would be accepted as a Playwright Capable of Development (PCOD), and could also join Mensa.

As a cross-check, personality profiles for each candidate would be constructed to see how well they matched up with a Composite Playwright's Profile (e.g., inordinate number of odd jobs held, MFA from Yale, etc.).

Personality conflicts can disrupt the process, so a judgment should be made regarding a playwright's compatibility with the artistic leadership of the theater. The comprehensive Compatibility Assessment (CCA) would compare the attitudes and interests of the playwright to those of the artistic leadership. All aspects of the developmental process would be covered, from overall aesthetic concepts to whether or not it would be necessary to order both red and white wine at a working dinner.

To properly process and constructively critique the vast number of unsolicited manuscripts, a team of genetic engineers would be commissioned to duplicate the chromosomal map of David Emmes and Martin Benson, the artistic directors of my theater, the South Coast Rep. Then a team of readers who could consider scripts with Emmes' and Benson's sensibilities would be cloned. Ancillary costs, such as who pays for the clones' keep during childhood and adolescence, college tuition, and the fact that Emmes and Benson might be retired before the clones are old enough to assume their duties, mark this notion as one needing more discussion.

A key element in the developmental process is the relationship between the dramaturg and the playwright. A positive tone is vital here; unfortunately, it is not always achieved. How can success in these relationships be predicted?

Dupont could create a special typing paper—Literary Litmus/Bond (LL/B)—which would absorb the playwright's persona from the secretions and vital juices left on the paper in the course of manuscript preparation. Random pages from scripts scheduled for development could be applied to the tongue of the proposed dramaturg in a variation of the litmus test. If the page turns red—acid—another dramturg is sought. If blue, a basic medium is indicated, and the dramaturg is assigned to the play.

Well, these are just a few ideas. Perhaps someone else can continue the effort to bring technology into play developemnt. At least the door has been opened.

Somewhere between limitation and fantasy would be these possibilities at South Coast Rep:

Put playwrights on a salary (say $15-20,000 annually) to write plays.

Produce selected new plays on SCR's Mainstage. They are fully designed and built, and the playwright is in residence during a six-week rehearsal period. Top actors are cast. The production plays two weeks of previews (no notices — it doesn't open) and then ceases. Sets and costumes are stored for six months to a year while the playwright rewrites and revises. The production re-enters rehearsal with the new script, then officially opens as part of the following year's season.

On SCR's Second Stage, cast top actors in new plays using top designers with adequate budgets. Plays are rehearsed in the east-European manner for three weeks until the actors are at a run-through status. Rehearsals stop while the playwright revises based on what the run-through demonstrates. Rehearsals resume when the rewriting is completed. This process is repeated until the play is thought ready to open.

Though it is interesting to consider new ways of doing things, the usual result is a renewed understanding of why we do what we've been doing. While SCR generally subscribes to the development process used at the O'Neill Conference and other theaters, certain guidelines and principles stressed by Producing Artistic Director Emmes and the literary department have evolved.

Commitment and Trust—SCR is interested in long-term relationships with playwrights. Never judge a playwright unfavorably on the basis of one play. Always judge a playwright favorably on the basis of one play (if the writer succeeded once, he or she can do it again).

Interest—Respond vigorously to plays which excite you, however imperfect. Respond politely to plays which fail to stir or otherwise interest you, without lengthy comment or critique (even though the playwright or agent asks for it). Comments from disinterested sources often cannot help being gratuitous, like trying to make constructive suggestions for a dish you found tasteless ("It certainly looked nice on the plate . . . mebbe a little garlic salt?").

Patience—Take sufficient time to develop new work. The quickest way to bury a new play is to produce it before it is ready.

Play Your Role—During the process, be sure to protect the playwright from ourselves. State the play's problems as perceived without offering solutions (unless asked). It's the writer's play.

Commission New Work—Link playwrights with SCR's artistic directors and staff directors on projects of mutual excitement. Upon making a commission agreement, assign a director who works with the playwright from first draft through the play's opening. Assign the best directors you have to develop plays.

Do Second Productions—While SCR enjoys premieres as much as any theater, second productions are equally exciting. Plays tend to need at least two full productions before they sort themselves out. Second productions, with the playwright in residence, are still part of the development process.

Chemistry—If a playwright is supported properly, there should be good working relationships among participants in the development process. The playwright is the controlling artist, and open, personal relationships with other colleagues will encourage them to offer reactions and opinions freely. Similarly, the playwright ought to feel free to engage in constructive argument without fear of jeopardizing current or future projects. If any of the relationships suffer problems, the dramaturg functions as an ombudsman and mediator.

So we continue to worry about where new plays will come from. We do all we can to encourage talented playwrights to practice their art. For the sake of the American Theater, we say, and that's true enough. But we also make those commitments selfishly, because doing new work is the most challenging and exciting activity theater has to offer.

Interview with Mako:
The East West Players

James F. Dean

East West Players in Los Angeles is one of the nation's leaders in producing and developing Asian American theater, if not *the* leader. The company of dues-paying members perform, work on crews, and help maintain the theater and office. Classes are offered, including some training in clasical Kabuki and Noh theater techniques. More importantly, however, the actors have an opportunity to work in plays that deal specifically with the Asian American experience.

This focus on Asian American culture dictates special needs in terms of dramatic material. Literary management becomes not so much a task of selecting plays for a season, but actively searching for and, sometimes, helping create appropriate plays.

Mako, the artistic director and one of the founding members, was asked about the origins of the group, its changing needs, and how the theater works with playwrights. He spoke very openly and clearly about where the group gets its material, what is looked for in playwriting, and the current theater season at East West Players.

The interview was conducted in the theater near the set for *12-1-A,* a play by Wakako Yamauchi currently in production. The transcript of the interview has been edited in two ways. Some of my questions have been changed from mumbled half-thoughts into complete sentences. Mako's responses have been left unedited for the most part, but some paragraphs have been moved around so that related or connected thoughts follow each other.

QUESTION: Why was East West Players formed? Because there were actors with unfulfilled needs? Or were there Asian American plays waiting to be produced?
MAKO: I think to answer the question we have to go back to the very beginning. We have to go back to 1965 when our company was formed, founded. Since all of us who were founders at that time were actors, I would have to classify our theater as "actors" theater, as opposed to "directors" theater or "writers" theater. So, in that sense, our needs are so wide and varied, also our backgrounds and training are so varied—even though all those people were so-called professional actors, but professional in the sense of working

in television and motion pictures. Ninety percent of those people never had any kind of experience on stage. Even at that time, I felt a need to train the actors that we had to represent Asian American strata of this American society. So, it became a kind of a workshop situation for about first few years, and we got funding from Ford Foundation to train our actors for two years. So, during that time our company grew from six people to about thirty.

About that time we ran into problem of lack of material. In other words, material that we could relate to. Materials that we could identify with. We used to do a lot of adaptations of classics. For instance, let's say, *Servant of Two Masters* by Goldoni. We assume that . . . We impose that there was a Chinatown in Venice. So, from there we changed — not changed drastically, but we made adjustments — in terms of each character without really tampering with the main text. *Twelfth Night* was kind of a weird experience, in the sense that we just didn't succeed. This director was trying to bring in all sorts of Middle East influence . . . trying to introduce various Middle Eastern cultures and ethnicities and mannerisms. It just didn't work out.

There was a time within our company not to recognize Asian American movement, especially in terms of art. What is Asian American art? We do recognize Japanese art or Chinese art or Korean art, but what is this Asian American stuff, you know? But at the same time, the whole thinking began to evolve much more . . . Why are we here? What do we have to do? What do we want to do? And all those questions came to a point where, yes, it is important to convey Asian American experience in theater form to non-Asian audience in this country. When I say non-Asian audience . . . there are Asian American audience whose thinking is very much non-Asian. So, we need to educate our own people as well as reaching out to non-Asian audience. And we have to educate our actors.

In order to do that we had to develop writers. One of the things we did with Ford Foundation grant was to establish a national playwriting contest to which writers like Frank Chin from San Francisco and Momoko Ito from Chicago submitted their work. They shared the first honor, so to speak. We continued with the playwriting contest for, I would say, about five or six years, and after that we began to rely on various funding sources to continue. Rockefeller, National Endowment for the Arts.

QUESTION: The contests were one source of plays. Now that the

East West Players are more widely known, playwrights must be sending you their scripts. What happens to these?

MAKO: What happens here is my assistant, Alberto Issac, reads all the scripts. He makes recommendations to me, and only then do I begin to read and select from that screened material.

QUESTION: Is there any particular voice or kind of play you're looking for?

MAKO: I like to sense the playwright's point of view, subjective point of view. If that is honestly reflected in the writing, then I would begin to consider that particular piece. The pieces without strong point of view, I'm not quite sure . . . If premise or characters are interesting enough, then I might impose my own point of view on top of it and begin to think, "Will it work for our audiences? Will it work for our actors?" I begin to wrestle with questions like that, and then I decide to do it or not to do it.

QUESTION: Do you find, say, novels or short stories and ask people to dramatize them?

MAKO: We have done that in the past. With, for instance, John Shiroda's *Pineapple White.* We commissioned him to write it in play form. And Wakako (Yamauchi, *And the Soul Shall Dance,* printed in this issue) same way. This year we have commissioned Ed Sakamoto, whose play we'll be doing following *12-1-A, The Pilgrimage,* the effect of internment to Japanese Americans.

QUESTION: Have individual actors in the company been encouraged to write?

MAKO: Dom Magwili has written a few things for us — as well as another company up in San Francisco, the Asian American Theater Company. There are a number of actors who have written something.

QUESTION: Has the company written any shows collectively?

MAKO: We've done it a couple of times. We've tried a couple of times, but it wasn't successful. We learned from each project, but, still, collective writing presents a problem. It needs really . . . Somebody has to make that decision. And if writer doesn't make that decision or take a point of view, it becomes very hazy. It pleases everyone, but to what extent? I don't think that's ideal form of writing — writing theater piece, anyway.

QUESTION: There are a few other theaters which primarily do plays about Asian American life, including the Asian American Theater Company in San Francisco, the Pan Asian Repertory Theater in New York, and some connected with colleges and universities in

Hawaii. I've been told that 90% of the plays on this "circuit" originate at East-West. Is there an exchange of plays between these theaters?

MAKO: Not so much active exchange, but there is exchange. It's like once a playwright writes a play — before we know it, the play is already going to be done in Seattle, Hawaii, or what have you. We have, at this point, no control over the project, so to speak. Unless it goes up, in other words, to a better production (ie, to a full Equity production).

QUESTION: The theme of this season is the internment of the Japanese in camps during the second World War. The poster for the season titles the season "Kidoairaku." What does that mean?

MAKO: It applies to four basic human emotions in terms of Japanese theater: *Ki,* happiness; *Do,* fury; *Ai,* sorrow; *Raku,* enlightenment.

QUESTION: So, all of these emotions, without being imposed on the plays, are what are experienced by watching the plays. This range of emotion is experienced, even in the camps. How was the decision made to focus on one theme? Has this been done in the past?

MAKO: This was the first season we decided to stick to one theme. I've always wanted to do plays based on the camp experience, but I never did have enough materials. Some materials that I did come across were, I thought, not quite pertinent. In other words, somebody imposing a certain formula upon internment experience, you know, like *Romeo and Juliet.* Love affair between outside and inside the camp. So, in that sense, we never did have enough material. It just so happened that I knew Wakako wrote *12-1-A* for Mark Taper a couple years back. She was given a grant, Rockefeller grant, from Mark Taper to write this, but they decided not to touch it, for whatever reason. So, I knew there was one play, which was this one. And then I ran into *Station J* (by Richard Franz who lives in New York) which was the play which opened our current season. I decided we could build *Christmas in Camp* ourselves somehow. It was kind of a collective effort, but writer in charge of that was Dom Magwilis, who is a member of our company. And the fourth one, Ed Sakamoto's piece which is not yet completed, but . . . so. The first time in my life I felt like we could do a full season, and full season is not quite enough to explore this whole issue.

QUESTION: So, each play has been developed from a different perspective. Is that because the various writers and actors come from different backgrounds?

MAKO: Frank Chin is a good example. Born and raised in Oakland right next to Black section and so on and so on and so forth. A lot of our people have led somewhat sheltered life as opposed to his background, you know. But, at the same time, Frank was never interned because, number one, he was too young. But why does he write? Why does he keep harping about concentration situations? Whereas, why is it our people who have actually spent some time in concentration camp do not write at this point about their experience or their parent's experience or what they saw? Like *12-1-A* is a good example. Finally, finally, she felt she had to write something. Because she was there.

QUESTION: After seeing the play, *12-1-A,* it was a surprise to learn that Wakako Yamauchi is a woman in her fifties. The writer seemed to be very young.

MAKO: Well, I think she's a very pure person, even though she's fifty-three, so in many ways she's naive. Naive about life, naive about professional writing. So she still maintains that youthful, romantic notion of character, situation, premise, and it's just the way she is. You can't expect a person like that to write like Frank Chin, and vice versa.

QUESTION: Wakako adapted some of her short stories into plays. Did she find this difficult?

MAKO: The very first one we did, *And the Soul Shall Dance,* was the most successful one. And, number one, the reason it was successful was that she was able to work with a couple of . . . myself and co-director for about eighteen months before we went into rehearsal. We went through about four or five drafts. But that's what is missing in other of her adaptations.

QUESTION: Is *12-1-A* an adaptation of a story as well?

MAKO: No, not this one. She did a thing called *Music Lessons.*

QUESTION: That's an adaptation?

MAKO: Yes. I think even now as I compare the two, short story and the play, I am still drawn to the short story because it has more to offer. It stimulates my imgination more than the play.

QUESTION: The program notes mention *Wind Dances* by Diane Aoko. What is that?

MAKO: *Wind Dances* is a play in progress. So, it's a sort of mini-production. We just want to take a look at the play with actors onstage, and so forth.

QUESTION: Was *Oofty Goofty* (by Frank Chin) the same?

MAKO: Yes, play in progress.

QUESTION: How is this set up? Do you set up readings as the plays come in?

MAKO: We set it like a year in advance as to what we're going to do. Unless something extraordinary comes along, we try to stick to the schedule. This year we will have done three plays in progress. The third one is unscheduled, but I just wanted to get it done this year.

QUESTION: From the workshops do plays go into full production?

MAKO: No, not yet. It makes it easier for us to function now. For instance Frank would always like to develop something here. I think that's number one. I enjoy that process, so I try to get as many actors involved in that play in progress situation. Otherwise, a lot of times people tend to think "Play in progress? We don't have to do our best!" You know, but that's not the point. Unless we do our best, we will never see the best of Frank Chin or whoever. Some of our actors are beginning to understand that process and are beginning to enjoy that process as well.

QUESTION: What would you consider to be the goal of East West Players, to get the plays written as well as to do them?

MAKO: Yeah, I think it goes hand in hand. As I said, this company was founded by a group of actors, and it still remains the actors company. But actors and writers have to go hand in hand, without written materials, actors cannot function. So, our goal is that in time Asian American writing becomes part of American theater scene, part of *whole* American theater scene, because you start talking about Asian American-ness or Asian American theater and people will say, "What's that? I mean, is there such a thing?" Whereas now I think most of non . . . most of the American people would agree or have to recognize it's true that there is a Black American theater and Black American literature. And I think that's what we're trying to do. Developing actor is one thing, but we have to go a step farther into essence of theater by trying to develop writers, so that ultimately we do become part of American theater.

QUESTION: Do the playwrights and the actors work together — aside from the workshops?

MAKO: It all depends on the chemistry between the writer, director, and actors. For instance, guys like Frank Chin would just rewrite like crazy, you know, he would come in with like twenty, thirty pages overnight, whereas some writers would take out one word, insert two words in lieu of . . . So, it depends on the writer and director to conduct this whole rehearsal procedure.

QUESTION: How long is the rehearsal period?

MAKO: Six to four weeks.

QUESTION: That's not a long time. Are the playwrights working all the time during rehearsal? It's not like the author submits the play, and that's it? Sometimes, nobody wants to see the writers.

MAKO: No. I personally don't like that process because every problem that the actors go through I want writers, the playwright, to see it for himself or herself, so we can talk about what we can do. Even when I'm working at the Public Theater in New York and what not, I do the same. I try to maintain my pace. Instead of "We have an opening in four weeks!" —The hell with the opening! We've got to work first, and let's see what happens.

So, usually, I have fun during the rehearsal. I mean, hopefully, more than myself, actors as well.

QUESTION: Several Asian-American playwrights have been able to see more than one of their plays produced at East-West.

MAKO: I hope that the atmosphere or environment here is a positive one so that, in other words, we do not walk away with bad vibration. I think we try to remain as positive as possible because we know that there are so few Asian American writers who write about Asian American experiences. We feel we have to nurture them as well. We need them. Maybe that's why we keep going back to some writers.

Interview with Oliver Hailey:
Workshops in Los Angeles
Grace Woodard

I found Oliver Hailey on a ladder in his garage cleaning out the paint closet. It was a perfect setting for talking about playwrights' workshops — it felt like down-home country nestled right there on the lower rim of the San Fernando Valley. Hailey, who speaks with a West Texas drawl, has inherited the Mountain Men's gift of spinning yarns. He has written for theaters from Melrose Avenue in L.A. to Broadway, as well as for the tube and film, picking up Drama Desk and Vernon Rice Awards along the way.

In Los Angeles, Hailey has participated in or helped to organize playwrights' workshops at several small theaters. Although "name" playwrights are often said to be associated with various workshops, seldom do we hear of playwrights with Hailey's experience and success seeking out the workshop process time and time again. As I spoke with Hailey, I learned that he enjoys writers and workshops, although he has his saturation point. For him, it is the work that matters. It's the coming together for readings and discussions that he thrives on.

What follows is an edited version of our interview.

On Playwrighting: Playwriting cannot be taught. Playwriting is something you learn for yourself with guidance. At the workshop, we just encourage people to write. Writing, writing, writing. That is what's useful. And sometimes a deadline, the pressure of it, can also be helpful. I don't believe a play can just be read. It must be heard. I don't let anyone submit a play to me to be read to find out if they're acceptable.

Some Workshop History: I began with a group at the Circle Theater in Hollywood about three years ago. We took an option for a year at the Circle and we fully produced three plays and did over eighty readings. All work was heard, not just read. Well, the year was expensive. My wife and I had put in several thousand dollars which we did not expect to get back, but by the end of the year I was just plumb tuckered out. Then one day we were approached by Laura Zucker from the Back Alley. She and Allan Miller were interested in starting a writers' lab and offered the organizing of it to me. It seemed like a good idea. They would be able to foot the bills and there was also the possibility of productions at the Back Alley.

So . . . I called about a dozen playwrights I knew and respected. Among them were Beth Henley, Ernest Thompson, Paul Zindel, Sam Bobrick and Ron Clark. And so we all met and started at the Back Alley. People heard about it, asked if they could come, and we let that happen very freely. At one point we had two groups meeting at the Back Alley on alternating Thursdays, to accomodate the quickly growing numbers. Well, I was wearing out, so we cut back to every other Thursday and combined the groups.

The Back Alley Theater Workshop: The current workshop is not exclusionary although we began with more established playwrights. The process here is the one I prefer, and it seems to work. I think it is the ideal place for a play to develop. The audience (of playwrights) is very alive and will give you feedback which is crucial for a play's development.

It's a totally playwright-oriented workshop. Other playwrights' workshops I've been involved with, the Actors Studio and Theatre 40, were both actor-oriented. The playwright was an addendum. Here the rules are few. There is no leader, the playwright moderates. It's communistic. (He laughs.) We keep administration to a minimum. It is my theater and I am an autocrat. (He laughs.) But we do try to get a consensus, and try to be reasonable within bounds if a decision has to be made—date changes, etc. . . . We have very few rules. The playwright may not read his own play. John Gassner at Yale said "I let you read your plays but that is cheating. You bring something to your play no one else ever will. And you don't listen." So we don't have playwrights read their own works. And actors may not stay for the discussion.

The Set Up—Thursdays: Currently we meet every other Thursday at which time no more than twenty minutes of a long piece is read. The next week the writer can bring in another twenty minutes or the same piece. We suffer from short attention spans. We're all little Richard Nixons. And we don't want to make each other crazy. And the writer is solely responsible for the casting and the discussion which may or may not follow the reading. It is up to the playwright. There is no co-moderator. We have no attendence requirements. You can come or not. Some playwrights come only when their work is read.

"We don't Encourage Pain": The playwright can end the discussion at any point. People are open to criticism, and by and large the criticism is excellent. We encourage honesty from a positive point of view. We are interested in protecting the playwright so he doesn't get so lacerated he can't crawl back to his typewriter. We share tips and there are positive strengths to be gained from associating with others who are trying to do what you are trying to do.

Sundays: Sundays are for full readings of pieces that have previously been read in twenty-minute segments. Again, the playwright controls the evening, from inviting the audience, casting the play, to even excluding the playwrights from attending, if he wishes. The writer can insulate and incubate forever. Nobody high-powered has to show up. Friends can come one Sunday, and do a repeat the next week for potential producers. And if the play is well received, conceivably it can be picked up. If there is commercial interest, we give the writers our blessings. Since the writer controls the evening and can select his audience wisely, we support whatever he or she wants to do.

After Sunday Night: We had a new playwright, a man who has done a lot of directing. He wrote a brilliant first act. We all went through the roof. He came back with an even better second act. It had a Sunday reading. Now the Back Alley is going to do a full production, and it came very close to having it taken directly to New York. So plays can take off or they can sit there. It's the people who come to the Sunday readings who can be important for the play, who might be willing to produce it, rather than agents who matter.

Director/Playwrights: We are lucky in that we have our share of playwright-directors—Allan Miller, Jered Barclay, a young man from Chicago, Bruce Hickey and Dona Cooper. They are available to help the other writers.

24 Hours: We do not do exercizes. The writing here is self-starting. However, for guidance we are trying a project called *24 Hours,* in which plays of five minutes are written for every hour of the day. No restriction on form or subject matter. The hour simply has to be mentioned at some point. We are hoping to present the evening in the fall, perhaps make it an annual project.

Struggling and Working Playwrights: The rubbing shoulders between the working playwright and the struggling, more inexperienced writer is helpful to both of them. The more established playwrights frequently get impatient with the people who are less experienced. They don't groove on it. They want excellent work immediately or they're bored very quickly. But they are not that willing to expose their own work, so we have found a mix is so much much better. The established writers come in only when they feel they have something to share, such as Paul, or Beth or Ernest sharing their experiences. They come when they want or need a meeting. What keeps the group going are the new playwrights, those who have something to win or to prove. You just can not second guess who will turn out something good.

Plays for Los Angeles: Los Angeles is a good enough market for plays and it's getting better all the time. It's becoming like Off and Off-Off Broadway. It's going to surpass New York. Los Angeles is a creative town. The more people who work in the theater and love it, the better. Nothing can help us more than good plays. The only thing that can help is good work. I've seen enough bad plays to last me a life time. What's exciting is to see a good play. You carry it around for days. There are a lot of theaters and a lot of interest in new plays. There are a lot of avenues open to new and more established playwrights. By and large we are blessed.

A Parting Shot: I covet my time and I encourage that in the playwrights. We're not very social (at the workshop). We do our work and then go home. Sometimes we have craft discussions, but I hate long-windedness, though you'd never guess it with my carrying on here (laughter.)

On that note the interview concluded. The paint closet was now organized, and Oliver Hailey had to go in and rustle up some chow.

Interview with Drury Pifer:
Early Days at Berkeley Stage

WEST COAST PLAYS: You were a literary manager at The Berkeley
    Stage Company, 1974-1977. What were some of the problems
    you faced?

PIFER: At Berkeley Stage we shared out jobs back then so it was
    difficult to know where the artistic director began and the
    literary manager ended. Because I was a writer I did end up
    doing most of the reading. Especially when we got more
    organized. Our problems were no money and hundreds of plays
    to read.

WEST COAST PLAYS: How many scripts did you get in a year?

PIFER: My last year I counted near a thousand.

WEST COAST PLAYS: How do you deal with that many scripts
    intelligently?

PIFER: I'm quite sure you don't. Some people think you are looking
    for a play that will fit your actors, your space, your directors,
    your audience. The truth is I was looking for playwrights. One
    good play doesn't mean much. I wanted to develop the
    playwright. Recognize the person who was right for our theater
    and stick with my choice.

WEST COAST PLAYS: Is that what you did?

PIFER: Conditions were chaotic. No money of course. All of us
    trying to do five or six things at once. I was new to theater. My
    lack of theater experience at the time gave me a case of galloping
    insecurity. But I could see that a theater that does living
    playwrights is not the same as one that sticks with the dead. And
    I could see that in the U.S. theaters and playwrights had grown
    incompatible. None of us, I'm sure, had reckoned on the kind of
    hard work it would take to get new work up to the mark. The
    irony is that theaters with the least resources are the ones who
    find themselves with the future of American theater in their
    hands.

WEST COAST PLAYS: So how did you wind up choosing your plays?

PIFER: Directors who had done good work elsewhere might show
    up with a play, or actors would come in with a playwright.
    Ideally, we should have picked a series of plays that made it clear
    to audiences what kind of theater we intended to be, and then
    gone out and found directors. But we'd built the theater with no

money whatever. We started it by writing letters to friends asking for donations. I'd met Angela Paton and Bob Goldsby when Bob directed a play of mine for the Magic Theater and Angela acted in it. Anyway, a friend of mine, Lew di Sibio, helped me build the theater itself. This was strictly small time. Once we'd got the walls up and the plumbing in people began to come around and help. We owed those people a lot and naturally we wound up disappointing most of them. Given the nature of the thing it was very difficult establishing a direction.

WEST COAST PLAYS: Are you saying you had difficulty establishing the identity of the theater for audiences?

PIFER: Something like that. The idea was to do new work. And by God we did do new work with a vengeance. More new plays in 1976 than any other theater in the country, so we were informed by Theatre Communications Group. We were willing to try almost anything. And I suppose no one quite knew what we were because we didn't know ourselves. For me it really was like the beginning of the world with all the elements flying about. As the elements began to separate I gradually saw what to do in both my own work and in the work of the theater. It became clear to me that the identity of a theater is determined by elements which must all be there, and these include playwrights whose work fits artistic ends the director of the theater is working toward.

WEST COAST PLAYS: Did you work to that end then?

PIFER: It was pretty clear from reading all those scripts that the plays a working theater needs are not going to show up in the mail very often. This is not because there is no talent out there. Playwrights need to be attached to a specific theater with specific actors, directors, the whole shebang. What's an actor without a production? What's a play without a production? The playwright is one more actor in the company. Keep him or her out and you've got a yolk with no shell and no development.

WEST COAST PLAYS: Do you mean theaters should not accept plays through the mail?

PIFER: Plays through the mail provide a window to the outside and a good literary manager will look for the kind of talent, the style that feels right for his or her particular theater. Say you come across a brilliant new play written in a style reminiscent of Polish expressionism. What American theater, what American audience will be ready to meet the thing on its own terms? Too much originality may damn a play as easily as too little. Original playwrights need new theaters for their work as a rule. Existing theaters get socked into existing modes of theater. They think they're looking for well-wrought, original plays, but really they're looking for the well-wrought same old thing with a new gimmick. Intensity scares us. Pity and terror we'd prefer to avoid. But a theater without pity and terror only patronizes its audience. And of course you don't arrive at pity and terror by stumbling on it in the mail, handing it to a couple of actors for a three week rehearsal, and then sitting back while the audience has convulsions.

WEST COAST PLAYS: How did you handle new plays you liked?

PIFER: No new play is liked by all concerned. Some playwrights are very impressive of course and people will admire the work as a matter of course. I'm not being entirely ironic. Most people don't know what to make of new work. It's strange, often. It's usually not finished. It's certainly not the masterpiece to which we've all grown accustomed by hanging around Ibsen, Shakespeare and Chekhov. We've even grown used to putting down half of Shakespeare and most of Ibsen, and some of us have grown to love our own opinions even more than theater itself. We go to the theater to sharpen our teeth, not to immerse our sensibilities in a new vision of things. Actors and directors who do new work in small, understaffed, poverty-stricken theaters are going to have it tough, because new work means vulnerability for all concerned. The only insulation they have is intelligence, time, and money. All hard to come by. New plays may imply a new kind of acting. If the writer is any good the work will stretch the actor. A stretched actor is a vulnerable actor. Here he is doing a very difficult role in some unknown play and perhaps making a fool of himself doing it. When you handle a new play and develop its author you're involved in a complex balancing act with no net below. It's easy to talk about readings, consultations, workshops. These are mechanical features, getting a text ready. The real work is making the thing accessible, finding a director who can do it. The terrifying thing about doing new work is the sure knowledge you've got to let writers fail before they'll learn enough to succeed. All this at the expense of the actors.

WEST COAST PLAYS: How can you possibly run a theater on failures?

PIFER: Most of our failures packed them in. Some of our successes were almost unattended — for instance our production of David Rabe's *Sticks and Bones* that got invited to the Venice Biennale.

WEST COAST PLAYS: So what is failure then?

PIFER: Bad work. Embarrassing work. If the subject's right you can still fill the house. And then who's to say it's bad? Well I will still say its bad. How did it get on if it is bad? Easily. Inevitably an artistic director makes commitments. When a project begins to go bad after weeks of work, perhaps after years of waiting, do you alienate a valuable director and good actors and maintain artistic standards? Or do you do the inferior work even though everyone will suffer? Inexperienced artistic directors find themselves in this situation all the time. It becomes doubly perplexing when you put the thing on and people love it.

WEST COAST PLAYS: So were you wrong for having put it on?

PIFER: You were wrong, I think, for not having seen the problem long before it came up. But in a way this is a false problem. The real solution is to do plays that are right for your theater. Right for your actors and production people and space. Nowadays. there are so many styles and standards that no one person can possibly approve or understand them all. And we approved too many. Too many people had no idea what we were getting at. We would have done better sticking at some single kind of theater or theme. Feminist theater or metaphysical theater. Something identifiable. I'm sure we gave both our actors and our audience too much to handle. We spread ourselves thin. We made the great liberal mistake of being too all-inclusive. The trick is to consult the dark flame of conviction inside you and move out very slowly from there. Your playwright may not be anyone else's idea of a playwright. But, if you're any good as an artistic director, in time everyone will want your playwright. If you know the real thing when you see it. Unfortunately it takes wisdom, time and support from outside.

WEST COAST PLAYS: In your view, new work will never pay it's own way?

PIFER: Nothing of real value pays its own way. Children don't pay their own way. Science. Medical research. Schools. Libraries. Parks. The truth is nothing that increases our enlightenment comes free. Artists, like scientists, are magicians who can turn almost nothing into something overwhelming given the chance. Theater is this kind of magic and the people who do it do more, I'm sure, than we know. Or can know.

The Padua Hills Playwrights Workshop and Festival

Susan LaTempa

Murray Mednick, artistic director of the Padua Hills Playwrights Workshop and Festival, has explained the purpose of this annual gathering of theater people: "We want to continue to examine the creative processes of playwriting and playmaking—especially with regard to the awareness of space—and to continue to evolve new methods of teaching the art."

This will be my second year of participation at Padua Hills, and as I begin to plan and anticipate the coming weeks of workshops and rehearsals, I naturally think of my responses to the previous summer's sessions. Mostly I remember a sense of dignity: dignity for the students who gathered at Padua from all over the country, dignity for the playwrights who were extended complete artistic control as teachers and as playmakers, dignity for the actors and other theater people who have found their own compelling rewards for participation in this radically different laboratory for playwrights.

The Padua Hills Playwrights Workshop and Festival is a two-part event. Ten students are accepted each year for the Workshop, which is the core of the event. "We have striven for a natural balance between practice and teaching, the one not necessarily separate from the other," says Mednick. "Therefore, the nobility and creativity of teaching as an art in itself is given new life. Partially because of this, we find that an atmosphere of equality and maturity arises which is difficult to discover elsewhere in theatrical circles. This, in turn, allows us to probe rather deeply into such questions as 'integrity,' 'honesty,' etc. and, at the same time, to provide a real place for new, younger, or 'unproduced' playwrights with something real in them."

This year, the Workshop will also include a special apprentice program for four returning students, who will be guided by staff playwrights in the development of a collaborative work.

Both students and apprentices are instructed by the staff playwrights, most of whom are simultaneously preparing a play of their own for presentiton during the Festival, which is held during the two weekends following the four weeks of the Workshop. Plays are not submitted, accepted, or rejected for the Festival. Playwrights are invited to Padua, and, says Mednick, "the Festival grows out of work done by the community." Many playwrights write or develop plays from scratch during the Workshop.

Three playwrights who share a committment to explore the process of teaching form the core of the Padua staff: Murray Mednick, Sam Shepard, and Maria Irene Fornes. Each year, each of them has led several workshops, and they have presented plays at the Festival — Shepard once, Fornes three out of the first four years, and Mednick each time.

The Padua Hills Playwrights Workshop and Festival began in 1978 when Mednick, who was teaching at the University of La Verne (La Verne is a small town about an hour east of Los Angeles), invited a small group of writers and actors to spend several weeks together, working with students and experimenting with plays.

The workshops and rehearsal took place at the site which gave the Festival its name — the Padua Hills Theatre, a cluster of adobe buildings situated in the foothills of the Sierra Madre Mountains north of La Verne. The Padua Hills Theatre was a dinner theater from 1932 to 1974, home of the Mexican Players, but the gasoline shortage forced its closing. When Mednick first saw the site it was being rented out on a day-to-day basis for weddings and other festive occasions. He arranged for use of the buildings and grounds during the six-week summer period of the workshop and festival. The 300-seat theater has remained unavailable to the group because of insurance restrictions, but this limitation has turned out to be an asset, informing the spirit and molding the personality of the festival.

Uninhibited by the idea of non-traditional performance spaces, and haunted by the beauty of the outdoor and indoor sites available, the writers have ignored the empty auditorium. Instead, they have staged plays under the arching branches of the olive trees, on the dusty red clay "plain" below the grove, in the jumble of wood and concrete that is the loading dock at the back of the kitchen, on a small outdoor stage in the courtyard, on the polished wood floor of the dining room. Each year, playwrights not only select the sites for their performances, but often write their plays under the influence of a particular space. They are restricted only by the need to accomodate about one hundred audience members, and they must be able to restore the site to its previous condition.

The works have accordingly been deeply affected by the

environmental possibilities. Characters drop from the trees or emerge from pits in the ground; works are written with twilight or sunset or deep darkness in mind; gardens are planted as sets; themes and mysteries emerge from a site.

.When I was invited to participate in the Padua workshop and festival, I was unaware of the extent to which Mednick, as Artistic Director, treats the invited playwrights as he himself expects to be treated. Put simply, he extends complete artistic control, as teachers and as playwrights, to his colleagues.

After working in Equity waiver theater in Los Angeles for several years, I thought of "artistic control" as something film directors fought for after reaching a certain plateau of success. After all, the emerging playwright's process of getting plays produced is one of seeking approval, not taking control. And while I secretly considered myself a theatrical (as opposed to literary) artist, I didn't question current "truths" which were at odds with my sense of a playwright's role. I listened when I was told (over and over) that I shouldn't direct my own work. I struggled to make my visions clear without stage directions because I knew that actors were taught to ignore them. I agreed that if a production of a wonderful play wasn't satisfactory, it might be because the playwright hadn't been able to "get it down on paper" and that the ideal play was "director-proof."

At Padua, things were different. Murray never read the script, never put himself in a position of judging my work. I'd been invited, and welcomed, and I was on my own. He encouraged the playwrights to direct their own work, he encouraged the playwrights to cast from the company of actors in residence, he reminded the playwrights that there was little or no production budget for each show—but it was really up to you.

"Hey," Murray explains, "I'm doing a theater piece. It's in my head, it's on the paper. I gather whomever or whatever I need to help me get it on the stage. If you want a director, get a director to help *you* achieve your vision. Or get a drummer, or a choreographer, or an actor, or whomever you need."

What, then, was it like to have artistic control? First, it was *fluid.* It was easy to change and adjust and mold the production. The script, so recently written, and the staging were of the same cloth. When I saw, for example, that my plans for the garden that was being planted to function as a set were too grand, it was a simple matter to scale down the set and adjust the script. In another example, there was a character—a zucchini—whose role and function would have been difficult to verbalize and was in fact, unclear to me for a time. I was under no pressure to cut the character or define the role, and it was possible to let the *play* bend around the part. Casting was (excuse the pun) organic, not arbitrary. Before I began to write I knew the work of many of the actors who would be in residence, so I knew what kinds of performance were possible and probable and experienced no frustration on that count.

It was *fast*. I like to work quickly. Here I didn't have to wait, politely, through the weeks or days of vagueness while a director familiarized him or herself with the script. I didn't worry about "imposing" my interpretation on someone else so I didn't hesitate to volunteer information to the actors that I might have waited for them to discover in another situation—although I welcomed the burrowings and discoveries of the actors and relished their panache.

Third, it reinforced my belief in my own work. Directors and theater administrators who didn't get the joke had made me begin to wonder if there *were* a joke. At Padua, I was pleased to find from audience response during and after the play that most people perceived, with me, the events of the play. How they interpreted those events varied delightfully.

Having artistic control is not simply a matter of directing your own work. I plan, in the future, to work often with other directors. And I plan to request and listen to script criticisms from people I respect, and to compromise and negotiate in regards to spaces and other elements of production. I'll probably even grit my teeth and tell myself it's not worth getting into a discussion when an administrator or an actor pedantically points out that my play lacks "conflict." But I will remember that it is possible to make a play as an artist.

At Padua, teaching is considered part of the art. "The whole reason for the workshop is for everybody to refresh themselves," says Mednick, "The teachers here don't start from a position that they *know*. We're trying each time to start from scratch, to explore where the music and the vision come from, to reinvestigate the source."

Playwright development at Padua, then, has to do with a personal and continuing effort both for professionals and for students. "I'm not interested in being a producer," says Mednick, "I'm interested in being a playwright."

Sundance: The Utah Playwriting Conference
Al Brown

Every so often in everyone's life, in spite of all the lovers you've lied to or taxes you've cheated on, everything goes right. Everything works. Your life makes sense. That's what happened to me during July of 1980 at the first Utah Playwriting Conference held at the Sundance Resort in Provo Canyon.

The Utah Arts Council decided that instead of awarding prize money for a new play that they would go the whole nine yards and give three playwrights the chance to work on their scripts in an environment unconcerned with production, focused instead on process. They felt too often new plays were not given a chance to develop. That they were rushed. The fact that a play is a collaborative effort was ignored.

The first step was to hire a producing director for the Conference. Applications were sent out across the nation and after interviewing several people the Arts Council's playwright's committee selected John Dennis, a director at the Mark Taper Forum in Los Angeles.

Scripts were the next priority. They were sought from all over the country. The reading committee's criterion was to select a script that would benefit from two weeks' work in the mountains. They weren't looking for finished scripts. They were looking for plays in mid-process. According to deadline, nine scripts were selected as semi-finalists. These scripts were given readings at Theater 138 in Salt Lake. The judges, who were comprised of conference producing director John Dennis and local theater professionals, selected three finalists. Gaylen Nielsen, Aden Ross, and I were, before we knew better, the lambs for the slaughter.

The next step was a production stage manager. Richard Serpe from Los Angeles was selected. Richard, in turn, came to Salt Lake and selected a stage manager for each play. Dramaturgs were next. John selected Russell Vandenbroucke from the Taper and Ann Cattaneo from the Phoenix in New York.

Then directors, and as any playwright knows you occasionally must tolerate a director. Burke Walker of the Empty Space Theatre in Seattle and Michael Leibert of the Berkeley Rep were selected by John Dennis. Well I should say they were invited to participate, and wouldn't you know it, they accepted.

Then John Dennis auditioned actors in Los Angeles, Seattle, and Salt Lake. He selected ten and, as usual, they expected to be paid. That brings up another point. The biggest reason that the Utah Playwrighting Conference was such a success was the volunteer feeling among so many people in the administration of the program. Not everyone was paid but everything was done first class. There is no substitute for a group of people who want to do something right.

July rolled around and it was time to do it. Miraculously, everybody arrived on time. We began on a sunny hot Monday afternoon reading all three plays with everyone concerned in attendance. There were thirty of us and it seemed like it took no time for all of us to get to know one another. And what was really remarkable was the feeling that everyone liked one another.

We were put up in cabins. (Real rustic-type cabins with fireplaces and martini pitchers.) We were for the most part housed by show. Actors, stage manager, playwright, and director all living either in the same house or in one close by, and believe me for the playwright that's heaven but not always for the actor.

Three a.m. I wake up Tony Papenfuss who played Hughes in my play *Back To Back*.

"Hey Tony, think this joke'll work?"

"Huh?"

"Charlene's got this friend. She'll be out of traction by the time we get home."

"GET OUTA HERE!"

"He loves it. Now, I'll try Nathan."

I wake up Nathan Cook who played Verville in *Back to Back*.

"Hey Nathan, how 'bout this one? I used to try to sing like that till I heard that dude Beethoven went deaf . . . . Pretty good, huh? . . . Nathan? . . . Nathan?"

The playwrights were nicknamed. I was "Underground" due to the fact my play *Back to Back* takes place in a hole in the ground. Gaylen Nielsen was the "Mole" since he revelled in his basement room, beating up his Smith Corona. He did emerge frequently for meals and to hand out rewrites and his play, *R.F.D.*, is a poetic and painful story of a man trying to return home. Aden Ross was called "Rewrite." Members of her cast told me they expected her to start rewriting the phone book next. Her play *Oedipus Unbound* takes a different look at the Oedipus story and not just from a mother's point of view. It's a stylized, honest-to-the-point-of-being-mathematical, look at who we are. It has been subsequently produced at Louisiana State University.

Our days were filled with rehearsals, (10 A.M. to 1 P.M., lunch 1 P.M. to 2 P.M., then more rehearsal from 2 P.M. to 6 P.M., then dinner and then optional rehearsls or martini races till bedtime) flys, mosquitoes, sweat, more flys, an occasional movie star, more flys, sunburn, genuine moments of honest-to-God creativity and ground squirrels who kept reminding us that afterall it was their land and would we please keep the noise down.

We rehearsed outside. I recommend that to anyone. With an aspen forest in front of you and Mount Tipanogas in back of you it's very hard to get yourself not to believe that creativity, nature, and the human heart aren't all one in the same. Watch an actor under a scorching sun, fighting the sweat and flys, trying to remember the line, trying to offer an idea to change the line, and subsequently giving you the line not out of his mouth but out of his frustration and energy. Watch that for two weeks and try not to be humbled, thankful, and amazed at the wonder of human beings.

To be more succinct about what went on at Sundance in 1980 let me put it this way: We got up in the morning, had some breakfast, went up on the side of a ski hill, rehearsed a scene, changed a scene, threw out a scene, built a scene, laughed our butts off, cursed the flys with theatrical vehemence, went and had lunch, went back to the rehearsal site, screamed at the flys some more, improvised some scenes, cut some scenes, rehearsed some scenes, threw out some scenes, laughed a bunch more and then said the hell with it and quit for a while and went back to the cabin and played with the script, had some dinner, relaxed, and then I went up to my room to rewrite what we had done that day so we could do it all over again tomorrow.

It was the best time of my life.

At the end of the two weeks we had a staged reading for the public and over four hundred people came up the canyon. It was a great big roaring success.

For two weeks I got to indulge in the human potential. I'm forever grateful to the Utah Playwriting Conference.

And now two years later I get to go again. If there's a Santa Claus he must be a playwright.

This summer I get to join playwrights Gil Smith, Toni Press, and Paul D'Andrea.

The concept and overall responsibility of the conference has changed. This year the Sundance Institute has taken over the administration of the conference and has instituted different guidelines.

This year the emphasis is on taking a concept and turning it into a play. That is, showing up with a rough first draft and seeing where it can go.

Unfortunately, information about this change in concept was circulated incorrectly and many finished plays were received. They were included in the judging and the four plays for this July are at various stages.

I will be going in with a very rough first draft of a play dealing with what I see as the loneliness of our times.

My idea for this new play is based on a newspaper article I saw a few years back. The article was about a hermit out in the Nevada desert who killed three people. I don't necessarily want to write about this particular story but about a conflict that this article brought me to think about. Is it the loneliness of insanity or the insanity of loneliness that drives us to an act of desperation.

I already have the beginning, middle, and end of the play. What I need and what we'll do at Sundance is build the characters of four people and put them into the situation I've dreamed up. Will it work? I honestly don't know and that makes me both excited and scared. But I guess that's what creativity is about. Somewhere in between fear and confidence lies that little creative bug that keeps flitting around trying to get out.

And that's what Sundance offers the playwright. The chance to get at those bugs inside you. The chance to have actors, stage managers, and directors drag you along until you finally see what was already in front of you.

At the final get together at the first Playwrights Conference Robert Redford said something to all of us that has really stuck with me. He said that as long as he was in charge of Sundance it would be a place for people to "dare to be wrong."

Well, this summer four playwrights are going to dare to be wrong but somehow I have a feeling that everything's going to turn out right.

Duck Hunting in Marin:
On the Second Shepard Workshop
Scott Christopher Wren

"Language has to be discovered, not structured," Shepard explains. "There are modes of expression lying dormant and every once in a while something is triggered and they become accessible to us. We need to learn how to open that channel." Shepard believes that theater is the one form open to real adventure, as it can move into the world of the mysterious, the unknown. He suggests that perhaps new voices are needed in theater, urging us to explore the huge territories not even touched upon yet.

It is almost two years since Sam Shepard made that comment during the playwriting workshop he led at the Bay Area Playwrights Festival III in 1980. It was published in *West Coast Plays 7* as part of "Camp Shepard: Exploring the Geography of Character," an article which grew out of my participation in that workshop. Shepard's urging seems no less vital today, and his challenge to explore new theatrical territory has been met by the direction the Playwrights Festival has taken since.

Festival IV, held in August 1981, was a major departure from its predecessors. As a result of a long and hard-nosed evaluation, the Festival moved away from producing fully-mounted plays to concentrate on the development of new work. Rather than soliciting plays, the Festival this time solicited writers, who in turn defined their projects. Emphasis was on the process of creating plays, presenting short pieces only a few times, and with minimal technical resources. We wanted to create an environment in which to experiment—especially to explore opportunities for writing beyond the territory of the conventional play, to question the impulse of writing itself, to examine what it means to be a playwright in these times. We realized that earlier Festivals had duplicated the work of the established Bay Area theaters that were already doing full productions of new plays. The Festival could serve the complementary, and neglected role of a community focussed on inceptive work, work which could go on to fuller productions in other theaters if the merit were there.

The Festival title, "Duck Hunting in Marin" came up jokingly one afternoon at the end of an exhausting planning meeting. But the more we thought about it the more it seemed to sum up the festival's intent perfectly. When the announcements for Festival IV were published with this title, reactions ranged from raised eyebrows to glances of inquisitive non-comprehension. But there was the occasional chuckle of understanding, as when Murray Mednick (playwright in residence) first read it and said, "Yeah, isn't it the truth. It really is a lot like a duck shoot. Sometimes there are ducks and sometimes not, and sometimes you hit them and sometimes not."

The Festival had a similar and purposeful uncertainty to it. Nothing was predetermined. There were, initially, no scripts. The work was subject to constant change and revision. The name of the game was trusting writers enough to take artisitc risks. Why? Because if the Festival could create and maintain this spirit of "real adventure," as Shepard called it, the nature of the work produced could be much more exciting. Discoveries could be made, possibly even new ground broken. On one front, experienced playwrights could share their expertise with students (in workshops) as well as with colleagues, and on the other front they could probe and refine new avenues of investigation through creating and performing work.

Six artists in residence (Joseph Chaikin, Laura Farabough, Chris Hardman, Murray Mednick, John O'Keefe, and George Walker) led workshops and created theater pieces during Festival IV. And Sam Shepard again led an invitational workshop with some twenty playwrights, about half of whom were Camp Shepard veterans.

The first workshop meeting had the familiar signs of the year before: all looked quiet, anxious, expectant, and had next to no idea what they'd be writing. The venue had moved from a theological seminary to a high school, and this year Shepard wanted to meet indoors. Any significance to this, I wondered? Probably. The multi-colored plastic scoop chairs and the bright, quasi-orange carpet complemented by flourescent lighting was a far cry from the sunny lawn of the seminary. "Airport lounge" pretty much captures the feeling.

While the summer before Shepard had us working on a wide-ranging and eclectic series of exercises, this time he wanted to hone down to real specifics. Getting in touch with "voice" was still his central concern, but this time he said he wanted "to provide an extremely limited structure for us to work inside of." So why not meet inside as well? Our lounge was an extremely limited structure (slightly mitigated when we kept the lights off) and affording a view of the unlimited and unstructured sky.

Shepard's proposition was to write five-minute monologues. He suggested we think about music as a possible element, as long as it didn't require electricity or any sophisticated technology (no tape recorders). Why monologues? Shepard felt they force a writer to focus on basics: "Dialogue makes dramatic tension—or apparent dramatic tension—too easy. Too often dialogue reduces itself to just banter." So far so good. But then he abruptly asks us if we have any questions. Questions? About what? Silence cuts the room. Puzzled expressions. Before anyone can muster a sentence out of the vacuum, Shepard pulls a little notebook out of his back pocket and tells us he has a few things we might consider when approaching our monologues. First, he wants us to think about them in terms of a "Speaker." The Speaker being simply one who speaks, as in a spoken work, *sine qua non* of theater. I like its implication of something active and present—present tense—manifest. Then, true to form, Shepard has a whole list of his own questions:

1. Who is the Speaker and who is the Speaker addressing? Is it between the Speaker and himself, the Speaker and the audience, or the Speaker and another? If the latter, who or what is the other?

2. What is the Speaker's predicament with the audience? Is the audience voyeuristic, listening, not listening, intellectually or emotionally involved? He emphasizes that the Speaker must be brought into a relationship with the audience and that regardless of what the situation is we shouldn't lose track of the exchange with the audience.

3. What is the state of the Speaker? (Physically, emotionally, intellectually.)

4. Where is the Speaker in time, space, history?

5. Who does the Speaker serve?

6. What is the Speaker's purpose in being there?

7. How many levels does the Speaker exist on?

8. How do you want the Speaker to be understood?

9. Is the Speaker alone? To what degree is the Speaker alone? (With the audience? With himself? Or is he just pretending to be alone?)

10. Is there a disguise or mask to the voice of the Speaker? Is the Speaker making up the voice or is it the one he/she uses when alone?

   a. Does the Speaker know his/her own voice?

b. If the voice is a disguise, can you peel the fake one off and get the real one to come through now and then? Is the Speaker using language as a mask to some purpose, and if so, what?

11. Why is the Speaker speaking? What is the impulse to get the voice to hit the air?

12. What is the language *not* being heard? How does the Speaker connect with the silent implications of what is spoken?

13. What is the Speaker connected with? (Weather, seasons, age, sex, etc.)

A *few things* to consider, he said. Shepard's talent for understatement is not limited to his playwriting. As I glance at my furiously scribbled notes I notice a place where I've written Suspect instead of Speaker. It seems to fit. The object being to find out if the Speaker is who or what he says he is. I begin to imagine an interrogation along these lines: "Did you get a good look at the Speaker? Would you recognize him again? Was the Speaker acting suspiciously?"

As Shepard finishes going over his list he looks up matter-of-factly. Pause. "Okay?" he asks us, completely earnest. Involuntary smiles break out across the room. Why sure, fine. You bet! Everyone is intrigued by the pitch of the questions, not sure what to make of them, but engaged. Finally, Shepard mentions in passing that he wants us to consider acting in our own pieces, or at least directing them ourselves. Energetic fear pervades the room as the first meeting breaks up. Now all we have to do is write something, direct it, maybe perform.

During the next two weeks Shepard's questions provided a rich axis for discussion. All of the writing was done outside of the sessions which were devoted to reading and discussng the drafts of our monologues. We all read our own work at least two times. The notion of the Speaker was always predominant, so much so that there wasn't a single monologue that referred to the Speaker by a given name.

Though a number of Shepard's questions can be translated into the terms of conventional dramatic analysis—as in "What is the language not being heard?" (Subtext) or "Why is the Speaker speaking?" (Motivation)—Shepard is getting at something deeper. In the latter question, for example, he is referring to far more than standard psychological explanations of behavior. "What triggers the language?" he asks, "in that particular moment?" he adds, thereby moving the question toward a phenomenological consideration of the actual event on stage and the immediate predicament of the Speaker. In this regard, Shepard frequently used the term "eventfulness"—which extends from the smallest activity (a door opening, perhaps) to the largest (a roof falling in)—as a way to express whether we'd fully captured a single moment or a tangible quality in the monologues. He was very specific in noting when certain modes of expression or actions seemed integral to a piece and when they felt "gratuitous" or "laid on", as he put it.

But Shepard was quick to point out that eventfulness is not the result of merely external circumstances. He noted that, "Sometimes language causes itself—a lot of the time." Implied here is an invitation to follow the voice, to sense something unknown and get on its trail, ultimately trying to penetrate its mystery. "To follow the mystery of it is the key," he notes, but then cautions, "The mystery has to be sincere; it has to have integrity. True mystery comes from a kind of tension and the tension is when two elements come into contact, which means that the Speaker is *up against something*."

This comes down to an excruiating question of why the Speaker speaks, specifically and totally in the Speaker's own terms. What is the justification for not remaining silent or for being there at all for that matter? In our writing, this led to a constant examination of what exactly the language of speech is. Shepard emphasized, time and again, that playwriting too easily uses thought and not speech. Rather than remain true to a voice, writers often get into making their own statements which then come out as "big ideas," as abstractions imposed on the work. This jars the listener, pulling him out of the internal dynamics of the play by commenting on it. As the workshop progressed, we began to sense, almost physically, the distinction between parts of the monologues that were external and those parts which investigated the much subtler conditions and states of the Speaker. It would sound as if the laid-on voice were suddenly coming out of the loudspeaker.

Importantly, Shepard is concerned that this investigation not be purely a private process which excludes the listener. Through all his initial questions and subsequent responses to the monologues was a constant awareness of the audience and a recognition that the Speaker is not only in the presence of, but in a relationship with, the audience. This is not just an *a priori* assumption but an acute awareness of the audience's immediacy. Shepard felt that a critical requirement for theatricality is the ability to open itself up and let the audience in; it is not being read or projected on a screen, but is happening in that very moment on stage.

The issue is *relation,* he stresses, and that's a tough nut to crack because it is all too easy to talk to no one and about nothing. Shepard feels that writers have to pay a certain price to deal with something fully in their work. He warns that, "You can justify something until the cows come home, but to have a reason or *not* to have a reason isn't eough. You have to really be up against something and have enough air around it (in the writing) so we (in the audience) can connect with it."

While Shepard believes that "emotions" (he emphasizes the word as if suspicious of it) have their place in a piece of work, he feels that it is more important to get to a place where an audience has *feelings* about it. But "big emotions," like big ideas, put an audience off as there is no way to connect with them. Shepard explains: "The Speaker can be tense or upset or whatever, but true feelings are triggered when the audience feels together with the Speaker in a situation; in the same boat. When that happens the emotional shit falls away and we are into something new." He pauses a moment then adds, "This can change what is communicated. Beyond a statement." Implied here is the writers' willingness to make discoveries, to be able to question their own understanding or points of view on something. The ultimate question for Shepard is, "Do you want to stay on one side of it yourself, or let us in and meet it? And if you're going to meet it then you're going to have to pay for it!" He smiles. We laugh.

Shepard later explained that his intention in the workshop was to have the playwrights deal with "the real manual labor of craftsmanship, to stick within a limited frame and sweat it out. " And to sustain even five minutes of material within these perimeters was a tough challenge. It was an entirely different proposition from writing a monologue within the context of a play where characters, situation and plot have already been established. In five minutes we had to deal with solo pieces which were complete dramatic entities. This didn't leave room to wander. The writing had to be right down to the bone, as one speck of fat stopped the movement of a piece dead in its tracks.

So we wrote and brought in drafts and read them aloud, and

threw them out and started over, and then started over again, and read them, and threw them out, and re-wrote and revised and sweated it out. But there was always the feeling, however dim at times, that the work was gradually getting closer. Shepard's feedback was amazingly on target. As someone would begin to read he would drop his head slightly, completely focused on listening. Afterwards, we would all offer our reactions, but sooner or later Shepard would always come to the heart of the matter. And once we all got used to his vernacular—a short-hand vocabulary we quicky developed—discussions were very specific, responding to a writer's intent and execution. The term with the most currency after voice was undoubtedly "stakes." What are the stakes for the Speaker? By stakes Shepard did not mean elaborately concocted character rationales, plot justification, or thematic generalizations, but simply what are the stakes for the Speaker at the very moment of speaking? Why bother?

Shepard believes that such stakes exist and are implied by the language itself—its tone, pitch, rhythm—as if it were music. If the right elements are present in the voice, then the play's statement will be there also—implied and within the piece, rather than laid on and external. As with music, it is easy to discern what is false or phoney right away, instinctively. And even when Shepard felt that certain monologues were getting closer to their targets, he always urged the writers to go further with them. In every case, if a writer was on to something there was a taste to it, however vague, in the beginning. His reactions and suggestions were geared towards how to hone it down—completely up-front feedback, yet always supportive.

The final two weeks of the workshop were spent working with actors on the monologues, doing still more re-writing. Shepard and a number of the directors from the Festival came in at various times to watch rehearsals and would offer suggestions. In the end, only one playwright braved it and decided to act in his piece, but we all directed our own work. This was important for us to do and was possible, given the limited format of short pieces. Directing forced us to step back and look at our work differently, and also made it mighty clear from the beginning that we really had to know what the monologues were about if we were to communicate our intentions to the actors. So directing was healthy not only in terms of making us struggle first hand with the problems directors face constantly, but also for the insights it gave us into our writing. In this context it wasn't a question of making something work, but rather of asking, "Is it right?"

Sixteen of the monologues were finally performed during the Festival. They were done with minimal lighting and virtually no props or costumes. For myself, having participated in both of Shepard's workshops, this was the culmination and realization of approaches developed the previous summer. It was a time to call into question and re-examine basic impulses and to focus on nuts-and-bolts issues of playwriting amid critical, yet supportive community of writers. As before, Shepard never advocated any particular style. He posed some fundamental (and universal) questions and encouraged us to find and refine our own voices.

As he said towards the end of the workshop, summing up his intentions and capturing the Duck-Hunting-in-Marin spirit, "the important thing is the tracking down of the voice. You're bound to go off up a lot of blind alleys, but it's the tracking down of the voice that's important. If something is there, then you have to hunt it, and the question is how to become a more determined hunter."

POSTSCRIPT: AN APPROACH TO UNCHARTED TERRITORY

The success of Shepard's workshop and as well of work developed by the other artists in residence, confirmed and solidified the Festival's commitment to this kind of open inquiry. First and foremost, this emphasis involves trusting and respecting the playwright as primary artist, both as writer and conceptualist. Certainly, there is a lot of talk in most theaters about serving playwrights, but in practice it often amounts to serving the theaters. To seriously support playwrights means presenting their plays on their own terms and giving them the freedom and support to realize them fully, come what may. But this does not mean setting them adrift: critical feedback is essential to the process.

This commitment has further translated itself into the Festival's encouraging playwrights to direct their own work. During Festival V *all* of the work presented will be directed by its authors, with a staff of a half-dozen resident directors to provide support.

In addition, the Festival is encouraging playwrights to create works for particular performance spaces, natural terrains, visual environments, or musical scores. Tamalpais High School, site of Festivals IV and V, features an indoor theater, outdoor amphitheater, and other found spaces suitable for performance. In this

regard, Festival V will explore possible syntheses between performance art / visual theater and playwriting, with a group of
writers working on pieces responding to a landscape environment
created by Alan and Bean Finneran of Soon 3. In addition to the
Finnerans, visual artists Chris Hardman (Antenna) and Laura
Farabough (whose Nightfire production of *Surface Tension,* which is
presented in this issue, was created for Festival IV) will again be
artists in residence.

Obviously, the success of such an endeavor requires careful
attention to the selection of Festival artists. While not engaging in
formal script solicitations for production consideration, the
Festival staff does read a large number of scripts and keeps close
tabs on productions and performances by Bay Area theater artists.

Serving the Bay Area is a primary mission, and here the Festival
is able to bridge a gap which exists, bringing together artists who,
because of their commitments to particular theater groups during
the regular season, otherwise would not have the opportunity to
work together and share ideas. And the Bay Area is further enriched
by the Festival's invitation of playwrights and other theater artists
from across the nation. Thus Festival V will include actor / director
Joseph Chaikin, playwright and literary manager Richard Nelson,
and three of the artists from the Padua Hills Writers Conference
(see Susan La Tempa's article in this issue) Murray Mednick,
Martin Epstein, and Maria Irene Fornes, will present work and lead
workshops. Also, two playwrights from New Dramatists, a
playwrights development organization in New York, will be in
residence during the Festival in an exchange program which will
enable several Festival writers to work in New York the following
year.

Finally, with an intensive, four-week program oriented towards
work in progress, the Festival is an ideal environment in which to
offer workshops for theater students and professionals. Artists in
residence perform the dual roles of creating theater pieces and
leading workshops in performance, directing, and playwriting.

These many projects and directions are all linked together by
their common emphasis on experimentation, some of which is
avant garde and some within the context of established forms. The
work-in-progress orientation of the Festival allows playwrights
the freedom, in a low-pressure atmosphere, to explore new ways of
working. Since each work is presented only a few times the worry
about critical and box-office success is minimized. Audiences are

educated to the benefits of taking a chance on unknown kinds of work. And plays developed at the Festival can go on to full productions at other theaters — indeed more than half the work premiered at Festival IV was subsequently produced elsewhere.

Central to this approach is what might be called theatrical research. Laboratory is a term often used to express this concept, but it has besn so overused in theater that all specific meaning has been stripped from it. Research is here used in the creative sense — primary source investigation, conducting experiments. And the primary theater artist is the playwright, if we broaden that term to include creators of performance art and visual theater. This implies expanding the artistic role of the playwrights beyond the proverbial page, to involve them in directing, design, and other aspects of theatrical endeavor.

In terms of the uncharted territory out there, theater is still sailing the high seas, seeking a shorter route to Asia for the spice trade. But wait until North America gets discovered. Wait until it discovers itself!

Three Festival Monologues

Kick the Can
Elizabeth Wray

A woman turns over a large food can with her foot. She turns it over again, then touches it (like touching home base) with her toe.

Home. (*Laughs.*) I remember I used to like to cook. I had a lot of cans on my shelves. I used to walk into my pantry and just stand there in the middle of all these unopened cans. Tomato sauce. Spanish olives. Anchovy paste. It was reassuring. Knowing there were all these meals just waiting there on the shelves. Waiting to be eaten. Just waiting there.

(*She kicks the can.*) I never felt that way. That way makes me want

---

to puke. I used to walk in that pantry and take off all my clothes and open up all those cans and pour that stuff all over me. Yeah. Creamed corn sliding down my thighs. And smushing all that white meat out of the red beans, rubbing it in. And those little slimy things. Those oysters. Putting them up inside of me. Then popping them out. Putting them in. Popping them out. Then the best part — waiting there for my man to come find me. My man to come looking for his dinner and instead, find his dinner there dripping off of me. And saying to him: dinner's ready.

(*Bringing the can back to home base.*) GET OUT OF HERE. She's the part of me who likes to wander off. SO GET LOST. I'm through with her. (*Pause.*) Because of her I lose things. Because of her wandering off. One day I come home and my man's gone. Because of her wandering off. After something *big.* BIG. Oh yeah, her latest adventure was a real biggie. Wandering off to become a real live rock 'n role star in Butte, Montana. With that burned out rockabilly band. Yeah. She made a big impression on those out-of-work pit miners. Standing there in that red light on that dirty white linoleum wedge of a stage singing (*She sings.*) "Last chance, Texaco . . ." Living out some truck-stop fantasy. Surrounded by a herd of miners' sons with their caved-in eyes staring blanks through her. Yeah, that was *big* time. And then the best part — coming home and her man's gone. And every single last stick of her life with him is packed up and gone. (*Pulls note out of her pocket.*) Except for this note stuck underneath that can. (*Reads note.*) "Welcome home, babe. Hope you found what you were looking for." (*Pause.*) So what's she going to wander off from now? Hunh? (*Laughs.*) She's been had. I mean, what's the point of wandering off if there's nothing left to wander off from? (*Pause.*) Just you and me, can.

(*She kicks the can.*) She doesn't know nothing about wandering. She don't know shit. She's the part of me who sticks around and digs herself into a hole. WANNA KNOW HOW FAR I CAN GO? She's got no idea how far I can go. I can go to the other side of the desert. Over the mountains of Mexico. I can go down deep into the jungle of Mexico. I can go to a little hotel full of green and purple birds. My hotel. And I can fuck men that change colors like ripening papayas every time my fingers dig in. I can sleep in the stump of a 5000 year old bristlecone pine and dream about the age of ice and the first lizards and the last warm valley. That's how far I can go. And if she could ever get it up to come that far to find me, she'll open up the door of the little hotel and I'll be sitting there. Yeah. In my shorts. With the can—full of everything I've seen. And she'll know *she's* been had. It's her who's been had all along. (*Crossing to can.*) She won't be able to help herself. She'll cross the room and take this can. And she'll drink down the sweet cosmic juice.

(*She drinks. She spits.*) It's just a can. It's a goddamn can. It doesn't do things to *me*. (*She places the can upright on the ground.*) I do things to it. It's all that's left to do things to. (*Pause; laughs.*) I could cook in it. I could wash in it. I could store things in it. When I get some things to store. I could paint it purple, with little green stars, and store pencils in it . . . .

Great! She'll make herself a little boring life, just like the one she had before. Then before too long I'll be itching to leave it again. (*Slight pause.*) Hey, I wanna just get out of here. There's nothing left.

She takes note out of her pocket, wads it up and throws it back over her shoulder. She starts to kick the can but instead kicks the air. She walks away, stops, turns around and comes back to the can.

I could make a big tomato sauce. Lots of grated garlic and zucchini. I could invite my friends, the ones that are left. Yeah, I could invite the ones that are left for supper. I could fill them up. We could talk. I could push back from the table and watch them talk. Slow, like you do after a meal. Then I could go out on the back porch and let her imagine all the other things she could be doing, all the other places she could be living. All the possibilities under the stars. And then I'd go back inside and say goodbye and watch my friends walk out and disappear one by one down the street. With my tomato sauce in their stomachs. Helping them get through the night. (*Pause.*) That would be something.

The Autophobic
Scott Christopher Wren

As the lights come up a man is sitting on the floor resting against the upstage wall. He is sitting at an angle facing stage left, and talks to someone stage right. The tone of the speaker should be matter of fact, which should work against the material. Nothing should be put on it, he's just telling his story, he's got it down cold

I hate accidents. (*Pause.*) But I'm always . . . I'm plagued by them. My life takes place in snatches between accidents. I squeeze it in. (*Looks at listener.*) Barely. They crash over you like a wave or like . . . like an avalanche. You never know when. They just come up. Surprise you when you least expect it. The crucial moments always come outta nowhere. Shaving in the morning, you slit your jugular vein. Drop a cigarette and burn your house down. Spill a beer and break your neck. (*Looks at listener.*) But this is the biggee. Oh boy, I bought this one. I'm just driving home. Nothing monumental. Just driving home after the bars closed. Done it a million times. Streets are practically deserted. Look down to find a goddamn cigarette and BOOM! An accident happens. It wasn't my fault. I should'a never—. I turned the corner, slow. Didn't see the stop sign. It was late, dark. She just came outta nowhere. I swerved, drove the sedan into a travel agency. Thought I missed her. Got out and god! There she was laid out on the pavement. It looked bad. (*Pause.*)

See, I've been accident-prone ever since I can remember. Christ, I came into the picture by accident. My mother didn't realize she was pregnant. And ever since then it's been . . . dangerous. A series of close calls. So now I imagine them on purpose, conjure up hypothetical situations. Not that I'm paranoid. That's all behind me now. This is a technique. If I've already anticipated it, the accident can't happen to me. The target . . . I had to get outta there. (*Pause.*)

You wanna sit down? Sorry, you'll have to sit on the floor. I got ridda the furniture, nothing but hazards. Took all the doors off too, after my hand got slammed. (*He rubs it.*) She's probably okay. (*Pause.*) I bet you don't know what the leading cause of accidental death is? Traffic! It's lethal. Avoid it. Best way is to stay off the streets entirely. I'm not going out again . . . Ever! There's nothing you can't have home-delivered. You place the box in the center of the room. Open it slowly. Inspect the contents. So far so good. Everything's in order. One by one you pull the bones out of the chicken. Count 'em. Then chop it finely just to make sure. No knives. Use a comb. Count the bones again. Okay, you're ready. Use your hands. No silverware. Wait! Only one hand. Take very small bites. Chew thoroughly. Eat everything. Then count the bones again. Fine. You're home free. Dispose of them. Then you take a long cool drink to celebrate. (*Pause.*) And you choke on the ice. Ugly. Insensitive. Choking is a cruel killer. I've stopped eating solid foods altogether. She should'a looked before —! (*Pause.*)

Look, let's face it. Potential causes of accidents are infinite. But there is a foolproof way to protect yourself. I invented it. The John Glenn method. You remember John. He slipped in the shower and broke his back after being the first man to orbit earth. How'd it happen? Easy. He didn't pre-plan. John was originally going to take his shower earlier. But the phone rang. He should'a never answered it. Allowed the unknown to creep in for a second and (*Snaps fingers.*) he had an accident.

You wanna know the secret? Simple. Number one, accidents are surprises, right? So, you get there before they do. Wait for them. See them coming. Eliminate the surprise element and you put accidents out of business. (*Pause.*) She should'a pre-planned. (*Pause.*) And two, don't, I repeat, don't respond to stimuli. Stimuli move in and take over. Pronto! They don't need much. Stimuli can thrive anywhere. Keep the shades down, don't use appliances, get rid of furniture, and don't make loud noises. Eliminate stimuli-breeding areas and you cut down on potential causes. (*Pause.*)

It's hot in here. (*Runs his hand through his hair, notices his hand and looks at it.*) Ah, where was I? Oh yea, accidents happen while you're pre-occupied. Stay in the present. And above all watch your hands. Just look at them. (*Looks at listener.*) Come on! Closely. (*He concentrates on his hands.*) Make absolutely sure you know where they are at all times. See those thumbs, all those fingers. They're

enemies. Always want to touch things. (*Starts touching his body.*)
Feel, fondle, caress, stroke, strangle. (*Pulls hands off his neck.*) Like
I said, keep track of your hands at all times. When they're not
absolutely essential keep them in your pockets. (*He grips his knees.*)
And never, never, never close your eyes. Keep blinking to a
minimum. Of course, this eliminates sleep. I've been up for
days . . . She'll be alright. (*Pause.*) I mean, anything can happen
when you're asleep. And what can yo do about it? Wake up? (*Sighs.*)
It's all over! (*Pause.*) But nothing's sneaking up on me now.
Nothing! I've got it covered. Completely. No surprises. (*Whispers.*)
No stimuli. (*Lights fade.*)

Five by Six
Dana Foley

nobody will find me down here
doubt anyone will look
five rows across
six deep
that makes thirty sets
thirty sets
of eyes
covered by thirty white sheets
the way ya put a jacket
over the cage of a parakeet
let the bird know it's time to sleep
otherwise
ita just keep talkin
an starin
the blind stare
of a dumb bird
till it just keeled over an died
from sheer exhaustion

like a go go dancer
who done one too many a shift
bet you there's one right now
out in jersey
who been paid her money
had her after-work drink
bars getting ready to close
chairs stacked on tables
cages cleaned out
last guy paid for his last pinch
plug pulled to the jukebox
lights turned off
cept for the red exit sign
but there's no gettin out for her
not tonight
i don't wanna put my clothes back on
i don't wanna go home
it's too late the busses have stopped running
someone stole my fire extinguisher
there's no puttin me out tonight
tonight ladies an gentleman
i want to introduce
pasaic's bird of paradise
watch her flap in the wind
watch her cut the wind
watch her cut the wind with her hips
watch her rip zippers zip zippers
spark the unsparked
stomp on the unstomped
to the beatin
to the beat of the unbeat in
they turned the music off
but ya can't turn me off
i'm gonna dance to the unbeat in
beatin
beatin
to the beat
of broken bottles bein swept off the floor
to the beatin
to the beatin of scum bein wiped off the walls
to the beatin

to the beatin
i can't stop
to the beatin
to the beatin
i can't stop
to the beatin
to the beat of alla your unbeatin hearts
my party is down here with you guys
stop laughin slim
i could be a dumb bird if i want
ain't you never seen a girl in her slip before?
nothing to be embarassed about
i know alla you guys are naked under those sheets
can't see nothin anyway
you're all dead
thats why i like you guys you know
cause you're honest
specially you slim
you let me be just who i am
keeps your hands to yourself
not like those guys upstairs
put their hands
all over me
just cause i like to dance
sometimes I just gotta dance
an their eyes peel off
pop out
roll on the floor
like black eight balls
lookin for their hole
an i dance harder
an their eyes roll
richochet up my dress
but do they ever ask to dance wit me
or go for a walk
oh no
an i dance harder
for the sake of the show
an their eyes roll
an i dance harder
an their eyes roll

like glass marbles
let out the bag
an i dance harder
smashin them
grindin
them into the ground
i want to go slow slim
but sometimes i can't stop
i want to dance a slow dance
with nobody lookin
to go fast
i wanna dance wit somebody slim
boy i bet you were a real looker
when you were alive
oh go on
i could tell
i ain't blind
must've had it rough though
your liver's shot to shit
no i'm sorry
we don't have to go into it
there's not much time left anyway
shut-up danny-boy
i'm not talkin to you
well anyway
i just wanted to let you know
you been a real friend to me
you don't make me feel crazy or weird
ya let me dance fast
ya let me dance slow
an more important
sometimes I feel like i don't gotta dance at all
like i could dance wit you
sittin real still
not movin a muscle
to the beat of the unbeatin
heart
slim
i'm gettin cold
you know an i ain't gonn see you no more
tomorrow

we're supposed to quarter the skull
an then in the afternoon
work on your heart
an after that
it's down the hall
in little pieces in plastic bags
an i thought maybe i could do something for you
you know how those hamburger hands hack away at you
an i thought maybe
i could cut your heart out
myself / here / tonight
you know as a friend
sorta like the last dance

Catholic Girls
Doris Baizley

Catholic Girls was first produced at the Forum Lab of the Mark Taper Forum, in Los Angeles, produced by Susan Albert Lowenberg and L. A. Theatre Works on October 10, 1979 with the following cast:

BLACKIE	Belita Moreno
MARYCLARE	Lisa Jane Persky
ANNA	Sharon Barr
SKIPPER/PRINCE	Darrell Fetty
MAMA	Madge Sinclair

Music by Richard Weinstock
Lyrics by Doris Baizley *with* Richard Weinstock
Directed by Jeremy Blahnik
Set and lighting by Barbara Ling
Costumes by Victoria de Kay
Musicians: Gary Grimm, Maurice Killao, Mark Milner
Maggie Rosten, Richard Weinstock

A revised version was produced at the Odyssey Theatre, Los Angeles, by the L. A. Theatre Works on April 4, 1981, under the title *Hearts on Fire*. The current text, though it reverts to the original title, is a revision of the 1981 script.

TIME

An Easter weekend.

PLACES

Boston, Florida, and the Cafe of Miracles.

Catholic Girls
Doris Baizley

ACT ONE

Lights up on the hospital in Boston. The window of an intensive care unit. Curtains drawn. BLACKIE *enters, wearing a white nurse's uniform dress. She smokes a cigarette.*

BLACKIE: He says: let me go. His lips barely move. I can't get close enough to him to hear it, but I can see. He says: let me go. Let him go? His heart is wired to a TV screen, he's drilled full of I.V.'s he's hooked up to so many tubes and wires, and pumps and hoses, he can't even lift his head. Nothing moves but his eyes.

MARYCLARE: (*Entering. Wearing the same uniform. Carrying a pile of linens.*) You shouldn't be smoking in uniform, Blackie.

BLACKIE: Just his eyes.

MARYCLARE: Don't let Anna catch you. (*She exits.*)

BLACKIE: Imagine— the last thing you see on earth is a fluorescent light and somebody's hands on a dial. The last thing you feel is a stainless steel needle . . .

ANNA: (*Entering. Wearing the same uniform.*) Linens. We need more linens.

BLACKIE: And the last sound you hear is a bleep on the monitor. I don't want to die in a hospital.

ANNA: She's impossible today. She keeps disappearing with the linens.

BLACKIE: I don't want to live in a hospital.

ANNA: Don't let Sister Daniel catch you smoking. (*She exits.*)

BLACKIE: (*Stamps out her cigarette.*) Not another day.

ANNA: (*Offstage.*) Maryclare?

BLACKIE: (*Looks to see if Sister Daniel is around, to make sure no one sees her.*) Sister? (*No answer.*) I can't hear my calling anymore, Sister. The vision's gone too. It's dark. It's nothing but walls, Florence Nightingale's dead, Sister. I have to get out. I need a vision. Give me a vision, okay? I'll kneel if I have to. (*She kneels. Looks. Nothing.*) I'm kneeling . . . I'm ready.

Lights come up on BLACKIE's *vision. It begins as a standard religious vision.* BLACKIE *kneels and prays as a tall, veiled, feminine figure appears behind her. It is the silhouette of the Blessed Virgin, Queen of Heaven.*

BLACKIE: (*A chant.*)

>You surpass all mankind in beauty.
>Your lips are molded in grace.
>So you are blessed by God forever.

MAMA: (*A chant.*)

>You have loved right and hated wrong.
>Your God has anointed you with oil.

BLACKIE:

>The Queen stands at your right hand, arrayed in gold.

MAMA:

>Hear, oh daughter, and see.
>Turn your ear.
>Forget your people and your father's house.

BLACKIE:

>The Queen stands at your right hand, arrayed in gold.
>She stands in gold, shining.

The woman of BLACKIE's *vision lowers her veil to reveal herself as* MAMA, *a nightclub singer, wearing a spangled gold dress, a crown of gardenias in her hair, and carrying a microphone.*

MAMA: (*Sings.*)

MIRACLE CAFE

>For slippin' out I'm
>Slippin' on some
>Blood-red lipstick,
>Some lacquered red nails,
>And my dragon-red heels,
>Satin spikes—
>I like the way it feels . . .
>
>In Mama's Miracle Cafe,
>The burning heart's own cabaret,
>You'll find a club so hot
>The dance floor flames with passion
>And hear my band of angels play.

In Mama's Nightclub of Delights
We'll fill your eyes with wondrous sights,
And in a flash of horns of gold
And drums of thunder,
Your long lost dream will come alive.

Go through the smoke to find the fire,
If you are lost you're on the way,
Mama's Cafe never closes,
Come to me . . .

(*To* BLACKIE, *over music.*) Don't be frightened if Mama's leads you
to the edge of town where it's dangerous after twilight. They'll
tell you nobody goes there. Never after dark. It's way beyond the
city limits. They'll say you're not allowed. They'll call it a
dream. But you know it's there. And you know the danger is just
where you're going . . . you're ready . . . (*Sings.*)

Come on and step out,
It's time to put on
The blood red lipstick,
The lacquered red nails,
And the dragon red heels,
Satin spikes —
You'll like the way it feels . . .

In Mama's Miracle Cafe
It's always hot salvation day.
You'll get your crown of ruby, long-stemmed roses,
And sing while Mama's angels play.

Go thru the smoke to find the fire
If you are lost you're on your way.
Mama's Cafe never closes,
Come to me . . . to me . . . to me . . .

(*Blackout on* MAMA. *The vision disappears.* BLACKIE *runs off.*)

Lights up on the kitchen of the nurses' apartment. Boston. MARYCLARE
sits in front of a sunlamp. She is very still, turning her head occasion-
ally. She wears a white robe, a bandana, white socks, and slippers, and
eye-protectors. She buffs her nails.

MARYCLARE: (*Singing softly, to herself, a 50's tune.*)

ALL NIGHT LONG

All night long,
One night together.
All night long
Can't last forever
But with a love this strong
I know it can't be wrong
So no matter what they say
We'll stay in love this way
Everyday
All night long

BLACKIE *enters, from her room, wearing a kimono over a black bathing suit, sunglasses, sandals. She places herself near* MARYCLARE, *trying to get some light from the lamp. She joins in the singing. They get into it. Very 50's.*

MARYCLARE & BLACKIE:

All night long
I want you near me.
All night long
I'll love you dearly
And with a love this strong
I know it can't be wrong
So no matter what they say
We'll stay in love this way
Everyday
All night long.

MARYCLARE: We're good.
BLACKIE: We're getting better. Let's work on it. Let's make it perfect. We'll sing forever. I had a vision, Maryclare. Back at the hospital.
MARYCLARE: I know.
BLACKIE: You saw her too. Maryclare, did you see her?
MARYCLARE: Anna said you ran out.
BLACKIE: Mama?
MARYCLARE: What?
BLACKIE: Nothing. Let's sing "A Thousand Stars in the Sky."
MARYCLARE: I don't know the words.

BLACKIE: Oh. (*Silence.* MARYCLARE *massages oil on her hands.* BLACKIE *sits up suddenly.*) What's that?

MARYCLARE: Just the wind.

BLACKIE: No. The scent . . .

MARYCLARE: Oil.

BLACKIE: Jasmine?

MARYCLARE: No.

BLACKIE: Lily of the Valley?

MARYCLARE: Rose.

BLACKIE: Tuberose or plain?

MARYCLARE: Plain.

BLACKIE: It's always plain.

MARYCLARE: It's Anna's.

BLACKIE: Did you steal it?

MARYCLARE: Blackie. You're blocking my light.

BLACKIE: Did you?

MARYCLARE: She gave it to me.

BLACKIE: Did you think about it?

MARYCLARE: She's getting rid of her wedding presents.

BLACKIE: She's always getting rid of her wedding presents.

MARYCLARE: This time she's really doing it. There's a rummage sale.

BLACKIE: You stole it.

MARYCLARE: Go to Hell, Blackie.

BLACKIE: Go to Hell, Maryclare.

MARYCLARE: Let's sing "A Thousand Stars."

BLACKIE: You could have lied.

MARYCLARE: I don't tell lies.

BLACKIE: You could make something up. Come on, Maryclare, make something up. Tell me something new. Tell me something off the schedule. We aren't in Boston. You dyed your uniform red. Let me hear something we don't know by heart.

MARYCLARE: Let's just sing, okay? You can teach me the words. Or I'll hum back-up. (*Nothing from* BLACKIE.) Blackie?

BLACKIE: Damn her! She keeps it so dark in here.

MARYCLARE: She does it to keep out the draft. Don't go in there. You'll freeze. Everybody's got the flu.

BLACKIE: All the windows shut. All the curtains drawn. You look out there and there's nothing but walls. Brick walls. Yellow Catholic hospital brick walls. You know what I heard on my unit today? The guy said: I'm ready to go. Let me go. And we won't let him. We're worse than killers. Angels of mercy.

MARYCLARE: Blackie's in a rage.

BLACKIE: If we could just get out. We could sing our way out. Break that glass with a note. Blast through that wall and fly.

MARYCLARE: You've lost your calling, haven't you?

BLACKIE: I'm throwing it away. You hate it too. I know you hate it.

MARYCLARE: I never had a calling.

BLACKIE: Then how can you do it?

MARYCLARE: I do it because I know someday I won't be a nurse anymore, and then I'll be happy.

BLACKIE: That's death.

MARYCLARE: Blackie.

BLACKIE: It's worse than death, it's murder.

MARYCLARE: Don't say that.

BLACKIE: It's suicide. We'll end up like Anna. I'd rather die than end up like Anna.

MARYCLARE: It's just the season. It'll be over soon. In like a lion and out like a lamb.

BLACKIE: If we could X-ray vision our way out; get in the car, fill it up, check the oil, turn the key and drive till we get to the end of the road.

MARYCLARE: To Florida.

BLACKIE: Yes. We could. We could do it. Florida's perfect. Florida for Easter Weekend. We'll take I-95 straight South.

MARYCLARE: I don't like driving at night.

BLACKIE: I'll do the night driving. You'll do the day. In twenty-four hours we'll be in the sun.

MARYCLARE: It is hot there now?

BLACKIE: It's always hot down there. It's tropical.

MARYCLARE: Blazing hot?

BLACKIE: Blazing . . . but soft. The ocean doesn't even have waves there. It has swells. You just lie down and she carries you . . .

MARYCLARE: She . . .

BLACKIE: La mer . . .

MARYCLARE: Would there be jungles?

BLACKIE: Oh, lots of jungles.

MARYCLARE: I don't like jungles.

BLACKIE: You've never been.

MARYCLARE: I don't like tropical plants. The scent's too heavy. Spongy surfaces. And vines winding around everything. It's too slimy. I'm sure there'd be snakes.

BLACKIE: You're afraid.

MARYCLARE: I wouldn't be comfortable.

BLACKIE: Nurse shoes are comfortable.

MARYCLARE: I like meadows.

BLACKIE: Big white spongy nurse shoes. Your feet could swell up and rot in there and you'd never even know.

MARYCLARE: Blackie . . .

BLACKIE: We'll sleep on the beach.

MARYCLARE: (*Recitation from French class.*) "Au bord de la mer . . ."

BLACKIE: Tres bien Marie Claire.

MARYCLARE: Merci Soeur Terese.

BLACKIE: She adored you.

MARYCLARE: Could we wear silk?

BLACKIE: Whatever we want.

MARYCLARE: We could put on silk dresses at night and go to a nightclub like college students. (*Pause.*) You love Florida, don't you Blackie?

BLACKIE: You think it's a dream.

MARYCLARE: It *is* a dream.

BLACKIE: Not this time, Maryclare.

MARYCLARE: Anna would have a fit.

BLACKIE: Anna never has fits.

MARYCLARE: We're supposed to help her with the rummage sale.

BLACKIE: That's not for two weeks, Maryclare.

MARYCLARE: She got a leg of lamb for Easter.

BLACKIE: She can freeze it.

MARYCLARE: I don't have a silk dress.

BLACKIE: Wear mine.

MARYCLARE: What about sweaters, for night?

BLACKIE: It's hot at night. Even when the sun's gone, you can feel it. It stays on your skin and changes you. You're a different color in the sun forever after that.

MARYCLARE: You love it so much and you've never even seen it.

BLACKIE: I've got the map in my brain.

MARYCLARE: It's so far.

BLACKIE: (*Working her way into a litany.*) We just take it one city at a time. Follow the road south. Boston to Providence. Providence to New Haven. New Haven to New York. New York to Washington D.C. Washington to Richmond, Virginia . . . Virginia to North Carolina . . . to Charleston to Savannah to Jacksonville to St. Augustine . . .

MARYCLARE: Heaven is the place of eternal happiness. The streets are of gold. The walls of sparkling gems; the gates of shining pearls . . .

BLACKIE: St. Augustine to Cocoa Beach to Vero Beach to all the beaches . . .

MARYCLARE: All the beauty on earth; fine dress, handsome people, a clear sky at night full of stars—bears no comparison to the beauty of Heaven . . .

BLACKIE: Jupiter to Juno to North Palm to West Palm to Palm to Del Ray to Coral Gables . . .

MARYCLARE: The blessed in Heaven are free from all evil. They see God. They are united with God in the most intimate Love.

BLACKIE: To the Orchid Jungle through the Cypress Gardens and into the Everglades then the Keys . . . We'll take one pack and two sleeping bags.

MARYCLARE: Maybe shawls instead of sweaters.

BLACKIE: Definitely shawls. (*They return to sunlamp.*)

BLACKIE & MARYCLARE: (*Sing more of "All Night Long."*)

> So let the stars fall down
> Out of Heaven tonight.
> What good are stars anyway?
> And if the man in the moon
> Isn't shining so bright,
> Too bad!
> Who cares!
> We don't need the moonlight
> To tell us to stay.

(*They stop singing, hearing* ANNA *offstage.*)

ANNA: Either somebody's going to freeze or somebody's going to burn.

BLACKIE: Can we choose? (ANNA *enters. She wears a heavy overcoat, woolen cap, gloves and boots. She carries a bag with her nurse shoes inside.*)

ANNA: Sister Daniel saw you run off.

BLACKIE: I'd rather burn.

ANNA: I'm not surprised.

BLACKIE: You never are.

ANNA: (*Goes to the refrigerator, opens it, looks in, closes it.*) Every Sunday I make a roast, a cake, lasagna, beef stew, applesauce, and hard-boiled eggs for the week. Every Thursday is supposed to be beef stew, and every Thursday somebody forgets to thaw it out.

MARYCLARE: Me.

BLACKIE: Anna's a man.

ANNA: Go to Hell, Blackie. I'm not a man.

MARYCLARE: (*Gives* ANNA *the chair.*) Give me your feet, Anna. I'll do your feet. (*She takes off* ANNA's *boots and massages her feet.*)

ANNA: Thank you. Thursdays are always the worst.

MARYCLARE: In cardiac it's Fridays.

BLACKIE: (*Comes to* ANNA *and rubs her back and shoulders.*) Did he die?

ANNA: God knows. Maureen's still out. I had to give meds on her floor and everyone spit juice at me.

MARYCLARE: I'd rather have them die.

ANNA: Maryclare!

MARYCLARE: I don't care. I hate spit. I'll never get used to it.

ANNA: There's worse.

MARYCLARE: I know, but don't you still hate it?

BLACKIE: She loves hating it. She loves it passionately.

ANNA: Blackie's a romantic. She'll tie me to the chair and make me a saint.

BLACKIE: You are and we adore you. The Patroness of Nurses.

ANNA: I can't be, that's Catherine.

MARYCLARE: The one on the wheel?

ANNA: No. Of Siena.

BLACKIE: The one who stayed in her room and bossed the Pope and gave herself the stigmata.

ANNA: Received. She received the stigmata.

BLACKIE: With no visible lesions. There weren't any holes in her hands.

MARYCLARE: Maybe she painted them on.

BLACKIE: With nail polish.

ANNA: Don't get started.

BLACKIE: I hate saints like that.

MARYCLARE: But after she died, they dug her up and her body smelled like roses.

BLACKIE: Violets.

ANNA: That was Teresa.

MARYCLARE: Oh no. Teresa came back from the dead in a shower of roses. The Little Flower in God's wreath. She was my favorite.

ANNA: I mean the other Teresa. Of Avila.

BLACKIE: Only she's not in Avila. They loved her so much they took her apart after she died. Her foot's in Rome. Her left hand's

in Lisbon. Her nuns kept her eyes and her heart and Avila didn't
get any. So poor little Terry goes wee wee wee—

ANNA: Calm down, Blackie.

BLACKIE: Cause she couldn't get home.

MARYCLARE: My uncle saw St. Anne's finger in Illinois.

BLACKIE: See? They're all over.

MARYCLARE: It's true. He's got a postcard.

BLACKIE: Appollonia's teeth . . . Agatha's breasts . . . Ursula's
heart . . . Lucy's eyes . . .

MARYCLARE: Blackie played Lucy at school. She wouldn't be a
whore, so they burned her. But she wouldn't burn, so they
stabbed her in the throat.

BLACKIE: You stabbed me.

MARYCLARE: I was the soldier.

BLACKIE: Till there was nothing left but her eyes . . .

ANNA: I'm sure you were good.

BLACKIE: The best saints burned and got blasted into pieces.

MARYCLARE: So if Catherine's Patroness of Nurses, Anna can be
Patroness of Head Nurses.

ANNA: Thank you.

BLACKIE: Our lady of the I.V.'s.

ANNA: Queen of the I.C.U.

BLACKIE: Martyred by spit.

ANNA: You never change.

MARYCLARE: Anna?—I'm sorry there's nothing to eat.

BLACKIE: She doesn't need to eat.

ANNA: We'll think of something.

BLACKIE: A miracle.

ANNA: I love you.

MARYCLARE: Anna?

ANNA: Take out the onions, Maryclare.

MARYCLARE: We're going to Florida. (*She runs offstage.*)

ANNA: And the eggs. Maryclare! (*No answer. To* BLACKIE.) She
keeps disappearing.

BLACKIE: We're going to Florida.

ANNA: Her linen closet's never straight.

BLACKIE: "Are you really going to Florida? When? How'll you get
there? Where will you stay? What will you wear?" Ask a
question, Anna. You never ask questions.

ANNA: I ask questions.

BLACKIE: Only when you know the answer by heart. Do you think
we're going? Don't you want to know?

ANNA: If you're going, you'll go. Then I'll know the answer and I won't have to ask.

BLACKIE: You don't even ask the patients. You tell them: you're in pain, I'll give you something for the pain; you want to sleep; I'll give you something to make you sleep.

ANNA: They are in pain.

BLACKIE: Do you ask?

ANNA: In the time it takes to ask you could lose someone.

BLACKIE: And the last thing they see is some rubber tubing and your back at the monitor.

ANNA: Florence Nightingale hates the machines.

BLACKIE: I do.

ANNA: She can stand the burning flesh, but she won't touch the computer. She rubs their backs, touches their sores, rips the bed linens into strips with her bare teeth, but she won't share the bedside with an I.V. If you want to serve, you serve. Without questions.

BLACKIE: I want the burning flesh. I want the bare teeth.

ANNA: We all had that dream, Blackie.

BLACKIE: I'll touch their sores. I'll wash their feet.

ANNA: You have to give it up.

BLACKIE: I love the sight of blood!

ANNA: Give it up.

BLACKIE: No.

ANNA: You can't go. We're short of staff.

BLACKIE: I'm giving it up. I'm ready to go.

ANNA: He missed his twelve o'clock injections and his three o'clock sponge bath. His nails haven't been filed since God knows when. She keeps disappearing. Now you. (*Pause.*) Maybe the passion is in the serving, in the sacrifice. You can love that. Can't you? (BLACKIE *exits.* ANNA *finishes her shoes, puts them away. She stands and talks to* MARYCLARE, *outside her door.*) Maryclare . . .

MARYCLARE: What?

ANNA: Tell me if you're going.

MARYCLARE: I'm thinking about it.

ANNA: Tell me what you're thinking.

MARYCLARE: (*Lowering her voice, imitating* BLACKIE.) "You stole it."

ANNA: You can tell me you're afraid.

MARYCLARE: No. Lower. More throat. "You stole it."

ANNA: You could ask for help.

MARYCLARE: "Go to hell, Maryclare."

ANNA: I'd like to help.

MARYCLARE: Yes, that's it. "Go to hell, Maryclare."

ANNA: Maryclare?

MARYCLARE: *You stole it.* (*She exits.*)

ANNA: (*Sets the table, continuing to speak to* MARYCLARE.) Driving at night is the most dangerous this time of year. You can't see the icy patches. Suppose you run out of gas on a weekend. The filling stations are closed. You'd be stranded on the road. You'd have to get a ride and you don't know who might pick you up. Maureen's cousin was beaten to death, hitch-hiking. So many nurses are murdered. Not just alone on the road. In their apartments. In groups. They attract attention. Men have fantasies because we know so much about them. We handle them. We bathe them. We turn them over. You can't walk down the street in uniform without hearing remarks. "Nursey, nursey, give me mercy." "Nurse, nurse, it's getting worse." As if they hate us for it. Maureen always says, never tell anyone you're nurses. (*She sits alone at the table. Dark except for candles. She waits. Listens for a sound.*) Maryclare? (*No answer.*) Blackie? (*No answer.*) Don't sneak up on me, please, I know you're here. (*Silence.*) You're laughing at me, aren't you? Where are you? (*Silence.*) Why don't you answer? (*Silence.*) When I put out the candles, you'll jump out at me like wild animals. Okay. I'm putting out the candles. Go ahead. (*She blows out the candles. Black. Silence.*) Blackie? Maryclare? I'm asking.

Blackout on ANNA *in kitchen. Lights up on the girls on the road, in their car.* MAMA's *music accompanies them: "Girls."*

BLACKIE: Yahoo! Texas plates. Texas plates are a sign!

MARYCLARE: What kind?

BLACKIE: Inter-state travel. Just us and the truckers eating up the road. Look up there, it's a silver tanker!

MARYCLARE: Liquid hydrogen. Flammable.

BLACKIE: I'll pass him and you wave.

MARYCLARE: You think we should?

BLACKIE: Why not? Wave to the flammable man from Texas.

MARYCLARE: I'm going to.

BLACKIE: Go ahead.

MARYCLARE: I'm really going to.

BLACKIE: Get ready. I'm passing.

MARYCLARE: I'm rolling down the window.

BLACKIE: Right *now!*

MARYCLARE: (*Waving.*) Hi, y'all! (*Lights blink. Air horn toots twice.*) I did it!

BLACKIE: Okay! Let's turn up those tunes. (*As* BLACKIE *turns on the car radio,* MAMA *appears.*)

MAMA: (*Sings.*)

GIRLS

Girls — catch a fast-living girl,
When they play they play hard,
When they go they go far.
I love those fast-living girls,
Got the wind in their hair,
Got you walkin' on air.
No diamond rings,
No apron strings,
Can keep her at home,
No clinging vine,
She doesn't mind
She's goin' alone.
So hold on tight for a nonstop flight
In her double time world
Cause she's a —
Fast-living girl.

Lights change. Very late night on the road. BLACKIE *drives.* MARY-CLARE *is getting uncomfortable in here seat.*

BLACKIE: It's the Chesapeake Bay! Baltimore and the South. We are leaving the North behind, Maryclare.

MARYCLARE: I'm thirsty.

BLACKIE: What's your favorite bridge?

MARYCLARE: I don't know.

BLACKIE: I love bridges.

MARYCLARE: I always say a prayer so there's not an earthquake.

BLACKIE: They don't have earthquakes in Maryland.

MARYCLARE: You never know.

BLACKIE: I bet they talk real Southern here.

MARYCLARE: (*Hopefully.*) Let's stop and find out.

BLACKIE: No more stops till Richmond. They'll talk real Southern in Richmond.

MARYCLARE: (*Annoyed.*) They better.

BLACKIE: Go to sleep. (*Pause. Then suddenly* MARYCLARE *screams.*)

MARYCLARE: Blackìe!!
BLACKIE: What!!
MARYCLARE: On-coming car with one headlight!
BLACKIE: So what!
MARYCLARE: It's bad luck. We better slow down.
BLACKIE: Not a chance.
MAMA: (*Sings the second verse of "Girls."*)

> Girls, all those hard-working girls,
> Winter, summer or fall,
> When they give they give all.
> I love a hard-working girl.
> Got a confident air,
> Knows she's going somewhere.
> No one-night stand,
> No part-time man
> Can lead her astray,
> Cause what she gets she never lets
> Some guy take away.
> You gotta be strong if you wanna belong
> In her over-time world
> Cause she's a fast-living, hard-working — girl.

Lights up on an all night market. A door. BLACKIE *and* MARYCLARE *come out through it.* BLACKIE *heads for the car. Fast.* MARYCLARE *walks slowly, sipping a coke. She tries out a southern accent.*

MARYCLARE: Let's just sit a second, Blackie, pleeeeeeese . . . ?
BLACKIE: Get in the car.

MARYCLARE: I declare I'm so sick of that old car I could scream.

BLACKIE: Quick, Maryclare.

MARYCLARE: What is it? What's wrong? Who's after us?

BLACKIE: Don't look behind you. And don't scurry. Just walk. (*They get in the car.*)

MARYCLARE: Somebody's following us, aren't they? I had that feeling.

BLACKIE: Look in the pack.

MARYCLARE: What for?

BLACKIE: Just look. (MARYCLARE *does. She pulls out two steaks.*)

MARYCLARE: Steaks! You've got steaks in here.

BLACKIE: Free.

MARYCLARE: Holy—!

BLACKIE & MARYCLARE: (*A routine.*) Smoke, cow, Moses, and Mary Mother of God!

MARYCLARE: Goodbye Richmond!

BLACKIE: Gateway to the Old South.

MARYCLARE: I thought that was Baltimore.

BLACKIE: That was Gateway to the South. Richmond's Gateway to the Old South. Then comes Charleston, Gateway to the Deep South. Then St. Augustine, Gateway to—

MARYCLARE: The deeper South.

BLACKIE: The Deepest South.

MARYCLARE: The bottom of the U.S.A.

BLACKIE: The tropics.

MARYCLARE: I hope nobody's after us.

She slumps down in the seat, and puts on sunglasses, sleeps. BLACKIE *continues driving, in a quieter mood as the sun rises. Music is softer now.* MAMA *watches.*

BLACKIE: We've got the dawn on our left, the night on our right, and empty highway up ahead. You should see it, Maryclare. It's all ours. (MARYCLARE *is sound asleep.*) I'm not even driving. It's the lines on the road, pulling us down, leading us on, filling our eyes with all the lights, all the signs . . . Just for us. Oh, Maryclare. I wish you could see it.

MAMA: (*Sings the third verse of "Girls."*)

> Girls, oh those soft-spoken girls,
> Like a sweet summer breeze
> They really know how to please.
> Boys love those soft-spoken girls,

Love their murmuring low
Even when they say no.
A mother's dream, like peach ice cream,
The way that she talks.
Patent leather and lace, a picture of grace,
The way that she talks.
Patent leather and lace, a picture of grace,
The way that she walks.
But don't be surprised if the look in her eyes
Makes your hair curl
Cause she's a fast-living, hard-working, soft-spoken—girl.

MARYCLARE: (*Waking up, grouchy.*) I've definitely got a fever.
MAMA: (*Sings chorus of "Girls."*)

Girls, I love all of those girls,
Workin' and playin'
I love them.
Boys, listen to me.
I know what I'm sayin'
Listen to me.
I know.
I've been a fast-living, hard-working, soft-spoken—
Girl . . .

Lights change. Afternoon on the road. BLACKIE *drives and reads from a guidebook.* MARYCLARE *puts on makeup to kill time.*

BLACKIE: Yargo Magnolia Gardens and Sunken Forest . . . Ferry-boat to Jeckyll Island . . . Crooked River turnoff . . . We're getting deeper . . .
MARYCLARE: I'm really sweating.
BLACKIE: St. Mary's! We're crossing the border.
MARYCLARE: The line.
BLACKIE: Huh?
MARYCLARE: Countries are borders. States are lines.
BLACKIE: Oh. (*She starts reading everything in sight.*) Tropic Motel and Surf Club . . . St. Anastasia Snake Farm . . . McFeary's Monkey Jungle . . . Potter's Wax Museum . . . See Richard Speck in the Chamber of Horrors . . . Mandalay Avenue Exit . . . Mosquito Lagoon . . . Astronaut Trail . . . Captain Avila's Recreation Pier . . . Bone Fishing . . . Banana River Rocket Museum . . . Golden Paradise Motel . . . St. Lucie

County Fair . . . Home of the Rattler Rodeo . . . Blastoff Cafe . . . Skyline Cafe . . . The Stardust . . . The Universe . . . Mama's — (*She stops suddenly, car swerves,* MARYCLARE *screams.*)

MARYCLARE: Keep your eyes on the road!

BLACKIE: (*Still reading the sign.*) House of fish.

MARYCLARE: What?

BLACKIE: Nothing.

MARYCLARE: You could've *killed* us.

Blackout on the car.

MAMA: (*Sings.*)

> Boys, listen to me
> I know what I'm sayin'.
> Listen to me.
> I know.
> I've been a fast-livin', hard-workin', soft-spoken —
> Girl.

Lights up on a gas station in Florida. A lighted gas pump and a banana palm. Yellow sunset. MARYCLARE *enters, dazed and out of breath.*

MARYCLARE: Hello. (*No answer.*) Yoo hoo. (*No answer.*) Gas station!

SKIPPER: (*Enters, wearing greasy overalls and a bright red baseball cap.*) Hey.

MARYCLARE: Hey. (*She looks behind her.*) She was right behind me. (*They both look. Nobody's there.* SKIPPER *stares at* MARYCLARE.) We have a flat tire.

SKIPPER: Oh yeah?

MARYCLARE: (*Bumps into the gas pump.*) Sorry.

SKIPPER: That's okay.

MARYCLARE: She can't stop moving. No matter what, she just hates to stop. She lets it get to empty — below empty sometimes, and she still won't stop. So when we were turning off at the turnoff, she couldn't slow down and she drove right into the curb. (*She sits down.*) I'm sitting down.

SKIPPER: Right.

MARYCLARE: I still feel like I'm moving. Fifty-five, sixty, seventy-five sometimes.

SKIPPER: No kidding?

MARYCLARE: Nope. And she won't let me drive because I stay at the speed limit, so she drove day and night straight through from Boston.

SKIPPER: I know some girls in Boston!

MARYCLARE: Nurses?

SKIPPER: Hey, great. You're a nurse.

MARYCLARE: I've got a cold. It was a mistake to come this far without a spare.

SKIPPER: You've got a great voice.

MARYCLARE: It's a sore throat. She kept the windows down.

SKIPPER: Yeah.

MARYCLARE: What?

SKIPPER: It reminds me of something. A singer maybe.

MARYCLARE: A star?

SKIPPER: Sure.

MARYCLARE: What kind?

SKIPPER: How about a Vegas kind?

MARYCLARE: That's crazy.

SKIPPER: In disguise as a nurse.

MARYCLARE: I'm really not a nurse.

SKIPPER: Okay. How about a nurse in disguise as some other kind of star? You choose.

MARYCLARE: I'm not a nurse.

SKIPPER: Either way it's interesting. Even if you weren't the only one here, I'd pick you out as the most interesting.

MARYCLARE: It's just my voice.

SKIPPER: It's more than that.

MARYCLARE: My dress?

SKIPPER: No.

MARYCLARE: Anna's perfume. Blackie hates it.

SKIPPER: She does?

MARYCLARE: Because it's Anna's I guess.

SKIPPER: That's not it.

MARYCLARE: My nails?

SKIPPER: Nope.

MARYCLARE: Oh well.

SKIPPER: (*After a pause.*) Take off your sunglasses. (*She stares at him, doesn't move.*) Come on. It's getting dark out. You're not a blind girl, are you? (*She turns away.*) No. I know that. Hey, I'm cool, okay? This isn't a move. I guarantee. No moves.

MARYCLARE: What leads us into sin? Temptation and sinful occasions lead us into sin. Where do temptations come from?

SKIPPER: Huh. Come on.

MARYCLARE: (*Takes off the sunglasses. Turns away.*) From the devil. From wicked fellow men. From our own evil—

SKIPPER: Yeah . . .

MARYCLARE: What?

SKIPPER: Pretty in the old way, with the eyes and teeth . . .

MARYCLARE: Lust of the eyes, lust of the flesh . . .

SKIPPER: The stage and screen type star, like the old movies at the drive-in, or the real old star-in-the-sky type.

MARYCLARE: And the pride of life . . .

SKIPPER: What?

MARYCLARE: (*To herself.*) Oh shut-up!

SKIPPER: No. It's true.

MARYCLARE: I'm sorry.

SKIPPER: I thought you'd say thanks.

MARYCLARE: Thank you . . .

SKIPPER: Skipper.

MARYCLARE: Thank you, Skipper. (*They shake hands.*)

BLACKIE: (*Enters with the tire and the two sleeping bags.*) It's real jungle, Maryclare! Banana palms and everything.

MARYCLARE: I know.

SKIPPER: You're Blackie for your hair, right?

BLACKIE: The gas man doesn't miss a trick. (*She gives him the tire.*) What about this?

SKIPPER: It's off the rim.

BLACKIE: Can you fix it.

SKIPPER: You need a new tire.

BLACKIE: Can you take us in town?

SKIPPER: I could, but it's closed.

BLACKIE: What about a mall?

SKIPPER: Same thing. They close up early for Good Friday.

BLACKIE: God . . .

SKIPPER: They've got a Passion Play on over in Black Lake.

MARYCLARE: I knew it was something.

SKIPPER: You can camp here if you want. There's room out back.

BLACKIE: We're sleeping on the beach.

SKIPPER: I wouldn't if I were you. You don't know what kind of weird things go on out there.

MARYCLARE: What kind, do you think?

SKIPPER: You know what turpentine workers are like?

MARYCLARE: No.

SKIPPER: Well, there's a lot of turpentine workers out there. They cross over Bithlo Road from the swamp to the beach real easy. Like snakes.

BLACKIE: We'll be okay.

SKIPPER: You hear screams some nights.

BLACKIE: We can take care of ourselves.

SKIPPER: They get real crazy at their club out there.

BLACKIE: Mama's?

SKIPPER: Somebody's. Especially on a big weekend like this. Easter and a launch to boot.

BLACKIE: Mama's Cafe of Miracles. A nightclub?

SKIPPER: I wouldn't know.

BLACKIE: You've never been?

SKIPPER: I've thought about it. That's about all.

BLACKIE: Let's go, Maryclare.

MARYCLARE: (*Stays put.*) We can't. No car.

BLACKIE: (*To* SKIPPER.) Could you take us?

SKIPPER: Well, see, I don't really know where it is exactly. There's a lot of clubs around . . .

MARYCLARE: And he has to stay here. What if somebody else comes . . .

SKIPPER: Yeah, it'll be easier when it's light.

MARYCLARE: We should wait till it's light.

BLACKIE: We've got the lantern.

MARYCLARE: But what if it rains?

SKIPPER: Right!

BLACKIE: I don't see any clouds.

SKIPPER: You never know this time of year.

MARYCLARE: Especially on Good Friday.

BLACKIE: (*Delighted by* MARYCLARE's *attraction to* SKIPPER.) I see . . .

SKIPPER: Last week we had sixteen inches, just like that. Rattlesnakes came right up out of the swamp and into people's kitchens. I shot one under the trailer.

MARYCLARE: There's always a storm on Good Friday. You know, Blackie. About the big one. When the sky grew dark at three o'clock. Tell him.

SKIPPER: Yeah. Tell me.

BLACKIE: (*By rote.*) "It became like night. A terrible earthquake cracked all the rocks and split the temple in two. And the graves opened and the bodies of the saints who slept arose and came out of their graves and went into the Holy City and appeared to many . . ."

MARYCLARE: She knows it all by heart.

BLACKIE: And the Five Wounds and the Four Last Things, the Fourteen Stations and the Fifteen Mysteries—

MARYCLARE: Let's sing it.

BLACKIE & MARYCLARE: (*Singing with schoolgirl voices.*)

IMMACULATE MARY

> Immaculate Mary
> Our hearts are on fire
> Thy title so wondrous
> Fills all our desire . . .
>
> Ave, ave, ave Maria
> Ave, ave, ave, Ma- ri- i- a.

SKIPPER: You're Catholic girls!

BLACKIE: Once upon a time.

SKIPPER: It's your lipstick. The way they put it on at the bus stop after school.

MARYCLARE: My mother's Fire and Ice.

BLACKIE: They're watching us from across the street.

SKIPPER: Then you roll down your uniform socks . . .

BLACKIE: They love the uniform.

SKIPPER: You're not like other girls.

MARYCLARE: He thinks we're nurses.

BLACKIE: Or secretaries, right?

SKIPPER: No. We think you're wild.

BLACKIE: How wild, pagan boy?

SKIPPER: Wilder than we are. You talk about kissing a lot. And sin. That's what the lipstick's for, isn't it.

MARYCLARE: Blackie saved all the pagan boys in our block. She baptized them in the basement.

BLACKIE: With a hose.

SKIPPER: She can baptize me any day.

BLACKIE: You know what happens to the damned in Hell?

SKIPPER: Tell me, Blackie.

BLACKIE: They burn in eternal flames.

SKIPPER: I'm burning, Blackie.

BLACKIE: You know what the bodies of the wicked will look like when they rise?

SKIPPER: I'm listening, Blackie.

BLACKIE: Hideous and loathsome. Worse than a rotten corpse in the grave.

SKIPPER: You better save me.

MARYCLARE: She says you're mad dogs.

BLACKIE: French kissing turns them into mad dogs.

SKIPPER: I'll be a mad dog.

MARYCLARE: She'll tie you up and make you bark.

SKIPPER: I'll bark. Come on, Blackie, tie me up. Tie me up like your saint guys with their clothes off. Come on. Catholic girls. Make me do it.

BLACKIE: Do what?

SKIPPER: What you do.

BLACKIE: What's that?

SKIPPER: Eat his body and drink his blood.

BLACKIE: You think a lot of thoughts for a mad dog.

SKIPPER: You really do it, don't you?

BLACKIE: Do we, Maryclare?

MARYCLARE: What?

BLACKIE: Eat his body?

MARYCLARE: Those are the Mysteries.

SKIPPER: Yes or no? (*Pause.*)

MARYCLARE: Yes.

SKIPPER: You are wild.

MARYCLARE: Blackie stole two steaks in Richmond, Virginia!

BLACKIE: Maryclare—

MARYCLARE: Red meat on Good Friday.

SKIPPER: Great. I've got a barbecue out back. And beer.

BLACKIE: It sounds like a party.

SKIPPER: It will be a party.

MARYCLARE: We're gonna party—

BLACKIE: Till we drop—

MARYCLARE & BLACKIE: Like flies!

SKIPPER: It is a party.

MARYCLARE: We *are* wild.

BLACKIE: We're getting there. (*They exit.*)

MAMA *enters. Music comes up under.*

MAMA: (*Refering to the effect the band's music has on her.*) When they do it like that, I just can't make my body behave. (*She sings.*)

DON'T DO IT

(*Chorus.*)
Don't do it
No, don't do it

> Please don't do it
> Even though you wanna do it.
> Don't do it
> Please don't do it
> Even though you know you're gonna die if you don't
> Do it.

I just can't make my body behave
When he's looking in my eyes, saying don't be afraid.
My soul says stop and my body says go.
Body says yes.
Soul says no.
You're gonna get in trouble,
Better take it slow
So —

      (Repeat chorus.)

It's so hard to do what you should.
Nobody ever told me it would feel this good.
Got me feeling so high and falling so low,
Angels frowning up above, devils grinning below.
Devils say yes,
Angels say no,
You're gonna get in trouble,
Better take it slow
So —

      (Repeat chorus.)

Light change to back of the gas station. A lighted barbecue. A junked car. While MAMA *sings,* SKIPPER *and* MARYCLARE *drink beer, watching* BLACKIE *dance by herself, twirling and holding up a beer can.*

SKIPPER: *(Holding up a sleeping bag.)* Spread out the bags. Blackie's gonna drop.

BLACKIE: I'm not gonna drop.

MARYCLARE: She's flying.

BLACKIE: Speed of light.

SKIPPER: She's gonna drop. *(He goes to dance with her, but she pushes him away.)*

BLACKIE: Not you, oil boy. *(She grabs* MARYCLARE.) Mercy Girls do Cath-o-lic dancing . . . (BLACKIE *and* MARYCLARE *jitterbug.)*

MAMA: (*Sings chorus of "Don't Do It."*)

SKIPPER: Mercy girls . . . Mercy babies . . . Dance with the pagan boy, mercy girls. Come on, Maryclare.

BLACKIE: Go ahead, Maryclare. Do it for the bad boys. Do it for the pagan babies. Do it for all the times Sister whipped poor Jimmie Flynn on the butt.

SKIPPER: Dance with the mad dog—

BLACKIE: The grease monkey—

SKIPPER: The attendant—

BLACKIE: Oh yes. The attendant. (*She leads* MARYCLARE *to dance with* SKIPPER. BLACKIE *spins around them.*)

MAMA: (*Sings chorus of "Don't Do It."*)

> BLACKIE *and* MARYCLARE *signal each other.* MARYCLARE *pulls* SKIPPER *down to his knees. She holds his arms as* BLACKIE *takes off his cap and pours beer on his head, then dances away.*)

SKIPPER: Bad babies. Bad, bad babies . . . (MARYCLARE *wipes the beer off his face. They kiss.* BLACKIE *is spinning, almost out of control.*)

MARYCLARE: She's gonna drop.

SKIPPER: Bag's ready.

BLACKIE: No bags. When I drop, I drop.

MARYCLARE: When she drops, she drops.

BLACKIE: I fall. (*She collapses on the sleeping bag and passes out.* SKIPPER *and* MARYCLARE *sit, drinking beer and staring at her.*)

SKIPPER: All the way.

MARYCLARE: Yup.

MAMA: (*Sings chorus of "Don't Do It," slow.*)

> MARYCLARE *unfolds her sleeping bag and drags it away from* SKIP-PER. *She lies down and curls up on it.* SKIPPER *follows her, sits close to her, strokes her hair and her arms.*)

SKIPPER: Mary. Clare.

MARYCLARE: Yup.

SKIPPER: Mary . . .

MARYCLARE: For "bitter."

SKIPPER: And Clare . . .

MARYCLARE: For "light." She was beautiful.

SKIPPER: Who?

MARYCLARE: St. Clare. She ran away in her mother's wedding dress and all her pearls.

SKIPPER: Huh.

MARYCLARE: To meet Saint Francis in his church at midnight right in front of the altar. And you know what he did?

SKIPPER: What?

MARYCLARE: He undressed her.

SKIPPER: No.

MARYCLARE: Oh yes. Bit by bit. The sleeves and then the top part and the skirt and the stockings and then the slippers and the pearls.

SKIPPER: Everything?

MARYCLARE: Bit by bit. But he never touched her.

SKIPPER: He must have.

MARYCLARE: No. Never.

SKIPPER: He had to touch her neck to take off the pearls.

MARYCLARE: Nope.

SKIPPER: He had to touch her leg to take off her stocking. Just a brush.

MARYCLARE: Nothing.

SKIPPER: Just a little slip.

MARYCLARE: No.

SKIPPER: One button?

PHOTO BY CHRISTOPHER CASLER

MARYCLARE: Maybe one. (MARYCLARE *has been lying perfectly still,*
with her eyes closed, as SKIPPER *runs his hands over her body. Now he*
unbuttons the top of her dress as she continues.) She stood there
perfectly still with her eyes closed and he dressed her in a monk's
robe which she wore for the rest of her life and when she died all
the skin on her body stayed perfect and smelled like violets
because she was incorruptible and now she's the Patroness of
Television because her name means light which it is when you
leave it on at night and go to sleep . . . Skipper?

SKIPPER: What?

MARYCLARE: No more buttons, okay?

SKIPPER: What about inside?

MARYCLARE: Just no more buttons.

SKIPPER: Okay. (*He gets up. Goes to the junked car and opens the door.*
Interior light on the red leather upholstery.) Maryclare?

MARYCLARE: Huh?

SKIPPER: Lookit.

MARYCLARE: That's nice.

SKIPPER: Come on.

MARYCLARE: Okay. But no more buttons.

SKIPPER: No. (MARYCLARE *and* SKIPPER *go into the car. Close the*
door. Light goes out.)

Lights up on the kitchen in Boston. Bright blue light as ANNA *opens the*
refrigerator. She stares into it. Then begins taking things out and
throwing them away.

ANNA: Rotten lettuce . . . Rotten melon . . . (*She takes out meat*
and smells it.) It's gone bad. (*She throws it away.*) Asking for
maggots. (*She takes out a carton of milk. Smells it. Throws it away.*)
Spoiled. They let everything go. (*She takes out an apple.*) Half-
eaten. They have no idea. They never finish. They leave things
open. They run off. Oh sure, they think they'll finish it later,
but they don't. Then it goes bad. It spoils everything around it.
(*Throws out more things.*) Don't get mad, Anna. Anna's a man.
Anna's a cold bitch who freezes everything. (*Pause.*) I'm trying
to save it. (*Suddenly begins throwing everything away until the*
refrigerator is empty.) Everything goes, before it rots. It's the only
way. (*A glass bottle breaks as she throws it in the trash, she reaches*
down to pick up a piece and cuts her hand.) Damn you! (*She slams the*
door shut and exits as light goes out in kitchen.)

Light up on the gas station. BLACKIE *wakes up and suddenly, as if from a bad dream. She hears a horrible growling sound coming from* SKIPPER *in the car. Then it quicly turns into his and* MARYCLARE'*s giggles.*

MARYCLARE: (*From the car.*) Be quiet. She'll hear us.

SKIPPER: She doesn't mind.

MARYCLARE: I do.

SKIPPER: What's the matter. You think she'll tell on you?

MARYCLARE: I'd kill her.

SKIPPER: *Mad dogs!*

MARYCLARE: (*Really mad.*) Shut up. (SKIPPER'*s growl. Then silence.*)

BLACKIE: It's all wrong here. We better go back.

MAMA: (*Suddenly appears.*) Not yet. You haven't met my band.

BLACKIE: Mama?

MAMA: Introducing the Cafe of Miracles' Band of Angels: Victor Ruiz on the keyboards, Stevie Michaels on the cello, Bernard Thomas on percussion, Johnny Blue on the guitar and my best friend, Sweet Gabe Lawrence on sax . . . They're all my boyfriends, right boys?

BAND: Right, Mama.

MAMA: You gotta give it all to get a hand, right boys?

BAND: Right, Mama.

MAMA: Go all the way out or give all the way in. We give it all, and it's all for you.

BAND: For you.

MAMA: My lipstick, my shoes, my gown . . .

BAND: For you.

MAMA: My nails. My lashes.

BAND: For you.

MAMA: To adore . . .

BAND: For you.

MAMA: My hands . . .

BAND: For you.

MAMA: My throat, my lips, my teeth, my voice . . .

BAND: For you . . .

MAMA: It's all insured and willed to science. Chicago gets the bones. Johns Hopkins gets the nerves. The eyes go to Miami. I'd like to keep them seeing the tropics. But there's plenty to go around. I'm planning on spreading myself as thin as I can. Ashes at sea is nothing. I'll be thinner than air. And the only part that

won't disappear, is the part you can't see. The part of me I'm
giving you now to take home . . . is my song. (*She sings.*)

CARRIED AWAY

When summer flowers fill the air
Breathe in their sweetness, I'll be there
Lost in love so deeply
You'll be carried away
Carried away.

And when the winter winds begin
Sweet love, say yes, sweet love, give in
Into love completely
And we'll be carried away
Carried so far away.

No matter how the seasons change
Believe in love
And it will see you through the hardest days.

And when we've nothing left but dreams,
Unfolding sails on unknown seas,
I will hold you sweetly
And we'll be carried away
Carried so far away.

(*The last part of the song she sings to* BLACKIE, *and remains onstage
watching.* MARYCLARE's *face appears in the car window. She knocks.
She whispers.*)

MARYCLARE: Blackie?
BLACKIE: Maryclare.
MARYCLARE: I'm scared.
BLACKIE: Okay. Let's go.
MARYCLARE: We're loaded, aren't we?
BLACKIE: No. Come on.
MARYCLARE: (*Gets out of the car.*) Is this a dream? Are we sleeping?
BLACKIE: No. We'll wake up on the road.
MARYCLARE: What road?
BLACKIE: To the beach.
MARYCLARE: In the middle of the night?
BLACKIE: It's not far. We can walk.
MARYCLARE: I don't know.
BLACKIE: Yes you do. Come on, Maryclare. We're missing every-
    thing.

MARYCLARE: What?

BLACKIE: The ocean, the stars, everything.

MARYCLARE: I don't remember . . .

BLACKIE: I know.

MARYCLARE: Get me out of here.

BLACKIE: I will. But you'll have to get up.

MARYCLARE: (*Sits and stares at the car.*) Shouldn't we say something?

BLACKIE: Do you want to?

MARYCLARE: I liked him.

BLACKIE: Go ahead.

MARYCLARE: We shouldn't have stayed.

BLACKIE: Are you coming or not?

MARYCLARE: It's so dark. I can't see.

BLACKIE: Follow me. (*She starts out.* MARYCLARE *stays back.*) Yes or no, Maryclare?

MARYCLARE: What must we do when we find ourselves in an occasion of sin? When we find ourselves in an occasion of sin we must leave it at once.

BLACKIE: What, Maryclare?

MARYCLARE: Nothing.

BLACKIE: Follow me. Yes or no?

MARYCLARE: Okay. (*She exits with* BLACKIE.)

SKIPPER *watches from the car. With the door open. The red light on in the interior. He shuts the door.*

MAMA: Okay boys, take ten.

Blackout.

ACT TWO

Light up on a hot dog stand. Dawn. A lighted sign and picnic table. Phone booth opposite. MARYCLARE *is talking on the phone.* PRINCE, *a county beach-cleaner, sits at the table, eating and watching her. He wears a jump suit uniform, has a metal detector and two canvas bags with him.*

MARYCLARE: Anna— ? I just wanted to say— to say. Well, yes, it's beautiful. Oh. Very comfortable. Yes. Old-fashioned. There's a big porch overlooking the sea. Yes. Lots of wicker and potted palms. The room is blue. Very very pale blue. (*She slaps a mosquito on her leg.*) Yes. Right now. She's downstairs in the dining room. And oh yes, they have these white gauze mosquito nets over the beds. Yes. Very breezy. (*The table is filling up. Members of "The Band" come out, sit, eat hamburgers and cokes and look out at the sky.* BLACKIE *comes out last, sees* MARYCLARE, *who stops quickly.*) Yes and — oh. We have to go. Swimming. No. We won't get too much. Bye . . . Anna? We'll bring you presents. (*She hangs up. Puts on sunglasses. Goes to table, finds no place to sit. Takes a tray and sits on the sleeping bags, across from the table. Everybody watches her until she sits. Then they look back up at the sky.* BLACKIE *watches them. A long silence as they sit and watch.*)

PRINCE: It's late.

BAND 1: They're holding for the cloud cover.

PRINCE: It's not going up.

BAND 2: It's going up.

PRINCE: How do you know?

BAND 2: I've got the feeling. It's right for it. (*Silence as they keep looking.* BLACKIE *looks at them.*)

BLACKIE: What is it?

PRINCE: Apollo something.

BAND 2: No. It's a Titan, this one's going to Venus, isn't it?

BAND 1: I don't know. Somewhere out there.

BAND 2: Venus.

BLACKIE: What's Venus?

BAND 2: The launch.

BLACKIE: There's going to be a launch? Right now?

PRINCE: There was. Supposedly.

BAND 2: There will be.

BLACKIE: A blastoff?

BAND 2: Any minute.

BLACKIE: With astronauts?

BAND 2: Yeah.

BLACKIE: They're going to Venus?

BAND 1: Somewhere out there . . .

BAND 2: Any second. (*They wait. Nothing happens.*)

PRINCE: It's a no-go.

BAND 2: They're just holding. Conditions have to be perfect.

BAND 1: Yeah . . . Yeah . . .

BAND 2: They know what they're doing.

BLACKIE: Maybe they're counting down right now.

BAND 2: Right.

BLACKIE: Five, four, three, two . . .

BAND 2: It's gonna happen!

BLACKIE: One! (*Silence.*)

MARYCLARE: (*Suddenly.*) Don't look right at it! You'll get blind spots.

PRINCE: That's the *sun.*

MARYCLARE: Oh. (*The* BAND *resumes eating.*)

PRINCE: (*Packs to go.*) It's a definite no-go.

BAND 2: They let me down.

PRINCE: Cheer up. I found a ruby earring out there yesterday. A real one. (*To* MARYCLARE.) You wanna see it?

MARYCLARE: No, thank you.

PRINCE: This one goes with the treasures. (*He puts it in the small canvas bag on his belt and exits.*)

BLACKIE: You're a band. I can tell by your instrument cases. See, Maryclare? (MARYCLARE *refuses to look.*) It's Mama's Band: You're from Mama's, right?

BAND 1: (*Amused.*) Mama's.

BAND 2: (*Playing along.*) Sure, everybody's from Mama's.

BLACKIE: The Miracle Cafe, right? I know it's out on Bithlo Road, but where is that exactly? Is it the part that goes through Black Lake or the part that goes toward the airport? On the map it branches off.

BAND 1: Bithlo Road?

BLACKIE: Yes. Is it in Black Lake?

BAND 1: Forget Black Lake.

BLACKIE: It's beyond Black Lake?

BAND 1: Way beyond.

BAND 2: (*To* BAND 1.) That's a good one.

BLACKIE: The swamp side or the beach side?

MARYCLARE: (*Disgusted.*) Blackie.

BLACKIE: We sing, you know. Maryclare and I, we're singers. We're great at Fifties stuff, right Maryclare?

MARYCLARE: (*Looking away.*) I guess so.

BAND 2: (*Looks at the sky. No action. He's about to leave.*) I've had it.

BAND 1: I'm outta here. (*Neither one moves. Each takes another bite of hot dog.*)

BLACKIE: (*Rushes into action. Sets herself up in front of them and starts singing "All Night Long."*)

> All night long
> One night together.

All night long
Can't last forever.
But with a love this strong
I know it can't be wrong,
So no matter what they say
We'll stay in love this way
Everyday—
All night long—

(*The* BAND *continue eating. Hardly notice.* BLACKIE *doesn't let this stop her.*)

All night long
I want you near me.
All night long
I'll love you dearly
And with a love this strong
We know it can't go wrong
So no matter what they say
We'll stay in love this way
Everyday—
All night long.

(*Desperately signalling for* MARYCLARE *to join her.*)

So let the stars fall down
Out of Heaven tonight.
What good are stars anyway?
And if the man in the moon
Isn't shining so bright—
Too bad—

(*She signals and gets nothing from* MARYCLARE.)

Who cares—
Who cares—
We don't need the moonlight
To tell us to stay—

(MARYCLARE *keeps eating and looking away.* BLACKIE *stops.*)
Usually Maryclare comes in on backup. What do you think?
BAND 1: You better ask Mama.
BLACKIE: Is she coming here?
BAND 1: **Mama?**
BLACKIE: Yes.
BAND 2: Oh no. Mama never comes out on a launch day, does she?

(They start playing a game back and forth.)

BAND 1: Right. Mama's accident prone.

BAND 2: Since the fall.

BLACKIE: What fall?

BAND 1: When she fell.

BAND 2: Forty-five feet. Right off a ramp.

BLACKIE: In a show?

BAND 1: Rehearsal.

BAND 2: Yeah. Looking for her light.

BAND 1: They had to rebuild her face.

BAND 2: From scratch, just about.

BAND 1: But her throat was untouched.

BAND 2: She said it was a miracle.

BAND 1: "Untouched."

BLACKIE: So that's how the cafe got it's name.

BAND 1: What?

BLACKIE: The Miracle Cafe!

BAND 2: Right.

BLACKIE: But you've never seen it.

BAND 2: Seen what?

BLACKIE: Mama's face. You've never seen Mama's real face. Don't you want to?

BAND 1: Why?

BLACKIE: I don't know. Just to—

BAND 2: Just to see it?

BLACKIE: Yes:

BAND 1: No. Not really.

BLACKIE: When can we sing for her?

BAND 1: *(Packing to leave.)* Whenever.

BLACKIE: Tonight?

BAND 1: Sure. Why not.

BLACKIE: What should we wear? We should dress up shouldn't we?

BAND 2: That's a good idea.

BAND 1: Yeah. Right.

BLACKIE: We'll wear bright colors. Bright colors only for Mama! We'll shine for Mama.

BAND 2: *(Leaving.)* Shine for Mama.

BAND 1: *(Leaving.)* Shine for Mama . . .

BAND 1: *(Leaving.)* Gotta shine for Mama.

BLACKIE: *(Follows after them, shouting.)* We'll shine. We'll dress all the way up and shine for Mama. Tell her, okay? We'll be there tonight. We'll sing for Mama tonight! (*They are gone.* BLACKIE *comes back in and confronts* MARYCLARE, *who sits forlorn, holding her breakfast tray and looking out at the sky.*) You didn't come in.

MARYCLARE: This is the farthest away I've ever been.

BLACKIE: We'll go farther.

MARYCLARE: I don't know. (*Looking at the remains of the* BAND'*s meal.*) Hot dogs and milkshakes isn't breakfast.

BLACKIE: It's dinner. They're musicians.

MARYCLARE: In the morning you're supposed to have breakfast.

BLACKIE: Don't rule out on me, Maryclare.

MARYCLARE: Unless it's not morning because we haven't slept yet, so it's still last night and we're having breakfast in the middle of the night with the sun out. But if we sleep now and wake up and have breakfast later, it'll be dark and we'll be having breakfast in the middle of the night without any day in between.

BLACKIE: That's great. Maybe it's all one day.

MARYCLARE: It can't be. We have to sleep.

BLACKIE: It is for the astronauts.

MARYCLARE: We're not astronauts.

BLACKIE: And the band. They're up all day and playing all night. And the holy saints and the flaming martyrs, it's one big day for them. They don't close their eyes for a second. Even in the fire. They're standing there with the smoke going up all around them, and their eyes are wide open. They're looking right out. They're going to see their visions forever and all we've got is two days. You can sleep in Boston.

MARYCLARE: We could rest a little.

BLACKIE: We haven't got time.

MARYCLARE: Just a nap.

BLACKIE: No.

MARYCLARE: We're not saints and martyrs. And how do you know they're a band. You don't know. You just made it up because you want to see it like that.

BLACKIE: What's wrong with that?

MARYCLARE: You made a fool out of yourself.

BLACKIE: Okay. I'm a fool. Let's be fools. It's better than being killer nurses.

MARYCLARE: Blackie . . .

BLACKIE: Anna the big Snow Angel, sending them out on pain-killers, freezing them out alive. I'd rather be a real killer and burn.

MARYCLARE: She's not a killer. You're making it all upside-down. It's crazy. And it's too hot. It shouldn't be this hot in March. This place is like a furnace. It's crawling with ants.

BLACKIE: It's the tropics. We'll go farther south and get to the equator and it'll all be opposites. It's all upside down. Summer in winter, winter's summer, Heaven's red hot and Hell's ice cold . . . You ought to know you danced around the fire last night.

MARYCLARE: I did not. It wasn't me.

BLACKIE: Who was it? Your opposite? Your guardian angel?

MARYCLARE: I don't know. I don't know anything. I feel sick.

BLACKIE: Maybe she's sitting right beside you.

MARYCLARE: My guardian angel?

BLACKIE: Your opposite.

MARYCLARE: You?

BLACKIE: I'm your opposite. Sometimes I think we're exactly the same.

MARYCLARE: I always wanted to be like you.

BLACKIE: The bad girl with the low voice.

MARYCLARE: They say when you meet your opposite you disappear.

BLACKIE: Or else you go on forever.

MARYCLARE: You know why their eyes are open?

BLACKIE: Who?

MARYCLARE: The martyrs in the fire.

BLACKIE: Why?

MARYCLARE: Because the eyelids are the thinnest part. They burn off first.

BLACKIE: You sound like Anna.

MARYCLARE: It's true. You've been on the burn ward.

BLACKIE: That's not what I mean. Let's get dressed up. Bright colors only, for Mama's. Fire-engine red.

MARYCLARE: I don't have any fire-engine red.

BLACKIE: We'll go into town and get some.

MARYCLARE: We don't have enough money.

BLACKIE: I know that, Maryclare.

MARYCLARE: Then how'll we get stuff?

BLACKIE: I'll take care of it.

MARYCLARE: How?

BLACKIE: You'll see.

MARYCLARE: It's stealing isn't it? You're dragging me down. Holy Saturday is the day of deepest mourning. Our Lord is dead. It's

boiling hot in the middle of March. They're going to Venus.
Heaven's full of snakes and mosquitos. Good is bad and bad is
good at the equator. We can do anything. Let's call Anna and say
we disappeared.

BLACKIE: Let's forget about Anna.

MARYCLARE: She can burn our uniforms.

BLACKIE: Or freeze them and keep them forever.

MARYCLARE: Go to Hell, Anna! We'll be whoever we want. (*They
exit.*)

Lights up on the kitchen in Boston. A bright blue light as ANNA *turns
on a television. It illuminates the table, piled with appliances and
boxes. As suddenly as she tuned the television on,* ANNA *turns the
volume up full, then unplugs the set and puts it into a box.*

  *She plugs in an electric can opener. She turns it on. She turns it off.
She unplugs it and puts it into the box with the television.*

  *She plugs in a blender. She runs it at all speeds. She unplugs it and
puts it into the box.*

  *She plugs in a radio. She turns it up full volume, runs it to every
station on the dial then unplugs it. She puts it in the box.*

  *She plugs in a lamp. It goes on. She turns it off, unplugs it and puts it
into the box.*

  ANNA *stands. She takes the table cloth from the table, folds it up,
and puts it into the box.*

ANNA: Everything from the old life goes. (*Blackout on Boston.*)

Lights up on a dressing room in Florida. BLACKIE *opens a curtain to
reveal* MARYCLARE *in the cubicle, completely veiled with a big red
shawl draped over a coolie hat. She is framed by a three-sided mirror
with a fluorescent light.* BLACKIE *turns her around and poses her.*

BLACKIE: The Tibetan bride. (*She turns* MARYCLARE *around again.*)
The Moroccan princess. (MARYCLARE *starts posing on her own.*)
The Hindu god.

MARYCLARE: More bracelets. (*She holds out her arm.* BLACKIE *gives
her bracelets from a chair piled with things from the store.*)

BLACKIE: The veil is lowered. Flesh appears!

MARYCLARE: Give me more. (BLACKIE *does.* MARYCLARE *wraps the
shawl around her waist and begins moving her hips and arms.*)

BLACKIE: Turning into the Balinese Dancer . . .

MARYCLARE: That's good.

BLACKIE: Turning into something . . . Hawaiian . . . the virgin on top of the volcano!

MARYCLARE: Hotter! (*As* MARYCLARE *throws back the shawl and moves faster.*)

BLACKIE: Much hotter now. Getting very hot with the moves. Getting Spanish . . . faster than Spanish . . . Flamenco . . . meaner than Flamenco . . . Gypsy! (MARYCLARE *throws down the shawl and steps on it.*) Turning from Gypsy into something mean and lowdown. (MARYCLARE *lies down on the shawl. Poses.*) The All Girl Alligator Wrestler. The Snake Tamer of the Everglades.

MARYCLARE: Charmer.

BLACKIE: Right.

MARYCLARE: Give me the sunglasses.

BLACKIE: She demands shades. She's so bright you've gotta wear shades to look at her. (MARYCLARE *puts on* BLACKIE'*s sunglasses.*)

MARYCLARE: She's gotta wear shades to look at herself. (*More poses.*) Now the spikes. (*She puts on a pair of 60's heels.*)

BLACKIE: She's putting on her pumps. She's rising up out of the pit on her highest heels. Who could she be? In what form will she appear next?

MARYCLARE: (*Stands up.*) The Miami Beach Sightseer.

BLACKIE: I love it.

MARYCLARE: And a cigarette. Give me your smokes. (*She takes a cigarette, puts in her mouth and poses.*)

BLACKIE: Smoke from her nostrils . . . It's Dragon Lady.

MARYCLARE: (*Takes off the hat.*) Let me have your kimono. (*She puts on* BLACKIE'*s kimono.*)

BLACKIE: Dragon Lady turning into . . . turning into . . .

MARYCLARE: (*In a low voice.*) "They call me Blackie. Blackie, for my attitude, oil boy." (*She imitates* BLACKIE *and holds her in the dance poses from the night before.*)

BLACKIE: Mama's Little Flower, the most precious orchid in her corsage, the last cigarette in her silver case, the smallest spangle on her gown, the tiniest dot of polish on her little toe.

MARYCLARE: Oh, Blackie. Look at all these things. I want all these things.

BLACKIE: We can't take everything.

MARYCLARE: Why not?

BLACKIE: It's too much. They'll see.

MARYCLARE: No they won't.

BLACKIE: Maryclare.

MARYCLARE: I want everything.

BLACKIE: Pick one.

MARYCLARE: The shawl.

BLACKIE: Okay, we'll take the shawl. Take off that other stuff. Fold this up and put it in the bottom of the pack. Then we just walk.

MARYCLARE: What if they catch us?

BLACKIE: You can cry, can't you?

MARYCLARE: Yes.

BLACKIE: Good. You start crying. You say you didn't know.

MARYCLARE: I didn't know what?

BLACKIE: What you were doing. You say you got carried away by the beauty of the place.

MARYCLARE: I got carried away.

BLACKIE: Then you say you're a good girl.

MARYCLARE: I'm a good girl.

BLACKIE: You say you've never done anything like this before.

MARYCLARE: I've never done anything like this before.

BLACKIE: You ask them to forgive you.

MARYCLARE: Forgive me.

BLACKIE: And if worse comes to worse . . .

MARYCLARE: What then?

BLACKIE: You blame it on me.

MARYCLARE: You made me do it. You forced me. You tricked me into it.

BLACKIE: Yes.

MARYCLARE: He drags us down.

BLACKIE: What?

MARYCLARE: Nothing. I'm scared.

BLACKIE: Think of it as a gift.

MARYCLARE: It's gift.

BLACKIE: Let's go.

MARYCLARE: No. You go out first. I'll meet you at the beach.

BLACKIE: You'll do it by yourself?

MARYCLARE: Yes.

BLACKIE: It's more dangerous.

MARYCLARE: Go ahead. (BLACKIE *exits.* MARYCLARE *remains in the cubicle looking at herself in the three sided mirror.*)

Lights up on ANNA *in the empty kitchen, while the dressing room remains lighted.*

ANNA: Nothing belongs to us but our works, all works of mortification, all works of self-denial, all works of mercy. We can do nothing without God's grace.

MARYCLARE: It's a gift.

ANNA: The Heavenly gift, the nuptial garment, the most precious gem . . .

MARYCLARE: It's a gift from my hand . . .

ANNA: Which makes us holy and the children of God . . .

MARYCLARE: It's a gift from my hand and my hand is a gift from God . . .

ANNA: The more grace we possess, the greater will be our happiness in Heaven.

MARYCLARE: It's a gift from God.

ANNA: Obtained by baptism: of water, of blood, of desire . . .

MARYCLARE: You are blessed, Maryclare.

ANNA: And lost by mortal sin.

MARYCLARE: You are blessed! (*She takes everything in the room and stuffs it in the pack, the shawl last. She closes the pack and exits.* ANNA *carries out the boxes, empties the kitchen. Blackout on* ANNA *in Boston.*)

Lights up on the beach. BLACKIE *lies on her towel, taking in the sun and sleeping.* SKIPPER *enters and sits next to her, unnoticed. He holds his hand in front of her face to see if she reacts. She doesn't.*

SKIPPER: Catholic girls.

BLACKIE: (*Startled.*) What?

SKIPPER: You were out like a light.

BLACKIE: I'm sorry we left like that.

SKIPPER: Last night?

BLACKIE: I got scared.

SKIPPER: Of me?

BLACKIE: No.

SKIPPER: Then who?

BLACKIE: I don't know.

SKIPPER: That's okay. (*He lies back, taking in the sun along with her.*) This is it.

BLACKIE: You said it.

SKIPPER: Yup. (*Pause. Then he looks at her again.*) Your eyes are closed.

BLACKIE: No they're not. Light's coming in.

SKIPPER: (*Turning it into a game.*) What about mine? Open or closed?

BLACKIE: (*Looks over at him.*) Closed.

SKIPPER: Nope. Open a crack. (*Pause.*) Now what?

BLACKIE: (*Not even looking.*) Open.

SKIPPER: Wrong again. Completely black. (*He passes his hand over her face. No reaction.*) Like yours. (MARYCLARE *enters just at this moment as they appear to be in an intimate position with both of them lying down and* SKIPPER *leaning over* BLACKIE.)

MARYCLARE: What's going on?

SKIPPER: Jeeez!

BLACKIE: Holy—

MARYCLARE: Smoke, cow, Moses, and Mary Mother of God. (BLACKIE *and* SKIPPER *are shocked at* MARYCLARE's *appearance. She is dressed in a bizarre combination of everything she has stolen in town. Furious that* BLACKIE *has stolen her boyfriend, she sits on the beach at some distance from them and stares out at the ocean.*)

SKIPPER: And I thought Blackie was the wild one.

BLACKIE: Maryclare? (*No response from* MARYCLARE.)

SKIPPER: (*To* MARYCLARE.) See, I just came to say if you want to maybe come back tonight, there's a good view of the launch pads from my roof. They say it's going up tonight for sure.

MARYCLARE: That's nice.

SKIPPER: If you want to . . . Think about it.

BLACKIE: We can't. We're going to Mama's. (MARYCLARE *shoots* BLACKIE *a hateful look.*)

MARYCLARE: (*To* SKIPPER.) I'll think about it.

SKIPPER: I'll have your tire all fixed up and everything. (*Pause.*) We don't have to—you know—like last night—(*An embarrassed silence.* BLACKIE *looks at* MARYCLARE *who looks away.*)

BLACKIE: That's alright. It wasn't her.

SKIPPER: Who?

MARYCLARE: Go to Hell, Blackie.

SKIPPER: Well. Yeah. Okay, then. See ya. (*He exits.*)

MARYCLARE: You were trying to steal him.

BLACKIE: I was not.

MARYCLARE: You were stealing.

BLACKIE: I wasn't doing anything.

MARYCLARE: That's the best way. You steal him by not doing anything. You just *lie* there . . . the right way. I know. (*She smiles, turns to model her clothes for* BLACKIE.) I did it.

BLACKIE: You look it.

MARYCLARE: I went all the way. I was shaking at first. No, not shaking, sweating. First came the sweating, then the shaking. Thinking everybody's looking, everybody sees. Then I see they don't see. They're looking right at me. They're saying: come back again . . . have a nice day. I say thank you. I'm not shaking now. Not sweating. My hand's on the door, and it's cool. I've got it and they don't. I'm out the door and I'm flying. We're flying, aren't we, Blackie? Speed of light, right?

BLACKIE: Higher than the astronauts.

MARYCLARE: Oh yes. Much higher. We're looking down on them. We're waving goodbye. Goodbye, boys!

BLACKIE: Goodbye planets, goodbye stars.

MARYCLARE: Hello angels, hello archangels . . .

BLACKIE: And the Queen of them all . . . (*They sing as* BLACKIE *helps* MARYCLARE *disrobe. The stolen clothes are removed, a towel is spread out for her, and she lies down on it, in her bathing suit, basking in the sun, eyes shut.*)

BLACKIE & MARYCLARE: (*Sing.*)

> Hail holy Queen enthroned above
> Oh Maria.
> Hail Mother of Mercy and of love
> Oh Maria.
> Triumph all ye seraphim,
> Sing with us ye cherubim.
> Heaven and earth resound the hymn . . .
> Ave . . .

BLACKIE: The sun's our new boyfriend now, Maryclare. Put on some oil.

MARYCLARE: He loves the oil.

BLACKIE: We're slipping it on just for him.

MARYCLARE: To attract him.

BLACKIE: Mmmmm.

MARYCLARE: Now he's totally hot.

BLACKIE: Oh yes. And the heat—the heat's all over us. It's all we need to wear for him.

MARYCLARE: Our skin's the dress.

BLACKIE: A flaming red fire dress. A blinding flaming red fire dress.

MARYCLARE: Burning us till we peel.

BLACKIE: Burning each layer off till there aren't any layers left.

MARYCLARE: Till they can't tell us apart.

BLACKIE: All they find is a pile of bones and ashes on the beach.

MARYCLARE: But it smells like violets.

BLACKIE: That's good.

MARYCLARE: So they put it all back together and it's one *person*.

BLACKIE: She's got your hair. Your skin too. And your little feet. Those little toenails.

MARYCLARE: And your eyes and your voice. That's what I always wanted. I practiced at school. Remember when you said you saw Sister's hair? You said, "It's rat hair!"

BLACKIE: I did.

MARYCLARE: You said you saw it the night of the fire. The convent roof caught on fire and they all came out in their nightgowns. They tried to hide in the dark, but you saw it. It's rat's hair, you said. And her face, her face is pink wax.

BLACKIE: Perpetua?

MARYCLARE: Yes.

BLACKIE: She's so clumsy she started the fire. She bumped into a candle and her wimple caught on fire, but her face never burned . . .

MARYCLARE: Because it's wax.

BLACKIE: It just melted and dried in big, ugly lumps.

MARYCLARE: You said she only like basketball girls. You said that's what she is, she's a big clumsy basketball girl who's a nun.

BLACKIE: She liked you.

MARYCLARE: Everybody liked me.

BLACKIE: You were so Mary-like.

MARYCLARE: Even Christ on the cross. When I went up to the rail, he whispered to me.

BLACKIE: What did he say?

MARYCLARE: "Hello, Maryclare."

BLACKIE: No. He did not.

MARYCLARE: Yes. He said, "Help me."

BLACKIE: Help him what?

MARYCLARE: Help him down. He asked me to take out the nails and . . .

BLACKIE: And what?

MARYCLARE: He looked so cute. In his little cloth, and it slipped down a little just so you could see the sun-tan line, and he said "It's alright, Maryclare. You are blessed, Maryclare. Sister can't see. Father can't see . . ."

BLACKIE: See what? See what, Maryclare!

MARYCLARE: I've never told.

BLACKIE: It's okay. You can.

MARYCLARE: He'd come down and I'd kiss him. (*She waits for a reaction,* BLACKIE *is quiet.*) Every night. In my room. (*Still nothing from* BLACKIE.) French-kiss him.

BLACKIE: I wanted to die for him. And there *you* were—

MARYCLARE: I couldn't get caught. I didn't really do anything.

BLACKIE: I know. (*Sings to herself.*)

> "Too bad — too bad
> Who cares — who cares —"

(MAMA *appears as* BLACKIE *sings softly under:* "*All Night Long.*")

MARYCLARE: I'm sorry I didn't come in. When you sang back there. I'll sing with you tonight. Not just back-ups. I'll sing solos and everything. I'll sing as low as you sing. I'll sing lower. And hotter. I'll have the hottest, lowest voice they ever heard. And I'll get discovered. That fast. I'll be the hottest, fastest star in the world. They'll give me everything. They'll scream for me. They'll chant my name before I appear. They'll throw flowers at my feet. And I'll be so hot, I won't even notice. (MAMA *exits.* MARYCLARE *looks at* BLACKIE.) That's it, isn't it? I'm seeing your vision, aren't I, Blackie? (BLACKIE *lies with eyes closed, no response.*) Blackie, don't fall asleep, okay? (*She shouts.*) Blackie!

BLACKIE: (*Sits up, looks for* MAMA, *shivers.*) What?

MARYCLARE: Your eyes were closed.

BLACKIE: I'm freezing.

MARYCLARE: It's the sunburn.

BLACKIE: All of a sudden like that?

MARYCLARE: Your first day out you get too much, and then when it goes you freeze. (*She takes her white robe out of the pack.*) Wear my robe.

BLACKIE: (*Putting it on.*) This beach is hard as a rock. (*Light is fading.* BLACKIE *and* MARYCLARE *sit quietly looking out in different directions.* MARYCLARE *is becoming more and more nervous.*)

MARYCLARE: I see him again.

BLACKIE: Who?

MARYCLARE: The guy who's been following us.

BLACKIE: Nobody's been following us.

MARYCLARE: That's what you think. (*She takes* BLACKIE'*s kimono out of the pack and puts it on over her stolen clothes. She takes out the tire iron and holds it for protection.* PRINCE *enters.*)

PRINCE: Excuse me girls . . . pardon me. But it's almost dark.
  Officially that's closing time.
MARYCLARE: We're sleeping on the beach.
PRINCE: That's against the rules.
MARYCLARE: Blackie said we could.
PRINCE: Blackie?
MARYCLARE: She's a friend of ours up north.
PRINCE: Well, whoever she is, she's wrong about the rules. I won't
  say she was lying. She might have been mistaken, but when
  you're an official you hear a lot of lies. You say: no dogs allowed
  on the beach. They say: we haven't got a dog. And there's a dog
  sitting right beside them. Sometimes they walk away and leave
  the dog, just like that. Liars and jokers, all of them. If I had my
  way I'd dump them out with the garbage. You're the sisters I saw
  before, aren't you? In town.
BLACKIE: At the hot dog stand.
MARYCLARE: No.
BLACKIE: Maryclare?
PRINCE: Sure, the little girl in the blue dress.
MARYCLARE: No. Come on, Blackie. We're leaving.
PRINCE: Blackie? The real Blackie. Somebody got caught. Look,
  girls, I don't care what you do. Just pack up and move. It's for
  your own good. There's motels full of nuts out here tonight,
  waiting up for the big blast. I don't know what they see in it, but
  they'll do anything for a view. You can bet this bag'll be full
  tomorrow. (*He shows the big bag.*) This is for the garbage. (*He
  shows the little bag.*) This is for the treasures.
BLACKIE: We're going. We're on our way. (*She packs up.*)
PRINCE: You've got a place to stay?
BLACKIE: Yes. We're going to Mama's.
PRINCE: Your mother's? That's nice.
BLACKIE: Mama's Cafe of Miracles. On Bithlo Road.
PRINCE: Beg your pardon?
MARYCLARE: Don't tell him, Blackie.
BLACKIE: He's bombed, Maryclare. You can smell it on his breath.
PRINCE: Bithlo Road out in Black Lake?
BLACKIE: No. Out by the airport.
PRINCE: Why that's nothing but swamps out there. Your so called
  cypress gardens. Even the old timers get lost out there. That's no
  place for anybody. And it's off limits tonight. Pre-launch regu-
  lations. Within one mile of the site. There's no motels I know of
  out there.

BLACKIE: It's a nightclub. We're going to sing there.

MARYCLARE: Blackie!

PRINCE: A what??

BLACKIE: It's more like a friend's house.

PRINCE: Well. As long as you've got a place.

BLACKIE: We do.

PRINCE: Go ahead then. They'll be lighting up the launching pads soon. That's when all hell breaks loose. Someday that thing's gonna blow those jokers all over the county and I'll be the one picking up the pieces. I found a hand out there once.

BLACKIE: Let's go, Maryclare. (*She starts off with the sleeping bags and lantern.* MARYCLARE *stays back, holding the pack of stolen clothes.*)

MARYCLARE: (*Whispers so* BLACKIE *won't hear.*) I'm sorry I lied.

PRINCE: I know how it is.

MARYCLARE: I didn't mean to.

PRINCE: It's the holiday season. People get down here and they go a little too far.

MARYCLARE: I'm not like her.

PRINCE: And the tropical climate.

MARYCLARE: I'm the one you saw —

PRINCE: Beg your pardon?

BLACKIE: (*Offstage.*) Maryclare!

MARYCLARE: In town in the blue dress.

PRINCE: Oh, yes, you're a good girl underneath. They dress up like angels and act like whores. And the whores dress up and act like angels. But I can tell.

MARYCLARE: I dressed up. I danced around.

BLACKIE: (*Offstage.*) Maryclare?

PRINCE: What's that?

MARYCLARE: Nothing. I'm sorry —

BLACKIE: (*Offstage.*) Maryclare!

PRINCE: You take care now.

MARYCLARE: I am sorry. (*She follows* BLACKIE *offstage.* PRINCE *watches her go then exits in the opposite direction.*)

Lights up on the kitchen in Boston. ANNA *is dressed in her overcoat, sitting at the kitchen table writing a note by the light of the last lamp.*

ANNA: "Dear Blackie and Maryclare —" (*She stops and rips it up.*) No. "Dear Maryclare and Blackie — If you get back before I do —" No. They won't. (*She starts writing again.*) "Don't be scared by the light being on if I'm not here. I heard some noises last night

and I want them to think there's someone here. I'm going to
Easter Vigil with Maureen—the late service, so if you're here
and I'm not, don't worry, nothing's wrong. I've never lived here
alone before. I don't mind during the day but at night I hear
things. Then I look and there's nothing." (*To herself.*) I believe
that's worse than finding something. How can there be a noise
and then nothing? (*She stands up.*) Get on with it, Anna. Button
your coat, lock the door and get on with it. (*She does.*) That's the
ticket. (*She exits. Blackout on Boston.*)

*Faint light up on the swamp road. Dark night. Steamy. Swamp sounds:
water and night birds.*

BLACKIE: (*Offstage.*) Oh what a night for it. The darkest Saturday
   night for Mama.
MARYCLARE: (*Offstage.*) Do you see anything?
BLACKIE: The darkest night ever. (*Enters with lantern.*) She's more
   mysterious than I thought.
MARYCLARE: (*Enters barefoot, carrying her high heels.*) Listen!
BLACKIE: What?
MARYCLARE: I hear breathing.
BLACKIE: Everything's breathing out here.
MARYCLARE: I can't see.
BLACKIE: I'll turn off the lantern.
MARYCLARE: No!
BLACKIE: We'll see better without it.
MARYCLARE: No. (*She takes the lantern away from* BLACKIE *and turns
   to look behind them.*) The sign said Off Limits. (*She starts back.*) We
   shouldn't be out this far. (*She stands still.*) What if he's following
   us? (*No response.*) Blackie? He knows what I did. In town.
BLACKIE: Turn off the lantern. (MARYCLARE *does. Even darker now.*
   BLACKIE *and* MARYCLARE *are very still.*) He can't see you now.
MARYCLARE: It's all gray.
BLACKIE: It's the mist.
MARYCLARE: More like steam. (BLACKIE *starts to move away from
   her. She is frightened.*)
BLACKIE: Look!
MARYCLARE: Don't go—
BLACKIE: Look at the road, Maryclare. You can see it now in the
   moonlight. It's all white . . . mother of pearl. It's a pearl road,
   Maryclare!
MARYCLARE: It's cutting my feet.

BLACKIE: Put on your shoes.

MARYCLARE: They're too high.

BLACKIE: Walk on the side.

MARYCLARE: In mud? No thank you.

BLACKIE: I smell hyacinth. I bet in the daylight we'd see orchids growing.

MARYCLARE: I don't think the sun ever gets in here.

BLACKIE: The world before sun.

MARYCLARE: What if he's been following us the whole way? Was he the one at the grocery store. Remember, Blackie? Maybe Anna sent him. (*Pause. Nothing from* BLACKIE.) What was that sound?

BLACKIE: A frog out there . . . a bird taking off. Yeah . . . the one with the big wings. It's wings.

MARYCLARE: Snakes can fall out of trees in these places. That's what it sounds like.

BLACKIE: Of course her place would be out here.

MARYCLARE: Where? Just tell me where.

BLACKIE: I don't know yet.

MARYCLARE: I'm sure there's a snake in that tree.

BLACKIE: It's a vine.

MARYCLARE: It all smells stagnant. I don't like it, Blackie.

BLACKIE: Stay close . . . I'm here . . .

MARYCLARE: Wherever I touch it feels slimy. Like everything's rotting.

BLACKIE: That's how things grow here, out of their own dead.

MARYCLARE: It's bad.

BLACKIE: No . . .

MARYCLARE: We're lost, aren't we, Blackie? (*No response.*) I can't see the road anymore. Can you? (*No response.*) It's completely black. (*Pause.*) Say something. (*Nothing from* BLACKIE.) I can't see you. I can't see anything. There's no line. I can't tell what's land or water or anything. Even sky.

BLACKIE: Yes.

MARYCLARE: What?

BLACKIE: It's all washed together. There's no line.

MARYCLARE: Let's go back.

BLACKIE: Just like I dreamed it . . . No more lines. No light. No dark. There's not even black or white in the mist, just the road. I-95 straight south, as deep as you can get. That's where she's bringing us. Right into the deepest, darkest part of the planet.

Right up to her. Right into her heart, where everything starts growing.

MARYCLARE: I want to go back.

BLACKIE: There isn't any back. We're off the map, off limits. Don't you want to feel it? We're breaking all the rules to get here where there aren't any rules. No good, no bad, no boys, no girls, no day, no night. That's her secret. You have to go this far to get to her and it all starts. They go from here to outer space. You start singing here—you let out one note and it goes on forever. We can't stop now.

MARYCLARE: We have to.

BLACKIE: Just a little farther.

MARYCLARE: No. (*She reaches for* BLACKIE *and holds onto her, pulling her back.*)

BLACKIE: Let me go.

MARYCLARE: I can't.

BLACKIE: Stop it.

MARYCLARE: I can't stop. You made me. (*She tries to pull* BLACKIE *down.*)

BLACKIE: Maryclare! (*She pulls away and* MARYCLARE *falls.*)

MARYCLARE: I hate you.

BLACKIE: Get up. (*She tries to help* MARYCLARE *up.* MARYCLARE *holds onto her, pulling her down, hitting at her.*)

MARYCLARE: I'll kill you. Your hair, your voice, your eyes. Your things, all your things. You made me. Dress up and dance around the fire. Dress up and steal. Act like a whore. That's what he said. Like a whore and a dog in the mud. That's what you wanted—to drag me down. Making it sound so holy. And all you want is this. You just want to see me disgusting and dirty. Doing your sins for you.

BLACKIE: You're the one turning them into sins.

MARYCLARE: They are sins. Terrible sins. And I wanted them.

BLACKIE: Maryclare.

MARYCLARE: I wanted your sins. I took pleasure in them.

BLACKIE: You're soaking wet. (*She gets out a towel to dry her off. As she starts,* MARYCLARE *pushes her away.*)

MARYCLARE: I wanted to steal them from you. I wanted to see out of your eyes. I wanted to kill you and be you. You and your dreams.

BLACKIE: You loved me.

MARYCLARE: No.

BLACKIE: Look at me.

MARYCLARE: It was a dream, that's all. Where is Mama? Where is she? I don't see anything. There's no Mama. There's nothing here. It's all lies. All your lies.

BLACKIE: Just touch my hand, okay?

MARYCLARE: Lust of the eyes. Lust of the flesh. And the pride of life. I give them up. You and everything about you. I give it up. I didn't love you. You're not even a friend. You're nothing to me. I give you up. (BLACKIE *watches as* MARYCLARE *dries herself off with the white towel, then folds it into neat quarters and puts it down. Then opens the pack, takes out the stolen clothes, folds them into quarters and stacks them in a pile on the ground.* MARYCLARE *stands and takes the towel and wipes off her feet with the towel, then her hands. She looks at them.*) I'm not afraid. It's just water. (*She folds up the towel again into neat quarters.*) I know what to do. I know how to fold up the sheets just right and how to change the linens without disturbing the patients' sleep. And how to change the dressings without pain. I tell them a little story so they won't notice. And I know when they want someting to make them sleep. You need your sleep. That's the trouble with a vacation. You get over-excited and go without. But it can be fun for a few days. It'll make a good story to tell on the ward. They like to hear new things about the outside world. (*She puts the towel over the stolen clothes. She starts out, then looks back at* BLACKIE. *Gestures for her to come with her.*) It was just a dream to think of staying. (BLACKIE *refuses to join her.* MARYCLARE *takes the pack.*) They'll come and get you in the morning. You'll come back when it's light. (MARYCLARE *exits with lantern and the pack.*)

As BLACKIE *watches* MARYCLARE *exit, the light of the blastoff begins on the scrim behind her. It begins as a red glow which illuminates* MAMA's *face.*

MAMA: (*Sings.*)

DARK SIDE OF THE NIGHT

Cold and alone
You have made a bed of sorrows,
No dreams to lead you out,
You're on the dark side of the night.

Tears all gone dry,
So much time until tomorrow

Ghosts of all you lost
Wait on the dark side of the night.

Go into the dark.
To find the secrets of your heart.
No fear can burn you when you start
To love the fire.

Live inside the dark.
Light up the night inside your heart.
Burn through the darkness like a star
That lives on fire . . .

The fire of the rocket engines is projected onto the scrim between BLACKIE *and* MAMA. BLACKIE *sees her now, and begins moving toward her.*

BLACKIE: I see her, Maryclare.

The sound of the blastoff begins to build. MARYCLARE *enters downstage, wearing the blue dress and sunglasses. She looks out, away from the blast.*

MARYCLARE: Just as I was leaving, I saw the most amazing thing . . .
BLACKIE: The club is open, Maryclare.
MARYCLARE: A real blastoff from the Cape.
BLACKIE: She is ready and waiting. (*She keeps moving toward* MAMA.)
MARYCLARE: People were camped out all over the highway.
BLACKIE: The band is ready.
MARYCLARE: They stayed up all night to see it.
BLACKIE: They're all lining up to get in.
MARYCLARE: You could hear the countdown over loudspeakers.
BLACKIE: They're wearing their best perfumes to remember this night.
MARYCLARE: Then came the sounds of the engines.
BLACKIE: Her tables are set with the whitest cloth, her crystal ashtrays, her silver candlesticks, her golden urns full of lilies . . .
MARYCLARE: It was so loud you thought it couldn't get any louder, but it did.
BLACKIE: They're bringing her flowers and chanting her name.
MARYCLARE: You could feel the ground shaking under your feet.
BLACKIE: They're turning on her spotlights.
MARYCLARE: The steam from the engines went out for a mile around. It covered everything with a big white cloud. You could smell the fuel burning up.

BLACKIE: Pure white spotlights moving through the smoke.
MAMA: (*Singing under.*)

> Whispers of a sweet dark voice
> Reach through this veil of lonlieness
> And lead me into shadows
> Where I find you . . .
> Velvet arms of night enfold me
> Hold me here forever
> On the dark side of the night.
>
> Live inside the dark.
> Light up the night inside your heart.
> Burn through the darkness like a star
> That lives on fire.

MARYCLARE: (*Over the song.*) Then came the fire.
BLACKIE: Then her face.
MARYCLARE: You couldn't look right at it.
BLACKIE: Then her whole body in the light.
MARYCLARE: And when you did look at it, there it was . . .
BLACKIE: A crown of flowers on her head, a shining white dress, the microphone in he right hand . . .
MARYCLARE: The white rocket on top of the fire . . .
BLACKIE: And her arms wide open.
MARYCLARE: Going straight up.
MAMA: (*As* BLACKIE *reaches her.*)

> The dark side of the night
> Live on the dark side of the night
> Burn through the dark side of the night
> And live on fire . . .
> And live on fire . . .
> And live on fire . . .

MARYCLARE: And out of sight.
BLACKIE: Look at that fire. (*The fire is projected onto* BLACKIE *and* MAMA, *standing together, behind the scrim.*)

MARYCLARE *exits.* BLACKIE *and* MAMA *exit. Light of the blastoff fades on the stage, bare except for the towel over the pile of stolen clothes. Blackout.*
　　Lights up on the hot dog stand. Early morining. The band members sit at their usual places. One eats a hamburger, the other looks back toward the swamp, through binoculars.

BAND 2: Beyond recognition?

BAND 1: That's what the cops said. The road goes right to the site.

BAND 2: We're too close.

BAND 1: We're not that close.

BAND 2: It's like you can smell something bad out there.

BAND 1: I don't smell anything. (*He puts down the binoculars and resumes eating.*)

BAND 2: Nothing different?

BAND 1: (*Sniffing the air.*) Flowers or something. That's all.

BAND 2: Yeah, but like what if some of the ashes blew up here on the grill or something . . . (*He watches* BAND 1 *eating.*) What if they got in the burger meat . . . ?

BAND 1: There aren't any ashes in the burger meat.

BAND 2: She'd be in the burgers.

BAND 1: She isn't in the burgers.

BAND 2: You'd be eating her.

BAND 1: (*Puts down his burger.*) Shut up.

BAND 2: It could happen.

BAND 1: Forget it.

BAND 2: No kidding, it could. It bet it has. (*Blackout on hamburger stand.*)

> *Lights up on the kitchen in Boston. Everything is packed in boxes for the rummage sale.* MARYCLARE *sits at the table in her nurses' uniform, writing out a checklist.* ANNA *enters, also in uniform, carrying* BLACKIE's *kimono on a hanger. She also carries a pile of* BLACKIE's *clothes over one arm. There are three cardboard boxes on the table: things to sell, things to save, and things to throw out.*

ANNA: She loved this kimono! (*She holds it up and whirls it around.*) How much, Maryclare?

MARYCLARE: What?

ANNA: Should we ask.

MARYCLARE: I don't know.

ANNA: Twenty-five, I think. Twenty-five sounds right. I'm surprised she didn't keep it. (MARYCLARE *watches as* ANNA *carefully folds the kimono into quarters and puts in the box for sale.* ANNA *holds up* BLACKIE's *black shirt.*) Her shirt. Fifteen?

MARYCLARE: Fine.

ANNA: Write it down. We have to keep the list or we'll forget. (MARYCLARE *writes it down.* ANNA *folds up the shirt and puts it in the Sale Box.* ANNA *holds up* BLACKIE's *blue jeans.*) What about these? Save, sell or throw them out?

MARYCLARE: Save.

ANNA: Oh yes. For rags. I couldn't find any rags for the silver. I couldn't find anything when you were gone.

MARYCLARE: I'm sorry, Anna.

ANNA: I know (*Suddenly* ANNA *rips the jeans in half.*) One leg's enough for that. (*She puts the leg in the Save Box and the other leg in the throw away box. Then holds up* BLACKIE's *sandals.*) The sandals. Worn.

MARYCLARE: Five. (ANNA *places the sandals in the Sale Box. She holds up* BLACKIE's *scarves.*) Her famous scarves.

MARYCLARE: Five.

ANNA: Each?

MARYCLARE: Yes.

ANNA: Good. (*She folds each scarf and places them in the Sale Box, one at a time. Last of all,* ANNA *holds out* BLACKIE's *sunglasses toward* MARYCLARE.) What do you think?

MARYCLARE: Maureen asked for them.

ANNA: In case she's discovered.

MARYCLARE: What?

ANNA: In case she becomes a star. Maureen can say "These were *her* sunglasses." Her trademark. Way back then.

MARYCLARE: Do you think—?

ANNA: You never know. I can see her starting out in that bar you talked about out at the airport. But it won't be long until she's discovered. She'll climb that ladder of success until she's a star.

MARYCLARE: She always had a beautiful voice.

ANNA: She wasn't cut out for nursing.

MARYCLARE: She was meant to sing.

ANNA: When they write about her, they'll say she started out as a nurse but that was only the beginning. She'll tour all over the world. We'll see her on television. And maybe she'll appear here someday— live, in concert. We'll send her flowers or a basket of fruit and she'll send us a note and a special pass to let us in to see her— in her dressing room. She'll wear the most beautiful costumes of course. And the audiences will be wild. They'll be clapping and chanting her name before she appears. Then all of a sudden it will get very quiet, a spotlight will come on— and there she'll be. (ANNA *folds up the sunglasses and puts them in the Save Box. She sits at the table.*) Give me the checklist. (MARYCLARE *stares out the window. As* MARYCLARE *and* ANNA *sit quietly at the table,* MAMA *enters.*)

MAMA: (*Sings.*)

> For slippin out she's
> Slippin on some
> Blood-red lipstick,
> Some lacquered red nails,
> And her dragon-red heels—
> Satin spikes—
> She likes the way it feels . . .

MARYCLARE: (*Looks out the window, then at* ANNA.) What? Did you . . .?

ANNA: What?

MARYCLARE: Nothing. It's just the wind. (ANNA *and* MARYCLARE *remain seated and still at the table.*)

MAMA *gestures offstage and* BLACKIE *enters in gold, with white flowers in her hair, carrying a microphone.*

MAMA: Greet her with music. Welcome her in. There's a new girl singing with Mama tonight.

BLACKIE & MAMA: (*In the spotlight. Sing.*)

MIRACLE CAFE

> In Mama's Miracle Cafe
> It's always hot salvation day.
> You'll get your crown of ruby, long-stemmed,
> Sweet red roses,
> And sing while Mama's angels play.
>
> Go through the smoke to find the fire
> If you are lost you're on your way.
> Mama's Cafe never closes
> Come to me . . .

(*They sing another chorus and* MAMA *exits.*)

BLACKIE: (*Sings alone. A capella. A long, winding chant.*)

> She stands in gold, shining . . .
> Silver and gold, shining . . .

Lights out on MARYCLARE *and* ANNA *in Boston.*
   Lights out on BLACKIE, *as she finishes the last note.*

The Reactivated Man
Curtis Zahn

The Reactivated Man was first presented at the Edward Ludlum Theatre in Los Angeles in April of 1965 with the following cast:

NILES	Joseph Donte
NURSE	Rebecca Evans
PAULA	Jean Field
NORM	Herschel Reiter
SLEEVE	Charles Thompson

Directed by Frank Bolger

SETTING

A dimly lit adobe in disrepair, near the sea, alone, and lighted only by candles and kerosene lamps. At center stage there is a set of French windows and a table. An operating table is at stage left.

TIME

The present. Whatever year it is at the time of performance. This text has updated certain topical references to 1982. Further updating should be carried out as required.

The Reactivated Man
Curtis Zahn

Two doctors are hovering over CHARLES NILES *on the operating table.*
PAULA NILES *and the* NURSE *sit at a table by window where coffee heats
over a candle. Low moody lighting.*

NILES: (*A poetic, slow, and sad monotone narration which he will use
throughout play during his "recounting."*) For the duration of that
hushed, hesitant, ominous night they kept taking it apart and
putting it back together again, while a shy moon came and
went, and an abusive surf thundered above the cries of marsh
birds in the great swamp.

Idly, the NURSE *has pushed open the french window, flooding room
with the theme song played on a nickelodeon.*

NORM: (*Sharply.*) Nurse! (*The* NURSE *closes window; music faint
again.*)

SLEEVE: (*To* NORM.) He's going out again, Norm.

NORM: Yes, yes, of course, J.E.

SLEEVE: It didn't take so much.

NORM: (*Argumentatively.*) And again . . . it *might* take much *more.*

SLEEVE: (*Rising.*) That's more or less what I said! (*Pause.*) More!

NORM: (*He stops work and faces* SLEEVE. *Heatedly.*) Not at all! You
said *less!* More than two hours ago you said *less!*

SLEEVE: *Wrong! That was more or less before we gave* him *more!*
(PAULA *registers concern at their bickering; the* NURSE *stolidly chews
gum.*)

NORM: Earlier!

SLEEVE: *Later!* We gave him *less.* (*A pause.*) *Then* more!

NORM: (*Starts to swing his Phi Beta Kappa key.*) I'm sorry! It's the
other way 'round!

NORM: *Which* way?

SLEEVE: The *other* other way!

NORM: (*In a fury.*) *Other* other way! What kind of talk is that? I
merely said . . . (*Pause.*) Then you said . . . (*Pause.*) Which
compelled me to . . . (*The* NURSE *knocks a bottle off table. The
splintering crash halts them.* NORM *wipes off a dripping morsel and
starts to work.*) I'll hear no more about it! The more you
rationalize, the less I listen!

SLEEVE: (*Starting to work.*) Agreed! And the *less* you listen, the *more* I realize you know *more* about *less* than anyone I know. (*He picks up an enormous electric drill and starts to hold it against* NILES's *head, then changes his mind.*)

NILES: I had come here for an operation of a most unusual and delicate nature. (*A pause. Then table swings around and he pops up facing the audience.*) I had finally decided to have it removed. That is, *Paula* had decided for me! (*Hot spot on* PAULA.)

PAULA: (*She leaps up as lights over operating area diminish and spot remains in her area.*) Charles! That's not *exactly* true!

NURSE: (*Calls to* NILES.) That's just like an abortion or anything else, sweetie!

PAULA: (*To* NURSE.) His name is Charles!

NURSE: Charley?! (*Now expansively.*) *Chuck!*

SLEEVE: You got hemorrhoids, you have them removed. Charlie!

NORM: Or another example . . . a retroactive esophagus!

NURSE: Or excessive *hair!* I used to have *loads* of it, Chuck! (*A beat.*) So you go to a doc to have anything removed you never wanted in the second place!

SLEEVE: Or a wisdom tooth! If you're smart, you get rid of wisdom tooths! (*Pause.*) Teeth!

NILES: (*Theme music rises, now in poetic recall again.*) They were all propping each other up with explanations and rationalizations. The doctor they referred to as "J.E." was named Sleeve. Doctor Sleeve, I presume. (*Light comes up on* SLEEVE. *He makes a modest bow.*) The other's name I never knew. He was just "Norm." And in a way he represented it—the norm.

NORM: (*Light comes up on him. He bows, then assumes a lecture stance, twirling his fraternity key.*) Uh . . . you can have your guilts removed two ways! Through psychoanalysis, as is well known, but which sometimes takes months or years, and it is . . . expensive—

NURSE: (*Exuberantly cuts him off.*) And half the time those darn old guilts just flare up again at some future time! (*She accidentally knocks a clock off the table, picks it up.*)

SLEEVE: (*Ignoring her scene.*) The other way is fairly new! A surgical operation on that part of the brain lobe where overactive guilts produce excruciating anxieties—

NURSE: (*Exuberantly cutting in again.*) There's a third way, Chuck . . . but . . . (*Pause, voice drops.*) I . . . I already tried it!

SLEEVE: Nurse!

NURSE: (*Apologizing.*) I was only going to tell him about heroin . . . (*Pause.*) and acid.

NILES: (*Weakly.*) What about them?

PAULA: Oh, Charles!

NURSE: They don't work. Because I used to be a hippy and . . . (*She pauses, realizing that* PAULA *is looking at her with incredulous interest.*) I mean, shit! I tried speed and grass . . . You name it!

NORM: Nurse!

NURSE: (*Impassioned.*) I'm telling it like it isn't! (*Pause.*) I mean, wasn't! The trip only lasts *a while!* Less than that, even! Then you're right back where you started — simply *loaded with guilts!*

PAULA: (*A pause; quietly.*) And this way is . . . permanent?

SLEEVE: Forever!

PAULA: And no . . . side effects?

NURSE: (*Enthusiastic.*) Look at me! Norm operated on me way back in *1971!* (*She bumps into a table, almost upsetting its contents. A weak, self-conscious smile now.*) Reflex action! (*Pause.*) I always do that when I think about 1971. (*The doctors force a laugh; she straightens the table. Theme music loudens again.*)

NILES: I listened to the marsh-birds cackling . . . sharing the joke. I heard the carnival music, braving the fog in some old forgotten seaport. (*Pause.*) And I suddenly heard Paula's doubts, beating around her eyes and ears. She said:

PAULA: (*To doctors.*) But you have to admit it's, well, it's not . . . natural.

SLEEVE: *Natural?*

NORM: So what's natural nowadays.

SLEEVE: Twentieth-century man is an automobile junk yard of surplus parts!

NURSE: Like I said! God gave me surplus hair . . . (*Pause.*) But no boobs!

SLEEVE: Nurse!

NURSE: So I had the former removed and the latter installed! (*Brightly.*) Norm fixed me with a matched pair! (*To* PAULA.) Incidentally, honey . . . if you aren't satisfied with the way God made you . . .

SLEEVE: (*Sternly, to* NURSE.) Miss Thanatopsis!

NURSE: (*Apologetically to* PAULA.) It's not God's fault! *Eveybody* makes mistakes! (NURSE *waits; doctors observe* PAULA *interestedly.*)

PAULA: (*Shakes head.*) Thank you. I . . .

NILES: (*Facing* PAULA.) She's perfectly satisfied—aren't you, Paula?

PAULA: Well . . . (*Pause.*) I . . . I haven't given the matter much thought. (*Smiles, gestures.*) Besides! It gives you an incentive to try harder . . . (NURSE *knocks another object over.*)

NORM: (*Tired, scolding tone.*) Nurse!

SLEEVE: (*A pause. Music swells.*) Uh, Mr. Niles . . . (*Another pause.*) What's your first name, Niles? Charles?

NURSE: Chuck!

SLEEVE: Chuck! Chuck, you should understand we're all here to carry on where nature left off . . . finish the job.

NORM: (*Cheerily.*) Add a little bit here, subtract a little there.

NURSE: And the brain's no different from the rest of the physiological body! Here we are in the present century and we got all those obsolete parts! An over-active recall. An incipient guilt lobe! (*Pause.*) I was simply loaded with guilts till I met Norm. (*Pause, now wildly.*) I couldn't even go to the bathroom if somebody was watching!!

Doctors show embarrassment. NILES, *for the first time, begins to get half off the table to say something, to stare at everyone.* PAULA *gets up, opens window pensively. The carnival music instantly floods room.*

SLEEVE: (*Assuming* NURSE *opened window.*) Nurse! (*Sees that it was* PAULA.)Oh, excuse me, Mrs. . . . Mrs. . . . .

PAULA: (*Closes window.*)Niles. Paula Niles, who tries harder!

NORM: I'm sorry, Mrs. Niles. We have to exercise every precaution.

PAULA: I know. The operation is illegal.

NILES: Illegal and *unnatural!*

NURSE: Well, of course, it's illegal, sweetie! Merely because AMA is aways fifty years behind the future! Reactionary old fogies!

NORM: All brain surgery was illegal once upon a time, Chuck!

NURSE: More recent than that even!

SLEEVE: *Abortions* were illegal!

NURSE: (*To* PAULA.) Incidentally, we used to do them too, until it . . . until it . . .

PAULA: Became legal?

NURSE: (*Drops a test tube.*) No! I mean, sure! (*Pause.*) Well, doctors have got to make a living just like everybody else. (*Inspired.*) There's no *challenge* in abortions! You see, Norm and J.E. are pioneers! They like to play around with the hidden, dark recesses of the mind! They're *hooked* on the *unknown!*

PAULA: (*Worried.*) The unknown?

NILES: Paula! I thought you said—

SLEEVE: Miss Thanatopsis. (*More sternly.*) Miss Thanatopsis!

NORM: All she's saying—

SLEEVE: She's simply pointing out that the medical fraternity is afraid of the human brain, sir.

NORM: Won't touch it!

SLEEVE: Unless it's some poor psychopath already headed for the electric chair!

NURSE: Or some homo they caught banging little kids!

SLEEVE: She means . . . (*Pause.*) The point is . . .

NURSE: Siegfried Frood was a pioneer! Only, instead of going in there with words, Norm and J.E. use a darn little old drill and an ear scoop!

SLEEVE: And it's permanent.

NORM: You don't keep coming back for therapy and forking over all the bread.

SLEEVE: He means—

NURSE: He means, the whole bottom's going to drop out of Froodian psychology some fine day!

NORM: It's a put on.

SLEEVE: A rip-off! (*Pause; now gravely.*) I'd be the last to disparage my esteemed colleague. However—

NORM: However, we know several psychologists who have just as many guilts as Chuck.

NURSE: For charging all that money!

NORM: *They* come to *us!*

SLEEVE: (*To* PAULA.) For the same, simple alteration we're performing on your husband.

NURSE: Actually, Norm and J.E. are heroes! (*Inspired.*) They could be *arrested* for what they're doing!

NORM: (*Modestly.*) Oh, come! Miss Thanatopsis!

SLEEVE: We just don't like to see beautiful people suffer! That is all.

NORM: We happen to believe in what we are doing. That is all.

NURSE: (*Reverently.*) There've always been martyrs in the world! Look at Lenny Bruce! Jesus Christ! (*Pause.*) Sun Moon! The Almighty works in mysterious ways. (*The window blows open, flooding the room with a crescendo of carnival music. All stare at the phenomena.* PAULA *calmly goes over and closes it.*)

SLEEVE: Uh, Niles—I mean Charles. You've had psychotherapy, right?

NORM: And it didn't help. Right?

PAULA: No!

NILES: Yes!

SLEEVE: Which?

NORM: Yes or no?

NILES: No! I mean, *yes!*

PAULA: No.

NURSE: They mean, after you spend all that money you still got guilts! (*To* NILES.) Huh? (*To* PAULA.) Huh?

NORM: Put it this way, Mrs . . .

PAULA: Paula Niles, who tries harder.

NORM: Paula—you got an earache you don't go to a headshrinker.

NILES: (*Weakly, far away.*) Maybe you do!

NURSE: Or a ruminating trombolises! Guilt is actually a disease! Like syphilis or anything else!

NILES: (*A wail.*) I don't *have* a guilt complex! (*The* NURSE *drops another bottle. The doctors stand aghast.*)

SLEEVE: According to patient's case-history, he was virtually immobilized by guilts. (PAULA *and* NILES *shake their heads.*)

NORM: Patient was unable to cope with environment in normal manner.

NURSE: Can't eat Kentucky Fried Chicken without he throws up!

PAULA: Neither can I. Is that abnormal?

NILES: Besides . . . we're vegetarians.

PAULA: For humanitarian reasons.

NURSE: You're both confusing me! Humanitarians don't eat chickens—right? Then why do vegetarians eat vegetables?

SLEEVE: Nurse! Bring me patient's behavior pattern.

NILES: I don't *have* a pattern.

NURSE: That's right, Charlie! (*To* SLEEVE.) He does everything ass backwa- . . . I mean . . . (*Impetuously inspired.*) He *improvises!*

SLEEVE & NORM: (*In unison.*) He what?

PAULA: My husband—he has to stop and think about everything. He—

NURSE: (*To doctors.*) Practically everything *you* do, he shouldn't! (*The doctors appear offended.*) Chuck believes in *honesty!* (*They are more offended.*) He believes in *humanitarianism*—despite he eats vegetables.

NILES: There is a difference between guilt and conscience.

NURSE: Chuck gives it away to the poor! (*Pause.*) Money, not sex!

SLEEVE: The point is —

NORM: The point is —

NILES: Let me explain. Guilt is —

PAULA: Oh, Charles.

NURSE: Sweetie! We're all trying to help you!

NILES: I just want to explain one thing.

PAULA: Charles, you've explained it all a thousand times! To me! To the children! The neighbors! The income tax collector.

NILES: Paula —

PAULA: Explaining doesn't buy shoes for the children! Explaining doesn't meet the payments on the house.

NILES: Paula! The house was your idea in the first place!

PAULA: But you agreed to it!

NILES: And I agreed to come *here*. Nevertheless . . .

PAULA: Nevertheless our bank account is overdrawn again. Why? Because you can't conscientiously do this kind of work! Or that kind of work! Because it might be dishonest or helping the war! Or — (*She breaks off conversation.*)

NURSE: (*To* PAULA.) I know just how you feel. I had several boyfriends that didn't believe in work! Dozens!

NILES: I do believe in work! Paula means —

NURSE: He means work that doesn't hurt anybody!

SLEEVE: What kind —

NORM: Is that?

NURSE: Work that doesn't cause war. Or violence. Charley wouldn't hurt a flea — right? (*Glance at* NILES.)

SLEEVE: Wouldn't?

NORM: (*Moves menacingly to* NILES.) Not even if it came up and bit you?

SLEEVE: (*Makes as though to slap* NILES.) Not even if it bit you?

NURSE: He'd turn the other cheek!

SLEEVE: Which cheek?

NURSE: He's one of *those.* He don't believe in violence.

SLEEVE: Oh! (*To* NORM.) He's one of *those!*

NORM: I heard you. (*Threateningly.*) Mr Niles! Suppose I started to hit you! What would you say?

NILES: I'd say, (*Pause.*) please don't.

NORM: That's all?

NILES: I think so. (*Pause.*) Yes!

SLEEVE: You wouldn't hit back?

NILES: (*After a pause.*) No, sir, I . . . I . . .

NURSE: (*Enthralled.*) He's *really* sick!

PAULA: As you said, he is one of those. (*Pause.*) So am I. At least we have that in common. (*All are caught by surprise as* SLEEVE *slaps* NILES. NILES *recoils. But makes no effort to retaliate.* PAULA *watches very calmly.* NURSE *is shocked.*)

NORM: You wouldn't even defend yourself? (*He slaps* NILES. NILES *ducks, trying to avoid being struck, but shows no anger, only pain. Both doctors alternately hit* NILES. *However, now they seem weary of the game.*)

NURSE: He's really got it bad.

SLEEVE: Most advanced case I've ever seen! (*As a final test, he whirls, as though to strike* NILES *again.* NILES *stoically faces him.*)

NORM: Obviously, psychoanalysis didn't help at all. (*He also starts to strike* NILES.)

SLEEVE: Obviously!

NURSE: Obviously!

NILES: (*A wounded shout.*) But it *did!* (*All turn around, startled.*) I got rid of certain *guilts.*

NORM: Then, why, may I ask . . . ?

NURSE: Sweetie! You're not coming clean!

NILES: But, then, there was this *new* guilt.

SLEEVE: It is my absolute understanding—

NILES: (*He waves them silent.*) I know! But then, there was this *new* guilt! (*Impatient, impassioned.*) The *cost!* (*He tries to climb off table; they work at restraining him.*) Have *I* the right to spend sixty-five dollars an hour on psychiatry when other people are *really* sick? Or hungry?

SLEEVE: (*A pause; now with mock cheer.*) Well! That's a new angle!

NURSE: You go to a head-shrinker to get cured of one thing, and—

NORM: Exactly! I have always steadfastly maintained consistently—

SLEEVE: Exactly! But *who* are these hungry people, Charley?

NORM: Yes! Quite! But where are they? Do you see any, J.E.?

SLEEVE: Not at all! I see rich, pampered bastards trying to overthrow the government.

NORM: Ever see a hippie that wasn't getting unemployment insurance? (*Pause.*) Miss Thanatopsis, do you know any poor people in dire need of medical attention?

NURSE: (*Holds up a finger.*) Only one! That's why I didn't marry him.

NORM: Where are these people, Mr. Niles?

NILES: Everywhere! The people who live on the other side of the billboards. (*Doctors and* NURSE *look to* PAULA *for an explanation.*)

PAULA: My husband feels —

NILES: (*Cutting her off.*) Two-thirds of the world is underfed! There is *one* doctor for every million persons! (*Affixes glance on* SLEEVE. *Now looks accusingly at* NURSE. *Hysterical shout.*) There is a critical *population explosion!*

NURSE: Don't look at me, Sweetie. (PAULA *goes back to table by window.*)

NILES: (*To all of them.*) There's but one reason I'm here! Your operation is cheaper than psychoanalysis.

NURSE: Or heroin, Sweetie.

NORM: (*Swinging his key.*) You want to be rid of nagging guilts?

SLEEVE: You remove that small knob on the brain that causes the trouble. (*He holds up a jar and points.*)

NORM: From the *northeast* section of the brain. Smack in front of your anti-cerebellum unicoxus.

SLEEVE: Just south of the homo intellectus. (NILES *and* PAULA *hear the words with dutiful doubt.* NORM *swats a fly. They observe this also.*)

NURSE: (*Demonstrates with fingers.*) No bigger than a mosquito bite! (*Joyous wonder.*) Under the microscope it looks like a tangled-up tiny portion of spaghetti with clam sauce!

SLEEVE: (*Noting that* PAULA *and* NILES *recoil.*) Nurse! Bring me a *recall.*

NURSE: (*Heading for mantel where jars are lined up.*) Yes sir. (*To* NILES, *over the shoulder.*) Yet a great weight's been lifted right off your mind!

NORM: (*Swats at another fly.*) All of us have had ours removed.

SLEEVE: *All* of us. Actually, Miss Thanatopsis' was over-enlarged. Size of a cockroach!

NURSE: (*Returning with jar.*) Because I hated my parents.

PAULA: (*Newly interested.*) And you don't hate them now?

NURSE: (*Shakes her head violently.*) I never *think* of them now. (*The window blows open again, bringing the carnival music in loudly.* NURSE *crosses and closes it.*)

SLEEVE: (*Philosophically.*) It used to bother me, seeing sickness and poverty.

NURSE: Me too. I used to cry *daily*. Even after I dropped out.

NORM: It is man's destiny that his world shall always be filled with trouble. To survive, one must protect oneself, physically *and* mentally!

PAULA: (*Jumps up agitatedly.*) But we know all this! (*To* NURSE.) Everything's been settled! Why are we standing here talking?

Impulsively, she turns and opens window. No music. Only sounds of frogs, surf, marsh birds, crickets. Lights go out briefly. Marsh sounds continue as NILES *narrates.*

NILES: (*Poetic "narrative" tone.*) And so, while the doctors labored over me, my innermost thoughts came and went under a counterpoint of frogs and carnival music while strange faces scowled in the flickering light. (*Part laughingly.*) It isn't quite true that I'd agreed to having my soul shorted-out. My conscious mind said "yes." The tongue. The lips. And I believe the latter smiled even. But deep in the subconscious, that bathospheric volcano of righteousness, there was resistance. It was this they were after.

Nickleodeon music erupts; it is suggestive of Victorian bordello piano jazz. Strobe lights produce a "quickie" effect like old time movies. Doctors move with exaggerated speed as they drill, saw, pound the patient. NURSE *moves jerkily to and fro, carrying things; at the end of refrain, entire company freezes as a still-life.*

NORM: (*Excitedly.*) I think we've got it this time, J.E.! Really I do!

SLEEVE: Of course!

NORM: Really I do! I really think we've got it!

NURSE: (*Gloriously.*) Oh, doctor!

SLEEVE: (*Peering inside skull.*) There it is! It was right there all the time. Next to the libido!

NORM: The libido was over-active!

NURSE: They always are! Remember that used car salesman? I *never* —

NORM: (*Cuts her off.*) Nurse! Did you sterilize my wire cutters?!

NURSE: Natch! And the pliers.

SLEEVE: (*Stands back, waits.*) Well? *Now?*

NORM: (*Lights cigarette.*) I . . . I thought I'd make a few exploratory probes first.

NURSE: (*Nods emphatically.*) We got loads of time! It's only four AM.

SLEEVE: (*Lowers voice.*) Obviously it's going to be difficult to get past the patient's *recall.*

NORM: (*A cautious glance at* PAULA, *who appears to be asleep sitting up.*) Obviously.

NURSE: (*Peering into* NILES's *skull again.*) It's a whopper if I ever saw one.

NORM: (*Lowered voice, watching* PAULA.) I thought I'd circumvent his memory by going in close to the motor nerves. (*Coughs.*) Of course, I'd use my number four iron. I'd follow through with clamps.

SLEEVE: (*Cautioning.*) And if the motor nerves —?

NURSE: (*To* SLEEVE, *a worried whisper.*) Remember what happened to that broker?

SLEEVE: (*Leans closer to her;* NORM *cannot hear but is suspicious.*) Eh?

NURSE: (*Whispers with a cautious glance at* PAULA.) That tall fellow from Pierce, Fenner, Merill, Lynch and whoever it is. Something got shorted out. Every time he rode in a taxi, he urinated.

NORM: (*Overhears; angry.*) Nurse! Bring me the micrometer! (*To* SLEEVE.) You have to take risks. Nothing ventured leaves a guilt complex running 'round.

NURSE: Too much conscience makes a dull boy! (*Lowered voice.*) His wife says they're absolutely overrun with mice.

NORM: (*Questioningly.*) MMmmmmmmmmmmm?

NURSE: (*To* NORM.) He can't kill anything! Too *conscientious.* (*Pause.*) And he's failing in business.

NORM: (*Sarcastically.*) Imagine! J.E.!

NURSE: (*Oblivious to his tone, nods vehemently.*) And they had to borrow on their house!

NORM: (*Mocking sternness.*) Doctor Sleeve! Am I to understand from this ravishing young creature that the Horatio Alger success story no longer works? (NURSE, *embarrassed, drops hammer.*)

SLEEVE: (*Professing alarm.*) It sounds extremely un-American! I was taught that honesty and virtue were second only to charity!

NURSE: (*She catches on, but is determined to go on with her point.*) She said he lost forty-five hundred last month. Turned down a big deal because it sounded dishonest! They got three kids and a beat-up old Chevy station wagon and she may have to go to work.

NORM: J.E.! This should be reported to the President!

SLEEVE: Or the FBI! It sounds suspicous to begin with.

NORM: Honest *business man!* Must be from some retarded country!

SLEEVE: Typical charity case. Doesn't know how to lie or cheat!

NURSE: (*Stubbornly.*) As a matter of fact, she said he *gives* a lot of their money to charity. I mean, do-gooder causes.

NORM: Diseased conscience. Used to be a familiar type around here.

SLEEVE: (*Laughs.*) Nowadays they just get ulcers. Or cancer . . .

NORM: (*Laughs.*) Or swallow happiness pills.

SLEEVE: (*Laughs.*) Or attach a hose to the exhaust pipe.

NORM: (*Rising laughter.*) Or endow a medical foundation.

NURSE: (*Laughter.*) Or join the Republican Party.

SLEEVE: (*Laughter.*) Or the Communist Party!

NURSE: (*Laughter.*) Like that engineer from Passaic! After the operation he became a White Muslim. (*All laugh loudly;* PAULA *awakes but they don't notice.*)

NORM: (*Mock seriousness.*) Of course *some* businessmen can just turn off their conscience until *after* they've made their killing.

NURSE: (*Laughter.*) And *then* jump out the window!

SLEEVE: (*Laughter, tears.*) And into the pscho ward . . .

NORM: (*Hysterical laughter, tears.*) Stopping to see a head-shrinker on the way down.

They figuratively roll with laughter. PAULA *stands up, opens window. Instantly the nickelodeon music drowns out the laughter and lights go out.*

NILES: (*Poetic narrator recount, vaguely.*) One seems to move horizontally in and out of worlds that ignore each other; time returns delicately, and begins to feel its way backwards into memory. (*Pause.*) And the listener stands, while archaeology goes by, throwing over its shoulder those things which were good or evil, or guilty and frightened, or shameful and triumphant.

The doctors had pulled my past into the future and would freeze it there while Paula prepared for the thaw. A new part of me had invented anger now, and this was directed at my wife. (*Pause; spiritedly.*) Yes! The operation was her doing! I *had* to blame *someone!*

NORM: (*Quickly, loudly.*) Only the insane man blames himself! It's *normal* to blame others, eh, J.E.?

SLEEVE: Right! (*Humorously.*) And I'm going to blame *you* if the patient's motor nerves get fouled up!

NORM: (*Humorously.*) So, do I care? (*Pause. Coyly.*) That is, unless the operation you performed on *me* wasn't entirely successful!

NURSE: (*Good-humoredly.*) In which case you can blame *him!* (*Indicating* SLEEVE.)

SLEEVE: (*Humorously.*) And *I* don't care, unless Norm's little job on me didn't do all it's supposed to do.

NILES: (*Narration, but thoughtful, questioningly.*) But what about Paula? I seemed to be lying there, watching love drift away while images of other girls, other times, crowded in, smiling.

NURSE: (*Crowding in, smiling.*) It'll all be over soon, Charley!

NILES: (*Stirs suddenly, addresses this directly to the* NURSE.) Some day I'll meet you in a cocktail lounge and neither of us will recognize myself. (NURSE'*s smile freezes embarrassedly, then returns in force, but with a glance at* PAULA.)

SLEEVE: (*Quickly to* NURSE.) What's he saying?

NILES: (*Sits up quickly; in a declaration.*) Paula will have to have hers out, too! (*All four attentive.*) The operation! (NILES *waves a scalpel which alarms all.*) Otherwise she'll suffer! She'll have guilts for talking *me* into it. (*Jumps off table.*) She'll have to have *hers* remo- . . .

NURSE: (*Interrupts*—; *takes his arm.*) Sweetie! (*Coaxing him back.*) It's okay to blow your top but you got to take it easy!

SLEEVE: (*Cryptically.*) The top of your head's over there on the mantel!

NURSE: And your recall.

NORM: (*Sharply.*) Nurse! Did you remember to put his recall up there next to his memory? (NURSE *knocks over a lighted candle.*)

NURSE: I forgot. Sorry. (NURSE *picks up candle, races over to mantel with another jar, places it beside the other.*)

SLEEVE: And in the jar with the proper label! I don't want him remembering things before they *happen!*

NURSE: Yes, sir. (*Musingly, lowered voice.*) There's something wrong with my motor nerves today. (NURSE *busily gets patient back onto table.* PAULA, *overhearing her remark, stares at her.* NORM *picks up a rather large hand-drill.*)

SLEEVE: (*To* NORM.) Really, you're not going to use a three-quarter inch drill?!

NORM: (*Lowered voice.*) The other's broken.

NURSE: (*To* SLEEVE, *confidingly, mincingly.*) That hard-headed contractor we did last week.

SLEEVE: (*Exchanges shrugs with her.*) It's going to be hell when we re-wire his nerves again. (*Peering into skull.*) Lot of moral fiber there.

NORM: (*Coming around to other side.*) Look, J.E., I'm coming in from the front. Then I'll work up until I run into your pinking shears.

SLEEVE: Fine! (*Dryly.*) And be sure you know what you're cutting! The last time you chopped off a piece of my fingernail. (*Sound of frogs croaking as* PAULA *opens window. They glance at her, she closes it.*)

NILES: (*Dreamily; narrative voice.*) I may never know now which things I imagined, and which were real. Since the operation, people have insisted that I dreamed up the entire thing . . . doctors, nurse, power-tools and all.

NORM: (*Excitedly; he has heard.*) J.E.! Notice something?!

SLEEVE: I'm noticing!

NORM: He's ahead of us!

SLEEVE: Ahead of us! We've advanced him several weeks!

NORM: Because of the pressure! Take out your ballpoint pen and try that darning needle.

SLEEVE: (*He does. The patient reacts.*) He predicted we might have to use the electric sander!

NORM: How deep are you in there? Here. (*He produces an ordinary yardstick and hands it to* SLEEVE.)

SLEEVE: Don't you have anything smaller than that? Where's the tape-measure?

NORM: It's got blood on it.

SLEEVE: (*Shrugs, and inserts yardstick.*) Inch and five-eighths, give or take a little. Nurse! Take the hydrometer and see if my battery's up!

NURSE: (*Does.*) Yes sir. (NURSE *glances at* PAULA *who is extremely disturbed by the haphazard procedure.*)

SLEEVE: Sooner or later I'm going to have to insist that we find ourselves a set up with regular electric current.

NURSE: (*Calling to Doctor.*) One of your cells is dead. Otherwise, you're okay.

NILES: Thank you.

NURSE: Sweetie! I was talking to . . .

NILES: (*Cuts her off: vague, wandering.*) Where am I *now?* I hear music.

NURSE: It's the carnival, Chuck! Near town.

NILES: Let's go! (*Pause.*) *What* town?

NURSE: (*Evasive; a glance at doctors.*) Just a town . . . (*Pause.*) How does your head feel?

NILES: What's ahead?

NURSE: (*Comfortingly, friendly, baby talk.*) A head's the thing that sits on your neck and causes all the troub- . . .

NILES: (*Blurts, cutting her off.*) I know that! I mean, *ahead!* The future! (*Pause; now softly.*) I feel the future.

SLEEVE: (*A glance at* NORM.) Yes . . . ?

NILES: Is it over?

NORM: What? (*As in "Is what over?"*)

NILES: (*Feebly.*) War.

NORM: (*Questioning glance at* PAULA. *She comes up toward them.*) Which war?

NILES: Any war, I guess. (*He slumps back. They manifest discouragement.*)

PAULA: (*Figuratively shaking her head in doubt.*) I don't see any change yet.

SLEEVE: (*Nodding in agreement.*) He's not *ready* yet.

NORM: (*Serene, takes a few lecturing steps.*) We've temporarily shorted out the past. You noticed the feeling of lightness upon the part of the patient? (PAULA *appears doubtful.*)

NURSE: As though an awful burden was gone! (*Pause.*) He was happy as hell for an instant!

SLEEVE: But there remain the present and future. The present, in these types, inevitably presses for the *future.* And the future remains dark until we have scraped clean the damaging tissues of collective guilt.

PAULA: But suppose—

NURSE: I know it sounds complicated, but J.E.'s right.

SLEEVE: Sometimes, just cutting out a few milligrams of *recall* does the job. Say, the patient is suffering from some unpunished personal guilt . . .

NURSE: Like child molesting! (*Notes* PAULA'*s reaction.*) Or joining some . . . some subversive organization.

NILES: (*To himself.*) I . . . didn't . . . join . . . because of Paula.

NURSE: (*With quick cheer.*) That's as good a reason as any, Chuck!

NILES: (*Hasn't heard her.*) I'm guilty for *not* joining. Paula's guilty for not *letting* me.

PAULA: Charles!

NORM: Joining what?

SLEEVE: Joining what?

NORM: The Auto Club?

SLEEVE: The Auto Club?

NILES: (*He doesn't hear them. Drugged, slurred speech.*) But now . . . ever'thing's . . . going to be all right . . . all right . . . all right . . . (*Pause.*) For me, that is . . . for me . . . that is . . .

Faintly is heard a few bars of the forlorn nickelodeon theme-song music.
PAULA *stiffly heads for the window: dejected, hunched, with Kleenex.*
Doctors freeze as a tableau. Suddenly, PAULA *runs to window and throws*
it open. Instantly, loudly the "quickie" music comes on again. The doctors
and NURSE *again move quickly, jerkily under strobe light, working*
feverishly with power tools, etc. Then music slows to half speed and all
mime in slow motion for a few beats. Then music slows distortedly like a
run-down phonograph and ceases. The tableau freezes. It resumes at
"quickie" speed once more and the frenzied ballet under strobe light goes on
until PAULA *marches jerkily to operating table, turns, marches back to*
window and closes it. This stops the music.

   Momentary blackout.

   Lights come on to reveal doctors relaxed. NURSE, *with fly-swatter is*
creeping around floor, swatting at cockroaches. PAULA *sits alert, tense,*
waiting.

SLEEVE: (*Going over to corner, pulls out a dart game.*) That'll hold him
   for awhile!
NORM: That it will! (*He gets out a comic book.* SLEEVE *begins throwing*
   darts at target. Pause.)
PAULA: Is it . . . what happens now?
NURSE: They got to wait until the ice cubes freeze his obbligato.
PAULA: The what?
NURSE: (*Shrugs.*) I never can remember that word. (*Pause.*) Want a
   fix? (PAULA *shakes her head.*) Like to share a joint? (PAULA *shakes*
   head.) Gin? Coffee? Tea? . . . How about a burrito . . . only I
   can't heat it because we've got to use the gas later for the
   blow-torch. (NORM, *reading, bursts out laughing; he will continue*
   to do this intermittently. PAULA *notes this casualness with*
   astonishment.)
PAULA: (*Now back to* NURSE's *statement.*) Did you say . . . blow-
   torch?
NURSE: (*Throws up hands.*) No! You're right! I meant soldering-
   iron. (*Waits; explains.*) They have to solder his you-know later
   on. Otherwise—
SLEEVE: Miss Thanatopsis! Did you remember to get Plastic Wood
   when you were in town?
NURSE: Natch.
SLEEVE: And the thumb tacks?
NURSE: Natch. (*Pause.*) No! I remembered. But then I forgot.
   We've paperclips though. *Loads.* (NORM *laughs loudly again,*
   terminating the problem.)

PAULA: (*Uneasily watching the two unconcerned doctors. To* NURSE.) Uh, they didn't do anything yet. Right?

NURSE: Right. J.E. always makes a few practice tries first. Every brain's a little different than different ones.

PAULA: Will he feel it . . . when they cut?

NURSE: Not like the way pain is. He'll do a lot of fighting and begging. But it won't actually hurt.

PAULA: Will he . . . Will he talk much?

NURSE: (*A shy laugh.*) You'll hear words you never dreamed that yet existed! (NORM *laughs loudly;* PAULA *realizes he is still reacting to the comic book.*)

PAULA: Will he say a lot of derogatory . . . (*She suspects* NURSE *doesn't know the word.*) a lot of unkind things about me?

NURSE: Natch! But it doesn't mean a thing! Actually, they're only arguing with themselves. It's because of this split-level personality.

PAULA: Hmmm?

NURSE: (*Laughter.*) That's what J.E. calls a schizoid. (*Pause.*) When you get in there, the unconscious is triggered and it starts a fight with the conscious. (*She pauses as both watch.* SLEEVE *brings out a badminton set.*) Damndest thing you ever heard! It sounds like two different persons coming out of the same tongue! (*Pause.*) *Three* persons! Four! Once we had a boy from Kansas that suddenly started talking Chinese! Once we had a redneck farmer that all at once thought he was a black guy on a slave ship. He . . . (*Abruptly pauses; remembering something important.*) Hey! Incidentally, you forgot to remember to fill in that part of the questionaire where it says about *"color."*

PAULA: (*Bitter; contemptuously.*) I couldn't think of a color.

NURSE: (*Surprised.*) Hmm?

PAULA: Color. True blue? Red? Yellow? (*Pause.*) He doesn't believe in fighting for his rights.

NURSE: You're putting me on.

PAULA: I was putting you off.

NURSE: (*Warm and sympathetic again.*) I don't mind. That questionaire asks a lot of personal shit. (*Pause.*) You, uh, left out a lot.

PAULA: (*Grim laugh.*) I wanted to pass him off as a square instead of a freak. I was afraid the doctors might be prejudiced . . . unsympathetic.

NURSE: (*Heartily.*) They couldn't care *less!* You pays your money and you . . . (*She breaks off; shock registers.*) Hey! (*Lowers voice.*) I forgot to get the money from you! Norm and J.E. will—

PAULA: (*Shrugs helplessly.*) I don't—(*Pause; gestures.*) It's all in Charles' pocket. Nine hundred.

NURSE: (*Glancing at doctors and* NILES.) Wow! My memory . . .

PAULA: Shall I go over and—

NURSE: (*Cuts her off with violent head shake.*) Jesus! If they ever found out I forgot something like that—

PAULA: Don't worry about it. We'll slip it to you later.

NURSE: (*Unconvinced; wondering what to do.*) Yeah, but Chuck might . . . (*Pause.*) Sometimes they—

PAULA: (*Lays a friendship hand.*) Don't worry! Charles may be a lot of things but he's not a crook.

NURSE: (*Vague; still concerned.*) Yeah.

PAULA: That's his problem. He's *too* honest.

NURSE: Yeah.

NORM: (*To* SLEEVE; *looking up from comic book.*) Hey! Know what Linda Lovelace does with her time when she's not busy eating?

SLEEVE: Of course! (*He picks up a dart and starts throwing it at an enlarged photo of Sigmund Freud.* NORM *goes back to his reading.*)

NURSE: (*To* PAULA.) Uh . . . when did Charles begin to decide to let it all hang out?

PAULA: Mmmm?

NURSE: What I mean is, when did he start to put it all *together.* (*Pause.*) For instance, this vegetarian trip?

PAULA: (*Shrugs.*) Who knows! Who knows when something changes inside us? (*Pause.*) The fact is, Charles used to be crazy about hunting and fishing. He was an expert shot. We had deer, quail, pheasant . . . you name it! Then, one night at dinner he suddenly looked at me with a strange expression! (*Pause.*) He looked at me and said, "I heard it quack!"

NURSE: (*Puzzled.*) What?

PAULA: *Quack.*

NURSE: Quack? (*She does.*) Quack! Quack! *Quack?* (*The doctors stare at her;* NILES *stirs.*) Like a duck? (*Waits.*) Well?

PAULA: It was on the plate. (*Pause.*) Cooked. (*Pause.*) The duck.

NURSE: (*Long, long pause.*) Oh. (SLEEVE *puts darts aside, starts bouncing a badminton shuttlecock on the racquet.*)

SLEEVE: Hey? You guys want to join in? We got extra racquets. (*He playfully bats one at* NURSE. *He bats another at* PAULA, *who shakes her head but manages a civil smile.* SLEEVE *retrieves the shuttlecock and bats one at* NORM *who irritably swings at it with his comic book.*)

NURSE: (*Answering* PAULA's *disapproval.*) They like to relax once in awhile. It's really important *therapy!* (NORM *leaps up, seizes a racquet and savagely bats one at* SLEEVE's *head.*) I know it probably seems strange.

PAULA: Nothing seems strange any . . . (*Breaks off.*)

NORM: (*Chasing* SLEEVE *with racquet.*) Olé! (SLEEVE *darts behind* NILES. NORM *starts batting just over* NILES *head.* PAULA *registers fear.*)

NURSE: (*Admiringly.*) They *really* like to relax! (SLEEVE *and* NORM *become aware of the impression they are making and move away from* NILES. NURSE, *remembering her thoughts, confronts* PAULA.) Uh . . . why is it you didn't want Chuck to join the radical movement?

PAULA: The what? (*Now uncomfortably.*) It's a very complicated story.

NORM: (*Dancing around, batting.*) Olé!

NURSE: According to the questionaire you're from a wealthy family. (*Pause.*)

PAULA: (*Cryptically.*) A *long* way from it now!

NURSE: And Chuck was poor. And radical?

PAULA: (*Nods.*) But I was *rich* and radical. (*She gets up. Paces.*) They make the best kind! The rebellious offspring of upper middleclass families.

NURSE: (*Doubtfully.*) Yeah. Well . . . They do?

PAULA: But they get over it quickly!

NURSE: (*Suddenly disturbed and curious.*) Why?

PAULA: (*Gesture of helplessness.*) I don't know. (*Beat.*) Maybe it's some kind of unwritten tribal law. (*Beat.*) Survival of the fittest. Natural selection.

NORM: (*Again he darts precariously close to* NILES *to bat the shuttlecock.*) Olé!

SLEEVE: (*As* NORM *misses.*) Touché!

NURSE: (*Believes she understands; nods.*) Well my dad owned a laundramat. I hated every minute of it.

PAULA: (*Disturbed, watching* NORM.) Mmmm . . . (*Pause.*) You what?

NURSE: I dropped out. But then after awhile I began dropping *in* again.

SLEEVE: (*To* PAULA *and* NURSE.) Anybody for a shot of one-ninety-eight proof laboratory alcohol?

NURSE: (*Starts to respond; catches herself on seeing* PAULA. *Righteously.*)
   I'm on *duty!* (PAULA *shakes her head. Politely.*)

NORM: I will. With ice.

SLEEVE: Ice? We used it all. Remember?

NORM: So? (*He crosses to* NILES *and reaches inside his bandaged head as*
   PAULA *stares, carries cubes to sink, rinses them off, pours two drinks.*)

NURSE: (*Oblivious to* PAULA's *shock.*) I even joined the flower
   children. Nevertheless . . .

PAULA: Mmmmmmmm? (*Forces herself to be polite and attentive.*)
   Excuse me. I missed that.

NURSE: *Flower* children. Until they started ripping each other off.
   (*An impassioned gesture.*) Everybody's the same! Even if they *are*
   different! (*The teakettle is starting to whistle. She removes it. Comes
   back to* PAULA. *Now shyly.*) Would you like to hear my final
   conclusion bout *everything?*

PAULA: (*Vaguely.*) Yes. (*Now with sincere eagerness.*) Yes. I would!

NURSE: Just this! No matter where you are on the outside. When
   you look back inside, then turn it inside out, you're right back
   where you started on the outside!! (*The teakettle falls from her
   hand. Immediately, and for no apparent reason,* NILES *begins to hum
   "Yankee Doodle."*)

NORM: Nurse! (NURSE *quickly grabs kettle and starts for operating
   table.* NILES *goes on humming.*) No! No! Not yet! Paperclips 'll do!
   (NURSE *rummages through a not-clinical-looking bucket.*)

NURSE: (*Shaking head.*) How about bobby pins? (NORM *nods. She
   pulls two or three from her hair. Hands them to him. As he twists a
   turniquet around* NILES's *head, the tempo of the tune slows, much like a
   phonograph record running down.* SLEEVE *assists. Together, they twist
   until the tune stops midway.* NURSE *hands* SLEEVE *the kettle which he
   pours through a funnel atop* NILES's *head. There is a reaction, then
   stillness.* NURSE *to* PAULA.) They got to melt the ice.

PAULA: Oh.

NURSE: (*Sits with* PAULA.) Ummmmmm . . . is Charles musically
   inclined?

PAULA: (*Stares for a long time.*) Not if you mean "Yankee Doodle." I
   never heard *that* before!

NURSE: (*Nodding.*) That's what I mean! They usually sing the
   opposite kind of music they like when the ice cubes begin to melt.
   (*Pause.* PAULA *looks dumbfounded.*) You know? (PAULA *smiles;
   shakes her head.*) Chuck was a little early. Unless it melted before
   it should . . . (PAULA *waits.*) The *ice* . . . (PAULA *is bewildered,*

but nods her head agreeably.) I'm glad he sang "Yankee Doodle" instead of Rachmaninoff. Or Neil Diamond. He's *resisting.*

PAULA: (*Nervous glance at operating table.*) But what about . . . afterwards? (NURSE's *cup falls to floor. Again, she seems unaware until sound of impact. The doctors react to the sound.*)

NURSE: (*Picking up pieces.*) Gee!

NORM: Dr. Sleeve! The gravitational pull seems most excessive today!

SLEEVE: It's the time of the month, sir! Saturn's directly in line with Jupiter. There's a flood tide!

NORM: And a pregnant moon!

NURSE: (*To* PAULA *examining broken cup.*) Gee! (*Shrugs.*) Sometimes you — (*She breaks off, embarrassed.*)

PAULA: (*Charitably changes subject.*) Tell me more about this music thing.

NURSE: Oh sure! Take me for instance . . . I was way into Bob Dylan and Janis Joplin before I had my operation. (*She falls silent.*)

PAULA: Yes?

NURSE: (*Triumphantly.*) Now I can't stand them! *That* was *music?* (*She falls silent again.*)

PAULA: Well . . . ? What do you prefer now?

NURSE: (*Righteously.*) Lawrence Welk! Stravinsky! Burt Bacharach! (*She observes that* PAULA *seems distressed.*) You never know! *Always!* (NILES *suddenly sings the suggestive words of a current hard-rock song. Doctors leap up and tighten clamps.* NILES *is jerking to the beat; with great effort they hold him down. Again his singing grinds to a slow halt like a run-down phono record. The* NURSE *tries to smile for* PAULA's *reassurance.*) That's a good sign! Because he isn't finished yet! He'll probably be humming Strauss waltzes by the time they put him all together! (*She notes that* PAULA *is in no way reassured.*)

PAULA: (*Long pause.*) Well?

NURSE: I'm not getting through?

PAULA: You're getting through. It's just —

NURSE: (*Sees the light.*) We don't groove! You're a . . . (*Pause.*) You come from a different . . . (*Pause.*) Your family, probably . . . (*She breaks off,* PAULA *waits.*) I was spaced out. Born that way! I took the trip . . . Drugs! Flower child! Groupie . . . (*She paces.*) Whereas you . . .

PAULA: (*Long pause; quietly.*) *I* was a groupie. (NURSE *appears uninterested, she does not believe this.*) Yes! (PAULA *now leaps up and starts to pace;* NURSE *withdraws. Impassionedly.*) Not so far back as you might think! Me! I was one of the post-pubic camp followers who yank beads and earrings off rock and roll heroes! Me — (*A low moaning from* NILES *stops her;* NURSE *glances at* PAULA *questioningly.*) There wasn't any Charles Niles then! Only a beautiful unformed boy who played bass! And I? I was just the girl next to ten thousand other girls who dwelt within that private, vacant city of the mind they call 'youth.' (*She waits for* NURSE *to absorb this.*) We thought we could put it together by letting it all hang out! With or without a bra.

NURSE: (*Surprised, but laughs.*) That's good! Because you can laugh —

PAULA: (*With unexpected fury.*) It was excruciating! They were Gods . . . up there on that platform! Wild! Unattainable! Trampling all the rules! And all that unleashed electronic power . . . that unerring beat that shook your glands. (*The doctors are fascinated; they move towards her.* NILES *stirs.* NURSE *is bewitched.*) It turned you into jelly . . . and a million vaginas opened and waited! No . . . begged! Mine was one of them. (*Aware that she's becomes a spectacle,* PAULA *hesitates.*)

NURSE: Go on!

PAULA: (*More down to earth.*) It was the Children's Crusade, 1960. The bloodless revolution! We were out to overthrow order, discipline, responsibility! Work became a dirty word! Success was obscene! (*Rising crescendo.*) All you had to do was *be* . . . be there . . . drowned in the mass hysteria of failure worship!

NURSE: But it wasn't failure! It was hero worship! The guys up there on the bandstand —

PAULA: (*In fury*) And why! Because God was permissive! Indulgent! You didn't have to comb your hair! Wash your clothes! You could slurp coca cola and pop bubblegum! No dishes to wash! No chores! No rules! All the pleasures and privileges of being grown up without the work of getting there. (*The doctors have become so entranced that they're unaware of* NILES*'s writhing.*) Why! Why? Because some adolescent oracle came up with the marvelous idea that you could create your hero in your own image and likeness! Father and Mother were past thirty! Bourgeois!

NURSE: They were what?

PAULA: Square. No communication! The truth was to come from freaks in soiled leather pants . . . babbling in monosyllables.

(NURSE, *aware of* NILES's *distress, glances at doctors. They hurry over and start to administer.* PAULA *somewhat purged, and embarrassed, tries to force a laugh. Now in lower tones.*) Well. (*Pause.*) That's about it.

NURSE: Please! You were going to tell me what happened.

PAULA: (*Almost to herself.*) Yes. I was, wasn't I?

NURSE: Why you stopped. Being a groupie . . .

PAULA: (*Reluctantly, from deep within.*) Oh, seven years is a long time! (*Suddenly recharged.*) I'll *tell* you what happened! It happened at Woodstock! There was this boy that played . . . bass? With his hair in a pony tail, and standard dark glasses and fuzz, so all you saw was his mouth, which was exactly like Peter Fonda's. (NURSE *sits, but on edge of chair.*) Grim and curled. Sneering at all the falseness of the world. Later . . . well, later . . .

NURSE: Well, what's wrong with sneering at the falseness of the world?

PAULA: It had nothing to do with the falseness of the world!

NURSE: (*Gets up, glancing nervously toward doctors.*) So what happened?

PAULA: I'm trying to tell you what happened! I followed this boy around Woodstock! Even Santa Ana, California. I think he even recognized me once or twice . . . Of course, with those black glasses you can't tell. They all might be looking straight at you . . . or everybody, for that matter. But something jolted me. I felt God looking straight through me and liking what he saw. I promptly soiled my underpants.

NURSE: (*A wild laugh. Then cuts her laugh quickly on seeing* NORM's *glance.*) Go on. (*Waits.*) At least it shows you had feelings. (PAULA *reacts.*) So what happened?

PAULA: (*Gets up, slowly walks toward window; alone, voice rising.*) The guitar player was screaming into the microphones, and gyrating, trying to make his pants fall down still farther. And the bass and treble were coming out at a volume you wouldn't believe . . . and everybody on the platform was caught up in a crescendo! Where it all *was!* And the multitudes on the grass . . . or on grass . . . or both . . . or acid . . . the world was united . . . moving as one . . . led by the mad Gods right over the cliff! We'd 've gone anywhere with them. (*She stops; tense, abstract.*)

NURSE: (*Caught up.*) Well? Well?

PAULA: Somebody pulled the plug. (*She starts to laugh; the sound is angry, wicked.*)

NURSE: Did what?

NORM: Nurse! (*She leaps up but cannot move until she hears the rest.*)

PAULA: Some weirdo had climbed up on the back of the stage and disconnected the amplifiers. (*She is almost screaming with rage.*) You know what happened?! You want to know what happened when all that phallic power went dead? You saw a group of pallid, pockmarked anemic little boy freaks! The guitar was a shrieking mouse! The guitar sounded like a goddamned toy ukelele! You couldn't even hear the bass player! (*She pauses.* NURSE *wildly gestures her to continue.*) They stopped. (*Pause.*) A piteous band of unkempt, pallid, insecure, dull, third rate —

NORM: (*Interrupts with a bellow.*) *Nurse!* (*And the nurse jumps.*)

PAULA: The bottom dropped out of the world. I saw myself, mirrored back — (NURSE *lingers now, overwhelmed.*)

SLEEVE: *Nurse!*

NURSE: (*Starts toward doctors; stops, in whisper.*) Uh . . . don't forget to remind me not to forget! The money! (*Lights dim. Carnival music; sound of marsh birds and crickets.*)

NILES: (*Again, poetic recitation.*) And so, at last, the patient was pronounced ready. He had heard the strange dialogue between wife and nurse, watching anger take on the smell of fear. And the fear? It rode nurse's shoulders to the operating table where suddenly it leaped into the doctor's eyes. I stared it down: and the odor and the sound . . . but not with the ordinary senses. For it entered me through the top of the skull, assailing my exposed nerves of precognition.

NORM: (*Humourously.*) I'm starting the countdown, J.E. Lights! Action! (NURSE *pushes lantern to patient's head.*)

SLEEVE: Sooner the better! He's ahead of us again.

NORM: Practically into tomorrow! Bombs away!

NILES: (*Disclaiming poetically.*) It was all very good-humored. (*Pause.*) Later it would prove to be even more humorous.

SLEEVE: (*Watches* NORM *hover uncertainly over patient with icepick. The sight still revolts him. He lights a cigarette and walks to window, looks out, waiting.*) Well, Doc?

NORM: Well?

SLEEVE: *Well?*

NORM: (*Demanding, angry.*) *Well?*

SLEEVE: (*Furious.*) *Well?*

NILES: (*Declaiming poetically.*) Still he hesitated. He seemed to listen for the pounding sea a quarter mile away across windswept dunes. Then, sliding his Phi Beta Kappa key into his rear pocket — presumably so it wouldn't see what he was about to do — he turned on me with unleashed vigor! (*In silhouette against the rear walls we see the icepick plunge downward to patient's skull.* NILES *emits a bloodcurdling scream.* PAULA *leaps up.*)

NURSE: (*Tense, but game.*) Hold tight, darling! (NORM *plunges instrument again, patient screams again, but less urgently.* PAULA *back to audience, appears to vomit.* NURSE *sees this but remains at her post.*)

SLEEVE: (*Joyously.*) Bull's-eye, doctor!

NORM: *Two!* But it'll take more!!! (*Plunges icepick again. This time, patient's cry is a whimper.* NORM *starts to plunge again.* NILES *tries to move his head out of the way.*)

NILES: (*In a new, strange voice which will occur intermittently henceforth, the so-called Inner Voice of his subconscious which will now be in a stage whisper.*) Please! Gentlemen! I've never hurt *you!* I've never hurt anyone!

NORM: It's still alive. Take your screwdriver and push! No . . . more to the right! (SLEEVE *pushes screwdriver.*)

NILES: (*Inner voice.*) No! Other way!

NORM: (*Scoldingly.*) I said '*to the right.*' Not *left —*

SLEEVE: I *am* pushing to the right! Don't you know right from left?

NORM: Don't you? (*Holds up hand.*) This is my right hand! (*Holds up other hand.*) This is my *left* hand! (PAULA *listens with agitation;* NURSE *is used to this, but is concerned for* PAULA.)

SLEEVE: (*Imitates gestures of* NORM.) So? And this is *my* right hand! And this is my *left* hand! So if you tell me to push the goddamned screwdriver to the right, I push this way. (*He demonstrates.* NILES *moans.* PAULA *rushes toward them but stops helplessly.*)

NURSE: Wait! Norm! He's right! I mean *left!* I mean . . . (*She breaks off, addresses* PAULA.) The whole problem's simple! One of the doctors is *backwards!*

SLEEVE: (*Outraged.*) *Who* is?

NORM: (*Outraged.*) *Who* is?

NURSE: I mean —

PAULA: (*Furiously, uncontrolled.*) You're *facing* each other! Right for one is wrong for the other! I mean —

NURSE: She means *left.* If one says 'push to the right,' it means the other one's left! (*The doctors think this over in exasperated confusion.* PAULA *waits tensely. A long pause.*)

NILES: (*Cheerily.*) Boop! Boop! A Doop!! (*All astonishedly face him.*)

PAULA: (*Horrified.*) *Charles!!*

NILES: Boop-boop-a-doop!

NURSE: (*As doctors go into action, zestfully.*) He's in Outer Space already! Left was right after all!

NORM: Harder, J.E.!

SLEEVE: (*Twists,* NURSE *smiles.*) It just doesn't want to die!

NILES: (*Inner Voice.*) Kill me then! Go ahead! Try!

NILES: (*Calmly.*) The nurse's face smiled. She was unable to feel pain vicariously.

NORM: (*Calling.*) *Charles Niles!* Can you hear me?

NILES: (*Calmly.*) Which Charles Niles are you calling?

NORM: The other one! (*To* SLEEVE.) I think we've got it, J.E. Really I do.

SLEEVE: Nurse! The patient's Behavioral pattern —

NURSE: But he has no pattern, remember?

NORM: He had one in '45.

NURSE: It was removed in June, '46.

NORM: The fools! Didn't they replace it with anything?

NURSE: This cat's a stylist! He invents his pattern after the fact!

NILES: I would have laughed, but they had clamped my Sense of Humor onto my subconscious. All I could do was cry a little while they stood there, swinging their keys and storing up resentments.

SLEEVE: (*Probing with screw driver.*)

NILES: Mmmmmmmmm?

SLEEVE: Why haven't you supported your wife and family in the customary manner?

NILES: (*Inner Voice.*) Can't afford it. (*The* NURSE *angles around to see if she can get to his pants pocket for the money.*)

SLEEVE: You've a college degree in engineering? Why'd you leave a lucrative profession?

NURSE: (*Confidingly.*) There are certain things not shown in the case history.

NORM: (*Sarcastic.*) Imagine that, Dr. Sleeve!

NURSE: He quit a position with the government. Because it was *war work.*

NORM: (*Stops work.*) He what?

NILES: (*Inner Voice.*) *Missiles.* I got to thinking I was digging my own grave.

NURSE: He don't kill ducks or anything! Do you, Charles?

NORM: (*Sternly.*) Nurse! Don't coach the patient!

SLEEVE: You've got to be realistic, Mr. Niles! You've got to think of your wife and children.

NILES: (*Inner Voice.*) That's why I'm here.

NORM: J.E.! *Harder!* (SLEEVE *thrusts.*)

NILES: (*Inner Voice. Weak, gasping.*) Please! I mustn't die! (*Active Voice; harshly.*) You've *got* to! (*Inner Voice.*) You'll turn into a monster! The other half is always a monster. (*Active Voice; tautly.*) Shut up. Please.

PAULA: (*Anguishedly, lays hand on* SLEEVE.) Doctor! (*They stand back, irritated.*)

NURSE: He's doing just great, Paula!

PAULA: Are you sure? (*Pause.*) Are you sure it's all right?

NORM: (*Humorously.*) I've never lost a soul yet!

NILES: (*Active Voice; he jerks up.*) That's why I'm *here! To lose my soul!*

SLEEVE: (*Gesturing* NURSE *to get him down again.*) Nurse!

NURSE: (*Coaxing him back.*) Not your *soul!* It's just a little old pimple the size of a flea!

SLEEVE: *Unnatural growth!*

NURSE: Like leprosy or anything.

NORM: (*To* PAULA.) The soul will be left absolutely intact.

SLEEVE: Just like anybody else's.

NILES: (*Inner Voice.*) But he doesn't *want* a soul just like anybody else's!

NORM: (*In a fury.*) Oh? (*He applies a mechanic's wrench.* NILES *screams anew.*)

NURSE: (*To* PAULA *and all with hearty cheer.*) His *scream* is coming through just swell!

SLEEVE: (*Modestly.*) A bit strident! Left syndrome is severed, but—

NORM: (*Cuts in peevishly.*) Quickly now, J.E.!! Before it has time to recover! Nurse! (*She brings to* SLEEVE *an electronic-looking complex of wires and two chrome rods, attached by wires to a box.* SLEEVE *reaches into skull with the two probers, fixes them, waits. To* NILES.) Say something.

NILES: (*Hopefully.*) Mother?

NORM: (*Nods at* SLEEVE, *who tries a new position with the nodes.*) Go on! Anything!

NILES: (*Chants these words off precisely, loudly.*) Anything. Of. think. Can't. Boom.

NURSE: He's coming through backwards.

NILES: (*High, Germanic proclamation.*) Ach!

NORM: (*To* PAULA.) He was stationed in Germany during the Occupation?

PAULA: (*Shakes her head.*) He wasn't in the war. Conscientious objector. (*Pause.*) He speaks no foreign languages. (SLEEVE *probes again with the mechanism.*)

NILES: Forgive them for they know not what they do. (*All glance at one another.* PAULA *shrugs.* SLEEVE *tries again.*)

NORM: Mr. Niles, is there something important you would like to tell us?

NILES: (*Quickly.*) Mary had a little lamb. (NORM *gestures for* SLEEVE *to try another position. He does.*)

NILES: (*Impassionedly, almost pleading and sobbing.*) Mary! Mary! Mary! (SLEEVE *quickly moves the nodes.*)

PAULA: Charles!

NILES: (*Now cheerily and sing-song.*) Mary had a little. Mary had a little. Mary had a little. Mary had a—(SLEEVE *reaches around and tries nodes on another part of brain.*)

NILES: (*Conversationally.*) Why not, Alice? Isabelle? Barbara? Lucille?

NORM: (*Cuts him off. Sees* PAULA's *concern.*) You're fumbling, J.E.! Fumbling! (SLEEVE *goes around to other side of table and tries again.*)

NILES: (*Declaration, but as though surprised.*) I went limp on the courthouse steps! I went limp on the courthouse steps! I went . . . (SLEEVE *tries again.* NILES *continues in marchtime.*) Limp. Limp. Limp. Li- . . . (SLEEVE *tries again.*) Mary had a little limp.

NORM: J.E.! Damn you, J.E.! (SLEEVE *with exasperated look at* NORM, *tries again. Gets down on knees for better position.*)

NILES: (*In Castilian tongue.*) Ghandi! Es un pacifisto, no? (*Pause; dramatically.*)This above all, to thine own self . . . (SLEEVE *tries again. Laughingly.*) Mary tried non-violent resistance on me! (*Laughs. He continues laughing until* SLEEVE *removes the nodes.*)

NORM: (*Irritated, demandingly of* SLEEVE.) What *is* all this *drivel* you're getting me?

NURSE: But it makes sense! It's all part of his beliefs!

NILES: (*Without being probed.*) Megatons.

NORM: (*Leans over him.*) Yes?

NILES: They're not quite ready to take their place . . . megatons. (NORM *seizes the hydrometer. He aims it at* NILE's *brain, but waits.* NILES *sings to tune of "Over There."*) Ov-er-kill! Over-kill! Over-kill . . . over-kill . . . over—(NORM *squirts liquid from hydro-*

meter on NILE'*s head as though extinguishing a fire. Thoughtfully, after a pause.*) They turned the fire hoses on us in Mississippi.

NORM: They what?

SLEEVE: They what?

NILES: Fire hoses.

NORM: (*Humoring him.*) Oh. (*Doctors glance at each other as if patient is crazy.*)

SLEEVE: (*Humoring him.*) Oh.

NORM: (*Whispers.*) This will never do!

SLEEVE: Never!

NORM: Never!

SLEEVE: Never!

NORM: Never! (*Now with anger.*) You got his *responses* all fucked up!

SLEEVE: (*Angry.*) Oh I have, have I?

NORM: (*Snaps pinking shears dangerously.*) I knew it from the time he went "boom!"

SLEEVE: He what?

NILES: Boom! (NORM *resignedly picks up electric drill, turns it off and on.* NURSE, *anticipating that he is about to rectify a mistake wrongly diagnosed, puts hand on him.*)

NURSE: Wait! Please! Sir! Stop! He's coming through perfectly okay! The fire hoses . . .

PAULA: It's true! He was in the civil rights march down south! They used fire hoses to break it up. (*The doctors think this over.*)

NILES: (*As though lecturing.*) Peace begins and ends with the little things . . . such as not honking your horn, or killing the umpire. (*The doctors shrug this off, glancing at the two women, who nod understandingly.*) Peace is equality! Honesty! Justice!

NORM: (*Dryly.*) Brilliant deduction, J.E.!

SLEEVE: An amazing concept! Amazing! We've raised his I.Q. to 69.

NORM: Higher! I'd say 74!

NILES: (*Inner Voice.*) The problem is to love your neighbor.

SLEEVE: *Astounding!* I never thought of that! Did you, doctor?

NORM: *Never!* Did you?

SLEEVE: Never! How about you?

NORM: Never! What about you?

SLEEVE: Never! And you?

NORM: Never! Besides . . . I don't have any neighbors. Do you?

SLEEVE: Not I! Have you got neighbors?

NORM: No. Have you?

SLEEVE: No.

NILES: (*Inner Voice.*) Whole world is neighbor.

SLEEVE: Think of that!

NORM: I *am* thinking! Does he mean Japs, Wops, Democrats, Kikes, Krauts, Spics and Frogs?

SLEEVE: Or Commies, Greasers, Niggers, Rednecks, Southern Californians, Cops, Dagos, Seventh Day Adventists, or Hippies?

NORM: What about China? Russia? Cuba?

NILES: (*Inner Voice, but excitedly.*) Si! Es *verdad!!* (*He switches to Russian, German, French, Chinese.*)

NORM: (*Distressed.*) Goddamn it, J.E.! You've caused him to defect! (*Quickly the doctors bring out new power tools and gadgets. They twist and probe; then wait.*)

NILES: (*A new, fatherly, authoritative voice.*) Of course, one has to be practical about these things! Just because some half-baked religious zealot got goosed by a hippopotamus and . . .

PAULA: (*Screams.*) Charles! (*All glance at each other in astonishment. Smiles of triumph begin to register upon the faces of the doctors. NURSE is joyous until she sees PAULA's concern.*)

SLEEVE: (*Taking out a pencil and pad and taking a stance as though interviewing NILES.*) Care to add anything to that statement, sir?

NILES: (*Same new voice.*) Definitely! Go take a flying fuck at the moon! (PAULA *fights tears.*)

NORM: (*Utterly pleased and delighted.*) Well!

SLEEVE: Well!

NURSE: (*Radiantly.*) That's telling 'em, Chuck! (*Now to PAULA more subdued, apologetic.*) He's right in the groove! You *got* to be practical! (NURSE *drops pliers.*)

NILES: (*New Voice.*) Practical! (*Inner Voice.*) But loving your neighbor *is* practical. (*Doctors register disappointment. New Voice, like doctors'.*) Oh? (*Inner Voice.*) That time has come when it is cheaper to help your neighbors than to defend yourself against them. (*New Voice.*) That's some platitude, Charley!! Wow!!!

SLEEVE: Wow!!!

NORM: Wow!!!

NURSE: Wow!!! (*Aside to PAULA.*) Actually, I'm just kidding him along.

NILES: (*Inner Voice.*) Snap. Drap. Clapp. Bapp. Sap. Whap. Nap. (*Pause.*) Sleep. Creep. Deep. Beep. Gleep. (*Doctors make rapid adjustments with instruments.*) Coo coo! Poopoo!

NURSE: (*Turning back sheets; joyously.*) He's soiled his trousers already! Usually it takes *ages!*

NILES: (*Inner Voice.*) Hiss. Piss. Bliss. Kiss.

SLEEVE: (*Making adjustments.*) I don't want you free-associating yet, Mr. Niles.

NORM: (*Making adjustments.*) I don't want you free-associating yet, Mr. Niles.

NILES: (*New Voice.*) I don't want you free associating yet, Mr. Niles. (*Inner Voice.*) Wow! (*New Voice.*) *Wow!* (*Pause.*) Now! What's this threadbare old platitude about turning the other cheek? (*Pause. Inner Voice.*) Well, uh . . . (*Doctors and* NURSE *react excitedly to his hesitation. New Voice.*) All right, Niles. Come clean! (*Inner Voice.*) I . . .

NURSE: (*Cheerleaderlike.*) Come on, Chuck! Tell it to yourself like it is! (*Pause. She drops something.*) I mean "isn't." (*Pause.*) I mean *is!* (*Pause. They tensely wait.*)

NILES: (*Inner Voice.*) Why are you always dropping things or knocking something over? (NURSE *is stymied.* PAULA *glances questioningly at her. Doctors also react.* SLEEVE *knocks over a test tube.* NORM *drops his saw.*)

SLEEVE: (*Singsong.*) Charley! You're evading! *Evading!*

NILES: (*New Voice.*) Charley! You're evading! *Evading!* What about *peace?* Would you be peaceful if somebody tried to rape your wife? (*The three of them, encouraged by* NILES's *New Voice, wait with renewed hope. Inner Voice.*) I . . . (*Pause.*) Uh . . . (*Long pause.*)

SLEEVE: A *foreign* person!

NORM: Of questionable color!

NILES: (*Instantly; subconscious.*) I'd let him! (PAULA *winces. Doctors are outraged.* NURSE *shakes her head sadly. Suddenly, mysteriously, the windows fly open, flooding the room, loudly, with the theme music.* NILES *leaps from operating table.*)

NILES: (*New Voice; shouting above music.*) No! No! Like hell you would!

SLEEVE: (*Wildly; trying to hear.*) Nurse! close that window!

NORM: (*Calling.*) We've told you a thousand times . . .

NURSE: (*Rushing to window.*) I didn't open it!!!

PAULA: It was the wind!

SLEEVE: There *is* no wind!

NURSE: It won't close! (*Doctors agitatedly react, wanting to go and get window closed, but afraid to disturb instruments attached to* NILES's *head. Music continues to play at full volume.*)

SLEEVE: (*Shouting.*) Charles Niles! What were you telling yourself?

NORM: (*Shouting.*) About somebody raping your wife? (*Music stops as suddenly as it began; all glance toward windows.*)

NILES: (*New Voice.*) I'd beat the shit out of them. (*Music comes on; a fast, cheery beat of the nickelodeon tunes.*)

NORM: (*wildly.*) He's got it!

SLEEVE: (*Wildly.*) Freeze him right there!

NURSE *races to shelves, returns with what appears to be a spray can. Doctors excitedly aim it at* NILES's *head and set adjustments.* NURSE *does a few steps of whatever is currently called dancing.* PAULA *stares out window. Blackout.*

NILES: (*In the darkness. Subconscious; poetic recall.*) The newly awakened man . . . completely renovated and prefabricated . . . is aware first of a new girl.

NURSE: Come on, sweetie! Try!

NILES: And then, an old wife.

PAULA: Charles! Stop acting so silly! (*Lights come up. The doctors are smoking.* NILES *is propped up and reaching for a cigarette that* NURSE *holds out. But his hand keeps missing; it won't go where it should.*)

NURSE: (*Cheerily, to* PAULA.) Wow! He almost got it that time!

NILES: (*Poetic recall.*) They were trying to make me put it all together . . . but the birds of the marsh were gone, and the salt from the sea . . . And the music was gone . . . (*Pause.*) *Something* was gone . . . (NURSE *finally takes cigarette and shoves it between his lips.*)

NURSE: (*To* PAULA, *forced casualness.*) Sometimes it takes a little *longer* than sometimes. (*To* NILES.) Inhale! (NILES *unintentionally bites her finger; she screams.*)

NORM: (*Angrily throws down his cigarette.*) Shit!

SLEEVE: (*Whispers to* NORM.) Left side's still shorted out.

NORM: Right!

SLEEVE: Left!

NORM: Right!

SLEEVE: Left!

NORM: Right! (*The tempo of their argument becomes a beat, as though marching. This continues as* NILES *sings.*)

NILES: (*Hums and then sings.*) Tramp! Tramp! Tramp! The boys are marching . . . (*Angrily,* SLEEVE *reaches out and jerks the wires from* NILES's *head, 'disconnecting' him. His song winds down like a defective phonograph.* PAULA *is up, hovering worriedly.*)

NURSE: (*Cheering; consoling.*) Actually, it don't matter right now whether he leans left or right.

PAULA: But that's not—

NURSE: Right! What's important is they've completely disconnected the *Radical Middle!*

SLEEVE: (*Shouting, to cut off* NURSE.) Mr. Niles! Try your other hand!

NILES: (*Vaguely.*) Don't have any other hands.

PAULA: (*Minor wail.*) Charles! Doctor! (SLEEVE *picks up his arm, holds it straight out. It remains there. He moves it to several different positions. Each time, it remains stationary.*)

SLEEVE: Charley, move your arm. (NILES *does. With sudden, surprising force his stiff arm whacks* NORM *almost knocking him over.* PAULA *stares aghast.*)

NURSE: (*Quickly.*) He's resisting!

SLEEVE: (*Staring, happy recognition suddenly shows on his face.*) *Violently!*

PAULA: (*Amazement.*) Charles! (*To* NORM.) It's the first time he's ever done a thing like that! (*Pause.*) I'm sorry! He's . . . not himself!

NORM: (*Ruffled, but dignified.*) On the contrary, Mrs. Niles!!

SLEEVE: (*Excitedly.*) He *is* himself! (*Pause.*) Charley . . . (*He raises the other arm.*)

NORM: (*Demandingly.*) Niles, do you still love Reds? (NILES *wallops again. All scramble out of the way. He wallops again without help.* NORM *takes a stance, folds his arms, looks triumphantly at* PAULA.)

NURSE: (*A sly sideways glance at* PAULA.) Chuck! What do you think about guys that freaked out of the war by hiding in Canada? (NILES *gropes around, grabs a handful of instruments from the table and flings them across the room, seemingly at* PAULA.) Well!

SLEEVE: Well!

NORM: Well!

PAULA: Well!

NURSE: He wasn't aiming at you! His coordination—

NORM: Isn't very good.

SLEEVE: *Yet.*

NURSE: Remember?

NORM: (*Sidles up to* NILES. *Coyly.*) Mr. Niles! When was it you said you were going to join the American Nazi Party? (*They wait for a violent response which never comes. Slowly,* NILES's *right arm stiffens*

and he begins what apparently will become the Nazi salute; PAULA
registers horror. The other three have an "I-told-you-so" expression.
But the arm gets only half way to position and stops.)

SLEEVE: (_To break the deadlock._) Charlie! Answer me, true or false!
Ralph Nader would be a better President than Cesar Chavez.
(_Pause._) Unless Fidel Castro was permitted to run. (NILES
furiously throws things at PAULA _again._)

PAULA: Charles! It's me . . . Paula! (NILES _hears; stops. Then starts_
throwing things as fast as he can. She darts all over the room, dodging.)

NORM: (_Admiringly._) Look at that!

SLEEVE: Look at that!

NURSE: Look at that! He's actually _upset!_

SLEEVE: (_Laughs._) Over-compensating. They always do.

NORM: They always do. (_Pause._) Over-compensate.

NURSE: (_Nodding agreement. To_ PAULA.) Always they over-compensate. Over and over. Always and always —

SLEEVE: Over and over —

NORM: Always and always.

NURSE: (_To_ PAULA.) It's because they haven't replaced his memory
yet. (_Pause._) Actually, he's forgotten —

SLEEVE: To remember —

NORM: Who you _are_, Mrs. Charles.

NURSE: (_Correctively._) _Giles._ (PAULA's _expression tells her she's wrong._)
Riles. (PAULA _firms up her displeasure._)

SLEEVE: _Lyles._ (PAULA _almost sadistically shaking head._)

NORM: (_Sightly worried._) Pyle? (PAULA _shakes head._)

NURSE: Argyle? (PAULA _continues to shake head; it becomes a fas-_
cinating guessing game for the three.)

SLEEVE: Carlisle? (PAULA _shakes head. Long pause._)

NORM: (_Explorative._) Smith?

NURSE: (_Trimphantly._) _Jones?_

SLEEVE: _Brown?_

NORM: _White!_ That's it . . . _Mrs. Roger White!_ (_To_ SLEEVE.) Eh,
George?

SLEEVE: I'm Sleeve.

NORM: (_Dismissive._) Sleeve! George! All the same thing. (_A wink to_
PAULA.) Right Mrs. George? Names are a funny thing! (_He_
playfully buzzes the power saw near NILES's _cheek._) Right Mr.
Charles?

NILES: Igloo. (_The three hear this with disappointment._)

SLEEVE: (_Comes over threateningly._) Care to repeat that statement,
sir?

NILES: Igloo.

NURSE: (*Inspirationally.*) He's free associating again! Wow! He's trying to tell us!! These little icecubes sitting there next to his libido are cold!! (*To* PAULA.) Get it? Ice! Eskimos! *Igloo!* (To NILES.) Right, George?

NILES: I'm *Norm*.

NURSE: (*Inspirationally; to* PAULA's *concern.*) *Norm!* See what I mean! Free-associating again!

SLEEVE: Wants to be part of the *norm!*

NURSE: Like Norm! And Dr. Sleeve! (*Pause.*) Like *everybody!*

NILES: Igloo.

NURSE: (*To doctors; concerned.*) Should I . . . ?

SLEEVE: Remove the . . .

NORM: Ice? Not until . . . (*He moves to the control panel and touches knobs and buttons, watching and expecting physical reactions from the patient. He pushes a button;* NILES, *with electrode wires attached, leaps from chair.* NORM *pushes another button;* NILES *walks toward* NURSE. *He pushes another button;* NILES *stops. He pushes more buttons causing* NILES *to turn, stop, move, jump, sit, rise, walk.* PAULA *watches; winces.* NURSE *admires.* NORM *leaves control panel with* NILES *standing in middle of room and whispers to* SLEEVE; NILES *suddenly "starts up" by himself and heads for the* NURSE, *a curious look of lust on his face.*)

SLEEVE: (*Seeing* PAULA's *consternation.*) Hmmmmmmmmmmm!

NORM: *Hmmmmmmmm!* (*He leans over, pushes a button on the control.* NILES *is abruptly halted. Now with various button tunings, he makes him walk toward* PAULA. NILES *balks.* NORM *doubles the charge, jolting* NILES *forward. Finally,* NILES *stands before* PAULA *robot-like; remote.*)

SLEEVE: (*A shout; to alleviate delicate impasse.*) Charles Niles!

NORM: Charles Niles!

NORM AND SLEEVE: What are you going to do when you wake up?!

NILES: (*New voice; a hard stare at* PAULA.) What else? *Make money!*

SLEEVE: (*Pleased; but feigning skepticism.*) Oh?

NORM: (*Same.*) Oh?

NORM AND SLEEVE: And just how, may one ask, do you propose to do this?

NILES: (*Same hard stare at* PAULA.) Steal. Cheat. Rob. Mug. Murder.

PAULA: (*Her first indicative show of real anger.*) Don't look at me like that! I'd *never*—

NURSE: (*Quickly; cheerily.*) It's okay! He's *role-playing.*! (*Seductively to* NILES.) Aren't you, Charley? (NILES *responds to voice but stands threateningly.*) Tell her you're sorry, Chuck! Apologize! (NILES *remains immobile.*)

NORM: (*Fatherly; encouragingly.*) Charley . . .

SLEEVE: (*Same.*) We're all waiting, Charley. (*Long impasse.*)

PAULA: (*To all; demanding.*) Well? ? (*With a whispered oath,* NORM *steps to control panel and pushes buttons. He is trying to make* NILES *get down on his knees before* PAULA. *There becomes a Herculean struggle as* NILES *fights against bowing.* NORM, *grim and cruel, applies more electronic volume.* NILES *shudders, struggles, but each time is bent closer to the floor. Finally he is on his knees.*)

NURSE: (*Relieved, shaken. Forced cheer.*) There!

PAULA: (*Leaps up.*) This is disgusting!

NURSE: (*To* NILES; *feigns admiration.*) I *knew* you could do it if you tried, Chuck!

SLEEVE: (*Magnificently, to all.*) There's a man with a mind of his own! Bet we gave him 700 volts of electricit— (*He is cut off. A huge crash of thunder; lightning illuminates the outside window. All are visibly impressed. There is momentary silence.*)

NURSE: (*With uneasy humor.*) More than that! (*They laugh nervously.* NILES *struggles to get to his feet.*)

SLEEVE: (*In admiration.*) And still resisting.

PAULA: (*Angrily.*) Charles! Get up! You . . . you're . . .

SLEEVE: (*Aside to* NORM, *but meant for all ears.*) See what I mean, doctor? ! *Resistance!* He defies even the person he most loves! (*Pause, now intimately.*) *Niles* . . .

NORM: Niles . . .

SLEEVE: (SLEEVE *works with the controls so that* NILES *stands; he causes* NILES *to turn around facing them.*) Niles . . . exactly what are you going to do when you walk out of here? (*Pause.*)

NORM: A completely—

SLEEVE: Beautifully—

NORM AND SLEEVE: Reactivated—

NORM: Once again able to be of use—

SLEEVE: To the society in which he dwells! (*A long wait.* SLEEVE *rapidly begins pushing the button that controls* NILES.)

NILES: (*Suddenly, rapidly.*) Yes-yes-yes-no-yes-yes-no-yes-yes yes-yes-yes—(*Another crash of thunder; the mystique has an effect on them again, but they profess to ignore it.*)

NORM: (*Chuckling.*) Going to join the Yacht Club tomorrow, Charley?

NILES: (*Shakes head.*) *Golf* club. (*Pause.*) And the Ku Klux Klan.

PAULA: (*Concerned at this last.*) Doctor!

NURSE: (*Trying unobtrusively to get* NILES's *wallet from his trousers.*) It's all right! They always overdo when you first remove the pressure of moral behavior.

NILES: (*He grabs at* NURSE. *In a new, liberated, brash voice.*) You can say that again, sexpot! Come here! (*She eludes him.*)

NORM: (*Suavely; confident.*) Naturally, the first symptoms are *super* elation.

SLEEVE: They got to make up for lost time. (*He notes the lustful manner in* NILES's *action.*) At the moment, patient has an elongated pithecanthropus erectus. (NURSE *emits an embarrassed giggle;* NILES *eyes doctors with reproach.*)

PAULA: A what?

NURSE: (*Cheerily.*) And it's all kind of wonderful! (*Pause.*) You . . . you feel like everything belongs to you.

NORM: (*Heartily.*) And if it don't, you grab it anyway! (*Pauses; realizes this is wrong approach.*) Of course, when we put back the rest of the recycled parts, he'll calm down a little.

NURSE: They sandpaper the Recall just enough so that patient's memories are worn off.

SLEEVE: And we shellac the ego so that —

PAULA: You do what?

NORM: The *ego*. We coat it so that it can never again be tarnished by creeping morality.

NILES: (*Deftly, he has caught* NURSE's *arm; lowered voice.*) Look, Mata Hari . . . let's trip out! There's a carnival . . .

NURSE: (*Embarrassed; drops scissors; winks at* PAULA.) Not just now! There's work to do.

NILES: (*Aware of* PAULA's *angered disapproval. Lowered voice.*) Who's the Mother-Figure that keeps scowling? (*A flash of lightning illuminates the faces of doctors; they are shaking their heads and reveal failure.*)

NORM: (*Coughs; clears throat; with tired dismissal.*) Well, J.E., might as well button him up. Might we?

SLEEVE: (*Same paternalistic tone.*) That we might! I see no . . .

PAULA: (*Agitatedly.*) But wait! . . . But . . .

NORM: (*Not heeding her.*) Nor do I! I can conscientiously declare that the patient's Homo-Intellectus has successfully undergone a cortex transplant with almost no oraculear cerebellum! Even the *Unicus-Pavlov* is allegro non troppo . . . cum laud . . . give or take an erg or two!

NURSE: (*Really overjoyed.*) Wow! I hear you! Wow!!
SLEEVE: Wow!
NILES: (*A bewildered monotone.*) Wow.

Blackout. Then, a peal of thunder and total brilliance illuminates them momentarily in fixed tableau. The blackout then resumes; now is heard the plaintive nickelodeon theme song, faintly.

NILES: (*Poetic recall.*) And so, long after they had taken me apart, they were finally putting me back together again. It all seemed like a year made up of slowly churning moments . . . (*Pause.*) Eventually, the nurse went over to the mantel and picked up my past. Neatly sanded, of course, so that the sharp edges wouldn't hurt when they put it back. And now, again, I heard a lot of people talking about things that never mattered. (*Lights up.*)
NORM: Hydrometer working properly?
NURSE: Properly, doctor.
NORM: And the spark plugs?
NURSE: Filthy. Absolutely filthy.
SLEEVE: Use much oil?
NURSE: By the quart, no less.
NILES: (*Narrator's voice.*) With relief, I realized they were talking about the nurse's used car. There was a kind of small earthquake inside me when they gave me back my ego, but I didn't actually mind. They had skillfully removed that part of me which used to fear earthquakes. (NURSE *goes back and sits at table with* PAULA.)
NORM: Well, J.E., we'd better run one last test.
SLEEVE: One last test.
NORM: Right.
SLEEVE: Right.
NORM: Okay!
SLEEVE: Okay!
NORM: Can you hear me, Mr. Chuck? (NILES *doesn't.*)
SLEEVE: (*Correctively.*) Charles! Can you hear us, Mr. Charles?
NILES: (*New voice; furious.*) Charles Niles, you mental pygmies!
SLEEVE: (*Feigning admiration.*) Very adroit!
NORM: Very adroit! (*Pause.*) Very!
SLEEVE: Mr. Niles . . . what comes to mind when you think of wild-eyed radicals who'd steal your income tax money and . . .
NORM: And use it for socialized medicare?
NILES: Gas chamber.
SLEEVE: (*Deliriously pleased, but feigns shock.*) Oh, no!

NORM: (*Same.*) Oh, no!

SLEEVE: (*Feigning horrified concern.*) But what about their wives?!

NORM: (*Same.*) And children?

NILES: (*In fury.*) Let them starve!

SLEEVE: (*Coyly.*) Uh, is it true . . . and I have it on good authority . . . you'd sit back quietly and allow colored folk to move into your neighborhood? (NILES *pauses; they again worry.*)

NURSE: Chuck! He means *Blacks,* that is . . .

NILES: (*Starts angrily to leap from chair.*) Are you out of your *mind?!* You think I'm an idiot? Of course not!!! (*The doctors, arrogant and smug, slowly, triumphantly, step toward footlights and take a stance, swinging their scholarship keys counterclockwise. Lights slowly dim, revealing dawn coming through windows and doors; sound of birds and new morning sounds.*)

NILES: (*Poetic recall.*) Daybreak had begun its reluctant move towards the old adobe by the sea . . . and the first birds began to materialize among the trees. Objects were solid, began to claim shadow . . . and the shadows grew strong and began to assert themselves. (*Pause.*) When finally I awoke, I was pleased to discover that I had become somebody else.

PAULA: (*At bedside.*) Charles . . . how do you feel?

NILES: (*New voice.*) Like a million bucks! (*Pause. Poetic voice.*) I didn't bother to mention that I'd like to have it in unmarked currency, since I might have to steal it. The doctors shook hands with one another and thought of breakfast, possibly laced with 198 proof alcohol. Doctor Sleeve himself gave me his hand. (SLEEVE *does so.*) And inside it was a bill for $998.99.

NURSE: (*Helpfully; cheerily.*) Some of it's for labor, and some for parts. (NURSE *frantically signals to* PAULA *for the money.*)

NILES: (*New, brash voice; eyes the jars on the mantel.*) Yeah! But there's more parts left over than when you started!

PAULA: That's true! The guilt complex! And his Recall!

NILES: (*A harsh, bitter laugh.*) And my conscience! You could recycle it! And pawn it off on some unsuspecting sonofabitch.

SLEEVE: (*A withering glare at* NILES.) And *who* is going to come to *us* for a *conscience transplant?*

NORM: Market's glutted! Right, Miss Thanatopsis?

NURSE: (*Swiftly to mantel where she picks up the jars.*) Here! Be our guest! (NILES *accepts bottles; he stares at them, then at* PAULA *as though asking for an answer.*)

NORM: Nurse! Give him his change. (*To* PAULA.) We knocked off a

couple of bucks because we ran out of antiseptic. We only
used . . . (NURSE *vainly signals to* PAULA.)

NORM: (*Interrupts by snatching bill from* NILES's *hand.*) Incidentally,
sir, the operation's not tax deductible.

SLEEVE: (*In turn, snatches the bill from* NORM.) Thanks to a bunch of
lawmakers with moral hangups! (*He dramatically tears it into
small fragments.*) Nurse! *Give him his change!*

NURSE: (*Nudges* NILES.) Psssssst!

NILES: (*Reacts.*) What's bugging you, sex-bomb?

NURSE: (*Hoarse whisper.*) The *money!*

PAULA: (*Loud, clear, scornful.*) Charles! Give her the money! (*The
doctors react to this.* NILES *calmly gets out his wallet. He removes the
bills and holds them up for all to see.*)

NILES: You mean, *this?*

SLEEVE: (*Infuriated.*) Nurse! I've told you a thousand times—!

NORM: A thousand times! Never—but *never*—

SLEEVE: (*As they descend upon her.*) Always! Always be sure you—

NURSE: (*Backing away.*) I . . . that is, he . . . (*Passionately, to*
NILES.) Chuck! (*She reaches for it,* NILES *dodges.*)

SLEEVE: (*Trying to grab money.*) Look here, sir!

PAULA: Charles! Give them their goddamned money!

NORM: I must warn you, sir! (NILES *has leapt atop the operating table,
seizing the power saw enroute. He looks insane, gleeful, and dangerous.
they stand around him, uncertain what to do. Freeze position.*)

NILES: They were all staring at me as though I were somebody else.
(*He laughs hysterically.*) It was the funniest sight I ever saw.
Somehow . . . because I *was* somebody else all right . . . all
right . . . all right. (*Pause. The tableau suddenly becomes an active,
pleading, shouting cacaphony, mingled with sudden screeching of sea
birds, etc.*)

CACAPHONY: Come on Chuck . . . we're all tired . . . He's got a
sickness . . . He's not being himself . . . I knew it all
along . . . all this lofty hogwash about morals . . . We got
witnesses . . .

NILES: (*Gleefully insane.*) So call the police! (*A frightening laugh. He
leaps from the table, the power saw still in his hands. He buzzes it
threateningly.*)

NURSE: (*The only one not afraid. Embraces him; but convincingly.*)
Charley, please! For my sake . . . (NILES *returns the embrace
orgiastically—almost.*)

PAULA: Charles! You're sick! (NILES *suddenly releases* NURSE. *He puts down the power saw and moves ominously toward* PAULA *and the doctors. Majestically he tears the money into small shreds and scatters them.*)

NILES: (*He seizes* NURSE'*s arm firmly.*) Come on! For your sake! (*He forcefully guides her toward door; she hesitates, almost unsure, glancing at the others—then concurs. Doctors and* PAULA *block doorway, but yield to* NILES'*s threatening stance.*)

PAULA: (*Beseeching, a hand on* NURSE'*s arm.*) Please! (*She half spins* NURSE *around.*) Do you know what you are doing?

NURSE: (*A low, healthy laugh, sans malice.*) Natch! (*Pause.*) Didn't *you* know what you were doing?

SLEEVE: Nurse!

NORM: Nurse!

SLEEVE: You're hereby fired for unprofessional conduct while on duty! As of now!

NORM: As of *now!*

NURSE: I already quit! Come on, Chuck!

NILES: (*Fumbling in his pockets.*) I am . . .

PAULA: (*Knowing what he seeks.*) The keys! I have them!

NURSE: (*Holds up set of keys.*) The keys! I have them! To Dr. Sleeve's Rolls Royce! (*Laughing,* NILES *and the* NURSE *start through the door.*)

PAULA: Miss! (NURSE *turns; her glance is sympathetic.*) I thought you and I . . . I thought that you . . . (*Breaks off.*) . . . At least you would . . . (NURSE *shows many expressions—sympathy, warmth, sadness, a dismissive shrug.*)

NURSE: Have a conscience? (*She mimes the operation, pointing to her head, churning her hands, and finally with a shrug pointing to one of the jars on the mantel. The theme song is heard. A long pause;* PAULA *glances at* NILES.)

NILES: (*Moves toward* PAULA.) Well? (NURSE *waits: unsure of* NILES *but incapable of insecurity.*) Well?

PAULA: (*A voice of recognition.*) Only the children. (*Pause.*) And part of myself . . .

NILES: (*Soberly, as the* NURSE *watches, he picks up his jar from the table. He professes to examine at arm's length. He tosses the jar which* PAULA *catches.*) Tell them . . . tell *yourself* to always remember . . . this . . . part of myself! (NURSE *breaks out in a shy giggle—not cruel, not childish, but wonderously healthy and innocent. She is joined by* NILES *whose laughter is coarse and harsh, but also healthy and real. The doctors now laugh heartily and long.* PAULA *remains stoic.*

Seeing PAULA's *reaction, the doctors motion for her to get onto the operating table, getting their tools out, with elaborate gestures, preparing for another operation.*

Home Free
Robert Alexander

Home Free was presented at the Inner City Cultural Center—
San Francisco, in October of 1981 with the following cast:

REGGIE	A. Jacquie Taliaferro, Troy Cobb
STACKHOUSE	Richard Harder
MANDRIL	Mychal Chambliss
ALICIA	Ruby L. Braxton
FREEMAN	Melvin Paul Payne
LORAINE	Adilah Azikiwe
ALEX	Melvin Thompson
CEDRIC	J.P. Phillips
EXCEDRIN	Richard Harder

Directed by Ahmad Shabaka
Produced by Deborah Asante
Set design by Willian Watts
Sound design by Ahmad Shabaka
Lighting design by Jim Schelstrate

SETTING

The play is set in the modestly furnished home of Loraine Johnson,
located in San Francisco's Filmore district. The set includes a
livingroom, stage right, with a sofa and matching lazy-boy re-
cliner. The furniture should have a worn appearance. A new color
TV and stand should be conspicuously placed in the livingroom
area. A dinette set with four chairs should be placed center stage.
Far stage left is reserved to create the illusion of a prison cell. There
the stage should be somewhat elevated and rectangular.

CHARACTERS

ALEX: A middle-aged ex-felon returning home from San Quentin. Haunted by grim memories of prison.

LORAINE: Alex's wife, lonely, frustrated, tense, demanding, she has a reservoir of quiet determination.

ALICIA: Their daughter, a twenty-year-old sophomore at a local junior college. Bright, obedient, goal-oriented. Extremely excited by her father's homecoming.

REGGIE: A seventeen-year-old dropout who supports himself by selling drugs. He resents his father's return. Behind the macho front is a terrified, complex individual who wants to be loved, but is too afraid of loving.

FREEMAN: Alex's older brother, a responsible citizen who owns his own business. He has been a surrogate father to the kids.

STACKHOUSE and MANDRIL: Two of Reggie's friends. Stackhouse is the more sensitive of the two.

EXCEDRIN: One of Reggie's drug-buying customers.

CEDRIC: Alex's prison lover, he appears as a spirit haunting Alex.

DETECTIVE BROWN: A narcotics detective.

POLICEMEN: Walk-ons for a drug bust.

Home Free
Robert Alexander

REGGIE *is prancing around the livingroom dribbling an imaginary basketball. Being guarded on both sides by* STACKHOUSE *and* MANDRIL, REGGIE *goes up for a jump shot and holds his hands up, posing in a follow through. The boys have on funky playground attire.*

REGGIE: Swoosh! Face job.
STACKHOUSE: Nose job.
MANDRIL: Blow job.
STACKHOUSE: Snow job.
REGGIE: (*Resumes dribbling.*) Three seconds left in the game. The ball goes up top to Johnson. He dribbles twice to his right.
STACKHOUSE: Always to his right, he can't go left.
REGGIE: (*Jumps up.*) He shoots.
MANDRIL: (*Jumps up to block it.*) He misses.
STACKHOUSE: (*Pretending to rebound.*) Airball. Johnson blows the game. (STACKHOUSE *and* MANDRIL *slap five.*)
REGGIE: Blow my nuts.
MANDRIL: Blow it out your butt. (ALICIA *enters from the kitchen with a set of plates and lays them on the diningroom table.*)
ALICIA: Reggie, I thought you were gonna help me.
STACKHOUSE: Say mama, I'll give you a hand.
MANDRIL: You're too late, Stack, she's already spoken for.
ALICIA: Don't your friends have somewhere to go?
STACKHOUSE: Not me.
MANDRIL: Me either.
STACKHOUSE: I think I'll stay right here, Alicia, and watch you while you work.
MANDRIL: Yeah. Me too. Hey, you sure got a lot of plates. You expecting company? (ALICIA *and* REGGIE *look at each other.*) Am I invited?
STACKHOUSE: You're here, ain't you?
MANDRIL: Yeah, I'm here and I ain't ate all day.
ALICIA: That's not my problem.
MANDRIL: Come on Alicia, be nice to me.
STACKHOUSE: The girl don't know how.

ALICIA: Reggie, are you gonna give me a hand?

STACKHOUSE: Come on Mandril, let's make it.

MANDRIL: Now, man? Look, we just got here. Alicia, ain't you inviting us to stay for dinner?

ALICIA: No! (*She goes into the kitchen.*)

MANDRIL: Sho is cold in here.

STACKHOUSE: That's why we should make it.

MANDRIL: What's the deal with your sister, Reg?

REGGIE: Hell if I know. She's always tripping.

STACKHOUSE: Maybe it's that time of the month?

MANDRIL: Oh. No wonder she wants to throw "the kid" out. She ain't got no use for me right now. (ALICIA *re-enters with napkins and silverware.*) Say Alicia, you should have told me the timing was bad. I can come back next week.

ALICIA: What are you talking about?

MANDRIL: I'm talking about me and you baby and that good thing we got going.

ALICIA: You better get that fantasy out of your head!

STACKHOUSE: (*Giggling.*) Now are you ready to leave?

REGGIE: Hey, you guys can stay if you want to. Alicia, get two more plates.

ALICIA: You must be out of your mind!

REGGIE: These are my boys. They can stay if they want to.

ALICIA: I know mama is gonna go off, if they're still here when daddy gets here.

MANDRIL: You mean your pops got sprung? Why ain't you said nothing, brother?

REGGIE: I thought I told you.

MANDRIL: You ain't told me shit.

STACKHOUSE: You don't seem to be too thrilled.

REGGIE: (*Takes out a joint.*) It ain't a question of being thrilled.

ALICIA: Don't you think you should take a shower and change your clothes before they get here?

REGGIE: (*As he lights his joint.*) I'm not changing my clothes for nobody. Dig it?

ALICIA: Come on Reggie, act right, please.

REGGIE: Ain't you got something to do in the kitchen? Why don't you mosey on back to the kitchen, while me and the fellas smoke a joint.

ALICIA: Are you really gonna smoke that now? They might be here any minute.

REGGIE: They can get a hit. Do you want a hit? (*He blows a ring of smoke at her and laughs.* ALICIA *exits.*)

STACKHOUSE: (*Taking the joint.*) I say we smoke this one joint,

then get the hell out of here. When your folks get here, I want to
be in the wind.

MANDRIL: Well, I'm staying. That is, if my man Reggie really wants
me to stay.

STACKHOUSE: Come on Mandril, don't be an ape. Alicia's trying to
make this a special occasion. She don't need us around, spoiling
it.

MANDRIL: I leave if Reggie says leave. (*He takes the joint from*
STACKHOUSE.)

REGGIE: Tell you what, you guys stay, I'll leave.

STACKHOUSE: Come on Reg, be serious man. Go change your
clothes like Alicia said.

REGGIE: Do you believe this guy? He takes one hit and he starts
sounding like my sister.

STACKHOUSE: Look, this is gonna be your pops' first night home,
in how long?

REGGIE: Eight years . . . eight years since I've seen that chump's
face. (*Pause.*)

STACKHOUSE: That's a long time, man.

REGGIE: (*Taking the joint.*) Tell me about it.

MANDRIL: Man, can you imagine not being around any women for
eight years? I guess you play a lot of pocket pool, huh? And
handball. (MANDRIL *plays pocket pool with himself.*)

STACKHOUSE: Like you're doing now. You're around women every
day and you're still trying to get your first shot.

MANDRIL: I got my first shot in kindergarten.

STACKHOUSE: You mean your first shock. I know all about you and
the wall socket.

MANDRIL: But it does make you wonder what your old man will be
like. Prison does funny things to a nigger. Do you remember
Sonny Boy?

STACKHOUSE: He should. The nigger used to whip his tail every
day.

MANDRIL: Yeah, well he was in the joint.

REGGIE: (*Putting out the joint.*) That's just the place for him.

MANDRIL: Well, they got to his butt in the joint.

STACKHOUSE: Sho did. They turned my man out. Blood's a punk
now. A screaming sissy.

MANDRIL: Dig it. We saw blood the other day. Face was all soft and
smooth. His eyebrows was plucked and he had on mascara. He
came up to Stack, sacheying kinda sweet like and said, "Well
hello Stackhouse, it's been a long time, hasn't it? When do you
suppose we can get together, for old times sake?"

STACKHOUSE: You lying punk, you lying. That was you he was talking to.

MANDRIL: (*Sarcastic.*) Yeah Reg, you don't have to worry about Sonny Boy anymore, or should I say Sonny Girl?

STACKHOUSE: I'm glad your pops is coming home. I know you took a lot of kidding behind him being down.

MANDRIL: (*Laughing.*) Remember the one Eric told about your pops being the only prisoner left on Alcatraz? Now that's what I call solitary confinement.

STACKHOUSE: Would you stop being so ignorant?

MANDRIL: (*Still laughing.*) The way Eric tells it, your parents went to Alcatraz on one of them group tours. Your old man found a perfect opportunity to make a break from your mama. So he hid in the hole, but he got locked in and he ain't been heard from since.

REGGIE: It ain't funny, Mandril.

MANDRIL: I thought it was pretty funny.

STACKHOUSE: Nobody's laughing.

MANDRIL: Come off it man. I was only playing.

REGGIE: Maybe you play too much. (ALICIA *re-enters, with glasses and cups. She notices a napkin on the floor and bends over to pick it up, unaware that* MANDRIL *is staring at her rear end.*)

MANDRIL: (*Grabbing his crotch.*) Lawd, Alicia! Look at you. You gonna make somebody a fine little housewife someday. But until then, I got something for you.

REGGIE: Hey man, you stay away from my sister.

STACKHOUSE: (*Playfully.*) That's right. You don't want the old man coming in here catching you messing with his daughter. No telling what he'll do. (*Headlights flash through the window and dive across the room.*) That's him pulling up now.

MANDRIL: (*Mock fear.*) Hey Alicia, Reg, I was only playing. Don't put your old man on me. Please.

REGGIE: (*Looking out the window.*) Relax, fishlips. Its only Uncle Freeman. (ALICIA *exits to the kitchen.*)

MANDRIL: In that case we best be splitting.

STACKHOUSE: I'm glad you finally changed your mind.

REGGIE: Come on man, stay, so I won't feel outnumbered.

MANDRIL: Sorry blood, you've got to paint this scene by yourself. I'm sliding over to Larry's and getting some chicken and waffles.

STACKHOUSE: I heard that. I'm with you baby.

MANDRIL: Say Reggie, why don't you meet us in the parking lot after first period tomorrow? Bring a little something for the head.

REGGIE: You just make sure you bring plenty scratch. (FREEMAN *enters as the boys start their exit.*)

MANDRIL: Say Freebie baby, what it look like?

FREEMAN: Gonna look like death if you don't get my name right.

STACKHOUSE: (*Offering his hand.*) What's happening, cool? Pimp tap. (FREEMAN *ignores his hand.*)

MANDRIL: Soul clap. (*He gives* FREEMAN *the soul shake and doesn't let go of* FREEMAN's *hand.*) Say, that's a nice watch you're sporting, brother. One of those digitals.

FREEMAN: (*Pulls away from* MANDRIL *in a huffy manner.*) Look too long, you might get your face rearranged.

STACKHOUSE: (*Seriously.*) Say Freeman, how come I haven't seen you in church lately?

MANDRIL: (*Playfully.*) Yeah, what's the story, deacon? We're the church's truant officers. Don't tell me you've been too busy for God.

FREEMAN: (*To* MANDRIL.) Maybe you haven't seen me, because you haven't been there yourself.

MANDRIL: I was in church just the other night.

REGGIE: Was that you with that flashlight?

MANDRIL: Yeah, that was me.

REGGIE: I thought so. You can bring those goblets back anytime now.

MANDRIL: So you can steal 'em?

REGGIE: Hey you know, a little for you, a little for me.

STACKHOUSE: I guess you're real excited about your brother coming home.

FREEMAN: Yeah, I'm pretty excited.

MANDRIL: Quit lying. Everybody in the projects knows about the good deacon, who don't mind sneaking through his brother's back door.

FREEMAN: (*Annoyed.*) What are you talking about?

MANDRIL: I'm talking about you and Reggie's mama. That's what I'm talking about.

REGGIE: Quit talking about my mother, man!

FREEMAN: (*Grabbing* MANDRIL.) Why you little . . . I ought to break your face!

MANDRIL: Hey man, be cool, shit!

FREEMAN: (*Pushing* MANDRIL *down.*) Who do you think you are, talking that way to me? Get up! I said get up! (FREEMAN *snatches* MANDRIL *from the floor and drags him toward the door. He opens the door and tosses* MANDRIL *out.*) I don't want to see your ass around here anymore!

STACKHOUSE: I'm sorry . . . he—

FREEMAN: (*Cutting in.*) Get out of here!

STACKHOUSE: Yes sir. (STACKHOUSE *exits.* FREEMAN *slams the door behind him. He stares at the door for a moment. Slowly he turns around and faces* REGGIE, *who stares at him hatefully.* FREEMAN *looks away and crosses the room.*)

REGGIE: Guess there'll be some changes now that pops is back. Guess we won't be seeing you 'round so much.

FREEMAN: I don't see why not? Your pops is my brother. I can see my brother, can't I?

REGGIE: That's the killer. You been pinch hitting for your own brother.

FREEMAN: (*Matter of factly.*) Somebody was gonna have to.

REGGIE: What are you trying to say about my mother, man?

FREEMAN: (*Uneasy.*) Nothing! Can't we just change the subject?

REGGIE: (*Reluctantly.*) Change the subject to what?

FREEMAN: Basketball. How come you quit the team?

REGGIE: I don't need that shit. They need me more than I need them.

FREEMAN: What you mean, boy? That was your ticket to college.

REGGIE: Scratch college. I don't need it.

FREEMAN: What do you need?

REGGIE: I don't need nothing. I don't need nobody either.

FREEMAN: You need your head examined.

REGGIE: Don't worry about my head.

FREEMAN: What are you you gonna do after high school?

REGGIE: Who says I have to do anything? Can't I just be?

FREEMAN: Your mama ain't gonna support no parasite.

REGGIE: I'll take care of myself. Don't you worry about it.

FREEMAN: You a real smart ass, ain't you?

REGGIE: I ain't been going to school all this time to get dumb.

FREEMAN: No, it only worked out that way. (ALICIA *enters. She is visibly upset.*)

ALICIA: (*Looking down.*) Hello, Uncle Freeman.

FREEMAN: Alicia, what's wrong?

ALICIA: Nothing.

FREEMAN: You're crying. Come on, tell me what's wrong.

ALICIA: I heard the commotion between you and Reggie's friend. And this fool won't change his clothes. What's gonna happen when daddy gets here?

FREEMAN: We're gonna have a good time, that's what. (ALICIA *looks exasperated. She turns away, disturbed by* FREEMAN's *remark.* FREEMAN *goes to her and places his hands on her shoulders.*) You worry too much. Everything is gonna be just . . . just the way you planned it. Now stop worrying and give me a big smile.

ALICIA: I can't.

FREEMAN: Alright. Then give me a big frown. (ALICIA *smiles*.) I knew you could do it. You need a hand?

ALICIA: (*Sarcastic.*) I got it under control now, thanks to Reggie.

FREEMAN: So what's the story with Reggie here? How come he don't seem motivated to do nothing?

ALICIA: Reggie? I don't know. He's just another space cadet. Him and his friends be getting high, getting wasted. That's all they do.

REGGIE: Don't be spreading my business!

FREEMAN: (*Looking at* REGGIE.) Well he's gonna have to come back to earth real soon.

REGGIE: And who's gonna bring me down?

FREEMAN: Boy, why can't you be like your sister? She's using her brain making straight A's in college.

REGGIE: City College ain't no college. It's more like the 13th grade.

ALICIA: Well, I'm about to transfer. I got my acceptance letter today from USF. (*She picks up a letter off the table and hands it to* REGGIE. *He throws it down without looking at it.*) Go ahead and read it. It's probably the only time you'll ever see a letter like this in your life, Reginald! (REGGIE *exits.*) They're accepting all my credits too. They may even give me a full scholarship.

FREEMAN: So when do you start?

ALICIA: Next semester.

FREEMAN: I'm really happy for you.

ALICIA: I couldn't have done it without the support you've been giving me, Uncle Freeman, giving me money for books and clothes.

FREEMAN: Hey, you deserved all those things. I just hope you keep up the good work.

ALICIA: You know I will. (*The front door opens.* ALEX *and* LORAINE *enter.* FREEMAN *points to them.* ALICIA *turns around excited.*) Daddy! Is it really you? (ALICIA *throws her arms around* ALEX.)

ALEX: It's me alright. (*He kisses* ALICIA.) Damn, you look good! (*They continue to embrace for a few beats.*)

ALICIA: How come you wouldn't let me visit you the past two months?

ALEX: I thought it was best not to see anybody so close to getting out. You don't know how high I get from a visit, only to go back to the cell block. I swear, the last two months were the craziest of all.

FREEMAN: I heard on the news, you guys had another lockdown last week.

ALEX: Hey . . . let's not talk about that place. What's happening with you, dude?

FREEMAN: Business as usual.

ALEX: Thanks for all the books man. They might add a new library wing to the facility and name it after you. What are you . . . the book of the month club?

FREEMAN: So I sent a few books. No big deal.

ALEX: (*Kidding.*) You didn't have to read 'em all. I got your last letter too. What's that now? That's ninety-nine I owe you.

FREEMAN: Don't worry about it.

ALEX: You must get writer's cramp.

FREEMAN: I think about you a lot.

ALEX: I think about you a lot too. (*After a pause the two men embrace.*) It's great seeing you.

FREEMAN: You finally made it, man. I wish mama could have been alive to see this.

ALEX: So do I, man. (REGGIE *enters with a sullen expression on his face as* FREEMAN *and* ALEX *end their embrace.*) And who's this stranger?

REGGIE: (*With no enthusiasm in his voice.*) Hey pops.

ALEX: "Hey pops." Is that all you got to say?

REGGIE: Welcome home.

ALEX: Welcome home. He doesn't write. He never visits. Maybe once the whole time I was down. And he got the nerve to say welcome home.

REGGIE: So what should I say?

ALEX: For starters, how about, "I'm sorry, pops."

REGGIE: Well I ain't. Shit, what you been pumping him, mama?

ALICIA: (*Disgusted.*) I'm gonna put the food on the table . . . if you don't mind. (ALICIA *exits to the kitchen.*)

ALEX: Now boy, I want you to listen to me. I heard about the shit you been putting down the last two years.

LORAINE: Let it ride, honey. Deal with it later, okay?

ALEX: I can't let it ride. That shit you told me in the car has gone too far already. I got to catch up with it now.

REGGIE: It's too late. The race is over.

ALEX: The race ain't over.

REGGIE: It is for you old man. In a few more months I'll be splitting and you'll never see me again.

LORAINE: And where do you think you're going, young man?

REGGIE: Don't worry about it.

LORAINE: Boy, you ain't got a pot to piss in.

REGGIE: I don't piss in pots.

LORAINE: No, you just piss on people.

REGGIE: Then they should quit standing in my line of fire.

ALICIA: (*Re-enters with chicken and potato salad.*) Mama! Reggie! Quit fussing! That's all I can hear in the kitchen. Daddy is home . . . we're supposed to celebrate! (ALICIA *sets the platters on the table.*)

ALEX: Celebrate what? My own son making me feel like shit.

REGGIE: Well you ain't had to be here and take what I took all these years. Going to school, looking up on the blackboard and seeing "Reggie's daddy is a jailbird."

ALEX: You shouldn't have let it hurt you.

REGGIE: You don't know the abuse I've had to take. You don't know how many fights I fought.

ALEX: You think you fought fights? I guess I was doing easy time.

REGGIE: Scratch you, man. (*He picks up the plate.*) I'm eating in my room.

LORAINE: You're not taking that into your room. You eat with us or you don't eat at all.

REGGIE: (*Putting food on his plate.*) So who's gonna stop me, huh? (REGGIE's *eyes move from his mama to* FREEMAN, *then to* ALEX. *He stares* ALEX *up and down as he exits slowly with his plate.* ALEX *stands, shocked. Pause.* FREEMAN *comes to him and puts his arms around him.*)

FREEMAN: Hey Al, come on. Forget him! You're home now. You're home free. No matter what he says. Here, let me take your coat, Al. (FREEMAN *takes* ALEX's *coat.*) And you take a seat here at the head of the table. (FREEMAN *hangs up the coat.*)

LORAINE: Alex, I'm sorry honey. I'm sorry about Reggie.

FREEMAN: You can't be blamed for Reggie. Besides, he'll come around.

ALICIA: That'll be the day.

ALEX: Did you see that, Freeman? He stood there like I wasn't shit.

ALICIA: Look daddy, I fixed your favorite. Mama said you loved fried chicken, so I've been frying all day.

ALEX: Do you think I should go in there and talk to him?

FREEMAN: Just relax and forget about him for a minute.

ALICIA: I made some potato salad too.

ALEX: For a moment, I thought we were gonna go toe to toe.

ALICIA: Oh yeah. And today daddy, I got my acceptance letter from USF. Hey mama, show daddy my letter. They might even give me a full scholarship.

LORAINE: Look honey, Alicia got into USF. Didn't I tell you the girl was on the ball. Here, read it for yourself.

ALEX: (*Takes the letter.*) It's my fault man. That boy went through a lot of shit because of me. How do I make that up to him?

LORAINE: (*Pounding her fist on the table.*) Now wait just one minute! There seems to be two conversations going on here at once. Now can we all get on the same wave length for a second? Thank you.

ALEX: I'm sorry dear. It's just, well, you know.

LORAINE: Would you stop worrying about Reggie and read your daughter's acceptance letter?

ALEX: (*Glances at it.*) That's nice honey. Real nice. I'm proud of you. But let me read this some other time. Okay?

ALICIA: Sure daddy, sure.

LORAINE: Come on Freeman, everybody. Let's sit down and eat this good food before it gets cold.

ALEX: I see the place has undergone a few changes since I've been down. See you got a new color TV. You never told me about that, Loraine. When did you get it?

LORAINE: Last year, I think.

ALICIA: Last spring. Uncle Freeman gave . . . it to ma on her birthday.

ALEX: Oh yeah? On your birthday, huh? That's nice, Freeman. You got money to burn, huh?

FREEMAN: (*Nervously.*) I was overstocked at the store. We used to carry that model, but we don't anymore. You know how it is when you're trying to clean out your inventory, to make room for newer models. I was selling those things so fast I was

practically giving them away. Figured Loraine and the kids
could use one, so I saved the last one for them.

LORAINE: He's been real thoughtful. Every time we needed something he's been there.

FREEMAN: Hey, it ain't nothing. I mean, ever since Maggie took
off, I ain't had nobody to do anything for, except y'all.

ALEX: Have you heard from Maggie?

FREEMAN: Not one word. Look, let's forget about her. (*Pause.*)
Have you given much thought to what kind of work you'd like to
do? Things are pretty tight out here. You need to start looking
as soon as you can.

Lights come up on the jail cell. CEDRIC *enters, dressed in prison blues,
wearing a skull cap on his head.* ALEX *stares at him while nervously
feeling on a piece of chicken. Only* ALEX *is aware of* CEDRIC's *presence.*

CEDRIC: (*A sinister laugh.*) Boy o' boy. The man ain't been home a
hot minute and they're jamming him about finding work.
(*Pause.*) Hey lover boy, suprized to see me so soon? I told you I'd
be looking you up. (*He picks up a piece of chicken and bites it.*) Not
bad. Nice place you got here. You're moving up in the world.
You even got real chicken. No more mystery meat. Now all you
need is a job.

ALICIA: Daddy, why are you feeling on the chicken? (ALEX *slowly
puts the chicken on his plate.* ALICIA *and* LORAINE *look at each other,
perplexed.*)

FREEMAN: So what kind of plans have you made in terms of finding
work?

CEDRIC: (*Pointing at* FREEMAN.) Hey, fuck that! What are you
gonna do about this motherfucker? You need to kick his ass!

ALEX: Did I mention I got my AA degree while I was inside? I got
it in Business and Accounting. I know things are tough out
here, even without a record. But at least I got that piece of
paper. Now I'm gonna tell prospective employers I did
time . . .

CEDRIC: (*Cutting in.*) While they were making time.

ALEX: But I accomplished something inside.

CEDRIC: (*Shaking his head.*) You never were much on fighting, were
you?

FREEMAN: Hey, if you want to come back to work for me, just say
so. You can have your old job back. It'll be just like the old days.
I can start you at four-fifty an hour. I know that's not a lot. But
it beats nothing.

CEDRIC: Tell him to fuck off, Alex. What are you waiting for? Get up and hit him.

FREEMAN: You can start this Monday. What do you say?

CEDRIC: Didn't you learn anything while you were here? There's a knife next to your hand, Alex. Pick it up. Come on Alex, you can do it. Kill that bastard! I can't do it for you.

ALEX: (*To* CEDRIC.) I just want you to leave me alone, man.

CEDRIC: I can't leave you alone. I miss you too much. And I think you miss me too.

ALEX: (*Stands up.*) I want you out of my life.

FREEMAN: Loraine, would you say something to him?

LORAINE: Honey, sit down.

ALICIA: Uncle Freeman is only trying to help, daddy.

CEDRIC: Say Alicia, is Freeman banging both of y'all? (*Pause.*) Why won't you kill him, Alex? Look how he has taken over your family. What's the matter, are you afraid of being sent back here?

ALEX: I'll never go back! Never! You get that idea out of your mind.

FREEMAN: I'm not begging you to come back. Work for somebody else. See who'll hire you. When you find out how tough things really are, you'll wish you took me up on my offer.

CEDRIC: You'll be back. They all come back. You can't help yourself. I'm the warden of your dreams. (CEDRIC *laughs in* ALEX's *face, then folds his arms and goes into a freeze. A very smug look is on his face.*)

ALEX: (*At the top of his voice.*) I'm never going back to prison! Do you hear me? Never!

FREEMAN: Ain't nobody saying you is.

LORAINE: Sit down honey, we believe you. All of us are in your corner. We know you're going straight this time.

FREEMAN: Not with that attitude.

LORAINE: Come on and eat something. You've hardly touched your food.

FREEMAN: That's a lie. He felt all over his chicken.

ALEX: I'm sorry y'all, but I'm not feeling well.

FREEMAN: Maybe you'd feel better if I leave.

ALEX: No Freeman, don't leave. It's not you. I'm just tripping, that's all it is. I got a lot on my mind I'm trying to sort out. (*The doorbell rings.*)

ALICIA: I wonder who that could be?

LORAINE: Well, why don't you go see, honey?

ALICIA: (*Getting up.*) Okay mama. It's probably one of Reggie's friends. They're the only ones that don't respect the dinner hour.

LORAINE: They don't respect no hours if you ask me. Dropping in here all times of the night.

The doorbell rings again. ALICIA *opens it and* EXCEDRIN *enters wearing dark glasses, carrying a "boom box" stereo cassette player, blasting blaring disco music at top volume. He shouts above the music to be heard.*

EXCEDRIN: Hey Alicia, is my man Reggie home?

LORAINE: Young man, would you turn that thing off?

EXCEDRIN: (*Turns it down a little.*) You say something, lady?

LORAINE: Turn that music off, all the way off. You're giving me a headache!

EXCEDRIN: (*Turns it off.*) I'm sorry. Didn't mean to disturb you all while you's eating, but is Reggie home?

ALICIA: He's in his room.

EXCEDRIN: Cool. Don't bother. I knows my way. (EXCEDRIN *exits to* REGGIE's *room.*)

ALEX: Who in the hell was that?

ALICIA: Some dude named Excedrin. And don't ask me how he got that name.

ALEX: Is he one of Reggie's regulars?

LORAINE: This is the first time I've seen this one.

ALICIA: He's new in town.

ALEX: I know one damn thing, he ain't copping nothing here. Not tonight he ain't. I'm gonna bust in there and put an end to this shit, right here and now.

LORAINE: (*Stands to block his path.*) You're asking for trouble, Alex.

ALEX: You're goddamned right. This is my house.

LORAINE: It's Reggie's house too. No matter what he's doing, I'd rather have him doing it here, than out there in those streets.

ALEX: Shit like that belongs in the streets. Not in my house.

LORAINE: Don't expect to come home and right every wrong in one night. There's a lot of things wrong with this house that need your attention. Plaster is falling. The plumbing needs fixing. And I need some loving. Now, I can think of a thousand things you need to tend to.

ALEX: Look, I just got out on parole! I don't need that shit around me. I'm gonna find out where he's stashing his shit and I'm getting rid of it. This is my turf, I'm in charge here.

CEDRIC: (*Comes out of his freeze.*) Wrong Alex. This is my turf. I control the disorder in this ghetto madhouse! (CEDRIC *snaps his fingers and* REGGIE *re-enters with* EXCEDRIN, *crossing toward the door.*)

EXCEDRIN: Dig Reg, like I 'preciates you going out on a limb like that. Bending over backwards to do me a solid.

REGGIE: Well, what goes around comes around, I always say.

EXCEDRIN: Yeah, well I'll be right back at you. I'm a fix you up as soon as I can, okay?

REGGIE: Hey, don't sweat it.

EXCEDRIN: Thanks a lot Reggie. Pimp tap.

REGGIE: P.T. (*They do the pimp's hand shake. Then* EXCEDRIN *exits.*)

ALEX: (*To* REGGIE.) Who is that character and what did he want?

REGGIE: (*Obviouly high.*) You talking to me, old man? (ALEX *starts toward* REGGIE. FREEMAN *jumps up to restrain* ALEX.)

ALEX: I've had it with this old man crap. I'm gonna show you how old I am.

REGGIE: Well, let's see it, old man. Let's see if you got any fight left in you.

LORAINE: Honey sit down.

ALEX: (*Turns toward* LORAINE.) "Honey sit down, honey sit down." That's all you've said to me tonight. I've been down long enough.

REGGIE: I'll put you down for the count.

ALEX: You. You're too wasted to do anything to me.

FREEMAN: (*Holding* ALEX's *arms.*) Fighting him ain't the answer.

ALEX: (*Calmly.*) Hey, I'm alright. I'm cool. I'm not gonna hit him . . . I know all about the dope ring you've been running.

REGGIE: (*Sarcastic.*) So who doesn't? You want in on the action? (FREEMAN *slowly lets* ALEX *escape his grasp.*)

ALEX: (*Rational, he slowly moves toward* REGGIE.) Can't you take that shit somewhere else? Ain't you got no respect for this house, for this family?

REGGIE: (*Back against the wall near the door.*) I'm just trying to earn a living, that's all, minding my own business.

ALEX: (*Moving closer to* REGGIE.) But we don't know these people that be coming by the house. They don't mean us any good. All they care about is getting high. Suppose you ain't here and one of them goes off against your mother or your sister.

REGGIE: (*Crosses downstage center.*) When that happens I'll deal with it.

ALEX: (*Following* REGGIE.) And how is that?

REGGIE: We'll cross that bridge later.

ALEX: But it's upon us now. The code of the streets can betray your ass.

REGGIE: You ain't seen the streets in eight years. What do you know old man? (CEDRIC *laughs as* ALEX *starts toward* REGGIE's *room.*)

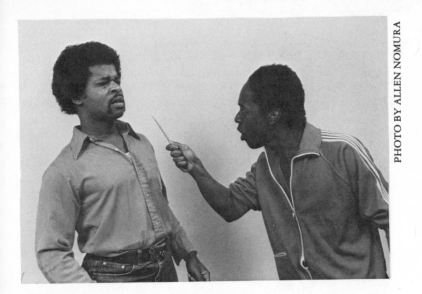

ALEX: I know how to deal with your black ass! I'm gonna find your stash and flush it down the toilet.

CEDRIC: That sho would be a terrible waste.

REGGIE: (*Whips out a switchblade.*) You ain't doing shit! I dare you to take another step!

LORAINE: Put that thing away! Are you crazy? That's your father.

REGGIE: As far as I'm concerned I ain't got no father. Now all of you get back. And you . . . you old man . . . come on and show me what you got!

CEDRIC: Look like you got problems. Things are going real crazy on the home front.

ALEX: Reggie, put down the knife. I'm begging you.

REGGIE: That ain't begging. You can beg better than that. Get down on your knees and beg.

ALEX: I'm not doing that.

REGGIE: I said get down on your knees!

LORAINE: Look Reggie, I'm down on my knees.

REGGIE: You won't get on your knees, huh? That's alright, I understand. Guess we all got our pride. don't we? Hey old man, don't come near my room. Understand? Nobody's flushing my stuff down the toilet. I got too much money invested to let that happen. We all got to protect our investments, now don't we? (REGGIE *exits to his room, still displaying his knife. He walks with a cool macho stride.*)

CEDRIC: (*Puts his hand on* ALEX's *shoulder.*) So, Alex, welcome home.

Blackout.

SCENE TWO

The following day, early afternoon. ALEX *is stretched out on the sofa, snoozing loud.* LORAINE *enters, wearing her trenchcoat. She spies* ALEX *asleep on the sofa and tiptoes toward him, quiet as a cat. She bends over and plants a soft, gentle kiss on his forehead.* ALEX *wakes up startled.*

ALEX: (*Sitting up with a start.*) Hey, what are you doing here? I thought you went to work.

LORAINE: Work can wait, honey. I decided to sneak home to be with my old man. What you been doing all morning, waiting for mama to come home?

ALEX: I just went downtown. Just got back a few minutes ago.

LORAINE: Oh, so that's where you were when I called. (*She starts unbuttoning* ALEX's *shirt.*) You just messing with my ambush plans.

ALEX: I guess I can redeem myself for last night.

LORAINE: Forget last night.

ALEX: That's not the way I planned it.

LORAINE: (*Kissing* ALEX's *face.*) Shhhhh. You be quiet.

ALEX: I'm sorry.

LORAINE: What's wrong?

ALEX: I'm afraid.

LORAINE: Afraid of me?

ALEX: Afraid of everything. I don't know if I can cope with it. Too many things have changed.

LORAINE: You'll get used to it.

ALEX: Suppose I don't?

LORAINE: I'll help you adjust.

ALEX: You ain't that great, Loraine. Nothing personal, but you ain't no saviour.

LORAINE: I kept this family together by myself.

ALEX: You did what you could. You saved Alicia, thank God.

LORAINE: Well, now that you're back, Reggie has someone to look up to. All he ever needed was his daddy. A man to put him on the right track. (ALEX *gets up and walks across the room.*)

ALEX: It's too late for me and Reggie.

LORAINE: It's not too late. It'll take time, but it's not too late.

ALEX: I can't deal with it. I can't do battle with him and put my own life back together. That's just asking too much. There's really no point in me even being here.

LORAINE: What are you saying?

ALEX: I'm saying too much has changed. This ain't the same place I left eight years ago and I'm not the same either.

LORAINE: Change is everyday, honey. Everyday.

ALEX: I don't know, Loraine. This morning I woke up depressed because I felt I didn't belong here. Not just because of Reggie, it's something else. Something I can't describe. I just know it's there. It stands between us. This vague invisible wall. I don't know, maybe I'd be better off if I just left California.

LORAINE: (*Coming toward him.*) Why are you so negative all of a sudden? Riding home last night you were full of hope, full of joy.

ALEX: I was lying to myself.

LORAINE: You are letting Reggie bring you down.

ALEX: It ain't just Reggie, Loraine, it's me.

LORAINE: (*Grabs him.*) I love you, Alex. I'm your woman, no matter what. I'm your woman and I love you. So tell me what's bothering you, Alex, please. I'm listening.

ALEX: I can't tell you, Loraine, I just can't.

LORAINE: Tell you what, why don't you let me fix you a drink and take you back to the bedroom. I could make you forget all your worries, at least for the afternoon.

ALEX: I know what you should do for yourself. Forget about me. Keep dealing with Freeman.

LORAINE: (*Turns away.*) What are you talking about?

ALEX: You know what I'm talking about. I peeped the game last night and I saw that same TV in a shop window downtown this morning.

LORAINE: So?

ALEX: I dug on the price tag and I know my brother. I know you must mean an awful lot to him. Hey don't worry, I ain't mad, I'm glad.

LORAINE: I don't know what you're talking about.

ALEX: I'm not dumb Loraine. I didn't expect for you to sit here eight years and dry up waiting for me. I expected you to deal with somebody.

LORAINE: You don't think very much of me, do you?

ALEX: It's not that. The joint taught me a lot about human need. What you and Freeman did, it ain't no crime. It didn't hurt nobody.

LORAINE: Because it never happened.

ALEX: Fess up, Loraine. Damn it, I said I wasn't mad. But you're making me mad pretending nothing happened.

LORAINE: Since you're so convinced, why don't you ask Freeman?

ALEX: Ask Freeman? What should I ask him? Hey brother, is it true you been trespassing on private property while I was away? Breaking and entering my old lady? Don't make me ask him, Loraine. I don't want to know the truth that bad. (*Long pause.*)

LORAINE: Look Alex, why don't I just go back to work. No point in blowing a day's pay here.

ALEX: Oh, so I'm not worth a day's pay?

LORAINE: It's not that, it's just that I came home to be with you, to make love to you, not to have my brain picked apart.

ALEX: Fuck it then. Go back to the man. Do your eight and skate. I don't give a damn.

LORAINE: (*Starts putting on her coat.*) Alright then. That's exactly what I'll do. I didn't have to put up with this for eight years and I don't have to put up with it now. (LORAINE *starts toward the door.*)

ALEX: Loraine wait! Don't leave. I'm sorry, I lost my head. Stay please.

LORAINE: Maybe you're right, Alex, maybe too many things have changed.

ALEX: Don't say anything. Just hold me please.

LORAINE: What's the matter?

ALEX: I need you to hold me. Please.

LORAINE: Sure. (*They embrace.*) You're trying to tell me something. What is it, honey? Go ahead, you can say what's on your mind.

ALEX: I need your help, Loraine. I was under a lot of heavy pressure the whole time I was inside. I did some things I didn't want to do.

LORAINE: You didn't kill somebody, did you?

ALEX: No, but I should have. You see, in the joint you become your reputation. (*The lights come up on the prison cell and* ALEX *slowly crosses to the jail cell as he delivers his speech. The lights fade on the living room as* LORAINE *sits.*) And you start making your reputation the very first day. Right from the jump they test you to see where you're coming from. I didn't come prepared to fight. I thought I could survive by making friends. Be a nice guy. Be cool with everybody. Be on no one's shit list. Do my time and get out. You have no friends on the inside. You only have enemies. If I had known then what I know now, I would have fought from the very first day. (CEDRIC *enters dressed as in the first scene.*)

CEDRIC: (*To* ALEX.) Hey you. Hey, you boy. Where you from? You hear me talking?

ALEX: (*To the audience.*) I should have kept on unpacking. I should have ignored him.

CEDRIC: Why don't you answer me, boy?

ALEX: (*To the audience.*) Cats are always trying to figure you out.

They don't like folks to be quiet, and off to themselves, oblivious to their madness. They want to wrap their madness around you, tie you with sick ribbons, just wrap you up in their shit.

CEDRIC: Where you from, boy? Don't I know you?

ALEX: You don't know me.

CEDRIC: Then I must know your mama?

ALEX: You know nothing about me.

CEDRIC: I know I know you. I know you know that I know you. What you in for?

ALEX: First degree murder.

CEDRIC: Don't bullshit me nigger. Why ain't you in the North Block?

ALEX: Because they reduced my sentence after they found out I only killed your mama.

CEDRIC: (*Running toward* ALEX.) Shit, nigger, I'll kill your ass. (CEDRIC *goes into a freeze.*)

ALEX: We would have fought and we would have fought. I might have fought him every day. I might have even killed him.

CEDRIC: (*Comes out of his freeze.*) Hey you. Hey you, boy. Where you from? You hear me talking?

ALEX: San Francisco, brother.

CEDRIC: Oh, the City. Welcome to Marin County, brother. Me? I'm Cedric. I'm from L.A. But I got people in the City. I got a few partners in here from the City. They're cool too. Do you smoke weed? (CEDRIC *takes out a joint and lights it, looking around for guards. The coast is clear.*)

ALEX: (*Hesitant.*) Sure.

CEDRIC: Say, what's your name?

ALEX: Alex.

CEDRIC: Alex. Alex in Wonderland? (*Laughs.*) I know I know you from somewhere. Your face sho do look familiar. Did you do a stretch in Chino?

ALEX: (*Taking the joint.*) Nope.

CEDRIC: How about Tracy or Susanville?

ALEX: Nope.

CEDRIC: Folsom? Soledad?

ALEX: I'm a first-timer.

CEDRIC: A first-timer? And you drew the Q? What you do, boy, commit mass murder?

ALEX: I did everything from passing bad checks to conning old ladies out of their Social Security. Even did a credit card scam. I was into it heavy.

CEDRIC: Had to be to draw such heavy time. This ain't the place for no youngblood rookie like you. You're locked up with murderers and rapists. You ever kill a man?

ALEX: Nope.

CEDRIC: Well, you may have to in here. Me? I've killed out there and I've killed in here. Many times. If it wasn't for me giving my shrink money, I'd still be locked down in the North Block with the rest of the misfits. Like, I been in more than I been out. I was damn near raised in the system. I finished high school inside. Even got a little bit of college. Don't know if I would have done that out there. (CEDRIC *picks up a picture form the table near* ALEX's *bunk.*) Is that your family? That's your son, huh? Yeah, he's real cute, looking good, just like you.

ALEX: I think he looks like his mama.

CEDRIC: Naw, he looks real cute, just like you. That's a fine family you got there. I ain't ever had no family. The state is my only family. From the orphanage to the Youth Authority, to the Penal System. The State been wonderful foster parents. Hey, these Nazis in here are crazy and them bikers too. They want to hurt the black man. But we don't play that shit. If they stick one of us, they have to lock us all down, because we be fighting for days. Black—White—that's the war around here. Hey, you hear that? They callin' us to line up for chow. Come on man, sit with me at chow. I'll teach you the ropes. Hang with me partner and you'll do easy time. I own these punk ass guards. I'm the Governor of this shit. Come on. (CEDRIC *exits.* ALEX *comes down stage center and addresses the audience.*)

ALEX: Like a fool I listened to him. I followed his lead. I smoked his cigarettes, unaware of the trap he was setting. The psychological trap. The game he was running. The technique he was unraveling. I felt comfortable when he was around, secure and protected. And I was like a frightened, pathetic mouse when away from his side. People were only friendly to me because of him and would only do me favors at his request. Without him I was either invisible or a target. Nothing in between. No friends, no enemies, just vultures preying on me, waiting for Cedric to slip. Waiting for him to let go. (ALEX *sees* CEDRIC *as he re-enters.* ALEX *runs to him.*) Hey Cedric, hey man, thanks a lot for coming to my aid out there in the yard. I tell you, that bastard might have killed me if you wasn't there. All over a silly game of basketball.

CEDRIC: (*Very solemn.*) I know.

ALEX: And did you see his bitch Duane jumping up and down and calling me a bitch? "Bitch, leave my ol' man alone. Foul him again and I'll pull your hair out bitch!" Wasn't that some sick shit?

CEDRIC: What's so sick about loyalty?

ALEX: Nothing's wrong with loyalty man. It's that faggot shit that's sick.

CEDRIC: What's so sick about it?

ALEX: A man making love to another man? Come on man, that ain't right.

CEDRIC: Do you see any women in here?

ALEX: (*Slowly, sensually mimes jerking off.*) No, but that don't condone that faggot shit. You know me, I prefer beating my meat. Shit, I mean, me and my hand be getting off. I get that vaseline and that Afro Sheen. And I flip through them girlie magazines. Black girls, white girls, Asian. In my mind I've been running the Baskin & Robbins of whore houses. Thirty-one flavors. And my favorite one be my old lady Loraine. Because with her, part of the fantasy is anchored in reality. My memory recalls the way it used to be. Her flesh on my flesh. Oh Loraine, Loraine, take away the pain. It be beautiful man, me and my hand. Except once or twice, I caught myself staring at my daughter's picture. My mind, my thoughts, shifting from Loraine to Alicia. I felt guilty at first. But I don't anymore. Oh Alicia honey, you're my favorite fantasy now. You're right up there beside your mother, right next to Loraine.

CEDRIC: And you think Mac and Duane are sick?

ALEX: At least my sickness is heterosexual.

CEDRIC: You never tripped on your boy Reggie?

ALEX: Are you crazy, man?

CEDRIC: Come on man, not once?

ALEX: You are talking sick.

CEDRIC: Hey, I could dig a little Reggie myself.

ALEX: You're serious, ain't you? I mean, you're not playing. You're really serious?

CEDRIC: Damn right I'm serious. And it's about time you got serious. You got some time ahead of you, boy. Let's see how long your hand and your pictures satisfy you. To hell with fantasy, give me some flesh.

ALEX: Hey man, get out of my cell talking that shit.

CEDRIC: You forget that this is the only world I know.

ALEX: So you fucked faggots, huh?

CEDRIC: Yeah, and I guess that makes me a faggot too.

ALEX: Get out of my cell, nigger! I don't play that faggot shit.

CEDRIC: I'm not playing either. I'm for real, Alex, as real as I can be. I'm not leaving. I'm having you, Alex. Either you be my wife or you bleed on my knife. Now come on, sweetheart, make it easy on yourself. I'd sure hate to mess up such a pretty face.

ALEX: You're not fucking me man. I'm nobody's sagoony.

CEDRIC: Come on man, don't you think I've earned it? And you know you want it too. You just don't know how bad you want it. Haven't I been a friend to you? I've spent time with you. I have comforted you. Who do you sit with at every meal? Who do you run to see when they unlock us every day? You enjoy being near me. You laugh at my jokes. You appreciate my wisdom. You look up to me. Admit it.

ALEX: I'll admit that I like you.

CEDRIC: Like me? Come on man. Admit I mean more to you.

ALEX: Hey man, I like you as a friend, man.

CEDRIC: You've enjoyed all the gifts I've given you. The cigarettes, you like smoking my weed, you like my friends, you like being known as my friend. You think that gives you status.

ALEX: Yeah, but Cedric —

CEDRIC: No buts here. I have often heard you say how badly you wanted to repay me, how badly you wanted to give me something, only you couldn't think of anything to give me. Now haven't you said that?

ALEX: Yes, I've said it man, but this faggot shit was not what I had in mind.

CEDRIC: In your own way, you have learned to love me, haven't you?

ALEX: In a man's way, yes, in a brother-to-brother way, but not in a sissies' way.

CEDRIC: Regardless of the way, you love me, right?

ALEX: Hey man, I'm your partner.

CEDRIC: And in your own way, you want to show me that you love me, right?

ALEX: You're putting words in my mouth.

CEDRIC: You want to comfort me, right?

ALEX: In a man's way, not in a faggot's way.

CEDRIC: You must also admit that you enjoy being under my protection. Am I right? You enjoy the strength I possess. That attracts you to me.

ALEX: I know you can kick ass.

CEDRIC: And you like the fact I can kick ass, right?

ALEX: Whatever, man, you distorting the shit.

CEDRIC: Fuck it man, I just want you to touch me with a soothing touch. Give me the gift of love, and I will return that gift.

PHOTO BY ALLEN NOMURA

ALEX: No man, I'm not doing that.

CEDRIC: (*Punches* ALEX *in the stomach.*) You don't have no choice in the matter. You do it willingly or you do it unwillingly. Just as long as you do it. Because a refusal means I'll break your neck. And I'll break your neck not because I hate you, but because I'll be angry at you and at myself for wasting my time the past six months I been thinking of things to do for you, and been sending you signals to show you my love, Alex. (CEDRIC *continues to beat* ALEX *up during this speech.*) But you've been blind to the shit, haven't you? So it has come to this. I want you to understand that I want to walk around this place with you at my side, proud of the fact that you are my sagoony. I want to put you on a pedestal. I love you, Alex. Even now when you are resisting. It's your innocence that I love. You might hate me at this moment, but when you leave here and return to face your wife again, you will have to admit to yourself that I have taught you a few things about life and love, if you let me. So why don't you just put down this macho front you're hiding behind and give me what I want? You know the choices, Alex, and you know the consequences.

CEDRIC *grabs* ALEX *by his belt buckle and pulls him toward him.* CEDRIC *brings* ALEX *to the floor and gets on top of him and begins to rape him.* LORAINE *stands. All stage lights flash in a rotating order as the two men turn toward* LORAINE *in a simulated humping motion.*

CEDRIC: Tell your wife that I have you now. Go ahead and tell her, tell her. Tell her that you will never be free. You will always be a prisoner here. Tell her. You will always leave a little piece with me. (CEDRIC *exits.*)

ALEX: (*Slowly rising and going to* LORAINE.) Loraine, please, don't stare at me like that. Just hold me, please. I need you to hold me.

LORAINE: (*Cold and distant.*) How long did it go on?

ALEX: Almost the entire time I was there.

LORAINE: Couldn't you have ended it?

ALEX: You don't understand. He would have killed me.

LORAINE: I don't know, Alex. Are you sure you didn't want it to happen?

ALEX: Loraine, I need your help.

LORAINE: It might be too late for my help.

ALEX: What are you saying?

LORAINE: I don't know how to deal with this.

ALEX: All I'm asking is that you try.

LORAINE: I don't know, Alex. I'm no saviour, you said that yourself.

ALEX: I guess you're gonna go to Freeman, huh? (*Pause.*)

LORAINE: (*Hesitant.*) I don't know . . . Maybe.

ALEX: So it happened? You did sleep with him?

LORAINE: Yes. I slept with him.

ALEX: So what are you gonna do? Are you gonna run to Freeman or deal with me and what I've become?

LORAINE: I don't know. (*Pause.*) Every time I came to visit you, I wondered what was happening to you. I always suspected something like this would happen. I just prayed and hoped that it wouldn't . . . that you were too strong to let that happen.

ALEX: At least I'm alive, Loraine. I came out of there with my life.

LORAINE: At some point you had to like what was happening.

ALEX: Like I'm sure you were liking it with Freeman.

LORAINE: Would you stop throwing that in my face? You can't make me feel guilty. Not after what you did.

ALEX: I don't want you to feel guilty. I just want another chance to make our marriage work. I'm just as confused as you are. (*Pause.*) I know I still have feelings for you and I want to make love to you.

LORAINE: I want to make love to you too.

ALEX: I know, but last night I kept . . . I couldn't get Cedric out of my mind. It was like he was there . . . watching us. I don't know if I'll ever be the same again . . . You still love me, don't you?

LORAINE: (*Hesitant.*) I don't know. I mean . . . I guess . . . maybe. I'm not sure. I don't know if I can love you that way again.

ALEX: All I'm asking is that you try. Can't you at least try?

LORAINE: Look Alex, I can't promise you anything, but I'm willing to give—

ALEX: (*Cuts in.*) I don't want you to feel sorry for me. I want you to try to make our marriage work because you want it to work. Not because you feel sorry for me.

LORAINE: Hey, stop talking. Let's just hold each other. (*They embrace.*) What do you want to eat tonight? I can go to the store and pick a few things up.

ALEX: Why don't we go out to eat tonight.

LORAINE: You really want to do that?

ALEX: Yeah. And maybe catch a movie.

LORAINE: Okay, it's a date. Hey, look, I'm going to go back to work.

ALEX: I thought you were gonna spend the afternoon.

LORAINE: (*Putting on her coat.*) I was, but I just want to . . . you know . . . get out, so I can think. You laid a lot of heavy stuff on me. I wanna be alone . . . to clear out my head. It'll do us both some good.

ALEX: You're right. Hey, before you go, how about giving me a kiss? (*As they embrace and their lips get close, the doorbell rings.*) Remind me to get that doorbell fixed.

LORAINE: Why, what's wrong with it?

ALEX: It rings at the wrong time. (LORAINE *opens the door.* EXCEDRIN *enters carrying his cassette recorder and dressed in the same manner as in the previous scene.*)

LORAINE: What is it?

EXCEDRIN: You know what it is lady. Where's the man?

LORAINE: You mean Reggie?

EXCEDRIN: The one and only. Is he here?

LORAINE: Of course not. He's in school, where he should be. And why would you come by here during school hours looking for my son anyway?

EXCEDRIN: 'Cause blood ain't in school.

ALEX: What do you mean by that?

EXCEDRIN: Just what I said. The brother ain't in school. Look, tell blood his main man Excedrin is looking for him. I need him to do me a solid.

ALEX: What kind of solid?

EXCEDRIN: That's between me and the brother, dig it?

ALEX: Hey look, just what in the hell do you want with my son?

EXCEDRIN: Let me see your shield brother, coming at me with all these questions. He's your goddamned son. Don't you know what the fuck he's doing?

LORAINE: Young man, cool it with that language.

ALEX: Look here boy, I don't want to see your face around here again. I don't want you or your kind coming to my door bringing that garbage into my house. You want to see Reggie, you look for him in the streets among the rest of the garbage backing up in the gutter.

EXCEDRIN: Hey man, don't pick your beef with me, brother. It's your son you need to holler at. Now until Reggie says otherwise, I'm a keep coming by here, 'cause blood don't do business on the street. (ALEX *pushes* EXCEDRIN *against the wall and pins him there.*)

ALEX: Are you dense, young man? Do I have to kick your ass to get my message through to you? I don't want you coming by my house again.

EXCEDRIN: Man, you're hurting my collar bone and tearing my shirt. I paid good money for this shirt. Hey man, I said you hurting me. I ain't no pain freak.

LORAINE: Stop leaning on him, Al. You're hurting the boy.

ALEX: (*Relaxes, lets go of* EXCEDRIN.) I just want to make sure he understands.

EXCEDRIN: Yeah, yeah, I understand, man. I ain't even know Reggie had an old man.

ALEX: What?

EXCEDRIN: As long as I been knowing blood, he ain't never mentioned his old man.

ALEX: How long you been knowing my boy?

EXCEDRIN: I don't know, about six months. Look, I'm new on this scene baby, I'm from back east. I'm from Deetroit, the motor city, baby.

ALEX: You run your game in Detroit, baby. Not here, understand?

EXCEDRIN: (*As he exits.*) Hey man, you talking loud and saying nothing. (ALEX *slams the door hard behind him.*)

ALEX: Did you hear that?

LORAINE: That's the way these kids are being raised. Look, I better get going back to work.

ALEX: You be careful out there. These creeps are crazy.

LORAINE: I know how to take care of myself. (*They kiss and* LORAINE *exits.* ALEX *sits down letting out a sigh. He picks up the newspaper and thumbs thorugh the want ads. He reads the want ads as* REGGIE *enters sleepily from his bedroom.*)

REGGIE: You're wasting your time old man. The want ads don't want nobody.

ALEX: (*Looks up startled.*) What are you doing here?

REGGIE: I live here, remember.

ALEX: Why ain't you in school?

REGGIE: I ain't been in school for over three months, old man. I dropped out, dig it? I quit.

ALEX: So you left this morning, then you came back while I was out?

REGGIE: Why are you tripping, old man?

ALEX: I don't want to see you messing up your life.

REGGIE: Well, it was messed up from day one when I was born into this family.

ALEX: You remind me of myself when I was your age. Mad at the world because you weren't born with a silver spoon in your mouth. You should have seen me, always ranting and raving. You see, back then, a black man had to take what he needed in order to survive. Wasn't nobody gonna give us nothing.

REGGIE: You think things are different now? Well they ain't. Nothing's changed.

ALEX: That's not true, Reggie. A kid today got all kinds of opportunity. Look at Alicia.

REGGIE: Everybody knows a sister will get a break before a brother. Besides, I ain't got time to go through all them head trips they be running everytime I try to land a gig. Wait 'til you get out there and see for yourself. They don't want you, pops, and they don't want me.

ALEX: That's bullshit, you just want life to be easy because you ain't got the discipline to struggle.

REGGIE: Why should I struggle, when I can push drugs and get over easy?

ALEX: Don't tell me about getting over easy, because it ain't easy wondering every time the doorbell rings whether or not it's the man this time. The whole time I was away I was afraid of what would become of you. I didn't want you to end up like this. I wanted your life to be better. I wanted you to have opportunities I never had. I wanted to live my life all over again, through you.

REGGIE: Well, I ain't going to be hanging around this scene much longer.

ALEX: I'm pleading with you, Reggie.

REGGIE: I like my life the way it is. So don't tell me what to do.

ALEX: You forget that I was young once, and had all the answers. Nobody could tell me nothing.

REGGIE: Pops, I appreciate what you trying to tell me. But I've already made up my mind. I like my way of doing things. Besides I'm making money, man. My own money. I ain't had to ask ma for nothing and I ain't had to take handouts from Freeman either. Now do you really expect me to give that up?

The doorbell rings. ALEX *answers it.* EXCEDRIN *re-enters with a white man dressed in casual clothes. They are quickly followed by other re-enforcement.*

ALEX: I told you not to come around here again.

EXCEDRIN: (*Flashes a badge.*) The game is up, Mr. Johnson. I'm Detective Harris with the Narcotics Unit of the San Francisco Police Department. And this here is Detective Brown. And there's the man we're looking for. Want to come with us Reggie? (REGGIE *makes a sudden move.* DETECTIVE BROWN *aims his gun at* REGGIE. *One officer makes* ALEX *put his hands on the wall, while the other searches* REGGIE's *room.*)

DETECTIVE BROWN: Freeze Reggie!

REGGIE: What is this?

EXCEDRIN: It's a bust. (DET. BROWN *puts* REGGIE *face down on the floor and puts the handcuffs on him.*)

DETECTIVE BROWN: You're under arrest for possessing and distributing PCP. You have the right to remain silent. Anything you say can and will be used against you in court. You have the right to counsel, if you cannot afford an attorney, one will be provided. Now that you've been explained your rights do you wish to make a statement?

REGGIE: You set me up, you punk, talking that brother shit.

EXCEDRIN: That's right. Every brother ain't your brother. Especially a little drug-selling punk like you. You sold one bag too many, junior. (*To* ALEX.) Your son here sold some bad shit to a kid who bugged out and is undergoing psychiatric care right now.

REGGIE: Money is money, old man.

EXCEDRIN: Get him out of here. (DETECTIVE BROWN *and* REGGIE *exit. The other officer comes out of* REGGIE's *room with a big cellophane bag of pills and pot.*)

POLICEMAN: I found the kid's stash.

EXCEDRIN: Good, they'll love this down at the lab. We're taking your kid downtown if you want to get him out, Mr. Johnson. (ALEX *doesn't answer, he just shakes his head, disgusted.* EXCEDRIN *and the other officers exit.*)

Blackout.

SCENE THREE

Several days later. ALEX *is snoozing on the living room sofa. As he sleeps he dreams. Lights come up on the jail cell.* REGGIE *enters, dressed in prison blues. He is visibly disturbed. He kicks his bunk.*

REGGIE: Damn these shrinks! What do they know?

CEDRIC: (*Entering.*) Hey you. Hey you, boy.

REGGIE: Are you talking to me, old man?

CEDRIC: You the only one here . . . Say, where you from, boy? Don't I know you?

REGGIE: You know nothing about me.

CEDRIC: Your face sure do look familiar. You got an older brother?

REGGIE: (*Jumps bad with an attitude.*) The only family I got is the Black Guerrilla Family. Is that enough brothers for you?

CEDRIC: (*Laughing.*) I know you.

REGGIE: I said you don't know me.

CEDRIC: Then I must know your daddy.

REGGIE: You know nothing about me!

CEDRIC: And I know that you know that I know you. What you in for, Reggie?

REGGIE: Who told you my name?

CEDRIC: Your daddy did. (*Long sinister laugh.*) Your daddy was the best sagoony I ever had. You should have seen your old man when I was teaching him the facts of life. I told him he only had two choices. He'd either be my wife or bleed on my knife. So what do you think he did?

REGGIE: Scratch what you did to him. You're dealing with me now.

CEDRIC: Like father like son, they say.

REGGIE: I'm nobody's sagoony.

CEDRIC: But you're the son of a sagoony. And I'm the faggot maggot on your back.

REGGIE: My back is already covered.

CEDRIC: Suppose I blow your cover (*He blows.*) away. Bye-bye Black Guerrilla Family. You see, there are still plenty around who'll testify that your daddy sho gave plenty head when he was here. Let's see if we can get you to do the same.

ALEX: (*Jumps up from the sofa.*) Don't do it, Reggie! Don't do it! Hit him! (*The doorbell rings.*)

LORAINE: (*Yelling from offstage.*) Honey, would you get that?

ALEX: Hit that bastard!

CEDRIC: (*Wiping* ALEX's *forehead.*) Hey. Relax, Alex. It's only a dream. (*The doorbell rings again as* CEDRIC *and* REGGIE *laugh in*

ALEX's *face.* ALEX *stands there in a confused state as* LORAINE *enters.*)

LORAINE: What's wrong with you? Didn't you hear the doorbell?

CEDRIC: You know something, Reggie, I think he's starting to get jealous. (CEDRIC *and* REGGIE *exit together arm in arm, their laughter trailing off. The doorbell rings again.*)

LORAINE: Honey, you're not having that dream again, are you?

ALEX: I'm sorry, honey, what did you say? (LORAINE *goes to open the door.*)

LORAINE: Maybe we should make an appointment to get your hearing checked. (*She opens the door and* FREEMAN *enters.*) Hi Freeman. Come on in.

FREEMAN: What took you so long to answer the door?

LORAINE: I'm sorry, Freeman, I was in the bathroom. Have a seat while I finish putting on my makeup. It should only take another minute. (LORAINE *exits.* FREEMAN *continues standing.*)

FREEMAN: Hey Alex, are you ready to go see about Reggie? (*Pause.*) (*Pause.*) What's wrong with you? You're sweating real hard.

ALEX: (*Sighs.*) Aw man. I just woke up from the strangest dream. I thought I saw Reggie with some dude I knew on the inside.

FREEMAN: Hey don't worry about Reggie. We're gonna get him a good lawyer.

ALEX: We can't afford a good lawyer.

FREEMAN: Look, business has been real good. We can work something out so Reggie can have the right kind of counsel.

ALEX: Did you get the bail money?

FREEMAN: Yeah, I got it.

ALEX: Good. You've done enough already. I'm gonna pay you back as soon as I can.

FREEMAN: Take your time. I'm in no hurry. (*Pause.*) I understand you got a little gig now.

ALEX: That's exactly what it is. A little poot-butt gig.

FREEMAN: You gotta start somewhere.

ALEX: But busting suds is nowhere.

FREEMAN: You know my offer still stands.

ALEX: And I'm still not interested. Why would you want to take another chance on me? Did you forget how I fucked things up the last time?

FREEMAN: I don't believe you're the same, Alex. I've got faith in you now. Besides, you're my brother and you're a little down right now. I wanna help you in any way I can.

ALEX: I don't think it would work, man. So let's drop it, okay.

FREEMAN: You really ought to reconsider.

ALEX: The discussion is closed.

FREEMAN: I'm only trying to help you.

ALEX: You wanna help? Then take a look at this stupid TV. We've been having a lot of trouble with the color lately. And sometimes the picture gets real dark and the thing starts humming real loud, like it's ready to blow up.

FREEMAN: I think the TV is fine.

ALEX: You haven't even looked at it.

FREEMAN: I don't have to. All I have to do is look at you. You wish you had given her that TV, don't you?(*Pause.*)

ALEX: How could you do it, man?

FREEMAN: Hey, look . . . I didn't want to bring this up, man. I was hoping to spare you the pain, at least until you got re-established. But since you've brought it up, we may as well deal with it. Loraine is leaving you, Alex. You might as well get prepared for that. I love her, Alex. And she loves me too. She's the reason Maggie left.

ALEX: I refuse to believe you're standing here telling me this to my face.

FREEMAN: Well, you better believe it, Alex, and you better start getting used to life without Loraine. I know you feel betrayed . . . like you've been done wrong. But when two people love and care for each other the way Loraine and I do, then sibling loyalty is thrown to the wind. Now, I have done my best to be decent about this situation, by offering you a job. I think you should take it, Alex. I'm willing to raise my original offer. I don't want to see you left out in the cold with nothing.

ALEX: (*Seething.*) Motherfucker, I ought to kill you. (CEDRIC *enters.*)

CEDRIC: This is it . . . the moment of truth . . . the moment of reckoning. Seize it! Don't let it escape your grasp.

ALEX: People get killed in the joint behind shit like this.

CEDRIC: That's right. A man has a reputation to protect. You can't let him walk around making his reputation off of you. I don't care if he's your brother. It's gone too far, Alex. You've got no choice but to kill him!

ALEX: (*To* FREEMAN.) You don't understand my world, do you? You don't understand the code of honor, people kill to protect.

FREEMAN: (*Hesitant, frightened.*) Killing me, Alex . . . what would that accomplish? (*Pause.*) You'd only end up doing more time.

ALEX: You'd like to see me get more time, wouldn't you?

FREEMAN: No . . . no, that's not true.

ALEX: Come on, Freeman, admit it. You enjoyed seeing me

incarcerated. You enjoyed sending me books and writing me letters, torturing me with your happy, successful life, out here in the free world. Admit it.

FREEMAN: That's not true.

ALEX: You get a certain sick satisfaction from it, admit it.

CEDRIC: Fuck that, just kill him!

ALEX: I'm not gonna give you that satisfaction. You're not worth killing. You're not worth pulling time for. If I learned anything from my incarceration, I've learned I'm a better man than you, Freeman. As far as I'm concerned, you're already dead. I don't have to kill you.

CEDRIC: (*Angry.*) You're the one who's dead, Alex. I gave you an order to kill and you didn't do it! Don't come back here! If you do . . . you're as good as dead! (CEDRIC *exits.*)

ALEX: I want you to forget about Loraine. Your relationship with her is over.

FREEMAN: Not until I hear it from her.

ALEX: You're begging for an ass-kicking. Save yourself a lot of trouble and take my word for it. (LORAINE *re-enters.*)

LORAINE: I'm ready. Sorry I took so long. (*Pause.*) Well . . . what's everybody standing around for?

FREEMAN: (*Hesitant.*) Alex was telling me, things were over between us. I want to hear your feelings on this.

LORAINE: Can't this wait until some other time?

FREEMAN: I have to know now.

ALEX: Go ahead and tell him.

FREEMAN: Don't be intimidated by him. Tell him of our plans to live together.

ALEX: You must be kidding.

LORAINE: This is really the wrong time for this. Can't we discuss this after we get Reggie out?

FREEMAN: Reggie can wait, damn it!

ALEX: You don't have to holler at her.

FREEMAN: Let's hear it, Loraine. I'm waiting for an answer.

LORAINE: (*Hesitant.*) Freeman, I'm afraid a lot of things have changed. I'm not leaving Alex. I'm staying.

FREEMAN: But you promised me you would leave him.

ALEX: Is that true, Loraine?

LORAINE: Yes, but I changed my mind.

ALEX: And why did you change your mind?

LORAINE: Because I realized how much I loved you, Alex. I've always loved you . . . even while I was seeing Freeman. I only . . . saw him . . . because he reminded me . . . of you.

(*Pause. After a few beats* ALEX *embraces* LORAINE. FREEMAN *has been rendered speechless. He stands there looking devastated.*)

FREEMAN: (*Hurting.*) We . . . we should go get Reggie out. (ALEX *and* LORAINE *end their embrace.*)

ALEX: Yeah . . . right.

FREEMAN: (*Refusing to look at her.*) Loraine, Alex and I can get him. We don't need you.

LORAINE: But I want to go.

FREEMAN: I don't want you getting in my car. (FREEMAN *exits.*)

ALEX: We'll try to be back as soon as we can. (*He embraces her again.*) Hey . . . it's gonna be alright. Don't worry. (*They kiss.*) I better go. (ALEX *exits.* LORAINE *closes the door behind him.*)

Blackout

SCENE FOUR

Late the same evening. ALICIA *is at the dining room table doing her homework.* LORAINE *enters wearing a robe. She carries hairgrease and a comb to braid her hair for bed. She sits next to* ALICIA *and starts braiding her hair as she talks.*

LORAINE: Alicia . . . Alicia.

ALICIA: (*Very much into her homework.*) What, mama?

LORAINE: I think you and I need to talk.

ALICIA: Can it wait mama? I'm trying to finish this paper.

LORAINE: I want to talk to you now. I've noticed a change in you since your father's been home.

ALICIA: What kind of change?

LORAINE: You've been acting real aloof. Like you don't want to be here.

ALICIA: Look, I'm just under a lot of pressure at school. I'm facing three deadlines and I'm worried, that's all.

LORAINE: Are you sure that's all it is?

ALICIA: Yes mama. What else could it be?

LORAINE: Sometimes I get the impression it's directed at me.

ALICIA: What would give you that impression?

LORAINE: I don't know. Maybe it's just me. Your father being back has forced me to take a hard look at myself, the type of mother I've been.

ALICIA: You've been a good mother, don't worry. I won't talk about you bad when I leave the nest.

LORAINE: You knew about me and Uncle Freeman, didn't you? (*A long pause.*)

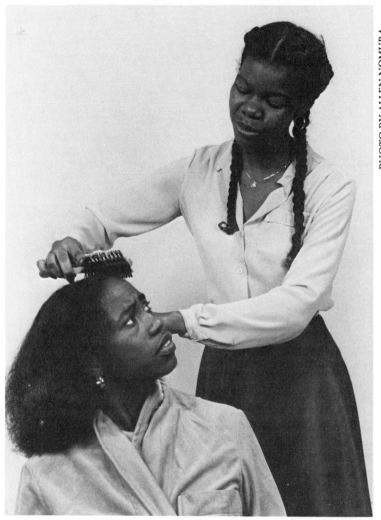

PHOTO BY ALLEN NOMURA

ALICIA: I sort of knew. I tried not to think about it. I mean, it's none of my business.

LORAINE: I'm really sorry if it bothered you. I did my best not to make it so obvious. Reggie knew too, didn't he?

ALICIA: Yes mama. So what about it?

LORAINE: He hates me, he thinks I'm a whore, doesn't he?

ALICIA: Isn't it a little late to be asking all these questions?

LORAINE: You know, I did my best to keep it from you. The whole time your father was away, no man ever slept in this house.

ALICIA: Mama, nobody's judging you. Would you please stop tripping?

LORAINE: I can't help it. Sometimes I think that if I had spent a little more time dealing with Reggie's needs, instead of my own, he wouldn't be in the mess he's in now.

ALICIA: You can't blame yourself for everything he does wrong, just like you can't take credit for everything I do right.

LORAINE: I can take some credit can't I?

ALICIA: (*Laughs.*) Sure, mama. Let me braid your hair. (*She takes the comb.*) Does daddy know about you and Uncle Freeman?

LORAINE: Yes, he knows all about it. He caught on when you told him that Freeman gave me that TV.

ALICIA: I'm sorry. So what was his reaction?

LORAINE: He was upset, but he forgave me. He figured I'd deal with someone. He just didn't figure it would be Freeman.

ALICIA: So what's gonna happen?

LORAINE: I can't say for sure, but your father and I are trying to work things out. This Reggie thing is hurting him more than anything. If Reggie ends up doing time it will just kill him. It will kill me too. What are we gonna do, Alicia?

ALICIA: I've been thinking about that a lot. You know we need to get Reggie a good lawyer. I'm willing to put off going to school, to help out in anyway I can.

LORAINE: You are going to school no matter what happens with Reggie.

ALICIA: Suppose I don't get the scholarship?

LORAINE: We'll make a way somehow.

ALICIA: But getting Reggie a good lawyer is more important than school.

LORAINE: The court can appoint him a lawyer.

ALICIA: Maybe they'll give us the same one they gave daddy.

LORAINE: That's enough from your smart mouth.

ALICIA: I've heard you say a thousand times, daddy had no business getting that much time. His only crime was being poor. Court-appointed lawyers don't care. All they want to do is work out a deal and get the thing over with.

LORAINE: I'm not going to sit here and argue with you. You are going to school and you are going to USF. I've done too much bragging on you, for that not to happen, understand?

ALICIA: Yes mama. You're the boss.

LORAINE: Damn right. What in the world is keeping them? Your father should have been back here with Reggie by now. (*Men's voices can be heard outside in the hallway.*)

ALICIA: I think that's them now. (ALEX, FREEMAN *and* REGGIE *re-enter.* REGGIE *is sulking with his head down. He has a patch over his eye.*)

ALEX: (*To* REGGIE.) I know one damn thing, you gonna get a job and pay your uncle back. I'm gonna see to that.

ALICIA: (*Jumps up excited.*) Uncle Freeman, you did it. You got Reggie out.

ALEX: Let's hope the boy here don't jump bail.

ALICIA: Reggie you had us so worried. What happened to your eye? (ALICIA *tries to put her arm around* REGGIE, *but he pushes her down.*)

REGGIE: Get away from me! I don't want nobody coming near me. (FREEMAN *and* LORAINE *respond to* ALICIA *on the floor.*)

ALEX: Hey man, what in the hell has gotten into you? We went out on a limb to get you out. So you show your appreciation by pushing your sister down. What kind of shit is that? She's trying to show you some love. Is it gonna kill you to let her touch you?

REGGIE: Hey man, just leave me alone, okay?

ALEX: (*Calm, restrained.*) Reggie, I'm begging you to turn your life around while you can or you'll end up in the slammer like me.

REGGIE: If I catch some time, it ain't no big deal. I'll do my stretch and get out. So don't worry about me.

ALEX: Reggie, doing time is not that simple. (*Pause.*) Do you know what a sagoony is?

REGGIE: Naw.

ALEX: Sagoony is the prison word for wife. A sagoony is a punk . . . a faggot . . . a wife who belongs to . . . who is the exclusive property of another inmate. A sagoony sleeps when his owner says sleep, he eats when his owner says eat. He can't go to the bathroom without his owner's permission. He can't even be seen talking to another inmate without rousing his owner's suspicions. (*Pause.*) There must be hundreds of boys behind those walls, that look just like you. Some of them are pretty tough. They run in gangs . . . they draw their strength in numbers . . . they survive by attacking before they get attacked. However, some are not so lucky. They come in alone . . . their backs unprotected. They become sitting ducks for the booty bandits, hoping to get the first crack at the new kid on the block. (*Pause.*) Reggie, I'm telling you all of this, not to scare you . . . I don't believe you could be scared . . . but because I love you and I want to warn you, 'cause where you're headed is governed by its own set of rules. You rape or be raped. You kill or be killed. It's a world where they prey on weakness. You see son . . . I was someone's sagoony. My mind . . . my body belonged to another man.

LORAINE: You don't have to tell him, Alex.

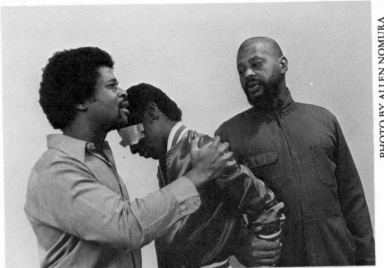

PHOTO BY ALLEN NOMURA

ALEX: But I want to tell him . . . I need to tell him. I have to tell it, Reggie, and I hope it does you some good.

REGGIE: (*Hurt.*) You telling me, you're a punk? (CEDRIC *enters and stands beside* REGGIE. ALICIA *turns to* LORAINE *crying.* FREEMAN *stands absolutely still.*)

ALEX: The word is sagoony, son. Sagoony.

REGGIE: Fuck you! Get the fuck out of my face, you faggot!

ALEX: What's the matter boy, you too ashamed to look at your daddy . . . too ashamed to hear how they turned a good man into a punk? Yeah, I know how you feel, 'cause you're the man around here. The big time dope pusher . . . the main man! Wonder how long you'd be a man in San Quentin, boy?

CEDRIC: Or should we say lady?

REGGIE: (*Turning away from* ALEX.) I bet they was all packing you in your ass at San Quentin. You must've been the sweetest bitch in the block. I bet there's graffiti all over them walls back there, about just how sweet a piece you can be.

ALEX: Yeah, I was sweet alright . . . getting punched in the butt, damn near every night. What else do you want to know, huh? Did I give head? Yeah, I gave head . . . gave flawless head . . . a mean blow job. Giving head was my speciality. This mouth would make 'em tremble and shake. I made the brother forget all about women. That's how bad I was. Look at me boy. Look at your daddy.

CEDRIC: (*Laced with sarcasm.*) You're one hell of a man to tell the kid that. More man than I'll ever be. (*Pause.*) I'm pulling for

you, Reggie. We sho could stand your face in the place. Niggers
would be clawing all over you.

ALEX: (*To* CEDRIC.) You ain't taking my boy.

CEDRIC: Let him make up his own mind. He can think for himself.

ALEX: I'm not gonna stand back and let that happen. (CEDRIC *and*
ALEX *circle* REGGIE, *while the others go into a freeze.*)

CEDRIC: Pass it on, pass it on. Pass the baton from father to son.
Pass on the great legacy.

ALEX: I'm not passing it on.

CEDRIC: Hey Reg, are there any more at home like you?

ALEX: (*Circling.*) Let go of him.

CEDRIC: You let go. You can't save him. We reserved him a cell.
Say Reg, see you when you get here. I'm getting a hard on just
thinking about it.

ALEX: (*Grabs* REGGIE *and hugs him tight.*) I'm not letting him take
you, Reggie.

CEDRIC: Too late, Alex. A hug does little good now. It's out of
your hands. It's all on the boy now.

ALEX: (*Slowly lets go of* REGGIE.) So Reggie, what's it gonna be?

Blackout